PARTING THE CURTAIN

PARTING THE CURTAIN

Propaganda, Culture,
and the Cold War,
1945–1961

Walter L. Hixson

St. Martin's Griffin
New York

ISBN 0-312-17680-5 paperback

Library of Congress Cataloging-in-Publication Data

Hixson, Wlater L.
     Parting the curtain : propaganda, culture, and the Cold War / by
Walter L. Hixson.
          p.   cm.
     Includes bibliographical references (p.) and index.
     ISBN 0-312-16080-1 (cloth) ISBN 0-312-17680-5 (pbk)
     1. United States—-Relations—Europe, Eastern. 2. Europe, Eastern—
Relations—United States. 3. Propaganda, American. 4. United
States—Foreign relations—1945-1989. 5. Cold War. I. Title.
IN PROCESS
303.48'273047—dc20   95-52253
                                                                                        CIP

Design by Acme Art, Inc.

First published in hardcover in the United States of America in 1997
First St. Martin's Griffin edition: January 1998
10 9 8 7 6 5 4 3 2 1

CONTENTS

List of Abbreviations vii

INTRODUCTION
Cultural Infiltration and the Cold War ix

CHAPTER 1
A Campaign of Truth: The Rebirth of Psychological Warfare 1

CHAPTER 2
Reviving the Voice: The Radio Cold War Begins 29

CHAPTER 3
Liberation Denied: The Twilight of Psychological Warfare 57

CHAPTER 4
From Revolution to Evolution: The Thaw in East–West
Cultural Relations 87

CHAPTER 5
"People's Capitalism:" USIA, Race Relations,
and Cultural Infiltration 121

CHAPTER 6
From the Summit to the Model Kitchen: The Cultural Agreement
and the Moscow Fair 151

CHAPTER 7
Six Weeks at Sokolniki: Soviet Responses to the American Exhibition . 185

CHAPTER 8
Conclusions: Militarization, Cultural Infiltration, and the Cold War . . 215

Afterword 229

Notes 235

Index 278

LIST OF ABBREVIATIONS

BBC	British Broadcasting Corporation
BRE	Brussels Exposition
CIA	Central Intelligence Agency
CP	Communist Party
CPSU	Communist Party of the Soviet Union
CPI	Committee on Public Information
CCF	Congress for Cultural Freedom
ECA	Economic Cooperation Administration
FEC	Free Europe Committee
GDR	German Democratic Republic (East Germany)
HCUA	House Committee on Un-American Activities
ITU	International Telecommunications Union
IIA	International Information Administration
MIT	Massachusetts Institute of Technology
MPAA	Motion Picture Association of America
NATO	North Atlantic Treaty Organization
NSC	National Security Council
OCB	Operations Coordinating Board
OWI	Office of War Information
OSS	Office of Strategic Services
PSB	Psychological Strategy Board
PWD	Psychological Warfare Division
PAO	Public Affairs Officers
RFE	Radio Free Europe
RIAS	Radio in the American Sector [of Berlin]
RL	Radio Liberation (renamed Radio Liberty in 1964)
SFRC	Senate Foreign Relations Committee
UN	United Nations
UNESCO	United Nations Educational, Scientific, and Cultural Organization
USIA	United States Information Agency
USIS	United States Information Service
VOA	Voice of America
VOKS	Soviet Society for Cultural Relations with Foreign Countries
VDNKh	[Soviet] Exhibition of the People's Economic Achievement
VFC	Volunteer Freedom Corps

Cultural Infiltration
and the Cold War

This study focuses on American propaganda and cultural infiltration targeting Eastern Europe and the Soviet Union from the end of World War II through the Eisenhower years. Although these efforts usually remained on the periphery of Cold War strategy, I have found that they were more significant than generally recognized. Washington sought to destabilize the Soviet and East European Communist Party (CP) regimes, first through "psychological warfare" and then through an ultimately more effective, albeit longer term, program of gradual cultural infiltration. Despite misperceptions and a lack of priority accorded to such efforts, Washington had succeeded in parting the "Iron Curtain"* by the end of the Eisenhower years.

I am concerned primarily with official U.S. government efforts to use propaganda and culture to challenge CP authority in Eastern Europe and the USSR. While I do pay attention to private initiatives and informal cultural exchange, my primary focus is on propaganda and culture as components of national security policy. I make no systematic effort to analyze how the Cold

---

*In recent years cultural historians have paid a good deal of attention to literary theory pertaining to the assumptions and hidden meanings of language, which must be "deconstructed" in order to be understood in a given context. Such thinking is particularly pertinent to the language of the Cold War, which can easily degenerate into a series of clichés, each highly charged with political meaning. To most Americans, for example, the term "communism" carries an emotional, pejorative meaning little connected with objective analysis of a theory of political, economic, and social development of human societies. For the same reason

War shaped American society, although some excellent scholarship exists on that subject.[1] Nor am I interested here in the impact of Soviet propaganda and cultural efforts in the United States, which appears minimal in any event.

Specialists in the history of the Cold War, like American policymakers themselves, have kept cultural matters on the periphery of their work. While American historians have analyzed domestic wartime propaganda, they have devoted less attention to its dissemination abroad. Despite some revealing scholarship on the impact of U.S. culture abroad in the prewar years, cultural diplomacy has yet to receive the attention it deserves.[2] No systematic study exists on efforts to use propaganda and culture as weapons in the Cold War. Memoirs and participant accounts dominate the literature on radio propaganda, the use of film, printed material, international exhibitions, and cultural exchange programs.[3]

A good case can be made for the value of a cultural approach to international history in general, and to the Cold War in particular. First, however, we must explain what is meant by the elusive term "culture," which one scholar has called, perhaps with only slight exaggeration, "one of the two or three most complicated words in the English language."[4] Progressively expansive definitions of culture transcend a narrow focus on works of a high artistic, literary or intellectual character. The broad anthropological "thick description" of culture, incorporating "all genres and modes," seeks to identify the "core values," "structures of meaning," or the "ethico-mythical nucleus" of a given society. Another definition, close to the one I employ here, views culture as "indicative of a way of life" of a group or society. Such a definition would include consideration of popular and consumer culture.[5]

While scholars study culture to understand individual societies, another level of analysis seeks to explore the transmission and dissemination of culture across international boundaries: in other words, "international relations as intercultural relations." At issue here is the "sharing and transmitting of consciousness . . . communication of memory, ideology, emotions, lifestyles, scholarly and artisitic works, and other symbols."[6] International historians, accomplished in studying the roles of power and economic forces in world

I have avoided such terms as "Soviet satellites" or "Soviet bloc." I refer instead to Communist Party regimes or to the Soviet empire.

In both the title and the text I employ the term "Iron Curtain," which I believe remains a useful metaphor for understanding the East-West division. Although "Iron Curtain" was a symbolic construction employed by Winston S. Churchill in an obvious Cold War context, the term nonetheless effectively characterizes efforts to shut off Western access and influence in Eastern Europe and the USSR, at least during the early Cold War years when Joseph Stalin remained in power. While the curtain could be permeated to varying degrees—that is, it was not really "iron"—the barriers established, and Western efforts to overcome them, are central to the history of the Cold War.

politics, have only recently begun to analyze what many perceive as the third layer of analysis, namely culture. Just as historians assess the rise and fall of states based on their military power and economic influence, the cultural influence of nations must be considered as well. "What historians can do," explains Akira Iriye, "is examine the evidence to see whether it may be said that in certain periods of history cultural issues do become critically important, even as in other periods security or trade may overshadow other factors."[7]

It is becoming increasingly clear that American mass culture has been one of the country's greatest foreign policy assets. Aided and encouraged by the federal government, cultural expansion has increased throughout the twentieth century. The emergence of the United States as the most advanced consumer society in the world accounts for much of the appeal of the nation's culture abroad. As Emily Rosenberg has explained, "Through the international marketing of consumer products identified as American, America itself became a code of modernity and consumer lifestyles." The nation's rise to world power was inextricably linked with the dissemination of images of affluence, consumerism, middle-class status, individual freedom, and technological progress. The appeal of American mass culture facilitated overseas expansion and identified the United States with progress. Not only in Western Europe but throughout the world cultural transmission facilitated the emergence of what Gertrude Stein, and later Henry Luce, called the American Century.[8]

The emergence of the United States as the preeminent global power after World War II sharply expanded opportunities for overseas cultural activity. In Western Europe, the process began with wartime Lend-Lease and escalated with the landing of U.S. troops, themselves powerful agents of cultural dissemination. With the onset of the Cold War, the Marshall Plan expanded economic and cultural influence in conjunction with the ongoing military occupation. U.S. economic aid and cultural expansion bolstered the anti-communist containment policy in Western Europe while helping to orient countries such as Italy, France, Austria, and Western Germany toward the West.[9]

In a pathbreaking study on American influence in postwar Austria, historian Reinhold Wagnleitner called attention to the "stupendous success" of U.S. popular culture in postwar Europe. Despite only limited access to American culture, Austrians came to associate the United States with "wealth, a comfortable standard of living for the masses, freedom, modernity, the culture of consumption, and a peaceful life." Wagnleitner's use of terms such as "coca-colonization" and the "*Marilyn* Monroe Doctrine" highlight the need to reconceptualize foreign policy with an eye on the impact of popular and consumer culture.[10]

To a greater extent than is generally understood, many of the same forces that influenced mass perceptions in Central and Western Europe shaped consciousness in Eastern Europe and the USSR. The difference is that U.S. culture filtered more slowly and encountered a great deal more interference during its transmission into the Soviet empire.[11] Despite the impediments placed in the path of ideas and information from the West, cultural dissemination gradually emerged as an important component of East-West relations. Because the Cold War was a military standoff, neither nuclear-armed superpower could risk direct conflict with the other (although proxy wars were, of course, intrinsic to the East-West struggle). Furthermore, animosity between the two superpowers inhibited trade and economic relations. As a result of these limitations, national security planners ultimately discovered that cultural interaction offered an effective way to influence the evolution of the CP regimes. Through a process of gradual cultural infiltration Americans could begin to export the symbols, lifestyles, consumerism, and core values of their society.

By the end of the Eisenhower years, U.S. propaganda and cultural dissemination had begun to influence mass perceptions throughout the Soviet empire. American officials, some more than others, realized that modern communications technology provided the means to circumvent the barriers of authoritarian states and appeal directly to the peoples inside the Soviet empire. Whereas traditional diplomacy centered on state-to-state relations, maximizing the importance of elites, technological advances made it possible to transcend governments and reach the masses of people, even those living in closed authoritarian states.

Washington's efforts to penetrate the Soviet empire proceeded haltingly because of both external and internal constraints. Employing closed borders, counterpropaganda, jamming of radio signals, and other tactics, the Soviet Union sought to counter Western cultural infiltration. With Soviet actions precluding cultural exchange in the early years of the Cold War, Washington employed propaganda and psychological warfare in an effort to undermine Kremlin authority. Having invested heavily in psychological warfare, Washington responded haltingly to renewed opportunities for cultural infiltration in the post-Stalin years.

Overseas propaganda and cultural initiatives received paltry funding in comparison with foreign economic and military programs. Many Americans sharply opposed the very concept of a democratic society engaging in propaganda, which in its essence entailed manipulation of mass opinion. The term "propaganda" possessed such a pejorative connotation that it eventually became necessary for its advocates to employ euphemisms such as "public diplomacy." Opposition also emerged from those who viewed culture as a preoccupation of elites or saw little evidence of its impact overseas.

Presidential leadership played a key role in both the scope and effectiveness of propaganda and cultural efforts in the Cold War. Both Presidents Harry S.

Truman and Dwight D. Eisenhower launched propaganda and cultural initiatives, but neither afforded such efforts primacy in overall Cold War strategy. Although Eisenhower in particular believed strongly that cultural infiltration would ultimately prove decisive in the Cold War, he failed to follow through on his own perceptions. This assessment calls into question some of the main arguments of "Eisenhower revisionism."[12]

The most sweeping constraint on a more effective use of the cultural weapon in the Cold War was the emergence of militarization as the dominant paradigm of postwar American diplomacy. Rooted in the World War II experience, militarization entailed massive armament in a quest for military superiority. As a corollary, Washington rejected negotiations with the enemy, whose "unconditional surrender" was to be secured instead. Demonization of the Soviets, and other CP-led regimes, focused mainly on promotion of worst-case scenarios of the enemy's intentions, such as the putative Soviet desire to overrun Western Europe. Such perceptions fueled a patriotic culture in support of unprecedented commitments of U.S. power overseas, including Washington's sponsorship of the North Atlantic Treaty and the establishment of a chain of military bases around the world. National Security Council Paper No. 68, signed by Truman after the outbreak of the Korean War in June 1950, authorized a three-fold increase in defense spending—up to $35 billion annually—establishing "military Keynesianism" as a central feature of the postwar "war economy." Militarization fueled a massive "defense" bureaucracy—or national security state—which collaborated closely with private industry to form a "military-industrial complex." The nuclear arms race embodied the ultimate expression of militarization.[13]

By stressing the Soviet military threat, and often declining to take advantage of diplomatic opportunities that might have produced broadened cultural ties, policymakers ensured that cultural initiatives remained on the margins of U.S. diplomacy. At no time from 1945 to 1961 did cultural diplomacy remotely approach in importance—as measured by the amount of attention and resources devoted to it—the larger Cold War policy of building alliances, amassing military force, and intervening to contain presumed communist insurgencies in the developing world.

Militarization dwarfed efforts to devise an effective cultural strategy and caused policymakers to lose sight of the struggle for "hearts and minds." The United States matched, or exceeded, Soviet militarization rather than pursuing an asymmetrical strategy that would have capitalized on U.S. economic superiority and the powerful allure of capitalist consumer culture. The State Department, wedded to conventional geopolitical thinking, was slow to comprehend the possibilities offered by cultural initiatives. As elitists and self-proclaimed realists, State Department diplomats tended to overlook the critical role that public opinion and mass culture played in world affairs. The Congress and the American public, sold on worst case scenarios of Soviet behavior, accepted Cold War militarization as the dominant paradigm of postwar foreign policy.

While militarization reflected a desire for preponderant power, Washington sought to undermine the Soviet and East European regimes by means short of war. What George F. Kennan termed "containment" was actually indistinguishable from "liberation," the strategy that Republican critics trumpeted to pillory the Truman administration.[14] While various officials, Republican and Democratic, may have varied in the means they would employ, they agreed on the end in view. Their aim was to apply external pressures, short of direct military conflict, that would promote instability behind the Iron Curtain with the ultimate goal of "rolling back" communism in Eastern Europe and, to the extent possible, in the USSR itself. In the early Cold War years, Washington policymakers viewed the struggle against Soviet power, and communist ideology in general, as America's "manifest destiny."

By the mid-fifties, psychological warfare had stirred unrest behind the Iron Curtain, but had failed to deliver liberation of the "captive peoples" of Eastern Europe and the USSR. As a result, U.S. policy began to shift toward an evolutionary approach emphasizing straight news and information programs, cultural exhibitions, and East-West exchange programs. Officials began to realize that Voice of America jazz programs and the "polite propaganda" of *Amerika* magazine could foster a more appealing image of the United States than anti-Soviet diatribes. Initially slow to respond to de-Stalinization and the cultural "thaw" in the USSR, Washington began to make inroads by the late Eisenhower years.

A breakthrough came with the 1958 U.S.-Soviet cultural agreement, followed the next year by the staging of the American National Exhibition in Moscow. All but ignored by diplomatic historians, the cultural agreement was a landmark achievement and arguably one of the most successful initiatives in the Cold War. In both real and symbolic ways, the American National Exhibition, which ran for six weeks in the summer of 1959, signaled the ascendancy of the West in the Cold War. Curious, teeming crowds responded enthusiastically to the unprecedented display of consumer culture in the heart of the Soviet empire. While a national exhibition could hardly change the course of the Cold War overnight, it highlighted Soviet weaknesses, and American strength, in the battle for hearts and minds. I offer the first comprehensive, multiarchival history of the U.S. exhibition, heretofore known only as the site of the famous Nixon-Khrushchev "kitchen debate."

While I confine my research to the Truman and Eisenhower years—for which a relatively complete documentary record exists—my argument can be projected into the future as we seek explanations for the end of the Cold War. The fall of the East European and Soviet regimes from 1989 to 1991 stemmed largely from economic and social stagnation, and ultimatley disintegration. The CP regimes thus collapsed from internal causes, with the economic decline certainly exacerbated, to be sure, by massive *Soviet* overinvestment in Cold War militarization.[15]

But internal social and economic decay of the CP regimes presents only part of the story. Western cultural infiltration of the regimes increased steadily throughout the Cold War. As their own social systems delivered stagnation instead of progress, and authoritarianism instead of political pluralism, residents of the Soviet empire gained ever increasing exposure to an alternative way of life. Modern communications, including radio, television, and film, as well as direct contacts through exhibitions, tourism, and exchange programs, were agents of Western cultural infiltration. Clearly, the relative weight of these forces varied between, say, Poland and Bulgaria, yet the main forces of historial change swept across the entire landscape of Eastern Europe and the USSR.

Although an explanation for the ultimate end of the Cold War takes me well beyond the scope of research in this volume, my purpose is to emphasize that any comprehensive explanation for the end of the East-West struggle will require serious analysis of the role played by Western cultural infiltration. Specialists in United States, European, and Soviet history will have to contribute to the effort. We need to learn more about the dissemination and reception of information and culture during the Cold War. I hope that this assessment of the formative years of cultural interaction—culminating with both a real and symbolic "parting" of the Iron Curtain—may serve as one of the building blocks of an emerging area of inquiry.

I have depended mainly on State Department and U.S. Information Agency records, supplemented by research at the Truman and Eisenhower presidential libraries, as well as an abundant secondary literature. Some documents cited herein, including CIA records, have been declassified as a result of my requests under the Freedom of Information Act. Documents obtained from archives in Moscow inform and enrich my analysis of the Soviet perspective on the 1959 American National Exhibition.

In the final analysis, the historian encounters the same dilemma that confronted U.S. psychological warriors: how does one gauge the impact of propaganda and culture inside the Soviet empire? I can, and do, demonstrate that Americans went to some effort to use those means to undermine CP authority, but the effectiveness of their actions is harder to assess. In part, I base

my conclusions on Soviet reactions to Western propaganda and cultural infiltration; on the results of observations by U.S. diplomats and public affairs
officers; on polls and surveys taken by American officials; and on letters and
debriefings of citizens, refugees, and émigrés. While I hope my argument will
be convincing, at the very least it should be suggestive to those asking some of
the same questions or contemplating kindred research on the impact of American culture abroad.

My personal experience with life in the former USSR informs this study.
In 1990-91 I spent ten months on a Fulbright lectureship at Kazan State
University, in the city of Kazan in the Tatar Republic, some 450 miles east of
Moscow. I did not conduct formal research in the USSR, but rather gained an
understanding of Soviet life that has provided me with a context for contem-
plating issues that otherwise would have remained simply mysterious.

During my extended stay in provincial Russia, I was struck by Soviet
images of the West and by the widespread appeal of market economics and
Western consumer culture.[16] By listening to VOA news programs on my
shortwave radio and watching American films dubbed in Russian, I got a sense
of what it must have been like to perceive the images and symbols of the West
as they filtered through the political barriers. During my stay in the Soviet
Union I took advantage of myriad opportunities to discuss with intellectuals,
workers, friends, and acquaintances the sources of their knowledge and attitudes
about the West. One close friend in particular, Leonid Sidorov, deserves special
mention. It was through discussions with Leonid, first in Kazan and then over
the course of the two years he spent in the United States, that I decided to study
the roots of U.S. cultural infiltration of Russia.

Generous research grants from the University of Akron helped make this
book possible. Scores of friends, colleagues, archivists, and family members also
faciliated my efforts. They include Betty Austin, Shelley Baranowski, Laura
Belmonte, Dennis Bilger, Charles Byler, Barbara Clements, Roger Creel, Mindy
Fetterman, Michael Flamini, Raymond Garthoff, Brian Himebaugh, William
F. Hixson, Robert S. Hopkins III, James Jensen, Deborah Kisatsky, Michael L.
Krenn, David Kyvig, James Leyerzapf, Martin Manning, Daniel Nelson, Christian F. Ostermann, Chester Pach, Thomas G. Paterson, David Pfieffer, Alexander Pikhovkin, James F. Richardson, Robert Schulzinger, Michael S. Sherry,
Holly Cowan Shulman, James Thompson, and William O. Walker III. These
individuals offered invaluable assistance, advice, and criticism, but should not
be held responsible for any factual errors, much less for matters of interpretation,
which are exclusively my own.

PARTING THE CURTAIN

ONE

A Campaign of Truth: The Rebirth of Psychological Warfare

Propaganda—the attempt to influence behavior by shaping the attitudes of masses of people—has always played a role in the conduct of U.S. foreign relations. Beginning with the American Revolution itself, propagandists used information and persuasion, most notably in the Declaration of Independence, to advance the cause of the rebellious colonies. It was not until World War I, however, that propaganda began to play a major role in U.S. diplomacy, both at home and abroad.

One week after intervention on the Allied side in April 1917, President Woodrow Wilson created the Committee on Public Information (CPI), headed by the energetic former editor of the *Rocky Mountain News,* George Creel. While the CPI focused initially on efforts to promote a domestic consensus among a public that had been sharply divided over intervention in the European war, the wartime agency soon shifted its attention to foreign audiences. The CPI used news articles, feature stories, movies, lectures, the telegraph, posters, signboards, a wireless cable service, foreign press bureaus, a film division, and leaflet-filled balloons. Creel and his co-workers displayed "utter sincerity" about their mission to promote democracy and anti-authoritarianism. Critics, however, blamed the CPI for disinformation that increased domestic tensions and spurred the postwar Red Scare. Congress withdrew funding for the CPI in the summer of 1919.[1]

The very term propaganda fell into disrepute during the interwar years. Its pejorative connotation stemmed not only from disillusion about U.S. participation in the European war, but from the activities of propagandists in revolutionary Russia and Nazi Germany. The Soviet and Nazi regimes were quick to exploit advances in twentieth century communications, especially radio and film, which sharply increased the speed, volume, and immediacy of the transmission of propaganda. After the USSR began shortwave radio broadcasting in 1926, Germany, Japan, Britain, and Holland quickly followed suit. Both the Soviets and the Nazis enlisted talented filmmakers in the service of state propaganda.[2]

Only under an emergency of the magnitude of the Second World War could the American public be convinced to support the revival of a government information program. On June 13, 1942, six months after the Japanese attack on Pearl Harbor, President Franklin D. Roosevelt launched the Office of War Information (OWI), whose mission was to explain government policy to the news media and the public, both domestic and foreign. Under the direction of Elmer Davis, a writer and radio commentator, OWI's Overseas Branch established 26 U.S. Information Service (USIS) posts in Europe, Africa, and East Asia. At home, the propaganda agency used all means of communication to exhort Americans to embrace Allied war aims, practice fuel conservation, launch salvage drives, buy war bonds, and support the war effort in every way. Aware that some 80 million Americans a week went to the movies, OWI not only produced its own films, but made Hollywood "a compliant part of the American war machine."[3]

While wartime propagandists used motion pictures, leaflets, and magazines to promote the national interest abroad, few doubted that radio was the most crucial medium in the overseas propaganda campaign. The Voice of America (VOA), inaugurated with a rendition of "The Battle Hymn of the Republic" on July 13, 1942, broadcast U.S. news and war aims 24 hours a day throughout the war. While the desire to advance the Allied cause united all propagandists, ideological disputes emerged over VOA's mission and the content of its programming.[4]

Opposition to the overseas program also materialized in the State Department, already resentful of Roosevelt for bypassing regular diplomatic channels. The Foreign Service professionals believed in elite diplomacy, rather than appealing to the masses, and viewed OWI propaganda as a disruptive force in the nation's foreign policy. In one of many such disputes, the State Department rejected an OWI pamphlet, *The United Nations Fight for the Four Freedoms*, which advocated self-determination in India, on grounds that it might "incite the Indians against the British." Such disputes reflected the waning influence of liberal propagandists, who had not wanted to see the war fought for the preservation of the status quo, including British imperialism in India.[5]

With the liberal agenda in retreat, "psychological warfare" gained prominence. Championed by William D. ("Wild Bill") Donovan, head of the Office of Strategic Services (OSS), psychological warfare encompassed a variety of activities, including propaganda in support of military operations; intelligence gathering; disinformation; sabotage; and myriad additional covert operations. "Bill Donovan," as one associate recalled, "is the sort of guy who thought nothing of parachuting into France, blowing up a bridge, pissing in Lutwaffe gas tanks, then dancing on the roof of the St. Regis Hotel with a German spy."[6]

Despite his swashbuckling style, Donovan failed to implement a coherent strategy of psychological warfare, which instead proceeded on an ad hoc basis. In Europe a Psychological Warfare Division (PWD) eventually coordinated operations, while a Pacific "psywar" network materialized but remained decentralized. The first Allied offensive, the TORCH campaign in North Africa, provided an opportunity to employ psychological warfare. Shortly after launching the invasion of North African shores in November 1942, General Dwight D. Eisenhower entered into an agreement with Admiral Jean Darlan, commander of the Vichy French collaborationist forces. Eisenhower granted Darlan political control of French North Africa in return for a pledge of full cooperation with the Allies. The agreement with Darlan (who was assassinated in December) facilitated Allied military strategy, and saved lives, but was denounced by critics as a compromise with fascism and a violation of the Four Freedoms.[7]

Washington opted for expediency over principle again by backing a new government named by King Victor Emmanuel III, a confirmed fascist, during the Allied invasion of Italy in 1943. While commitment to liberal principles waned, psychological warfare activities mounted. As the Allies fought their way across Italy, VOA conducted an anti-Axis propaganda campaign in which low-flying bombers dropped leaflets targeting both German troops and Italian civilians. In June 1943 alone, Allied planes dumped more than 35 million leaflets on southern Italy, Sicily, and Sardinia. Interviews conducted following the Allied victories in North Africa, Sicily, and Italy revealed that significant numbers of people had listened to Allied broadcasts, or picked up propaganda leaflets, and had been influenced by them. Following the capture of an Italian town, PWB immediately seized all films and replaced them with Allied propaganda drawn from 7,500 reels of "the very best" American films. In addition to the film, radio, leaflet, and newspaper propaganda, the Allies distributed massive amounts of food, medicine, clothing, and other relief supplies in Sicily and Italy. Pointing to "the ceaselessness and the scope of the operation," psychological warriors could "hardly describe the total effect of the day after day, week after week, month after month impact of a really tremendous propaganda program."[8]

The Nazis displayed their perceptions of the threat posed by Allied propaganda by instituting jamming of radio signals, authorizing the death penalty for listening to enemy broadcasts, and dispatching early morning crews to gather up freshly dropped leaflets. The U.S. propaganda paper *L'Amerique en Guerre* proved so popular in occupied France that the Germans printed a bogus version in an effort to sabotage its appeal. Similar papers were circulated in Norway, Spain, Ireland, and Germany itself, where *Sternenbanner* (Star Spangled Banner) encouraged German citizens to abandon their support of the Nazis.[9]

The most decisive Allied offensive on the Western front, the June 1944 cross-channel Normandy invasion, included a substantial psychological warfare effort. The PWD sent 27 million leaflets that argued that opposition to the huge Allied invading force was futile and 100 radio transmitters, printing presses, and mobile loudspeakers ashore with the D-Day landing craft. Allied psychological warriors exploited the July 20, 1944, failed assassination attempt on Adolf Hitler by calling on the German public to abandon its support of the unstable Nazi regime. In August the Nazi satellite government in Rumania, under a heavy Allied propaganda barrage, surrendered and declared war on Germany.

As in Europe, Allied propaganda in the Pacific theatre employed radio, leaflets, and newspapers to appeal to the mass public to abandon their support of Japan and its collaborators. Before General Douglas MacArthur's triumphant return to the Philippines, OWI propagandists sent thousands of "I Shall Return" leaflets and trinkets as well as the newspaper *Free Philippines*. With each victory in the Pacific, U.S. psychological warfare strove to convince the Japanese public that there was no dishonor in ceasing their resistance in view of Japan's inevitable defeat. Finally, in the wake of the devastating atomic bombings of Hiroshima and Nagasaki in August 1945, leaflets declared that "We are in possession of the most destructive explosive ever devised by man" and that further resistance was futile.[10]

By the end of the war propaganda had proven itself a useful complement to military strategy. With government propaganda and information programs controversial even in wartime, however, the end of the war not surprisingly brought intense pressure on the government to get out of the propaganda business. Congress proscribed a domestic information program, and only a minority on Capitol Hill and in the journalistic community advocated maintaining an overseas campaign. Most of those who expressed an opinion believed that with troops returning home after victory in Europe and Asia, the United States should also "disarm" its international information effort.[11]

President Harry S. Truman concluded that Washington still needed an overseas program, but that the wartime agencies would have to be replaced with new information services. On August 31, 1945, Truman issued an executive order abolishing OWI, noting at the same time that "the nature of present-day foreign relations makes it essential for the United States to maintain information activities abroad as an integral part of the conduct of our foreign affairs." The president declared that Washington would not try to "outstrip the extensive and growing information programs of other nations" but would do enough to present "a full and fair picture of American life and of the aims and policies of the United States Government."[12]

To oversee the transition to a peacetime program, Truman ordered the consolidation of all information activities under William B. Benton, an advertising executive and former university vice president who assumed the post of assistant secretary of state for public and cultural affairs. Compelled to make dramatic cuts to accommodate the end of the war, Benton slashed the OWI budget by 80 percent. VOA took the hardest hit, with much of its programming terminated and the number of employees cut from 11,000 to 3,000. After additional congressional budget cuts, the final 1947 appropriation of $25.4 million for information and cultural affairs represented nearly a 50 percent reduction from the $45 million appropriation in the 1946 budget.[13]

Despite opposition, Benton lobbied to gain support for a permanent information service. He declared that foreign peoples' awareness of the U.S. position in world affairs "must be based on education and on the dissemination of knowledge." Benton described the 1947 budget and level of overseas programming as "grossly inadequate. It is not only way below the level of activities of England and Russia, but it is far below what seems to me to be self-evident national needs." Given a lack of funds and of respect, Benton added, it was increasingly difficult to convince the most able men and women to remain in their positions in the government information service.[14]

After two years of mostly losing battles, a consensus emerged in 1947 to establish a postwar propaganda effort as a result of the onset of the Cold War with the Soviet Union. Information and propaganda would play a significant role in the East-West conflict. Already the mere announcement of the Marshall Plan to provide loans and support for European recovery had revived spirits and increased respect for the United States in Europe, a propaganda coup that could hardly be ignored in the Kremlin. The Soviets responded in September 1947 by forming the Cominform (Communist Information Bureau), which delivered propaganda broadsides against the Marshall Plan.[15]

With the Cold War all but declared by both sides, U.S.-Soviet cultural ties, which had expanded greatly during the war, deteriorated sharply. Although mutual hostilities in the wake of the 1917 Bolshevik Revolution had served to discourage cultural contacts in the 1920s, American movies, magazines, and consumer products trickled across Soviet borders. Following Washington's decision to afford the USSR diplomatic recognition in 1933, cultural ties increased through tourism and other activities promoted by organizations such as the American-Russian Institute. In 1938, however, the Soviets began turning away U.S. tourists and condemning Western culture as part of an anti-foreign propaganda campaign. The Stalinist purges and show trials and the signing of the 1939 Nazi-Soviet Pact undermined what limited progress had been made in East-West cultural exchange.[16]

The State Department, which did not form a division of cultural relations until 1938, had done little to promote such exchanges with any country, including most especially the detested Bolsheviks. World War II changed matters, however, in a process that began with Washington seeking broadened cultural ties with Latin America as a means of checking Nazi influence. Once the United States entered the war and embraced the USSR as its ally, Premier Joseph Stalin opened Soviet borders to Lend-Lease aid, as well as to music, films, printed materials, and American tourists. Particularly popular in the USSR were the musical scores circulated by OWI, including "Alexander's Ragtime Band," "Over There," "By the Light of the Silvery Moon," "White Christmas," and "Deep in the Heart of Texas." Moscow's jazz orchestras displayed unlimited demand for the American scores, which remained popular for generations.[17]

Film emerged as an equally popular medium for transmitting American culture in the USSR. Admiral William H. Standley, the U.S. ambassador in Moscow, remarking on "the interest of the Soviet people in all things American," developed as his "pet project" plans to "educate the Russian people about us through the selected use of motion pictures." By 1942, thanks to the efforts of OWI, American newsreels and feature films began to circulate throughout the USSR. Hollywood donated 40 of its most recent popular features to complement a series of OWI documentaries. Beginning in 1944, the State Department circulated *Amerika,* a slick magazine featuring reprints of articles from U.S. publications. Described by a *Time* correspondent in Moscow as "hot stuff," *Amerika* sold out its allotted 10,000 copies virtually overnight. In June 1947, after myriad American requests for expanded circulation, the Soviets authorized an increase to 50,000 copies.

The Soviet Society for Cultural Relations with Foreign Countries (VOKS) welcomed ties with Americans, sponsoring films, jazz group concerts, lectures, and exhibits of art and architecture. The works of Jack London, Mark Twain, Upton Sinclair, and Theodore Dreiser, among others, had long been popular throughout the USSR. The American-Russian Institute and other cultural groups promoted wartime academic exchanges, while other Americans, including tourists, chess teams, and athletes, toured the USSR. A Soviet-American conference on proposed student and teacher exchanges agreed that "a program of cultural exchange with the USSR was of the greatest importance in view of the necessity for better understanding between this country and the Soviets."[18]

As even Stalin himself admitted to U.S. diplomats during the war, the Soviet people were clearly enamored of American culture. By the fall of 1944, however, with victory in Europe virtually assured, the Kremlin took steps to reverse Western cultural infiltration of the USSR. By routing all exchange proposals through the Foreign Ministry, the Soviets centralized authority over cultural matters and ceased cooperation on a number of exchanges, including film and library materials. With the end of the war, scores of individuals and organizations requested State Department assistance in broadening ties with the USSR, but the Soviets remained obdurate. Washington worsened a deteriorating situation when the Justice Department enforced the exclusionary Foreign Agents Registration Act, which had been suspended during the war, against Soviet scientific and cultural exchange groups. That decision gave the Soviets an excuse, exploited by propaganda organs, to clamp down further on cultural contacts. In 1945 a U.S. embassy official in Moscow reported "insuperable obstacles" posed by the Soviet bureaucracy that precluded "even the most rudimentary cultural interchange."[19]

Soviet specialist Ernest J. Simmons, representing the American Council of Learned Societies, mounted a final effort to preserve Soviet-Amerian cultural contacts in the midst of rising Cold War tensions. Spending weeks in Moscow in 1947, Simmons negotiated with VOKS and Soviet government officials in an effort to maintain the student and professorial, book, and periodical exchange programs. Soviet rejection of this sincere and sympathetic appeal ended any hope of maintaining broadened cultural ties in the early Cold War. Rejection of Simmons's mission offered conclusive evidence of the Kremlin's quest to isolate the Soviet people from Western cultural influence.[20]

Obviously concerned about the impact of massive exposure to Western culture in the war years, the Kremlin launched a campaign to purge the USSR of foreign influence. In the late forties and early fifties, Soviet propaganda targeted jazz, "false films," and Western artists and writers. In Moscow, as many as a dozen plays at a time condemned American politics, racism, Hollywood culture, VOA broadcasts, Truman, and anti-communist congressional investigations. Soviet officials impeded the circulation of *Amerika*, prompting Washington to retaliate in 1952 by halting the distribution of Moscow's *Information Bulletin* in the U.S. While trumpeting socialist realism as the only legitimate art form, Soviet authorities harassed artists and composers whose work reflected "servility before contemporary bourgeois culture." They placed sharp restrictions on the ability of Soviets to maintain contact with foreigners, who were relegated to defined areas, harassed, and sometimes arrested. In the United States, the FBI hounded liberals and leftists who attempted to maintain contact with the Soviets, exercising a chilling effect on increasingly futile efforts to keep East-West cultural exchange alive.[21]

While attempting to purge Western influence inside the USSR, the Soviets stepped up cultural activity beyond their borders. In 1950, according to U.S. estimates, 17,000 foreigners came to the USSR on exchange programs, while 39,000 Soviets went abroad. In 1953, the number of individuals going to the USSR on exchange programs had increased to 45,000. By contrast, the State Department's Division of Exchange of Persons administered a program that sent only about 500 Americans abroad in 1948. As exchange programs gained an expanded role under the Truman administration, some 8,000 Americans went abroad in 1951, still well behind the Soviet effort.[22]

Fears that the USSR was gaining ground in the Cold War prompted increased efforts to mount an effective overseas cultural program. Claiming that the USSR spent more on cultural programs in France than the United States devoted to its entire international effort, the *New York Times* criticized "America's foolish disregard of the importance of the 'cultural offensive.'" Truman administration officials used similar arguments to appeal for increased congressional funding, warning that the Kremlin used international exhibits, film festivals, and exchange programs as part of its effort to destabilize non-communist regimes worldwide.[23]

Although postwar budget cuts limited efforts to promote U.S. culture abroad, the 1946 Fulbright Act was a significant exception. Named for Democratic Senator J. William Fulbright, former president of the University of Arkansas, the legislation was an amendment to the 1944 Surplus Property Act. The Fulbright Act established an educational exchange program financed by the foreign sale in nondollar currencies of surplus war material. The money would be used to provide scholarships for foreign nationals to study in the United States, and for American students, professors, and researchers to study overseas. A Board of Foreign Scholarships, appointed by the president, overseen by the State Department, and guided by private foundations, would administer the program. In 1948, 47 Americans and 36 foreign nationals participated in the program. By the 1990s the total number of participants had reached the hundreds of thousands.[24]

Fulbright was an early convert to the view that cultural and intellectual concerns, too often overlooked, were the equal of economic, military, and diplomatic matters in promoting the national interest. He feared that fascism and war had not only destroyed European facilities for cultural development, but had terrorized teachers and intellectuals. The exchange program would spread U.S. influence and help revive the European intellectual community. A precedent had been set by Herbert Hoover's Belgian Relief Commission, which in 1920 established a foundation that sponsored the exchange of hundreds of Belgian and American students. Since the sale of surplus property abroad, rather than any new appropriations, would finance the Fulbright program, it passed the 79th Congress with little opposition and almost no fanfare. "Whether or not it was admitted, or even recognized," noted one historian, "the Fulbright Bill provided for the creation of an overseas American educational imperium."[25]

Similarly, the United States strove to convert the United Nations Educational, Scientific, and Cultural Organization (UNESCO) into "a mouthpiece for the expression of American ideological interests." Washington joined UNESCO on July 30, 1946, but as the Cold War emerged, the Truman administration abandoned UNESCO's quest for a nonpolitical, multilateral program of educational and cultural advancement. Instead of promoting international understanding, UNESCO became a tool of Washington's campaign to attack communism and "integrate the free world." Benton was particularly keen on exploiting UNESCO's ability to reach millions of people, ranging from church groups to labor organizations, for the crusade against communism.[26]

The Fulbright program and UNESCO provided vehicles to expand American influence in the non-communist world, but cultural relations with the Communist Party–dominated regimes of Eastern Europe fell victim to the Cold War. In Prague, U.S. ambassador Lawrence Steinhardt favored extending the Fulbright program to Czechoslovakia, explaining in 1947 that it was "far more desirable to spread our culture in areas where [a] strenuous attempt is made to suppress and dominate it than in countries which are not in [the] Soviet sphere." As Cold War tensions mounted, however, officials concluded that conducting exchange programs with the USSR and Eastern Europe would be a sign of weakness and a form of appeasement. The State Department vetoed efforts by the Fulbright Board of Foreign Scholarships to negotiate agreements with the Communist Party (CP) regimes, while pledging not to interfere with private efforts.[27]

The failure of attempts to extend cultural influence into the USSR and Eastern Europe stemmed more from CP obstruction than from lack of effort. Various agencies and missions conducted informational and cultural activities aimed at sustaining Western influence. Much of the cultural activity flowed from the U.S. missions, but myriad unofficial groups such as the Red Cross, YMCA, CARE, American Friends Service Committee, and relief and refugee organizations also served to counter Soviet propaganda about Western intentions while lending moral and sometimes material support to opponents of Soviet hegemony. "Western missions, both humanitarian and diplomatic," the

Central Intelligence Agency (CIA) reported, "have served to sustain the people of Eastern Europe in their belief in the superiority of Western culture as well as to keep them informed regarding the actuality of Soviet aims." Perceiving the threat posed by both official and unofficial agents of Western cultural influence, the USSR launched a broad campaign to reduce Western influence. The CIA reported that the intensified Soviet campaign consisted of "harassing actions . . . against the U.S. and other non-communist nations, including the expulsion of certain Western cultural, religious, and humanitarian agencies, the curtailment of diplomatic activities, the trial and imprisonment of U.S. citizens."[28]

The anti-Western campaign began in late 1949 and culminated in February 1950 with the U.S.-Bulgarian suspension of diplomatic relations. Hungary requested that Washington reduce the size of its mission, whereas Rumania accomplished the same end by refusing to grant visas and by closing the cultural offices of both the U.S. and British legations. In Czechoslovakia, CP authorities lashed out at the Western missions, forced the closing of the USIS office, expelled the cultural attaché, and demanded that Washington reduce its embassy staff by two-thirds in view of its "anti-State" activities. Accompanying this activity, the CIA charged, were regular efforts by security forces to implicate U.S. personnel in various illegal activities.[29]

In concert with the campaign against the diplomatic missions, the Eastern European regimes mounted a concerted effort to drive out Western cultural and charitable institutions. By late 1948 Bulgaria and Rumania had closed all foreign-sponsored schools in their countries; most Western relief agencies, including UNICEF, the Red Cross, CARE, the Foster Parents' Plan for War Children, and the International Refugee Organization, had been driven out. A similar campaign, the CIA charged, had led to "ejecting or imprisoning nearly every Western journalist unsympathetic to their regimes." The anti-Western campaign included "subordinating the organized Protestant, Jewish, and Orthodox Churches to state control" as well as efforts "to detach the Roman Catholic clergy from the Vatican in order to organize them into national churches submissive to the state." The USSR simultaneously launched a "peace offensive" in which delegates at various international meetings and congresses blamed the Cold War and the threat of atomic weapons on Western imperialism.[30]

In the midst of the Soviet purge of Western cultural influence, the Republican-controlled 80th Congress responded to Truman's call for bolstering the overseas information program. Upon their return from a tour of Europe in January 1948, Republicans Senator H. Alexander Smith of New Jersey and Representative Karl Mundt of North Dakota declared that the Soviets were "directing a campaign of vilification and misrepresentation" in which the United States was the primary target. Washington had no choice but to "counteract the insidious undermining of the free forces resisting communism" and to explain U.S. "ideals, motives and objectives to a demoralized and groping Europe." Supporters of the call for a revived information program noted that Britain and France, despite their devastation and financial weakness, had mounted far more extensive propaganda efforts than had the United States.[31]

Bipartisan cooperation led to passage of the Smith-Mundt Act, which provided the overseas information program with its basic postwar legal foundation. Passed overwhelmingly by Congress on January 16, 1948, and signed into law by Truman 11 days later, the Smith-Mundt Act aimed "to promote the better understanding of the United States among the peoples of the world and to strengthen cooperative international relations." The legislation envisioned using all the tools of modern communications, including print, radio, film, exchange programs, and exhibitions, to disseminate information about the United States. While the Fulbright Act had allowed for exchange programs only with countries that possessed excess war material, the Smith-Mundt Act made the program global in scope and provided for continuing funding when the sale of the wartime surplus had been exhausted.[32]

Passage of the Smith-Mundt Act revived once-flagging U.S. efforts and established a foundation for efforts to promote propaganda and culture abroad. George V. Allen, a career Foreign Service officer who replaced Benton as assistant secretary of state for public affairs in 1948, called the Smith-Mundt Act "revolutionary," adding that "the real significance of the change which was made in the conduct of our foreign policy is not yet appreciated or even understood by many people." Under the impetus provided by the Smith-Mundt Act, Washington launched an aggressive campaign of anti-communist propaganda. U.S. efforts focused on uniting the "free world" and undermining the Soviet and East European regimes. For 1949, the first full year of operation under the new law, a $31.2 million appropriation represented a doubling of the money spent on the foreign information program the previous year, including $3 million for a radio relay program to revive the VOA.[33]

As with economic recovery and military assistance programs, the consensus to expand overseas information activities paralleled the rise of Cold War tensions. In 1948-49, the Czech coup, Berlin Blockade, successful Soviet test of an atomic weapon, and the "loss" of China to communism sent shock waves through the West. USIS posts emphasized putative Soviet aggressive designs as well as U.S. responses, such as the Berlin Airlift and the Truman Point Four program pledging technical assistance to developing countries. Deepening Cold War tensions silenced domestic critics of the overseas program, many of whom now conceded the need for resources to combat increasingly hostile Soviet propaganda.

While "containment" of communism has long been viewed as the essence of Cold War policy, Washington's aims actually transcended the purely defensive goals that the term implies. U.S. policy mirrored the advice of Soviet expert George F. Kennan, whose formulation of containment actually envisioned the rollback of Soviet hegemony. While rollback or "liberation" was the ultimate goal of U.S. strategy, at the very least Kennan anticipated a "mellowing" of Soviet policy. Kennan believed that the USSR, a fundamentally unstable regime, might soon be "overshadowed . . . by clouds of civil disintegration." Kennan and his colleagues envisaged the policy of "firm and vigilant containment" as a means to promote the disintegration of CP authority extending from Berlin to Moscow itself.[34]

By definition, the Cold War—a state of belligerency absent direct superpower conflict—established limits on overt American aggressiveness. Although Washington armed for war, it had no intention of starting a military conflict over Soviet hegemony in Eastern Europe. Even in the steps that it took short of war, the United States refrained from overt warlike behavior. In the mutual recriminations that emanated from both capitals, limits had to be adhered to if formal diplomatic relations were to be maintained. Few such restraints governed the *covert* behavior of the East-West rivals, however. In Washington, the creation of the CIA under the National Security Act of 1947 provided the bureaucratic structure required to launch a campaign of "peacetime" psychological warfare that aimed to undermine the Soviet and East European regimes.[35]

Creation of the CIA reflected a consensus on the need for a modern intelligence gathering apparatus, but the legislation also empowered the agency to perform unspecified "other functions." National security elites interpreted the clause broadly, eventually endorsing not only "black propaganda, primarily designed for subversion, confusion, and political effect," but also coups against undesirable governments and even assassination of foreign leaders. In December 1947 the NSC placed the CIA in charge of conducting covert psychological operations under State Department policy guidance. At the time officials were alarmed about Soviet efforts "to gain control of key elements of life in France and Italy."[36]

Washington responded with extensive economic aid, a concerted propaganda campaign employing news features and documentary films, and covert action. The latter included use of unattributed and subsidized publications, forgery, payoffs, and other forms of manipulation. CIA funds helped undermine the appeal of the French CP, but the Italian CP, large and well organized, appeared on the verge of victory—so much so that Kennan at one point called for a U.S. military occupation of the country. However, the promise of economic and military aid, and the growing appeal of indigenous anti-communist forces, led to victory by the non-communist center-right coalition in the April 18, 1948, Italian election.[37]

Psychological warriors believed the lesson of the French and Italian campaigns was that U.S. intervention in other nations' politics could produce victories over communism. Appealing for funds on behalf of an aggressive overseas propaganda program, OWI veteran Edward W. Barrett told a congressional committee that the "all-out psychological effort" had been responsible for the defeat of the Italian CP. He urged a worldwide psychological warfare offensive in which Washington would "go just about as all-out as we did in Italy."[38]

Citing the "vicious covert activities of the USSR," NSC 10/2 (June 1948) authorized a new CIA covert operations branch for which "the U.S. government can plausibly disclaim any responsibility." The measures short of war to be employed included "propaganda; economic warfare; preventive direct action, including sabotage, anti-sabotage, demolition, and evacuation measures; subversion against hostile states, including assistance to underground resistance movements, guerrillas and refugee liberation groups, and support of indigenous anti-communist elements in threatened countries of the free world." Legislation approved in 1949 authorized the CIA to spend money at the director's discretion, exempting it from the requirement that government agencies be accountable to Congress. Personnel and funds for covert operations increased, respectively, from 302 and $4.7 million in 1949 to 2,812 and $82 million in 1952.[39]

By the spring of 1950 an increasingly aggressive U.S. propaganda campaign attested to the emergence of a virtual crusade against communism. The Smith-Mundt Act had merely resolved the question of the *existence* of a government overseas campaign. A substantial increase in appropriations would be required to meet the new goal of making the overseas program an integral part of the broader national security policy of undermining Marxist-Leninist movements worldwide.[40]

The point man in the more aggressive Cold War propaganda campaign was Edward Barrett, a *Newsweek* editor who had worked closely with "Wild Bill" Donovan in World War II psychological warfare. Barrett, an Alabama Democrat, replaced George Allen (named ambassador to Yugoslavia) as assistant secretary of state for public affairs in February 1950. Experienced with wartime propaganda, and respected by influential journalists, Barrett was ideally positioned to direct the Truman administration's propaganda offensive.[41]

As part of "an all-out effort to penetrate the Iron Curtain with our ideas," Barrett sought increased funding and technical improvements to overcome a Soviet campaign of jamming VOA radio signals. He called for greater cooperation with U.S. allies, especially Britain and France, to counter Soviet propaganda and disinformation. Admitting that propaganda should not be considered a "magic weapon" that could bring a quick victory in the Cold War,

Barrett insisted nonetheless that it could serve as an important complement to the Marshall Plan. "The threat of Soviet-Communist tyranny cannot be met by material means alone," he declared.[42]

Several of Truman's top advisers endorsed the idea of a propaganda offensive, but it was Barrett who counseled the president to avoid using the insidious term itself. He had first advised "a bold new propaganda offensive, perhaps styled 'The Voice of Freedom,'" but finally settled instead on the slogan "Campaign of Truth." Truman chose to launch the campaign in a speech in Washington on April 20, 1950, before the American Society of Newspaper Editors, a group once openly hostile to a government overseas propaganda program. In his speech the president declared that the Cold War was "a struggle, above all else, for the minds of men" and that the forces of "imperialistic communism" were winning the propaganda battle through a systematic program of deceit and distortion. "Unless we get the real story across to people in other countries," Truman warned, "we will lose the battle for men's minds by default." The president called for a "sustained, intensified program to promote the cause of freedom against the propaganda of slavery."[43]

The Campaign of Truth emerged in the context of the Truman administration's sweeping review of U.S. diplomacy, one that culminated in the promulgation of the historic NSC Paper No. 68 in April 1950. Drafted principally by Paul Nitze, but based on previous State Department papers, the apocalyptic document asserted that "the issues that face us are momentous, involving the fulfillment or destruction not only of the Republic but of civilization itself." NSC 68 provided a conceptual framework that attributed all communist movements to a "Kremlin design," rejected negotiations with CP regimes, and ultimately sanctioned a more than tripling of U.S. military expenditures, including the cultivation of an arsenal of tactical and strategic nuclear weapons, the establishment and maintenance of a chain of overseas bases, and global intervention in other nations' internal affairs under the sacrosanct banner of "national security."[44]

Testifying in executive session before the Senate Foreign Relations Committee, Barrett explained that the Campaign of Truth flowed from the "inevitable conclusion" of NSC 68 "that the world situation was deteriorating and deteriorating rapidly. On the basis of that the President, on the advice of numerous people, reached the conclusion that we needed to step up [overseas propaganda] activities." More than a mere propaganda appeal, the Campaign of Truth was part of a broad Truman administration offensive that aimed to achieve a "preponderance of power" over the USSR and its allies.[45]

The Campaign of Truth signaled a renewed determination to undermine communism across the globe. Planning for the campaign entailed targeting key regions of the world and implementing a propaganda strategy to counter Soviet efforts. A country-by-country assessment identified a "hard core" region, consisting of the USSR and Eastern Europe; "the crucial periphery," including nations such as Thailand, Burma, South Korea, Greece, Turkey, and Yugoslavia; and "the danger zone," including Italy, France, India, Pakistan, Ceylon [Sri Lanka], Indonesia, and the Philippines. After identifying these regions, Barrett explained, plans were made to employ propaganda to assist in "rolling back, as far as you can do it psychologically, or helping to roll back, Soviet power." Plans called for destabilizing the Eastern European regimes, including efforts "to encourage and exploit defections, which can be awfully important on the propaganda front."[46]

The Truman administration received an unprecedented level of congressional support for the propaganda offensive. Avoiding the term itself, administration officials revived psychological warfare as a more compelling term in appealing for congressional funds. "In those days we found that money for pure information operations, for libraries in neutral areas, for sending American performers abroad, was very hard to come by," Barrett would explain later. "American congressmen, like Americans in general, were suspicious of anything that could be labeled propaganda," but "if you dressed it up as warfare, money was very easy to come by."[47]

William Benton, who had once held Barrett's position but now served as a democratic senator from Connecticut, emerged as the leading congressional spokesman for the aggressive propaganda campaign. Benton called for recognition "that the central issue of our time is intellectual and spiritual, and that the heart of the present conflict is a struggle for the minds and loyalties of mankind." Benton won widespread support for a Senate resolution calling for a sharply expanded foreign information program, "a Marshall Plan in the field of ideas." A parade of luminaries, including Dean Acheson, Dwight Eisenhower, John Foster Dulles, Walter Bedell Smith, Bernard Baruch, and David Sarnoff, testified in behalf of Benton's resolution in July hearings.[48]

Acheson, who normally displayed little enthusiasm for propaganda, appeared before the House Appropriations Committee in August 1950 to promote the Campaign of Truth as "a vital supplement to the military, economic, and political activities of our government abroad." The secretary of state explained that there were "large areas of the world where, unless we can do something about getting the story across, Soviet propagandists have no competition." Twenty-seven senators responded to Acheson's appeal by urging the president to embark on a "psychological and spiritual offensive against the Kremlin." Truman's congressionally mandated advisory commission on information also weighed in with a strong endorsement of an expanded propaganda effort. After the usual squabbles and cuts, the administration received nearly $80 million more than the regular appropriation of $32 million, including substantial increases for radio operations; press and publications; motion pictures; exchange of persons; and various additional cultural activities.[49]

The dramatic increase in congressional appropriations for the overseas program came only after the outbreak of the Korean War, which seemed to the Truman administration to confirm the darkest perceptions of NSC 68. When the war broke out on June 25, 1950, no one in the Truman administration doubted that Stalin had masterminded the attack. In fact, North Korea's Kim Il Sung had repeatedly pressed for the invasion and had gained Stalin's reluctant approval for it, at a time when an incipient civil war was already under way on the Korean peninsula. The Korean War assured congressional support for the Campaign of Truth. "It was conceived as an emergency program," Barrett explained, "and became a very special emergency program under the emphasis of the Korean outbreak."[50]

The intensification of the Cold War from 1948 to 1950, which culminated in the Korean War and the implementation of NSC 68, spurred a revival of psychological warfare dedicated to undermining the Eastern European regimes and ultimately the USSR itself. Truman's Campaign of Truth reflected a decision that a traditional information program was not enough, that a more aggressive propaganda policy would be required to undermine Soviet hegemony and deliver victory in the Cold War. What followed was a concerted effort to define and implement a psychological warfare policy that would achieve the ultimate goal of liberation.

As in World War II, psychological warriors employed a variety of means, including propaganda and covert operations. At the end of World War II psychological warfare had remained "a going concern," but after the dismantling of OWI it had "disappeared from the scene." As a result of postwar demobilization and the attendant budget cuts, psychological warfare had languished, explained analyst Edward P. Lilly, until "the realization dawned that here was a weapon which could be used in this twilight war zone in which we found ourselves living." The Cold War thus spurred a "renaissance" in psychological warfare.[51]

The revival of psychological warfare gained impetus from a special report the State Department commissioned from the Massachusetts Institute of Technology (MIT) on "the broad problem of how to get information into Russia." Project TROY, named, appropriately, for the legendary operation employing a wooden horse, brought together 21 scholars from MIT and Harvard in a study group that first convened in October 1950. Their principal aim, according to President James Killian of MIT, centered on "ways of getting information behind the Iron Curtain." The group addressed technical means of circumventing Soviet jamming and analyzed communications theory, psychology, and other aspects of information transmission.[52]

The top-secret final report of Project TROY, delivered to the State Department on February 15, 1951, provided "the intellectual framework for waging total cold war." Project TROY also served as a model of cooperation—or cooptation—between universities and the national security bureaucracy. Undersecretary Barrett praised the report for having "blazed new paths" while another State Department analysis called Project TROY the "principal research undertaken with reference to penetration of the Iron Curtain" and one with "vast implications for the overt propaganda program."[53]

After carefully analyzing all "methods of perforating the Iron Curtain," the study group advocated a psychological warfare campaign that "may yet achieve our purposes without armed conflict." Project TROY forwarded a thoroughgoing analysis of radio transmission, leaflet-filled balloons, and other propaganda programs. The group made recommendations concerning means of exploiting anti-communist defectors. TROY noted that U.S. material superiority "impress[es] the Russians," but should not be overtly emphasized so as not to alienate or prompt a defensive reaction on the part of a proud people.

Aside from its specific and technical recommendations, Project TROY contributed directly to the creation of a new entity to manage the disjointed U.S. psychological warfare effort. Calling attention to bureaucratic infighting and turf guarding among State, Defense, CIA, and other agencies, the study group concluded that "the parts are there—in separate agencies and departments—but the whole is not there." Absent a "coherent relationship under central direction" of the economic, military, diplomatic, and information services, "our political warfare will lack the striking power it needs today."[54]

Partly in response to these concerns, and convinced of the need for an expanded psychological warfare effort in view of the Korean War, Truman ordered the NSC to consider means to bring information, propaganda, and psychological warfare under one government umbrella. As a result, the Truman administration created the Psychological Strategy Board (PSB) and charged it with uniting the national security bureaucracy behind a campaign of psychological warfare. Established on April 4, 1951, the PSB was to report to the NSC on "national psychological operations." The agencies represented on the PSB were State, Defense, CIA, and the Joint Chiefs of Staff. The PSB had a full-time director—Gordon Gray, a former university president and retired secretary of the army—and could add representatives from other government agencies on an ad hoc basis. The PSB acted as "the nerve-center for strategic psychological operations," the "focal point . . . of activities to influence the opinions, attitudes, emotions, and behavior of foreign groups." PSB was to serve as a sort of clearing house that the President could quickly consult for an assessment of the nation's progress in psychological warfare. The CIA concurred "that the scope of the Board's responsibility is very broad and covers every kind of activity in support of . . . accomplishing the aims and purposes of NSC 68 and related papers."[55]

Creation of the PSB marked a watershed in the transformation of the postwar overseas program. "Psychological considerations" would now receive "concentrated attention at the most responsible levels of the Government." Enthusiasts averred that psychological warfare, once dismissed as "a minor but necessary adjunct to the handling of international affairs," had achieved equivalent status with diplomacy, economics, and military affairs in the structure of national security policy.[56]

Psychological warriors hoped that the PSB would, as propagandist Wallace Carroll put it, "fire the rocket to signal the opening of a major offensive." Carroll declared that it was the PSB's "'Manifest Destiny'" to ignite a campaign whose ultimate objective was the "rollback of Soviet power." The PSB worked in close association with the Project TROY group at MIT in continuing efforts to exploit "salients" in the Iron Curtain. The PSB also worked in concert with the CIA, whose funds paid PSB director Gray's salary.[57]

PSB priorities for the last half of 1951 called for shoring up economic, political, and military programs in Western Europe and Japan ("mopping up . . . in the free world"), but emphasized "offensive action against Eastern Europe." The psychological warfare plan centered around a destabilization program "to make East Germany a political, economic, and military liability to the Soviets." Plans included direct action against the Soviets through use of radio and other propaganda operations designed to "stir up maximum disaffection among the Soviet peasants and other groups." The global psychological warfare agenda included proposed campaigns in the Middle East and "a big psychological offensive" in East Asia.[58]

In October 1951, NSC 114/2 endorsed the PSB psychological warfare agenda, including efforts to promote the "ultimate liberation and identification with the free world" of the Eastern European regimes. The NSC paper advocated continued strengthening of the VOA, including more transmitting and anti-jamming equipment, as well as a strong effort in press and publications, motion pictures, libraries and information centers, educational and other exchange programs, and directed projects in special areas such as Austria, Western Germany, and Japan.[59]

Despite the favorable reception of some of its proposals, the PSB failed to achieve its "manifest destiny" of uniting the national security bureaucracy behind a coordinated psychological warfare effort that would force the retrenchment of Soviet power. Even had its aims been more modest, lack of adequate funding, disputes over representation on the PSB, bureaucratic infighting, and the general decline of the Truman administration's fortunes all conspired to limit the effectiveness of the psychological warfare effort. In his annual budget message to Congress in January 1951, Truman had requested $115 million for the foreign information program, but in October Congress appropriated only $85 million. By then Truman, battered over the inconclusive Korean stalemate, including his recall of General MacArthur, as well as allegations of communist infiltration of the U.S. government, could no longer inspire support for his diplomacy.[60]

Not only did the Korean stalemate continue to frustrate Americans but, as the PSB admitted in a status report to the NSC, "the Soviet grip in the Communist-dominated areas of Europe and of the Far East appeared to be even firmer at the end of the fiscal year 1952 than at the beginning." The overall psychological warfare effort was improving, but remained "inadequate for taking immediately effective action contributing to retraction of the Kremlin's power and influence."[61]

The PSB produced reams of studies, but failed to marshal the national security bureaucracy behind a coordinated effort. "Our psychological operating agencies are like bodies of troops without a commander and staff," a Defense Department official lamented. "Not having been told what to do or where to go, but too dynamic to stand still, the troops have marched in all directions." The PSB failed to achieve its goal of uniting the executive branch, State, Defense, all branches of the military, CIA, Congress, the Bureau of Budget, academic specialists, and corporate interests behind a campaign of psychological warfare. Bureaucratic disputes included CIA Director Walter Bedell Smith's rejection of Director Gordon Gray's request for PSB representation on the NSC. Denied the representation he deemed vital to achieving a coordinated psychological offensive, Gray resigned in May 1952 as PSB director after less than a year on the job.[62]

While the Cold War had ensured that propaganda would remain a part of national security policy, bureaucratic disorganization, jurisdictional disputes, and domestic politics plagued the U.S. effort. Under the Marshall Plan, for example, the Economic Cooperation Administration (ECA) publicized its own efforts to win the popular support of Western Europeans. The State Department complained of encroachment and duplication of information activities and proposed to absorb the ECA effort. ECA fought the proposal, asserting that because of the persistence of its traditional prejudice against foreign information programs, the State Department was "not able to operate as effective a propaganda program as ECA." Significantly, however, ECA officials said they would consider a merger under a new propaganda agency, divorced from the State Department.[63]

Threatened by the prospect of an independent information agency, the State Department mounted a turf-guarding campaign. Despite skepticism among professional diplomats regarding the utility of propaganda and cultural initiatives, the State Department did not want to lose its authority over such activities. On January 16, 1952, in response to renewed calls for creation of a separate information agency, the State Department announced the creation of a new International Information Administration (IIA), headed by an administrator who would report directly to the secretary of state and serve as chairman of the PSB. Barrett resigned as assistant secretary in early 1952, his role assumed, in effect, by the new IIA administrator, Republican educator Wilson Compton.[64]

This, the latest in a series of bureaucratic reshufflings that characterized the Truman administration's efforts to mount a coherent overseas program, failed to mollify critics of State Department control. Journalists, members of Congress, and anti-communist zealots continued to attack the VOA and other parts of the foreign information program. Benton, joined by Republican presidential candidate Eisenhower, among others, called for reconceptualization and bureaucratic reorganization of the entire overseas program.[65]

In 1951 Benton publicly advocated a separate agency devoted exclusively to overseas information activities. At his initiative, the Senate Foreign Relations Committee (SFRC) began investigating the existing information program on June 30, 1952. Six months later a bipartisan SFRC subcommittee urged a strengthening of the government overseas program as well as of private agencies that might aid in the propaganda campaign. The subcommittee, which included Benton, Mundt, and Fulbright, criticized duplication of services, especially the existence of separate information divisions in myriad government agencies, yet they opposed "divorcing the information programs of the United States from the Department of State as proposed in some quarters."[66]

While controversy swirled over the proper place for the foreign information program, Cold War militarization continued to dominate U.S. diplomacy. Funding for foreign economic and military policy vastly exceeded the resources devoted to the overseas information program. In 1952 Congress set appropriations for 1953 at $86.5 million, the approximate level at which they remained for the next two years. In contrast, NSC 68, the embodiment of militarization, envisioned a threefold increase in defense spending totaling some $40 *billion*. "The American people have not yet been asked to consider whether an investment in peace by communication and by education is remotely in a class with military and economic investments," Benton complained. "The voices in the field have been few and weak."[67]

IIA administrator Wilson Compton concurred. "As a nation we are not really trying to win the 'cold war'. We are relying on armaments and armies to win a 'hot war' if a 'hot war' comes. But winning a hot war which leaves a cold war unwon will not win very much for very long." Compton blamed the congressional parsimony on "a general apathy toward a Government program overseas, about which the public so far has little understanding . . . [and] which the people of the United States themselves never hear and never see." Public indifference could be overcome only when "our people get an understanding that winning a 'cold war' may be a practical way of avoiding or largely reducing the needs of continuous gigantic investments in means of 'hot war.'"[68]

Despite limited funding, the Truman administration had launched an aggressive program of psychological warfare that aimed to undermine communist movements worldwide. Although under fire and in disarray, VOA was still broadcasting to 100 countries in 46 languages; the U.S. press service supplied materials to 10,000 foreign newspapers a day; a motion picture service reached an audience of over 300 million in 1952; U.S. information centers could be found in more than 60 countries and 190 cities worldwide; and thousands of students, teachers, writers, scientists, artists, journalists, farmers, and labor leaders were participating in exchange programs. Considering that Americans had "started out in this business as amateurs," Edward Barrett believed that Washington had made "extraordinary progress" during the Truman years.[69]

The foreign information program played a marginal role in the 1952 presidential campaign. Denied the White House for 20 years, the Republicans savaged the Truman administration over the "loss" of China and the stalemated "limited war" in Korea. The GOP condemned containment as an "immoral" and "pantywaist" diplomacy that left the initiative with the Soviets while relegating the United States to a reactive posture. John Foster Dulles, the most prominent Republican internationalist, trumpeted "liberation" as an alternative to containment, as did author James Burnham in his influential *Containment or Liberation?*.[70]

Eisenhower himself quietly planned to elevate psychological warfare to the center of Cold War strategy. One subordinate recalled that the president possessed a "natural understanding of overseas opinion and world opinion, and the struggle that was going on between the East and the West for people's minds and people's adherence." Barrett made a similar observation, noting that Eisenhower "understood better than most" the importance of information and culture, both during the war and in his presidency. Theodore Streibert, whom Eisenhower would name to head the United States Information Agency (USIA), declared that "the President took a great interest in this, and he understood propaganda. . . . He was sensitive to it."[71]

Eisenhower and Dulles would elevate covert operations and the campaign for liberation to the center of the nation's foreign policy. Dulles charted an aggressive foreign policy that sought nothing less than "the disintegration of Soviet power," a goal that Eisenhower "emphatically endorsed." As a result of the "loss" of China and the stalemate in Korea, mere containment of communism had been discredited by 1952. Eisenhower himself embraced the concept of liberation and intended to use propaganda and covert operations to try to achieve it.[72]

Eisenhower had been enthusiastic about psychological warfare since his World War II command. "I don't know much about psychological warfare," he had admitted during the North Africa campaign, "but I want to give it every chance." After psychological warfare tactics had proven themselves in North Africa and subsequent campaigns, Eisenhower overcame "the original hurdle of soldierly distrust" to become a true believer in such tactics. He was particularly impressed by the effectiveness of British Broadcasting Corporation programs as well as clandestine wartime radio stations in undermining enemy morale and shortening the war.[73]

Eisenhower's wartime interest in propaganda and psychological warfare carried over into his own presidential administration. "In the final analysis," he explained, "public opinion wins most of the wars and always wins the peace." Eisenhower surrounded himself with committed psychological warriors, men such as John Foster and Allen Dulles, Generals Lucius Clay and Alfred Gruenther, Republican internationalist Nelson Rockefeller, and Walter Bedell Smith. The ultimate psychological warrior of the Eisenhower team, however, was C. D. Jackson, whom Eisenhower had named in 1943 to head the wartime Psychological Warfare Division.[74]

While Jackson described psychological warfare as "near and dear to my heart," actually it was closer to an obsession than a love affair. A vice president of Time-Life, Inc. at the time of the 1952 election, Jackson had maintained a close relationship with Eisenhower since their wartime collaboration. One administration insider described the two as "great friends," adding that Eisenhower displayed "enormous confidence in C. D. Jackson in the field of opinion-molding and propaganda and international actions and reactions." Eisenhower made Jackson the first special assistant to the president for Cold War planning, which provided Jackson an office in the White House.[75]

The triumph of the Chinese Communist Party followed by the outbreak of fighting in Korea had left Jackson in a state of virtual panic. Highly patriotic and a staunch believer in free enterprise, Jackson envisioned the spread of American values throughout the world. He feared, however, that communism, itself "a very dynamic idea," had begun to reach "well beyond the limits of Slavic desperation." Unless it undertook a campaign of psychological warfare to bolster allies and undermine CP regimes, the United States could see its world position erode. On the other hand, Jackson described himself as "steamed up by the conviction that World War III can literally be won without fighting it if Psychwar is used intelligently and boldly."[76]

The problem, to Jackson, was ignorance and lack of political will in Washington. "The gentlemen on the Potomac are so accustomed to failure . . . in psychological warfare that they are unable to recognize success when they see it," he complained in March 1952. Because the Cold War was "an unorthodox situation," few understood "the power or the potential of psychological warfare." A program backed by "adequate funds, no holds barred" and "no questions asked" was needed. But, Jackson lamented, "there is no Plan, and it is absolutely shocking." The entrance of Eisenhower into the presidential campaign, however, promised salvation.[77]

In May 1952, months before the election, Jackson kept Eisenhower apprised of a high-level meeting on psychological warfare at Princeton. Jackson organized the top-secret conference, the purpose of which was to produce a political warfare blueprint that could be laid on the president's desk the day he took office. Representatives from the State Department, the PSB, the CIA, radio propagandists, and academic specialists from Princeton and MIT—28 in all—met to discuss the problem. Adopting Jackson's own language, they agreed at the two-day meeting that "political (psychological) warfare, properly employed, can win World War III for us without recourse to arms." The Cold War planners declared that "in spite of our great pride of American salesmanship, the Russians have had it all over us in this department." Needed was "a more dynamic and positive policy" as "our foreign policy has failed to clearly enunciate a policy of determination to work for the liberation of the captive peoples of Eastern and Central Europe, without which our propaganda to this area has been seriously handicapped."[78]

The conference encouraged the emphasis on liberation in the presidential campaign. Eisenhower offered Jackson his "full endorsement" of the efforts to "discuss ways and means to improve our penetration of the Iron Curtain. I am sure that to win the peace, we must have a dynamic program of penetration designed to accomplish our objectives." In August, having reviewed the group's recommendation of a more aggressive strategy, Eisenhower thanked Jackson for the "extremely interesting material on the Psychological Warfare Conference at Princeton," which he judged "to be of the utmost significance."[79]

In his inaugural address, Eisenhower emphasized the need to "make more effective all activities of the government-related international information programs." He viewed these activities as central to the ultimate goal of undermining and defeating communism. "We are now conducting a cold war," he explained to a group of government propagandists in November 1953.

> That cold war must have some objective, otherwise it would be senseless. It is conducted in the belief that if there is no war, if the two systems of government are allowed to live side by side, that ours because of its greater appeal to men everywhere—to mankind—in the long run will win out. That it will defeat all forms of dictatorial government because of its greater appeal to the human soul, the human heart, the human mind.[80]

Eisenhower formed two committees whose reports would shape the administration's propaganda and psychological warfare agenda. One, the Advisory Committee on Government Organization, established January 19, 1953, and headed by Rockefeller, was to make recommendations on the bureaucratic structure of the executive branch. The other, chaired by attorney William Jackson (no relation to C. D. Jackson), a Princeton man and former CIA deputy director, was the president's Committee on International Information Activities. Eisenhower established the Jackson committee on January 24, asking that it submit recommendations after six months.[81]

The Jackson committee's somewhat innocuous formal title masked its real mission, which was to analyze "the entire range of national Cold War policies, covert as well as overt." The committee "was actually told in effect to study all aspects of our conduct of the Cold War," Jackson later explained. Many of its recommendations remained classified for decades. In addition to Jackson, committee members were Robert Cutler, Eisenhower's national security adviser; former PSB director Gordon Gray; business executive Barklie McKee Henry; Eisenhower aide John C. Hughes; OWI veteran C. D. Jackson; businessman Roger M. Kyes; and banker and advertising executive Sigurd Larmon. OSS veteran Abbott Washburn, formerly of General Mills, served as executive secretary. The Jackson committee conducted an extensive evaluation of existing policy, including more than 250 interviews, before submitting more than 50 recommendations in its June 30, 1953 report.[82]

The central conclusion of the Jackson committee was that psychological warfare should be integrated on an equivalent level of importance with political, economic, and military initiatives. The major contribution of the committee, William Jackson observed in 1956, "was its insistence that this area was not separate or separable in the organization and conduct" of foreign policy. The Jackson committee report opened with a reiteration of the NSC 68 mantra, namely that U.S. policy should be "based on the assumption that the purpose of the Soviet rulers is world domination." Because the primary threat was not military aggression but propaganda and subversion, the successful integration of psychological strategy was paramount. The United States would have to use the same means employed by the Kremlin to contain and undermine Soviet power. Should the West implement a successful approach and capitalize on its economic and cultural superiority, it could roll back Soviet power.[83]

The Jackson committee asserted that although U.S. national income was 3.8 times greater than that of the USSR, "the Soviet Union is spending proportionately forty times as much on overt propaganda as we are." Intelligence estimates indicated that the Kremlin employed 1.4 million "full time professional propagandists and agitators." While radio remained the primary medium of Soviet propaganda, publications such as the illustrated magazine *Soviet Union* and the weekly *New Times* circulated widely.[84]

As part of its call for a sweeping reorganization of the overseas effort, the Jackson committee advocated disbanding the PSB, which "possessed neither sufficient power to exercise effective coordination nor the techniques adequate to produce meaningful evaluations." The Eisenhower administration accepted the Jackson committee's recommendation to replace the PSB with a new Operations Coordinating Board (OCB), which was to provide for "coordination of departmental execution of national security policies." The OCB would coordinate planning between the foreign information program and covert operations under the auspices of NSC representatives from the highest levels of the foreign affairs bureaucracy.[85]

The most far-reaching result of the Jackson committee investigation was its acquiescence to the Rockefeller committee's recommendation that the overseas program be removed from the State Department and established under a separate government agency. Both John Foster Dulles and Rockefeller, chairing Eisenhower's Advisory Committee on Government Reorganization, advocated the change. Dulles and most State Department career diplomats wanted to be rid of the perpetual controversies associated with the foreign information program. On June 1, 1953, Rockefeller submitted his report recommending "a new foreign information agency" that would absorb programs dispersed throughout the federal government.[86]

The Jackson committee at first opposed the call for a separate information agency, declaring that it was based upon misconception. "Propaganda," the committee insisted, "should be a servant of policy and should therefore be clearly subject to policy guidance." The committee acknowledged that "antagonism on the part of political officers in the State Department toward the entire information effort and personnel engaged in it" was a serious problem. "However, we are not convinced that a remedy lies in separating IIA from the State Department and recreating it as an independent agency. The weakness and vulnerability of new, untried government agencies is attested by long experience; the history of OWI is instructive and discouraging on this point." A more "sound approach" was the retention of IIA in the State Department, but with the administrator accorded a higher rank. In its final word on the subject, however, the Jackson committee recognized "that there are strong arguments in favor of taking the information program out of the State Department." This was a reference to Secretary Dulles's sharp opposition to retaining the foreign information program. As a result, the Jackson committee made no formal recommendation on the proper place for the information program.[87]

Convinced of the centrality of propaganda to the overall Cold War effort, Eisenhower favored a strong information agency within the State Department. The president, however, bowed to the opposition of his secretary of state. A pattern had thus been set at the outset of the Eisenhower administration: the president, an enthusiastic proponent of the overseas program, compromised his own views in deference to Dulles, who perceived the information program as a nuisance as well as a potential threat to his own ability to conduct the nation's foreign policy. In approving the Reorganization Act creating the independent USIA, Eisenhower reassured Dulles that he would remain unambiguously in charge of the nation's diplomacy. The secretary of state had the authority to "direct the policy and control the content" of USIA. Eisenhower emphasized in a letter to department heads that the reorganization was "designed to emphasize the primary position of the secretary of state within the Executive Branch in matters of foreign policy."[88]

On June 1, 1953, Eisenhower announced the creation of the USIA in a special message to Congress. The new agency was to have a director and an assistant director appointed by the president and approved by the Senate. Congress approved the proposal and on August 1 USIA, incorporating all existing government information programs, came into being. Programs formerly under State Department supervision—including VOA, overseas libraries and information centers, the motion picture service, and press and publication agencies—came under USIA's authority. The mission of the USIA, whose director would report to the president and the NSC, was simply "to persuade foreign peoples that it lies in their own interest to take actions which are also consistent with the national objectives of the United States." It would implement the planning of the new OCB, based on policy guidance from the State Department. Educational exchange programs remained under State Department authority.[89]

Creation of the USIA, together with the report of the Jackson committee, marked a turning point in the postwar era. After years of fits and starts, campaigns followed by retrenchment, and myriad controversies and investigations, the overseas program had achieved a lasting bureaucratic foundation. Disputes, opposition, and disorganization would continue, but the essential bureaucratic framework finally had been established by 1953. The decision to remove the information program from the State Department, however, ensured a certain marginalization of the overseas effort. Contrary to the Jackson committee's wishes, psychological considerations would not assume a position as the vital "fourth area" along with economic, political, and military affairs in the nation's overall foreign policy. Despite his own belief in the centrality of propaganda, Eisenhower acquiesced to Dulles's desire for a separate information agency.

While the USIA would assume responsibility for overt overseas information initiatives, the Eisenhower White House would maintain direct control over covert psychological warfare operations. Such operations were at the heart of the Eisenhower administration's strategy to undermine the East European and Soviet regimes. More satisfying than mere propaganda, psychological warfare revived the sense of a wartime fight to the finish, a struggle that would conclude, like the last war, with the "unconditional surrender" of the enemies of the "free world." America's psychological warriors, committed to employing all the means available to destabilize CP authority, soon found that radio propaganda was the most effective tool at their disposal.

Reviving the Voice: The Radio Cold War Begins

Throughout his presidency, Franklin D. Roosevelt had skillfully exploited radio to address domestic audiences, yet the United States was the only major power without an overseas service when World War II began. On July 13, 1942, Roosevelt remedied the situation by issuing an executive order authorizing $5.4 million for construction of transmitters, thereby making the United States a permanent competitor in international broadcasting. The first Voice of America (VOA) broadcast aired in February 1942. Operating from a building on Manhattan's West 57th Street, the VOA broadcast 24 hours a day throughout the war.[1]

While the desire to advance the Allied cause united all propagandists, ideological disputes emerged between New Deal liberals and their opponents. Even though Roosevelt himself had proclaimed that the war had effectively terminated the New Deal, critics alleged that the VOA was a propaganda forum for a liberal domestic agenda as well as for the President's personal political ambitions. Critics savaged the VOA with an array of charges, including incompetence, wasting taxpayer's money, and being a haven for communists and sexual deviants. Right-wing columnist Westbrook Pegler characterized the OWI as a "hideout for privileged intellectuals, New Deal cowards, and communists."[2]

Liberals who perceived the VOA as a vehicle to promote international social reform on a world scale did dominate its broadcasts in the first year of the war, but their influence declined in 1943 with the waning of the New Deal and the political compromises associated with Allied military strategy in North Africa and Italy. Even more than the arrangement with Jean Darlan, the compromise with Italy's King Victor Emmanuel reflected the decline of liberal influence on U.S. wartime strategy. Before receiving a policy directive on the Italian surrender, VOA declared in a broadcast that Italy remained under fascist rule and quoted from a *New York Post* article describing Victor Emmanuel as "a moronic little king who has stood behind Mussolini's shoulder for 21 years." Lashing the VOA for allegedly undermining Allied military strategy, critics exploited the controversy to attack liberal influence in the OWI. Forced to respond to OWI critics, Roosevelt condemned the VOA broadcast, which *New York Times* columnist Arthur Krock blamed on "the personal and ideological preferences of communists and their fellow-travelers in this country."[3]

These wartime controversies, followed by postwar demobilization, threatened the existence of the VOA by early 1946. With the end of the wartime emergency, traditional suspicions of a government propaganda program resurfaced. Although forced to slash the budget, cut programming, and release thousands of employees, William Benton, assistant secretary for public affairs, fended off calls to shut down VOA. Accepting Benton's recommendations, Secretary of State James F. Byrnes urged President Truman to support "the continuance of shortwave broadcasting on a reduced scale until recommendations can be made." VOA continued to operate, albeit on a modest scale by wartime standards, while its ultimate mission remained uncertain.[4]

Journalists and media executives who had endorsed wartime propaganda now viewed a foreign information program as unwanted taxpayer-financed competition. In January 1946 the Associated Press and United Press, the nation's chief news-gathering agencies, discontinued their news services to VOA. AP president Robert McLean, publisher of the *Philadelphia Bulletin*, declared that the overseas program constituted a form of censorship, since propagandists omitted information that cast an unfavorable light on the United States. Walter Lippmann, the dean of American journalists, condemned the VOA as a "propaganda machine." By withholding and concealing unfavorable information, VOA engaged in censorship that Lippmann found incompatible with American democracy. Moreover, Lippmann added, "the roaring voices of our public life" could never be reduced to a single "voice" of America.[5]

Weathering the criticisms of Congress and the press, Benton garnered an appropriation of $7.8 million and 321 personnel positions for VOA in the 1947 fiscal year. VOA, which beamed broadcasts to Europe, Asia, and Latin America, received no money for new transmitters or upgraded engineering facilities. The programming fare included, in addition to news, round-table discussions, quiz shows, dramas, music, variety programs such as the "Jack Benny Show," and programs such as "Our Foreign Policy," which placed a benevolent slant on Washington's actions in world affairs.[6]

Although the passage of the Smith-Mundt Act in January 1948 ensured the preservation of an overseas program, congressional opponents continued to criticize VOA programming and demand budget cuts. In 1948 critics focused on a script from the VOA series "Know North America," which had aired on Latin American stations. The program, produced for the VOA by NBC, concerned Indians in the American West. In the script, the narrator observed that Indians still lived in the trans-Mississippi West, adding (apparently in an attempt at colorful aside) that "our Indian maidens run in races dressed in nothing but feathers."

House and Senate committees investigated such allegedly frivolous and offensive VOA programming. Senator H. Alexander Smith, one of the sponsors of the postwar information program, condemned a VOA broadcast on actress Lana Turner's wedding and honeymoon as "the most disgusting thing you ever read in your life, with the Voice of America singling it out and talking about a Hollywood movie actress who says she has had three or four 'experiences' before and he has too, 'but we are hoping this will work better than the others.'" Commenting on the features on Turner and the Indian maidens, Senator John Bricker of Ohio declared that he was "beginning to doubt the intelligence" of both the VOA and the State Department. "It looks to me like there is just an incompetence that can't be overcome." The furor over VOA programming produced sharp criticism of Benton, who soon resigned.[7]

Critics did have reason to question the competence of some VOA employees. Forced to compete with a thriving domestic radio industry, VOA employed writers, technicians, and broadcasters who were often inferior to those working at a higher salary for commercial stations. Critics also questioned the qualifications and priorities of the hundreds of émigrés whom VOA employed to conduct psychological warfare over the airwaves. The quality of VOA programming deteriorated further when NBC and CBS canceled their contracts with the station in the midst of the congressional investigation. Now operating on a skeleton budget, VOA faced the task of making up on its own the loss of the 75 percent of its programming that the two commercial networks had previously contracted to produce.[8]

Without the Cold War, VOA might never have recovered from the postwar setbacks. However, as East-West tensions mounted, radio emerged as virtually the only viable means of disseminating anti-communist propaganda. Indeed, U.S. national security planners ultimately concluded that shortwave radio broadcasts to the USSR could mount a challenge to Soviet hegemony.

In the late forties VOA's budget began to increase as it took on an increasingly prominent role in the ideological struggle with the USSR.

The inauguration of Russian-language broadcasts in February 1947 marked the beginning of VOA's emergence as a key weapon in the nation's Cold War arsenal. The conflict with the USSR encouraged professional diplomats, congenitally suspicious of the foreign information program, to see the merits of radio propaganda. Their support of VOA increased when professional diplomat Charles W. Thayer, who had served seven years in the U.S. embassy in Moscow, took charge of the Russian broadcasts.

Thayer, his staff of 12 permanent employees, and a crew of part-time assistants prepared sample scripts for the Russian broadcasts. A Special Advisory Committee, whose members included the prominent State Department Soviet experts Charles Bohlen and George F. Kennan, met weekly in Washington "to review scripts and transmit their suggestions and recommendations." The special committee also received reports attempting to gauge audience reaction inside the USSR.[9]

On February 17, 1947, after three weeks of rehearsals in its Manhattan studios, VOA beamed the first broadcast in Russian to three 85,000-watt short-wave transmitters in Munich. Both Bohlen and Kennan, seeking to avoid an unwanted "political stamp," advised against having a "high government official" inaugurate the broadcasts. Instead, the announcer gave the frequency of the VOA Russian program while explaining that the one-hour broadcasts would "consist of 15 minutes of news with special emphasis on news of America. There will also be a program of typical American music, and discussions of various problems of life in America and how we are endeavoring to solve them."[10]

As the Cold War escalated, culminating in the Czech coup and the Berlin Blockade in the first half of 1948, VOA gained acceptance as one of the few means available to challenge Kremlin authority behind the Iron Curtain. While it was difficult to determine the effectiveness of radio broadcasts, early indications suggested that the VOA served as an important counterpoint to Soviet propaganda. U.S. officials credited VOA and *Amerika* magazine (distributed in the USSR) with "diminishing the effectiveness of Soviet internal propaganda." Radio emerged as "the principal medium for the conduct of the Cold War, carrying the entire burden (with the relatively limited aid of *Amerika* magazine) of the psychological warfare effort behind the Iron Curtain."[11]

The first semiannual report of the U.S. Advisory Commission on Information, mandated by the Smith-Mundt Act, called attention to the vital role played by VOA. Following a tour of ten European countries in the winter of 1948-49, advisory commission member Mark May declared that VOA was "getting through to the people who have access to radio sets and many more by word of mouth." Calling VOA "by far our most important medium for bringing the message of America" to the people of East-Central Europe, May added that "its effectiveness has been testified to by thousands of letters, as well as by objective reports on the part of many intelligent refugees from those countries." In the ten months prior to June 1, 1949, foreign listeners posted 98,630 letters in response to VOA programming.[12]

The most telling evidence of VOA effectiveness, however, was the jamming of its broadcasts to Europe and the Pacific by the Soviet Union, beginning in the winter of 1948. Moscow signaled its intent the previous year when the journalist-novelist Ilia Ehrenburg attacked VOA, establishing the line to be followed by intellectuals. Jamming emerged in the context of the general Kremlin offensive against Western cultural infiltration (see chapter 1). By 1950 the Soviets indirectly justified jamming Western radio by charging the United States with "unceremoniously interfering with the radio services of the Marshallized countries, rebuilding them on the American pattern, and grabbing radio frequencies belonging to European broadcasting networks."[13]

The Soviets soon added British Broadcasting Corporation (BBC) frequencies to its jamming targets. Jamming intensified as Cold War tensions remained high over the ongoing Berlin Blockade and American airlift of supplies into Western sectors of the former German capital. The campaign to shut out Western radio broadcasts culminated in late April 1949, following Senate ratification of the anti-communist NATO alliance, when the Soviets unleashed what *Time* called "a mighty barrage of jamming" through an estimated 150 transmitters that "practically obliterated" VOA and BBC Russian language programming.[14]

The Kremlin leaders had left themselves vulnerable to radio penetration by building transmitters and marketing five million shortwave receivers to the Soviet public. Throughout the existence of the USSR, Soviet planners had perceived shortwave radio as an ideal means to establish communication links across the vast Eurasian land mass. But with eight million listeners, by VOA estimates, tuning into Western broadcasts, shortwave radio had become a strategic liability to the Kremlin. The Soviets rejected an outright ban on listening to Western broadcasts, and they did not require citizens to turn their radios over to the state, as in World War II. In 1951, however, the regime did forbid amateur radio operators from contacting people outside the USSR. The Soviets probably reasoned that a ban on listening would represent too open an admission of the regime's fears about Western cultural infiltration. A ban was also impractical: Nazi Germany had made listening to foreign broadcasts illegal and punishable by death, yet people had listened anyway. The Soviets condemned the Western broadcasts through state-controlled media, but did not outlaw listening. "To listen is not forbidden," noted one Soviet escapee, although it was certainly "not recommended."[15]

Soviet officials concluded that the best solution, despite the considerable expense that it entailed, was intensive jamming of Western broadcasts. The jamming, to which the Kremlin did not admit, typically entailed broadcasting signals on a wavelength slightly different from that used by the broadcast that was to be disrupted. The result of the two waves clashing was a high-pitched squealing or whistling sound that overwhelmed regular programming while causing listener discomfort. One source described the sound produced by jamming as similar to "the buzzing of a gigantic electric razor, mixed with a scraping noise and the roar of a squadron of B-24s."[16]

The intensified Soviet jamming, a product of careful planning, at first proved highly effective. Soviet jamming of Western transmissions required construction of hundreds of new transmitting stations in the USSR. The willingness to make the investment revealed the extent to which the Kremlin leaders perceived Western propaganda as threatening. The initial effort paid off, however, as Soviet jamming blacked out virtually all VOA programming for a week.

VOA administrators, writers, and editors had little doubt that jamming stemmed from Soviet officials' concerns about the positive impact of Western broadcasts. Intensive jamming did not prove that broadcasts were having the intended effect—the Soviets could have overreacted, or simply been behaving irrationally—but U.S. propagandists believed they were. "It was quite obvious that the jamming came in response to the effectiveness of our broadcasts," recalled Victor Franzusoff, who retired from the VOA in 1994 after 47 years with the Russian service. "It was hard to prove one way or another at the time, but in subsequent years many Soviet officials admitted to us that VOA had considerable influence on listeners." According to Franzusoff, who began as a newswriter in 1947 and eventually became head of the Russian service in 1978, "what they feared was that our broadcasts would change the understanding of world events on the part of the Soviet people and that this would erode their faith in the regime."[17]

Convinced that VOA broadcasts were making a favorable impression on Soviet audiences, the Truman administration implemented measures designed to counter Soviet jamming. First, Washington filed an official protest with the International Telecommunications Union (ITU), whose conventions on international broadcasting the Soviets had pledged to follow. Despite that pledge, jamming violated ITU agreements signed in Madrid (1932), Cairo (1938), and Atlantic City (1946). Washington's protests prompted international condemnation of the Soviet action and constituted a propaganda victory for the West.[18]

Despite the high cost of new facilities necessary to counter Soviet jamming, the Administration never seriously considered the option of abandoning its broadcasts to Eastern Europe and the USSR. Benton, now a U.S. senator from Connecticut, declared that capitulation to jamming would reward the Kremlin with "a tremendous propaganda victory," which it would exploit by claiming that VOA had stopped broadcasting because it "finally recognized that it had no audience in the USSR." Rather than abandoning its audience in the Soviet sphere, Benton advised, the VOA should redouble its efforts to penetrate jamming, thus convincing sympathetic listeners of its commitment to them.[19]

Efforts to counteract Soviet jamming played an important role in the Truman administration's propaganda offensive, the Campaign of Truth. Both the VOA and BBC launched a concerted effort to break through Soviet jamming. The effort included increasing the number of Russian broadcast frequencies to 61 for the Voice and 48 for the BBC. Both international radio services added new programming in Russian and the VOA began broadcasting its 2 1/2-hour Russian program on a 24-hour schedule. Soviet jamming would have to proceed around the clock, and on an increased number of frequencies, to disrupt broadcasts.[20]

VOA engineers developed additional means of circumventing Soviet jamming. One method entailed broadcasting a signal at two frequencies, thus requiring twice the number of jammers to disrupt programming. A game of cat and mouse ensued, with VOA engineers shifting signals and Soviet jammers scurrying to block the new signal. VOA could vary frequencies easily and often, thereby forcing the Soviet officials responsible for the jamming to increase and shift their jamming transmitters. George Herrick, a VOA engineer, explained that "sometimes we change frequencies right in the middle of a program. That throws the jammers off, and from what we hear, our Russian listeners have learned to twirl the dial to keep up with us."[21]

VOA engineers employed various devices, such as directional antennas and filters, aimed at reducing or removing interfering signals. Another effective device was a "clipper," which automatically cut out part of the lower tones of the human voice and reinforced the higher, more penetrating tones. VOA advised broadcasters to slow their delivery and speak in clear, deliberate tones. Yet another anti-jamming technique was to "cuddle" VOA broadcasts alongside regular Soviet frequencies. After identifying the frequencies of Soviet stations, VOA cuddled alongside them, so Soviet jammers could not block VOA broadcasts without blocking their own as well.[22]

The techniques and devices employed by VOA increased the percentage of broadcasts that got through to listeners in the CP regimes. Within a month of the onset of Soviet jamming, which had virtually silenced the VOA in late April,

25 to 50 percent of the broadcasts had been restored. The successful response spurred optimism. As Herrick put it, "We can lick the problem—at a price."[23]

Indeed, countering Soviet interference required heavy investment in new transmitters and other facilities. However, the most severe economic burdens fell on the weaker Soviet economy, since the expense of jamming the increased number of signals was far greater. Diplomat George V. Allen declared in November 1949 that the USSR devoted four times the capital equipment in transmitters and monitoring stations and ten times the manpower to block Western radio. "They would hardly go to this trouble if the programs were not effective," he added. According to a 1950 estimate, the USSR spent about $17.5 million a year on jamming—about equal to the annual budget of the entire VOA. "Can you imagine any regime spending the kind of money the Soviets spent on jamming if our broadcasts weren't having an impact?" asked Franzusoff.[24]

The most concerted effort to overcome Soviet jamming emerged from the planning sessions of Project TROY, the State Department-commissioned 1950 study by a group of Harvard and MIT scholars on means of infiltrating propaganda into the Soviet empire. Drawing on reports by technical experts from government and industry, the panel produced a "Ring Plan" for a series of high-powered, strategically located transmitters. The Ring Plan entailed sharp increases in transmitting facilities, on land as well as aboard ship. On April 4, 1950, NSC 66 embraced the call for maximum support of efforts to counteract Soviet jamming with new facilities. On September 27, 1950, Congress allocated $41.2 million—more than double the VOA budget—in startup funds for the Ring Plan alone. The radio Cold War was being waged in full force.[25]

Transmission of radio signals to the Soviet empire was no simple matter since an "auroral zone" of electrical disturbances in the atmosphere inhibited direct transmission across Europe. Because VOA signals had to be projected around the auroral zone, Tangier, Morocco, had long been the key transmitting site. In addition to bolstering the North African facility, VOA opened a new high-powered, medium-frequency relay station in Munich on September 1, 1949. Using funds allocated for the Ring Plan in 1950, the State Department initiated relay bases designed to enhance shortwave transmission to the Balkans at Salonika, Greece. Transmitters in Manila and Honolulu anchored East Asian broadcasting. By 1952 the USS *Courier* had begun broadcasting from the eastern Mediterranean. The specially designed ship remained moored at the Isle of Rhodes because international law proscribed broadcasting from international waters.[26]

VOA advised listeners of its frequencies and broadcast schedule in an effort to assist them in overcoming jamming, which it attributed on the air to "the over-all Soviet policy of isolating the Russian people from the rest of the world." In summer 1950, the Russian service explained that "in view of continuing Soviet attempts at jamming, the Russian radio broadcasts of the Voice of America are repeated by transcription uninterruptedly around the clock." The broadcaster then explained that the program was relayed on both short and medium waves, and provided a schedule before concluding: "Listen to the truthful information of a free radio! Listen to the VOICE OF AMERICA!"[27]

U.S. actions to counter jamming produced Soviet counter-responses, thus launching an action-reaction cycle similar to that which fueled the nuclear arms race. As the national security bureaucracy grew convinced of the efficacy of VOA broadcasts, increased funding revived the network from its near-moribund postwar condition. VOA would still suffer from budget woes, and endure public controversy, but had gained standing as a vital resource in the anti-communist crusade. Indeed, by the end of 1951 the Truman administration concluded that of all the possible ways to get information behind the Iron Curtain, radio represented "the only significant remaining program which effectively reaches the people of either or both the USSR and the satellites."[28]

Bolstered by the Campaign of Truth and the Korean War, VOA dramatically expanded its facilities and personnel in 1951. It developed a potential worldwide audience of 300 million. In 1951 Edward W. Barrett, assistant secretary of state for public affairs, announced plans for "doubling our hours of broadcasts and adding more than twenty languages to the VOA schedule" as well as increasing transmission and relay capabilities "as rapidly as possible." VOA expansion included establishment of regional broadcast operations, such as the Munich Center, inaugurated on October 1. By the mid-1950s, the Munich Center operated on an annual budget of more than $1 million.[29]

In the 1951 fiscal year, VOA sharply increased its daily programming and expanded from 24 to 45 the number of languages in which it broadcast. In addition to Russian, VOA now appealed to Soviet nationalities in the Estonian, Latvian, Lithuanian, Ukrainian, Georgian, Tatar, Turkestani, Azerbaijani, and Armenian languages. The VOA already broadcast to Eastern Europe in Polish, Hungarian, Albanian, Bulgarian, German, Rumanian, and Serbo-Croatian. New programs in Asia featured Malayan and Burmese. Secretary of State Dean Acheson sounded the aggressive tone of the new broadcasts when he opened the Tatar, Azerbaijani, and Turkestani services by expressing U.S. admiration of efforts to "maintain their religious traditions, their own way of life, despite the efforts of the communist regime to replace religion with godlessness, to replace the glorious histories of the peoples of the Soviet Union with the folklore of Stalinism."[30]

By the time the Eisenhower administration assumed office in 1953, VOA employed 2,000 persons, one-fourth of whom were foreign-born. Broadcasting in 46 languages, VOA devoted more than half its budget to Iron Curtain programming. In the 1953 fiscal year, VOA received appropriations of $6.5

million for broadcasts to the USSR; $4.1 million for Eastern European broadcasts; and $2.4 million for broadcasts to the People's Republic of China. Only $9 million of VOA's $22 million budget went to "Free World" broadcasting.[31]

While usually avoiding the florid rhetoric that often characterized Soviet propaganda, the essence of VOA's Iron Curtain programming was strident anti-communist propaganda. After Truman launched the Campaign of Truth, one Voice employee explained, the administration "expected us to 'make propaganda' and we made it. Anything more subtle than a bludgeon was considered 'soft on communism.'" VOA propaganda, heavily influenced by émigré broadcasters, was often crude. Much of it undoubtedly proved offensive rather than persuasive, especially among those committed communists who viewed émigrés as little more than traitors.[32]

Even those put off by VOA's strident anti-communist propaganda could ignore the political commentaries while tuning in to newscasts, feature stories, and music, all of which represented forms of cultural infiltration. A typical hour on the VOA schedule began with world news, followed by a feature, a commentary, an interview, music, and special programs, before returning to news at the top of the hour. VOA still presented straight news and features on the assumption "that people constantly exposed to communist polemics welcome factual reporting." Increasingly, however, VOA programming centered on "the weaknesses and evils of imperialistic communism." A State Department internal analysis of radio programming in the fall of 1950 emphasized the extent to which VOA had become almost an exclusive tool of the Cold War. "There is hardly an item that does not directly and explicitly bear on our Cold War strategy," the study concluded. VOA programming emphasized "the virtues of democracies with the vices of communist regimes" as well as "the inevitability of our ultimate triumph." It depicted the USSR as "the scheming villain . . . all black and sinister" while America "stands up against the powers of evil with unyielding determination and fierce goal-consciousness." The analysis found VOA's anti-communism so intense that it feared listeners might suffer from "propaganda fatigue. . . . The audience is exposed to an uninterrupted succession of purposeful messages without ever having the opportunity of a breathing space. It is an all-out offensive."[33]

VOA targeted Soviet intellectuals as those most likely to have access to shortwave radios and to listen to and be influenced by Western propaganda. A government-commissioned study at Harvard advised VOA to appeal to the Soviet intelligentsia, whose loyalty was "not all that the leaders feel it should be." Professionals, technicians, writers, and artists in the major cities, mainly Leningrad and Moscow, thus became the focus of VOA's attention. While VOA appealed to Soviet intellectuals, the Kremlin also targeted them by focusing its counterpropaganda on publications read predominantly by the intelligentsia. The Harvard study found that "the frequency of mentions of the VOA was markedly higher among those primarily directed to the special audience of the Soviet intelligentsia."[34]

American cold warriors analyzed the content and anticipated impact of VOA programs in an ongoing effort to make "an assessment of the USSR as a psychological warfare target." One major government study called radio "our best and more or less our only channel for direct communication" with Soviet citizens who had the access and desire to tune in Western broadcasts. While many of those listeners were CP members, and thus had to be "written off," the report found "room for optimism" since a large share of the audience consisted of opinion leaders drawn from the skilled workers and intelligentsia. If their faith in the system weakened, or if they nurtured pro-Western views, VOA programming would be creating "fundamental doubts about the regime in the minds of those citizens who are predisposed to doubt, and to support and strengthen this orientation in the minds of those already internally disaffected."

The study recommended that VOA's approach should be simple rather than "abstract or philosophical" and should seek to "tie in with thinking and sentiments which the audience can be presumed to already be doing or feeling." The "central theme" of VOA programming would be that "the hard working, long suffering, Soviet people have for more than thirty years made enormous sacrifices and endured untold hardships which should have yielded them a better life. Instead they have been robbed of the fruits of their labor." VOA's strategy would be to emphasize in the minds of listeners the contrast "between what *is* and what *could* be in the Soviet Union . . . if there were no communist government." Rather than emphasizing the virtues of the West, programming would focus on the weaknesses of the Soviet system in order "to create and foster doubt, as deep and as widespread as possible, in the minds of as many Soviet citizens as possible." The ultimate goal would be to foment an "internal migration" that would "build upon sentiments and attitudes which we have reason to believe are actually or potentially present in large numbers of Soviet citizens."[35]

Whenever possible, VOA launched its attacks on communism through the words of others, rather than through the commentary of the network itself. It quoted U.S. politicians, foreign leaders, UN spokesmen, and newspaper editorials, but gave most play to the statements of refugees from the CP regimes. The escapees' intimate familiarity with life in the Soviet sphere proved highly useful in VOA broadcasts. In 1951 the Polish service feature "Who Said It?" on one occasion asked listeners who was responsible for the statement, "Communism has brought with it a catastrophic reduction in the living standards of the

Polish people." VOA then told listeners that the statement had been made by three Polish fishermen who had escaped to Sweden.[36]

Scores of refugees possessed the knowledge, language skills, and zeal required to produce VOA's anti-communist programming. The East European refugees typically made little effort to hide their contempt for Soviet hegemony. Edward Barrett recalled the need "to restrain them from some of their fire-eating," which resulted in a decision to place an American in charge of every language desk. In addition to the strident anti-communism of the refugee producers and broadcasters, Western émigré organizations encouraged the hardline approach of VOA programming.[37]

While refugee broadcasts held out the vision of freedom in the West, VOA described the United States as "the Promised Land to refugees from communist tyranny." This commentary, emphasizing that "America has always been a land of immigrants," suggested that anti-Soviet defectors would be welcome in the United States. It pointed out that refugee resettlement programs had aided hundreds of thousands of recent immigrants to arrive on U.S. shores. Declining to mention legislation restricting certain immigrants, VOA emphasized the option of seeking refugee status "in preference to life under the communist yoke."[38]

VOA unleashed a never-ending stream of anti-communist propaganda. Its themes included refuting the misrepresentations of official Soviet history and the state-controlled press; emphasizing the regime's refusal to grant citizens the right to travel abroad; "slave labor" and collectivization; low wages and long working hours of men and women; privileges granted to CP members; limitations on the intelligentsia; denial of freedom of religion; and subjugation of ethnic minority groups. Reams of scripts in the VOA archives attest to the vituperative propaganda on these subjects beamed day after day into the Soviet empire.

Much of the programming to Eastern Europe and the three Baltic states focused on Soviet hegemony. "Today, prying the Iron Curtain open, we will gaze freely at Russia, at Eastern Germany and at the Moscow-occupied Baltic states," began a broadcast on the Lithuanian service. The program emphasized the denial of Lithuanian independence through its absorption by the USSR. Asserting that the Soviet system depended on forced labor, the broadcast declared "there isn't a family in the Soviet Union that does not have at least one person in slave labor camps." The program ridiculed Soviet propaganda that attempted to "show these dark days as sparkling triumphs," adding that "Hell remains Hell, even if painted in communist colors."[39]

Similar themes characterized VOA propaganda beamed to Eastern Europe. "Czechoslovakia has to serve as the arsenal of Soviet imperialism and aggression," the Czech service intoned. "It has to be exploited to the utmost from the economic, technical, and human point of view so that its industry and entire national economy should deliver to the Soviets the greatest possible amount of weapons, machinery and equipment for manufacturing arms." The Polish service featured a chronicle of Soviet-sponsored terror and oppression in a series entitled "Ten Years of Poland's Enslavement by the Communists . . . a history of Poland's bolshevization." Referring to labor camps and political prisons in Albania, VOA described them as "yet another aspect of the deep respect that cannibalistic communist regimes feel for the people."[40]

A constant theme of VOA propaganda to Eastern Europe and the Baltic states was Soviet collaboration with Adolf Hitler in the 1939 Nazi-Soviet Pact. On the thirteenth anniversary of the pact, for example, the Polish service presented "a dramatized documentary feature" on the treaty, which had led directly to "the rapacious invasion of Poland." VOA mirrored the rest of the American national security state in conjuring up an image of "red fascism," in which the Soviets and Nazis became almost indistinguishable. Like the Nazis, VOA declared, the Soviet regime was a "totalitarian state" that "engaged in continual warfare against the people" through means of "propaganda, unlimited terrorism, unparalleled isolation, indoctrination, and organization." VOA provided in-depth coverage of the periodic "nazi-type" political show trials, which it also sometimes attributed to "anti-semitism." Whatever the cause, "the very sight of communist wolves as they tear each other apart is worth the spectacle."[41]

VOA offered regular features such as the programs "Life Behind the Iron Curtain" and the satirical "Communist Paradise" to expose "the sham and hypocrisy of communism's pretense of a better life." The program "Do You Remember When?" highlighted the history of Soviet expansionism at the expense of weaker nations and alleged Kremlin violations of international law, while the program "Where Are They Now?" featured commentaries "on men who thought they could collaborate with the communists." One episode quoted the Czech liberal Jan Masaryk saying that "if the Western democracies stick to the old rule, live and let live, no insurmountable difficulties will be encountered." Masaryk made the comment before the 1948 Soviet-sponsored crackdown in Prague, in which he died mysteriously.[42]

VOA often asked authors, including the most prominent exiles and dissidents, to read excerpts from their works attacking communism. In 1950 the Czech service featured daily excerpts from *The God That Failed*, a book by six former communists. Arthur Koestler, Andre Gide, Stephen Spender, and others read their contributions on the air. From Pittsburgh, a spokesmen for the Slovak National Association then condemned "communist slavery" in Slovakia and pledged "to do everything to help our brethren across the Atlantic in their struggle to unfetter the shackles of godless communism and to enable them to emerge from darkness behind the Iron Curtain to the light of the civilized and free world."[43]

The contrasts between light and dark, good and evil, worship of God and atheism, were a staple of VOA broadcasting. VOA employed a Religious Advisor backed by a panel of three (one Protestant, one Catholic, and one Jew) who offered advice on scripts for VOA religious programming. A specialist with knowledge of the religion and culture of a particular country advised each VOA language desk. VOA advocated no particular religion, focusing instead on "religious persecution behind the Iron Curtain." It carried interviews with prominent clergymen, such as the preeminent U.S. theologian, Reinhold Niebuhr. VOA observed Christian, Jewish, and sometimes Islamic holy days, informed listeners about new translations of religious materials being denied to them, and encouraged the audience to maintain their faith until they could be liberated from "atheistic communism."[44]

Making use, whenever possible, of émigré broadcasts, VOA presented a Christmas Eve program to "occupied Estonia" in 1951 by the exiled Estonian Archbishop Johan Kopp. The sermon emphasized the existence of "nations without freedom of religion," countries in which "Christ's divine teachings are condemned and those who preach His word and believe in Him are persecuted. . . . God's temples are demolished or closed." Living under such conditions was "our dear Estonian homeland where there rules a foreign, unjust, godless, ruthless, and merciless force of darkness. There is no possibility of celebrating Christmas openly."[45]

While condemning the denial of religious and political freedom in Eastern Europe and the USSR, VOA emphasized the existence of democratic government in the United States. It glorified the U.S. electoral process, emphasized that the people selected their own leaders through free elections, and explained how local, state, and national governments operated within the federal system. VOA stressed that all political parties could freely participate in the electoral process, going so far as to declare in 1954 that "the Communist Party, on equal terms with other parties, enjoys all the rights and opportunities existing in a free country." The broadcast hastily added that "the American people do not sympathize with the ideas and actions of the Communist Party," but neglected to point out that the country had purged leftists from government, industry, and organs of culture.[46]

Central to VOA efforts to emphasize the contrast between freedom and tyranny was its programming on the role of a free press. VOA called its newscast "News from the Free World" and presented regular features such as "Review of the Free Russian Press." It relayed programs on the history of the emergence of press freedom in the West, contrasting that history with an August 4, 1918,

Soviet decree "forbidding the printing of so-called bourgeois publications." One broadcast ridiculed Soviet propaganda that "declared a long time ago that all inventions known to mankind are exclusively the inventions of the Soviet Union and czarist Russia. Haven't the Russians invented (if one is to believe Radio Moscow) the lightning rod as well as the atomic bomb, the samovar as well as the airplane, birch-tar as well as penicillin, not to speak of such minor things as radio, telephone, the electric bulb, and dialectical materialism?"[47]

VOA usually avoided tit-for-tat exchanges with the Soviet media on specific subjects, but did seek through its regular programming to counter Kremlin depictions of the United States as a land of "millionaires, gangsters, and oppressed workers." Broadcasts emphasized equal opportunity in the marketplace rather than the existence of classes of rich and poor. VOA presented features, such as interviews with FBI officials, to counter allegations about rampant crime. Most of all, however, programming constantly emphasized the higher standard of living, better health care, abundant consumer goods and leisure activities, and relative ease of everyday life in the West.

Occasionally VOA countered specific reports in the Soviet media, as was the case in 1950 when it refuted a *Pravda* article on slums in U.S. cities. Dismissing urban decay as a virtual creation of Soviet propaganda, VOA charged that the authors of the article had "rushed to the least-prosperous areas of New York—hunting for slums." VOA went on to belittle the very notion of journalism in the USSR, declaring that "Soviet journalists are well-acquainted with the latest party directives on how one must depict life in the U.S. The theme and slant are always there." In response to Soviet charges that U.S. newspapers were "mouthpieces for Wall Street," VOA explained that "the overwhelming majority" of U.S. papers were not published by the large chains, but by smaller ones. The radio network also emphasized that Soviet papers could be circulated in the United States, but the same was not true of U.S. papers in the USSR.[48]

Biting attacks refuting the general themes of Soviet propaganda regarding life in the West were a regular feature of VOA programming. "The Muscovite press, and along with it all the scribes in the Kremlin's pay in the subjugated countries, are carrying on a lively campaign to reveal—so they say—to the fortunate proletarians of the 'red paradise' the impossible living conditions of the workers in the United States," declared Rumanian radio. The VOA program emphasized "shortages and the fact that ration cards are maintained by the regime in countries like Rumania . . . which has never in its history known such poverty." In their preoccupation with the "manufacture of weapons of mass destruction," CP authorities were "sacrificing the production of consumer goods of prime necessity." Whereas Rumanian workers commuted on dirty, inefficient transportation, Americans drove their own cars. Rumanians had to stand in long lines to buy soap, whereas "in the United States every worker and office employee has his own bathroom, and soap is to be found free of charge in every public lavatory." At the end of the day, "the 'progressive worker' is forced to complete his Marxist education by listening to the bombastic speeches of the red propagandists; in the United States, the worker spends pleasant evenings in front of his television set, which enables him to know without restrictions everything that goes on in the world from the political, artistic, social or cultural point of view."[49]

American radio asserted that Western freedom fostered a thriving culture of artists and intellectuals, whereas the Soviet system stifled and often punished those with creative talent. The series "Communism and Russian Culture" detailed the suffering of artists and the intelligentsia. VOA constantly alluded to blatant Soviet misrepresentations and omissions about the past, while describing U.S. history in romantic terms. A feature on "winning the West" implied that it had been necessary to exterminate Indian tribes in order to make way for dams, water power, and thriving cities across the prairie. "Peace—long fought-for peace—has settled over the Missouri Valley," the program concluded.[50]

Eager to counter Soviet propaganda about the inevitability of conflict between capitalists and workers, the Czech service ran a series entitled "America, A Classless Society." The program advised listeners to "remember that capitalists—and especially American capitalists—are not so ruthless and selfish as communist propaganda describes them." Rather than exploiting their workers, "American capitalists raised the wages of their employees so that they could expand their enterprise." The achievement of economic growth by rewarding workers constituted "a feature of the American economy that surprises people who are accustomed to looking only through Marxist spectacles. They don't want or can't believe that both are winners: employers and employees alike." VOA never tired of offering comparative data on the economic situation of workers in the West and those under the CP regimes. Soviet listeners learned, for example, that whereas a worker in the USSR allegedly had to work four hours for a cup of sugar, the U.S. worker could earn one after only a minute and nine seconds of labor.[51]

VOA ignored the issue of strife between management and workers as well as income and social inequalities between men and women and whites and people of color. While avoiding the subject of minority groups in U.S. society, VOA featured as many interviews as possible with "Americans of Russian extraction, or with new immigrants, who can themselves tell about their life in the United States." One such interview featured Alexandr Lobanov, a 42-year-old Detroit autoworker, born in Kiev, Ukraine, who emigrated with his parents, went to American schools, and took a job with General Motors paying $96 a week. He told listeners his pay was "adequate," explained that he owned his own home, provided for a wife and two children, amassed some savings, owned a radio and television, took regular vacations, and belonged to a social club. "I have complete freedom of thought," he added. Another program, "Life Without Queues," featured the impressions of a Soviet émigré writer, who recalled standing in lines in the USSR, something he said he rarely had to do in the United States.[52]

In contrast to the happy collaboration between capitalists and workers in the West, VOA hammered away at the Soviet system founded on "slave labor." The Russian service declared that the UN and numerous private organizations had repeatedly been rebuffed in efforts to send an impartial commission to investigate Soviet labor camps. VOA condemned Soviet collectivization of agriculture and insisted that private farm enterprise remained more efficient. To bolster the point, VOA described U.S. supermarkets, constantly pointing out an abundance of easily prepared foods.[53]

On another program, VOA created fictional families to describe the way "ordinary" Americans lived. "The Smiths and Browns own a one-family house (there is probably a mortgage on it, but at very low interest), and own a car. The women like careers, but they are good mothers and wives, too, and work fairly hard around the house, although they have all manner of gadgets, frozen foods, and husbands who help with the dishes." *Time* observed that "in the Voice's otherwise true picture of the U.S., few couples ever get divorced."[54]

VOA rejected claims that socialist states took greater responsibility for health care than the capitalist West. The Albanian service declared that the CP regime there "pretends to be merciful and boasts that it is taking the proper measures to protect the people's health." In reality, the program asserted, "conditions of health in Albania have reached an alarming stage" as a result of shortages of qualified medical personnel and medicines. "To buy a single aspirin tablet, one needs a medical prescription and then must pass through a series of complicated bureaucratic steps that are sickening, to say the least."[55]

In addition to trumpeting the superiority of the U.S. economy and society, VOA vigorously defended the nation's foreign policy while condemning Moscow for seeking "world domination." The network depicted U.S. overseas activities, such as the Marshall Plan and NATO, as purely defensive reactions to Soviet aggression. The Atlantic Pact nations, as the Latvian service put it, were merely "continuing to build up their defenses against the communist aggression." VOA emphasized Western strength and resolve, declaring that "the number of well trained troops and divisions is growing. And so is the pooled force of the Atlantic nations under one international command."[56]

The Korean War dominated foreign policy discourse in the early fifties, providing regular opportunities to reassert putative Kremlin efforts to undermine world order. "A hard-hitting condemnatory approach appeared in political comments on Soviet totalitarianism and aggression in the Korean War period," a U.S. government-sponsored study of radio broadcasts concluded. Ignoring information that might suggest the conflict in Korea was in essence a civil war, VOA stressed that the war was an example of the step-by-step communist drive for world conquest.[57]

Frequently quoting from the speeches of Truman and Secretary of State Acheson, VOA emphasized the need for strengthening U.S. and European defenses in the wake of the red assault on Korea. As the war progressed, VOA reportage and commentaries emphasized that the UN (then being boycotted by the Soviet Union over its refusal to seat the People's Republic of China) had sanctioned U.S. intervention on the Korean peninsula. VOA bitterly condemned China for its November 1950 intervention on behalf of North Korea, and thereafter emphasized the need for increased U.S. military assistance to the "free" nations of Asia and the Pacific.[58]

As the war became a stalemate, VOA emphasized the U.S. commitment to stay the course to ensure the independence of South Korea. Reports stressed that the United States sought a negotiated settlement while the Soviet Union and China opposed such efforts. VOA vigorously countered Soviet allegations that the United States had engaged in bacteriological war in Korea. Myriad broadcasts focused on "communist mistreatment" of prisoners of war.[59]

VOA leavened its attacks on Soviet society and foreign policy with music and entertainment programs. The overseas service forged a good working relationship with the U.S. domestic radio industry, which contracted with VOA to broadcast entertainment programs abroad. As a result, some domestic radio productions—the Telephone Hour, the Hit Parade, University Theater, and Adventures in Science—became "as well known abroad as they are at home." Such programs conveyed the images, symbols, and ideas of a nascent campaign of Western cultural infiltration.[60]

The State Department constantly strove to gauge listenership and audience reaction to VOA programming. In neutral or Western-dominated countries, officials used the same methods to measure VOA's audience as the domestic broadcast industry. For example, polling in Western-occupied Germany found that "41 percent of the U.S. Zone's population listen to the Voice regularly or occasionally and most seem to like it." A poll by the High Commissioner in Germany tracked increases in VOA listenership in the months after the Berlin Blockade. Washington made the broadcast of VOA programs "an occupation requirement" of German commercial stations in Bremen, Frankfurt, Stuttgart, and Munich until 1951, when the German broadcast industry asked for negotiations to place them on a voluntary basis. Occupation officials granted the request after German broadcasters pledged to continue airing VOA programs since they "enjoy[ed] constantly increasing popularity."[61]

Polling and listenership surveys could not be performed to measure the size of the audience in the Soviet empire, but other means revealed that VOA was emerging as an effective tool of Western Cold War strategy. By early 1950 it was clear that the swift and increasingly well-funded response to Soviet jamming—taken in close cooperation with British officials—had allowed VOA to attract a growing audience. The State Department reported "widespread listening to the VOA despite the technical difficulties." Informal conversations and observations of diplomats and travelers in the USSR provided "evidence not only of relatively widespread listening to VOA broadcasts, but of permeation of the general line of the information included on these broadcasts." One report gleefully asserted that "everybody" in Siberia listened to VOA. By the end of the year VOA was printing 800,000 copies of its program guide and estimated its listening audience at 100 million worldwide.[62]

Officials based their estimates of listenership on letters received, the testimony of defectors, attacks on broadcasts in the Soviet media, and, whenever possible, direct observations of Western personnel. "The clearest and often the most moving evidence that the Voice has a deep influence all over the world," reported *Time,* "is furnished by the letters which reach Voice headquarters in New York." Within a year of the institution of Soviet jamming of VOA, more than half of a total of 105 letters received from Russian listeners gave "direct evidence of rather widespread listening to the VOA" despite the technical interference. By the end of 1951 VOA had received a total of 309,385 letters from around the world.[63]

In addition to letters, released German prisoners of war offered an important source of evidence about VOA listenership in the USSR. Following his return from the USSR, one German POW wrote that "there is no one who owns a radio (rather many people now) who does not know and listen to your transmissions . . . despite all the jamming." Another returned German POW told Voice officials that "your transmissions in Russian language are paid attention to and the Russians like very much to listen to them." The POW noted that his Soviet guards would stop their activities to listen to Western broadcasts. "Next day the party of course assured one another that it was a big twaddle what they had told on the Voice of America—but they heard it every one!"[64]

Perhaps the most revealing information about the listenership and effectiveness of VOA came from refugees. Teams of interrogators subjected defectors to systematic questioning about listening habits behind the Iron Curtain. From defectors, officials learned that a year after the institution of jamming VOA could be heard in 43 cities stretching across the USSR, despite jamming in 39 of them.

VOA listening was heaviest in Moscow and Leningrad, where officials gauged "average intelligibility" at only 25 percent as a result of jamming. An escaped Soviet engineer wrote that he personally knew more than a score of Soviet citizens, from workers to engineers, who listened to VOA. Interviews with other defectors "confirmed beyond doubt the fact that listening to VOA among Soviet military personnel, especially those on occupation duty, is widespread."[65]

Defectors surprised their interrogators by reporting that relatively few listeners feared reprisals or punishment. Many listeners kept the volume low and limited their conversations about listening. Overall, however, "the sources treated listening to VOA as a matter of fact . . . apparently 'everybody' is doing so" and "little actual danger seems involved." Years later, a professor at a Soviet university recalled that "it was assumed that teachers listened to the Western radio since their students did and it was their duty to expose to them the lies."[66]

Defectors also reported that the VOA minority language broadcasts inaugurated across the USSR in 1951 "have been highly effective." A physician from Tbilisi, Georgia, who left that Soviet republic illegally in September 1951, stated, for example, that he listened to both VOA Russian and Georgian broadcasts regularly and reported good reception despite jamming. "He stated that Georgian broadcasts made a deep impression even on Party members." The Georgians sometimes listened in groups, often when someone tuned in with the casual observation, "'We might as well hear what nonsense it says.' Of course, nobody is fooled—they come to listen to the VOA."[67]

Abundant evidence of Baltic and East European listening to VOA flowed from the testimony of defectors. Three Lithuanian fishermen who escaped to Sweden by boat reported regular listening. "They said that the fairly new Lithuanian programs are widely known throughout their country, and that VOA news is quite good despite jamming." Estonian escapees testified that "VOA broadcasts are listened to regularly in towns as well as in rural areas." A 24-year-old Hungarian émigré, who credited VOA with her "conversion" to the West, said it "opened my eyes as if coming from darkness to light." A Rumanian émigré declared: "I am telling you, there is no person who owns a radio set in Rumania who does not listen to London or America. Even the communists, because to tell the truth, the Rumanian communists are not communists." A Bulgarian émigré averred that "practically all the people are eagerly listening and waiting impatiently for the time of the broadcast. Even the communists listen . . . and often argue among themselves about certain news heard from the Voice of America." He added that people listened to the VOA "with absolute confidence" and "the news is immediately discussed and commented on following broadcasts." In Albania, the U.S. embassy reported on a favorable impression of the "objective presentation of news . . . and its documentation of the sufferings of the population in Albania." Similarly, the Belgrade embassy reported that "the eagerness of the Yugoslav people to learn about America continues to astonish us. . . . America is reaching directly into homes of Yugoslavs in villages and hamlets from Slovenia to Macedonia."[68]

Perhaps the most sensational incident reflecting the impact of the VOA in the Soviet sphere was the harrowing escape of a Czech "freedom train" in fall 1951. An engineer and fireman commandeered the fully loaded passenger train for a spectacular trip across the Czech border and into the American zone in Germany. Asked why he had been willing to risk his life in the escape, the engineer "replied that his inspiration came from listening to the Voice of America." U.S. propaganda did not urge such high-risk challenges to CP authority, but it gave top billing to the inspiring "story of freedom."[69]

Even though listening to foreign broadcasts carried the risk of fines and incarceration, thousands tuned into the Voice's anti-communist message. Listening was so widespread in Hungary in 1950 that state universities "inaugurated a 'political hour' in which the instructor puts his students through a daily catechism on 'why the Voice of America lied last night.'" In Rumania, the pro-Soviet regime limited circulation of radio receiving sets in favor of loudspeakers.[70]

Refugees declared that they had listened to the news on VOA, not only because it provided "a source of accurate information in the midst of a welter of communist propaganda and misinformation, but also because it keeps people in touch with events that sustain their hope for the future." The "intensely anti-regime character" of the defectors accounted for their preference for "the more hard-hitting VOA broadcasts" over the more straightforward style of BBC broadcasts. The analysis of refugee statements revealed that some regarded VOA broadcasts as "empty words," because the station failed to "set a date for military action against communism." Nevertheless, VOA was "quite generally praised for its resolute attitude and outspoken manner. The image of America most consistently held by this sample is that of a political liberator."[71]

In addition to letters and the testimony of Iron Curtain refugees, Soviet media attacks on American radio propaganda served as an important indicator of VOA effectiveness. Just as the institution of jamming attested to Kremlin concerns about the penetration of Western broadcasting, diatribes against the "lying transmissions of the Voice of America" convinced VOA officials that their message was getting through and having the intended effect on the audience. As one State Department official put it, the Soviet attacks on the VOA offered "invaluable testimony to the extent to which we continue to get through Moscow's jamming." Moreover, the media attacks "give us valuable advertising" with the Soviet public.[72]

Soviet attacks on the VOA attempted to discredit the broadcasts as the mendacious work of the American ruling class. One such representation, entitled "American Radio—Mouthpiece of Slanderers and Warmongers, Supervised by FBI and Un-American Activities Committee," asserted that "the true owners of the radio companies are in reality a small group of top-ranking millionaires, the Wall Street bosses, who determine the internal reactionary policy and the aggressive foreign policy." The average American regarded his own radio programming "with contempt and loathing" because of "the unbearable vulgarity of radio advertising, the wild howls of the jazz, the stupidity of the radio play, the false political commentaries." U.S. broadcasting companies could be counted on to "obediently fulfill all the directives of the secret police."[73]

Soviet propaganda also depicted the VOA as a desperate Western response to the failure of U.S. foreign policy and the nation's declining influence in world affairs. "The Washington politicians, irritated and discouraged by the systematic failure of their aggressive plans, are intently searching for a new means to impose their will on the peoples." Moscow radio sneered that the VOA trumpeted the "American Way of Life" as the cornerstone of its ideological propaganda abroad while attempting to conceal the "economic crisis and multimillion unemployment" endemic to the capitalist system.[74]

Western broadcasting became a cultural phenomenon in Russia, stimulating widespread discussion and even a play on the subject. In January 1950 the journal *Novyi Mir* (New World) reviewed a new play entitled "Voice of America." The production condemned the Western broadcasts, of course, but the review provided the State Department with a valuable indicator of the extent of the audience for Western broadcasts. "'The Voice of America'—to *millions* of Soviet people these words, with which the slanderous American broadcasts are announced, have become synonymous with lying and provocational fictions" [emphasis added].

U.S. officials combed Soviet sources such as *Pravda, Literaturnaia Gazeta* (Literary Gazette), and *Krestyanka* (Peasant Woman) for references to VOA broadcast effectiveness. In addition, the CIA compiled daily reports on all Soviet domestic and foreign broadcasts. From the beginning of VOA Russian broadcasts in February 1947 through July 31, 1949, the CIA found 302 references to VOA, "a relatively high degree of attention [which] indicates some concern about its possible impact." The survey found three times as many references to the VOA as to the BBC, revealing Soviet anxiety about the aggressively anti-communist U.S. network, as well as Washington's status as Moscow's chief global rival. The survey also found that "the amount of attention being given to the VOA in Soviet sources has been regularly increasing," including growing numbers of references to specific broadcasts. The number of references to VOA in the first six months of 1949 was twice the number that appeared in the same period in 1947. References to the VOA in Soviet-published material increased even more sharply following the institution of intensive jamming in April 1949.[75] By the early fifties, Moscow's propaganda sought to refute the VOA on a worldwide scale, but focused most especially on its counterpropaganda to Eastern Europe. In fact, monitoring revealed more than twice as many references to VOA in East European broadcasts as those in the Soviet Union itself. "This gives a clear indication of the concern felt by the Soviet leaders about the possible impact of the VOA on the population of the satellite states, and has obvious implications for VOA policy in regard to those broadcast areas." Hungarian, Rumania, and Czech state-controlled media condemned listening to the VOA, thereby acknowledging their concerns about its growing audience. When in February 1952 the Polish VOA accurately pinned the wartime Katyn forest massacre on the USSR, Polish state radio counterattacked against "the filthy Katyn provocation" by "The Voice of America—The Voice of Goebbels."[76]

The widespread listening in Eastern Europe and in the USSR itself reflected the success the Truman administration had achieved with its revived postwar radio propaganda program. In five years the VOA had emerged from a near-death experience to constitute the most effective tool in Western efforts to challenge Soviet hegemony over Eastern Europe and in the USSR itself. American radio had the Soviet Union on the defensive, as Kremlin counterattacks and the extensive—and expensive—efforts made to jam VOA broadcasts attested. A 1953 report concluded that the USSR had spent "some 70 million dollars in capital investment and some 17 million in yearly operating cost" on jamming. At the same time, the budget of the entire official U.S. broadcasting effort had been cut to $22 million. The investment obviously was "much more than balanced by the economic cost of the Soviet effort to keep these broadcasts (and those of the BBC) from being heard."[77]

The appeal of VOA propaganda attested to the vulnerability of the Soviet system. The weaknesses that the VOA exposed and thrived upon were the same ones, once fully matured, that led to the ultimate disintegration of Soviet power from 1989 to 1991. The lower standard of living and relative underdevelopment of the Soviet economy, especially the paucity of consumer goods it produced, compared unfavorably with the images of Western prosperity that the VOA attempted to conjure up for its audience. U.S. radio constantly linked the "good life" in the West with political freedom, capitalist economics, and democratic politics. "Our broadcasts described the way people lived" in the United States, Victor Franzusoff recalled. "It had to be clear to Soviet listeners that the lifestyle and standard of living of most Americans was a hundred times higher than their own."[78]

The VOA Cold War offensive in the Truman years revealed Washington's ability to capitalize on revolutionary changes in communications to infiltrate propaganda and cultural images behind the Iron Curtain. "It was easy to indoctrinate people in Soviet ideology before the war," Howland Sargeant, assistant secretary of state for public affairs, observed, "but since then [VOA and BBC] have made it considerably more difficult." Shortwave radio had broken Soviet efforts to monopolize information made available to the people. "Once that monopoly was broken," one U.S. propaganda study concluded, "the threat to it was much greater from materials which described life 'outside' in places like the United States. In this sense, then, the VOA seems to have the initiative in the propaganda battle, for life outside is the area about which Russians are most curious and which they are most eager to contrast with their own." Kremlin fear of alluring descriptions of Western societies was one of "the most striking findings" of VOA research. Those studies revealed that the Soviets attached "much more importance to countering the picture of American life given by the VOA than they do to countering the picture it gives of Soviet life."[79]

Soviet officials must have been chagrined to contemplate the extent to which VOA depictions of Western life passed from person to person, a phenomenon known as "whisper propaganda." From the Soviet perspective, Sargeant explained, it was "bad enough that individuals listen but the worst feature is that they are always running to friends to say, 'Did you hear that . . . ?'"[80] Lacking official and overt channels for disseminating the truth, explained another U.S. observer, "the Russian people have developed the world's most elaborate news grapevine. A rumor in Moscow spreads rapidly from Leningrad to Vladivostok." By such means, U.S. officials concluded, VOA propaganda reached greater numbers than its listening audience alone would suggest.

Radio cold warriors marked progress in the propaganda war despite domestic constraints. Indeed, domestic opposition threatened the VOA's ability to carry out its mission of propaganda and cultural infiltration. Becoming a nation virtually obsessed with communism in the wake of the "loss" of China and the Korean War, the United States indulged in a wave of anti-communist hysteria. Although the hysteria had deep cultural roots, one man, Republican Senator Joseph R. McCarthy of Wisconsin, came to embody the phenomenon. Beginning in 1950, McCarthy launched a series of sensational charges to the effect that communism was on the march as a result of treason within the upper reaches of the U.S. government.

Among McCarthy's charges was that the VOA had been infiltrated by communists. Announcing the opening of a Senate committee investigation in February 1953, McCarthy "plunged into a hunt for subversives among Voice employees." Informed that McCarthy was launching an investigation of VOA,

Secretary of State John Foster Dulles pledged to cooperate as long as the senator did not "unfairly try to blame him for things he has had nothing to do with." Dulles's response set a craven tone for the Eisenhower administration's response to McCarthy, whose reckless crusade would undercut the nation's overseas effort. Dulles ordered IIA administrators to forward materials to McCarthy and his ruthless young associates, Roy Cohn and G. David Schine, who conducted interviews with scores of VOA employees from a luxurious New York apartment. After first informing Voice employees that it was their own decision whether to meet with Senate committee investigators, the State Department reversed course under McCarthy's pressure and ordered compliance. "When the smoke cleared towards the weekend," *Newsweek* observed, "the [State] Department had capitulated to McCarthy on all points. For the present, at least, it appeared to be Administration policy to give McCarthy a free hand."[81]

The investigation focused first on controversy over the sites chosen for VOA transmitting stations before turning to charges of communist infiltration of the government radio network. As hearings opened in New York on February 16, 1953, Lewis J. McKesson, a former VOA engineer, testified that he had resigned over the squandering of $18 million in choosing failed sites for transmitters. McKesson attributed the decisions to incompetence, but McCarthy twisted his testimony to assert that pro-communist VOA employees had deliberately chosen the sites because they knew unfavorable atmospheric conditions would limit the effectiveness of VOA broadcasts. Cohn followed by blatantly misrepresenting the views of MIT's Jerome Weisner, head of the Research Electronics Laboratory, who was not called as a witness because he refused to buckle when Cohn pressured him to criticize the site selections. In fact, as Weisner had informed Cohn, most VOA engineers still defended the chosen sites as the most viable, but in the public hearings Cohn attributed to Weisner precisely the opposite viewpoint.[82]

In the second week the hearings shifted, in McCarthy's words, from "the sabotage of key transmitting stations" to investigation of "communist infiltration of key departments" of VOA. Nancy Lenkeith, a script writer for the French section, claimed to have been fired because she had written a favorable review of Whittaker Chambers's *Witness,* as well as for her refusal to join Marxist "collectivist groups." She explained that the former head of the Voice's French section invited her to join a collective and start bearing children, prompting McCarthy to interrupt with the warning that "many children are watching this program." It did not take long for neutral observers to conclude that Lenkeith, chain-smoking, rambling, and often incoherent, suffered from psychological problems.[83]

Next McCarthy attacked VOA's practice of quoting communists in its broadcasts. Despite protests from VOA broadcasters and editors, John Foster

Dulles had put an end to the practice, thus making it virtually impossible, as *Newsweek* observed, "to answer communist propaganda because the propaganda itself couldn't be quoted as a basis for refutation." Dulles remained "conciliatory" toward the Senate investigators, as the Eisenhower administration "evaded any evaluation of the McCarthy committee's operations." Republican Senator Robert Taft declared that McCarthy was being "very helpful and constructive" since VOA obviously was "full of fellow travelers."[84]

McCarthy plunged ahead, manipulating an offhanded comment by a Voice employee to charge that Roger Lyons, director of VOA religious programming, was an atheist. By the time Lyons appeared before the committee to plead with the senators to believe that he did, in fact, believe in God, the damage had been done. Next McCarthy destroyed the career of IIA deputy director Reed Harris, a 19-year government employee who had been called to explain why Hebrew broadcasts had been suspended. McCarthy avoided the real issue to focus on Harris's advocacy of liberal causes while a student at Columbia University 20 years before. Shattered by three days of brutal public interrogation, Harris resigned a few weeks later.[85]

Harris's was not the only head to roll. His superior, IIA head Wilson Compton, handed his resignation to Dulles during the first week of the McCarthy hearings. Charles Thayer, a West Point graduate and the architect of the VOA's Russian service, resigned from the Foreign Service rather than face a McCarthy hearing on a love affair he had had with a Russian woman during his prewar diplomatic service in Moscow. (McCarthy also targeted Thayer because he was the brother-in-law of Charles Bohlen, whose nomination as ambassador to Moscow McCarthy had failed to defeat.) George Herrick, the VOA's chief engineer and the architect of the successful efforts to overcome Soviet jamming, also turned in his resignation. Another VOA engineer committed suicide in the midst of the controversy over the transmitting stations.[86]

The highly publicized hearings produced no evidence of communist subversion of VOA, but undermined the structure, morale, and public support of the radio network. McCarthy, Cohn, and Schine dictated the outcome of the hearings through skillful calling of witnesses, controlling what material could be introduced as evidence, arranging for television coverage of sensational testimony, and willfully disregarding the truth. The committee refused to allow evidence that would cast doubt on its unfounded charges of communist subversion, but when it served their purposes allowed into the record classified technical data that could enhance Soviet ability to counter VOA broadcasts. In the wake of the fiasco, Dulles contemplated liquidating the entire VOA operation, but Eisenhower aide C. D. Jackson intervened, warning that "the repercussions outside the United States would be tremendous and almost entirely unfavorable."[87]

In the midst of McCarthy's sensational investigation of the VOA, the president's committee on foreign information issued its report, which offered several recommendations on overseas radio broadcasting. In contrast to McCarthy's assault on the VOA, the Jackson committee endorsed the network's role in the Cold War as well as its ongoing efforts to overcome jamming and measure audience reaction. In the wake of McCarthy's sensational attacks, however, the committee recommended that VOA change its name because the network had become "associated both in the United States and in many foreign countries with programs which have been widely criticized and discredited." The administration ultimately concluded that despite negative publicity, a name change would risk the VOA losing its loyal audience around the world.[88]

The most important Jackson committee recommendation regarding the VOA was that the network shift its emphasis to "objective, factual news reporting" supplemented by political commentaries. Psychological warriors worried about the appropriateness of the nation's official network engaging in hard-hitting propaganda attacks. The Jackson committee's recommendation, implemented by the Eisenhower administration, was that "VOA should stress directness in its approach, but should avoid a propagandistic note."[89]

The decision to tone down VOA broadcasts did not stem from a conclusion that aggressive anti-communist radio propaganda had been a failure. Quite the contrary, officials believed that the VOA, overcoming both domestic and foreign obstacles, had achieved a breakthrough in efforts to destabilize CP authority. While the strident anti-communist broadcasts undoubtedly offended many listeners, abundant evidence in the form of letters, interviews, and observations—as well as Soviet jamming and counterpropaganda—suggested that the VOA was having an impact on "hearts and minds" behind the Iron Curtain. While primarily a purveyor of propaganda in the early Cold War, the VOA had begun the process of infiltrating the images and symbols of Western culture behind the Iron Curtain. In the future, as the Jackson committee suggested, an emphasis on straight news and entertainment would enhance the VOA's credibility and popularity, making the station a more effective source of cultural infiltration.

While the VOA was to emerge as a dignified official voice, modeled after the more prestigious BBC, Cold Warriors had not by any means abandoned the campaign of hard-hitting anti-communist propaganda. Well before the VOA began its conversion to a more restrained approach, an array of U.S. backed, yet ostensibly independent, unofficial radio networks had launched their own campaign of aggressive psychological warfare.

THREE

Liberation Denied: The Twilight of Psychological Warfare

Once Eisenhower assumed the White House, C. D. Jackson urged the president to place psychological warfare at the center of Cold War policy, rather than maintaining it as "some kind of little informational freak quite separate from the major lines of U.S. foreign diplomatic and military policy." He urged the new president to get into "the real guts" of the matter by launching aggressive operations against CP regimes. Eisenhower, Secretary of State John Foster Dulles, and CIA director Allen Dulles shared Jackson's desires to overthrow not only CP regimes, but even moderate reformist governments. They authorized the CIA to do just that, fomenting successful coups that culminated in the installation of pro-American regimes in Iran in 1953 and Guatemala the next year.[1]

Not content with maintaining U.S. hegemony over peripheral regions, the CIA under both the Truman and Eisenhower administrations stepped up the campaign to destabilize Eastern Europe and the USSR itself. If nothing else, as the veteran diplomat Joseph Grew observed, "the busier we can keep the Bolsheviks in their own backyard, the less chance of their starting trouble elsewhere."[2] To that end, the CIA created and financed ostensibly private organizations with the mission of shoring up the anti-communist coalition in the West and other parts of the world while simultaneously seeking to undermine the Soviet and East European regimes. Such ostensibly private

President Dwight D. Eisenhower and his "psychological warfare" adviser, C. D.
Jackson, in 1953. The two were "great friends" who shared the view that
propaganda and cultural initiatives would play a decisive role in winning the Cold
War struggle for "hearts and minds." (Courtesy Dwight D. Eisenhower Library)

organizations, free from formal connections to Washington, could conduct a
more aggressive psychological warfare campaign than could official agencies,
while adding credibility to the notion of grassroots opposition to communism.

The Congress for Cultural Freedom (CCF), a putatively private group of
writers and intellectuals organized in Berlin in June 1950, was one such CIA
front organization. Staunchly anti-communist, the CCF, comprised of liberals
and democratic socialists, adopted anti-Soviet and anti-neutralist positions.
Members included prominent European and American anti-communist intellectuals such as Melvin Lasky, Arthur Koestler, Sidney Hook, Arthur Schlesin-
ger, and Raymond Aron. Estonian born Michael Josselson, who as executive
director became the driving force behind the Congress, was a CIA agent.
Beginning in 1953, the CIA covertly funded CCF anti-communist publica-

tions, including *Encounter* (British), *Preuves* (French), *Tempo Presente* (Italian), *Cuadernos* (Latin America), and *China Quarterly*. Not until a 1967 exposé in *Ramparts* was the CIA connection revealed.[3]

Thousands of refugees from the Soviet empire offered U.S. psychological warriors a propaganda asset they could not ignore. Not only did the refugees provide clear evidence of mass dissatisfaction with the Soviet-backed regimes, but valuable intelligence about East European languages, culture, and conditions. George F. Kennan urged creation of an ostensibly private corporation to assist refugees while mobilizing them into the anti-communist movement. The resulting organization, the National Committee for a Free Europe (FEC), was formally incorporated in New York on June 2, 1949. Sullivan and Cromwell, the Dulles brothers' New York law firm, filed the papers of incorporation. Allen Dulles, a Princeton graduate and OSS veteran, was the Free Europe Committee's first president before he became CIA director under Eisenhower.[4]

The radio and press division of the FEC, chaired by banker Frank Altschul, launched Radio Free Europe (RFE), an anti-communist émigré propaganda network targeting Eastern Europe. RFE modeled itself on wartime clandestine radio stations and on Radio in the American Sector (RIAS), the popular American station in Berlin. During the war, as the OSS veterans involved in RFE well knew, U.S. Armed Forces radio and clandestine anti-Nazi stations had aided the Allied cause. Eisenhower had personally supervised Radio 1212, the best-known clandestine station, which broadcast Allied propaganda from the Luxembourg border into Germany as part of battlefield tactics. After the war, RIAS emerged as a model for RFE plans to create a full-blown radio station, with complete broadcast facilities, studios, and transmitters.[5]

RIAS and RFE reflected the view of psychological warriors that the Voice of America, the nation's official overseas network, was ill equipped to conduct "no holds barred" propaganda. As Altschul explained in May 1950, because the VOA was "an arm of the government, it is not in position to engage in hard-hitting psychological warfare. A commitee of private citizens, on the other hand, would suffer from no such disability."[6]

The task confronting RFE was daunting. To foster the illusion of being a genuine private station, RFE would have to broadcast throughout the day, not just a few hours a day like the VOA and BBC. Its broadcasts, both technically and in their programming, would have to be of high enough quality to compete with the East European government stations. All of this would require extensive funding and a concerted effort to maintain the station's cover.

An elaborate fund-raising campaign, eventually dubbed the "Crusade for Freedom," provided the cover for RFE activities. Carefully organized by U.S. psychological warriors, the Crusade held rallies in cities across the United

States to raise "Truth Dollars" for RFE. General Lucius Clay, former head of U.S. occupation forces in Germany and hero of the Berlin Blockade, headed the Crusade's fund-raising efforts. Crusade rallies featured a replica of the Liberty Bell, chosen as the symbol of freedom. On October 24, 1950, at the end of the Crusade's initial tour, 400,000 witnesses attended a ringing ceremony at the bell's final resting spot, the Rathaus in West Berlin. American media, the Advertising Council, and corporations assisted in the fund-raising drive. Within two years the Crusade reported 25 million individual contributions. The elaborate public relations campaign generated hundreds of thousands of dollars in contributions, but that was not enough to cover even the costs of the Crusade itself. The U.S. government, using unattributed funds, continued its covert financing of RFE while the Crusade served as an effective cover and propaganda agent.[7]

On July 4, 1950, a little over a year after plans were conceived, RFE offered its first broadcast, beamed into Czechoslovakia through a new transmitter dubbed "Barbara." Broadcasts to Rumania, Hungary, and Poland followed within a month. Eventually, RFE added transmitters and broadcasts to Albania and Bulgaria. RFE's U.S. planning staff obtained expanded office space in New York's Empire State Building. The RFE broadcasts, featuring news and political analysis provided by Western news agencies, emanated from Munich, which offered the advantages of a large city close to the Eastern borders but far enough from the center of U.S. activity in Frankfurt to maintain the fiction that RFE was a private station. At the time, few plans existed for RFE's long-term viability. "It was still the established wisdom," one RFE veteran recalled, "that East European Communist regimes would soon fall . . . and that there would be no further need for an RFE."[8]

Altschul struggled to organize the émigré work force into a disciplined army of psychological warriors. He discovered that many émigrés with reactionary political views represented an "unpalatable past" rather than the liberal ideal the United States wanted to project to its East European audience as an alternative to CP authority. "It would be self-defeating," Altschul observed, "to attempt to expand the gospel of Twentieth Century liberalism through the recognized voice of nineteenth century reaction." The station's handbook noted that "RFE takes counsel with exile leaders and is respectful of their views, but its policy is not designed to further the aspirations of any single exile leader or party."[9]

RFE directors sought to steer émigrés away from appeals to the authoritarian past, but placed few initial restraints on their anti-communism. The émigré broadcasters and producers, embittered toward the Soviet-backed regimes, were "outspokenly belligerent," as one U.S. official put it. RFE employed harsh propaganda "to take up the individual Bolshevik rulers and their quislings and tear them apart, exposing their motivations, laying bare their private lives, pointing at their meanness, pillorying their evil deeds, holding them up to ridicule and contumely." Altschul admitted that RFE was "unhampered by niceties of intercourse. We enter this fight with bare fists." *Time* noted that the State Department welcomed RFE "as a freewheeling, free-speaking ally in the propaganda war."[10]

The official CIA handbook for RFE, issued in November 1951, authorized a focus on "the monstrous all-devouring ambitions of Soviet imperialism; the cruelty and unworkability of communist institutions, and the proven advantages of the democratic way of life." Broadcasts were to exploit every opportunity to point out lies, weaknesses, and repression, contrasting these actions with the moral, political, and economic superiority of the West. RFE propaganda dismissed Soviet "peace offensives" as propaganda ruses. Above all, RFE emphasized Western determination to undermine the CP regimes. The essential purpose of RFE propaganda was "to contribute to the liberation of the nations imprisoned behind the Iron Curtain by maintaining their morale and stimulating in them a spirit on non-cooperation with the Soviet-dominated regimes."[11]

After an initial phase characterized by virulent hostility, Walter Bedell Smith, Truman's CIA director, and C. D. Jackson, who became FEC president, toned down RFE broadcasts. They believed the station would be more credible if it adopted a less shrill tone. The CIA emphasized that greater subtlety would enhance RFE's ability to exploit the ongoing rift between Stalin and Josip Broz Tito, Yugoslavia's CP ruler. Tito offered a model of independent national communism that U.S. officials hoped the East European regimes might follow in breaking away from the Soviet empire. RFE guidelines called for an emphasis on Western receptivity to independent regimes such as Tito's, but the station was careful not to heap fulsome praise on the Yugoslav leader, who was, after all, a communist. The Yugoslav model was an important subject for RFE, but had to be approached with "delicacy."[12]

RFE guidelines targeted programming for East European youth groups, workers, and peasants, but the station refrained from directly addressing underground resistance groups. Avoiding political subjects, RFE appealed to Eastern European youth with programs on sports, entertainment, science and technology, and features on youth in the West. RFE offered invidious comparisons with life in the West in its programming targeting workers and peasants. Through its cultural, religious, and educational programming, RFE sought to "meet the spiritual and intellectual needs of its listeners." RFE broadcasters constantly emphasized their common national identity with the listener by calling their programs "Poles Speaking to Poles," "Hungarians to Hungarians," and so on. RFE programming was all the more effective because émigrés spoke "in their own idiom and with full knowledge of their [listeners'] psychology and background."[13]

By 1954 the Munich-based station broadcast anti-communist propaganda 20 hours each day throughout Eastern Europe. An expanding network of monitoring stations and informants enhanced RFE's ability to relay information and comment on conditions in Eastern Europe. The station embarrassed CP authorities by announcing breaking news, such as the death of Stalin, before official statements had been released. RFE maintained extensive files, as well as the "Black Book," a compendium of data on thousands of CP members, factory managers, and other authorities. RFE used the material to publicly identify police informers and to single out for criticism particularly stern factory managers and other officials.[14]

RFE's sophisticated information network, aided by hundreds of agents who had infiltrated the Soviet empire, enabled the station to disclose the identities of secret police officials. The station publicly identified agents to shatter their cover and warn potential victims. RFE called attention to a female agent who allegedly used sex to entrap opponents of the Czech regime. The station revealed the identity of a smuggler who took money from anti-communist Hungarians, promising to sneak them over the border into the U.S. zone of Austria, but instead routinely delivering them to the secret police.[15]

RFE's Polish service ruthlessly exploited the defection of Joseph Swiatlo, former deputy director of the notorious "Department Ten" of Poland's Security Ministry. On September 28, 1954, the day Washington announced Swiatlo's defection, RFE's "Voice of Free Poland" began a series of programs in which "Swiatlo personally exposed the activities, intrigues, and corruption of Polish regime officials." Swiatlo possessed intimate knowledge of the lives of all important CP and secret police officials. Between September 28 and the end of February 1955, RFE broadcast approximately 100 programs based on Swiatlo's revelations.[16]

In addition to the political programs, humor and variety shows commanded widespread listening audiences throughout Eastern Europe. The program "Polish Tea Party," combining comedy, singing, and a jazz band, was the most popular show on the Polish airwaves. Equally popular was the Czech program "Calling Communists," which featured satirical skits on "the communist way of life" as well as offering prizes of "nylon stockings, tobacco, and other items hard to get in the communist countries." Enthusiastic about RFE activities, John Foster Dulles observed that "we have been told time and again by responsible escapees from these countries that they attach high importance to continuing the radio programs which have been reaching the inhabitants."[17]

RFE's political disclosures and variety programming alarmed CP authorities, who responded with jamming and bitter denunciations over state-controlled media. A Hungarian government spokesman declared in a confidential memorandum leaked to the West that "the most dangerous effect of RFE's activities is that it results not in organized resistance, which is easily defeated and suppressed, but in atomized resistance, which is more difficult to control." When Soviet and East European officials complained before the UN and other international forums, Washington blithely responded that it could not control the activities of private anti-communist groups.[18]

By the time the Jackson committee surveyed the overall U.S. propaganda effort at the beginning of Eisenhower's presidency, RFE had established itself as a vital component of the anti-communist campaign. The network, employing 252 Americans and 1,526 foreigners, gathered information from eight news bureaus in Western Europe. In addition to its expanded programming, RFE operated 26 transmitters, including facilities in Portugal through an agreement with that country's ruler, Antonio Salazar. Unlike the VOA, RFE, operating in close proximity to Eastern Europe, provided "saturation broadcasting" that was "almost impossible to jam."[19]

The Jackson committee concluded that "the bulk of available evidence indicates that RFE is widely heard, particularly in its three primary target areas, Czechoslovakia, Hungary, and Poland, and that its programs are well received by its audience." As with the VOA, letters and defectors offered confirmation. For example, Marek Korowicz, a defector from the Polish UN delegation, told reporters in September 1953: "You have no idea with what longing we wait for information to be given us by Radio Free Europe. It is our only link with the outside world." After RFE reported his comments, Korowicz received several letters from his former students, some boldly through direct mail and others smuggled out of Poland.[20]

RFE was not the only radio operation launched by American psychological warriors. While RFE targeted the East European regimes, Radio Liberation (renamed Radio Liberty in 1964) sought to stir dissatisfaction and unrest in the Soviet Union itself. The ostensibly private RL thus joined the official VOA in a two-pronged Russian language propaganda offensive aimed at undermining Soviet authority. The American Committee for Freedom for the Peoples of the USSR, incorporated in Delaware in 1951, was the parent of Radio Liberation. Like RFE, RL received covert CIA funding under the cover of a dummy foundation. Its board of directors received guidance from the CIA and the State Department.

In 1953, former Truman administration assistant secretary of state Howland Sargeant became director of RL, which continued to receive CIA funding and oversight. RL employed 96 Americans and 218 foreigners in 1953. Even though RFE and RL were both CIA covert operations operating from bases in

Munich, little coordination, but some tension, existed between the two. Like RFE, RL staffers monitored broadcasts and combed the Soviet press for information to exploit in its own programming.[21]

Like RFE, RL received its impetus from anti-Soviet émigrés. Beginning with its first broadcast from Munich on March 1, 1953, RL set out "to utilize the forces of the Soviet emigration against the Soviet regime." The directors of RL experienced nothing but frustration, however, in their efforts to create a united exile organization. Pronounced conflicts between Russian and non-Russian nationalities were impossible to bridge. Moreover, émigré broadcasters often ignored guidelines set down by their American directors who, as one insider recalled, "went about their business in the sublime belief that they were running things." In actuality, "there were two worlds at RL, American and émigré."[22]

By the mid-1950s, at the impetus of policy advisor Boris Shub, RL had rejected hard-hitting propaganda, concentrating instead on raising "doubts in the mind of the individual who believes himself loyal . . . and to give the Russian citizen the materials for independent thought which he has been denied." RL strove to fill in "gaps" and provide alternative interpretations to those found in official Soviet news coverage. Its programming targeted a mass audience of soldiers, workers, peasants, bureaucrats, and the intelligentsia. RL made religious broadcasts "a continuing feature." RL presented regular interviews with prominent Americans, including Eleanor Roosevelt, Averell Harriman, Francis Cardinal Spellman, Norman Thomas, and Martin Luther King.[23]

Shub, a New Yorker whose father was a Russian émigré intellectual, stressed intellectual and cultural programming. A veteran of radio propaganda against the Nazis in World War II, Shub hoped to encourage anti-Sovietism among intellectual and cultural elites. Among those who appreciated RL's cultural programming was the bitterly anti-Soviet novelist Alexandr Solzhenitsyn, who declared years later after emigrating to the United States that he had been an avid listener of RL "from the start."[24]

The Soviets demonstrated their sensitivity to RL through constant jamming, denunciations, and intimidation. Under a Soviet five-year plan, an increased number of shortwave radio sets became available, thus enhancing RL's ability to reach its audience. The Kremlin responded with intensive jamming, which succeeded in limiting RL's audience. To counteract Soviet interference, Sargeant negotiated an agreement with Spanish dictator Francisco Franco for construction of a powerful new transmitter that became operative in 1960.[25]

Soviet media attacked RL mercilessly, describing its émigré broadcasters as traitors and "war criminals." Two RL staffers were murdered, presumably by Soviet agents. Others received threats on the lives of relatives still residing in the USSR. Despite jamming and intimidation, RL's audience grew. Throughout the 1950s and 1960s RL collected evidence of listenership based on interviews with Soviets traveling in the West. This "substantial body of authentic interviews" suggested an extensive audience for RL, one that may have rivaled that of the prestigious, and unjammed, BBC.[26]

In addition to RL and RFE, the CIA supported Radio Free Asia. However, the Asian anti-communist network received less funding and possessed weaker transmitting facilities in Manila than its European counterparts in Munich. Radio Free Asia sought mainly to bolster non-communist regimes rather than to undermine existing governments. U.S. psychological warriors badly wanted to employ radio to attack communism in China, but conceded that "listening facilities for the masses are severely limited."[27]

While radio clearly was the primary medium for conducting psychological warfare, the CIA covertly financed the Free Europe Press, which anchored anti-communist print propaganda. Print propaganda received fewer resources and had less impact than radio, which could more readily penetrate the Iron Curtain. The Free Europe Press published *East Europe*, a monthly magazine on satellite and Baltic affairs, printed in German, French, and Italian. It also circulated booklets such as "Studies in Communism," which condemned Marxism-Leninism. The Free Europe Press interviewed émigrés for knowledge about life in Eastern Europe. Their stories appeared in newspaper and magazine articles as well as in the monthly magazine, *News from Behind the Iron Curtain*.[28]

While much of its print material sought to bolster anti-communism in the West, the FEC also found ways to infiltrate printed propaganda behind the Iron Curtain. Balloons provided a cheap, expendable device for carrying reams of propaganda otherwise inaccessible to Eastern Europe. In August 1951, Crusade for Freedom chairman Harold Stassen joined C. D. Jackson, columnist Drew Pearson, and former General Mills executive Abbott Washburn, whose company had assisted in the design of the polyethylene balloons, in a formal ceremony near the Czech border in Bavaria. While sipping beer brought in barrels from Munich to mark the occasion, they released some 2,000 balloons into the air. From Bavaria the balloons, carried by prevailing winds over the Czech border, burst at an altitude of 30,000 feet, releasing thousands of leaflets. A typical leaflet read: "A new wind is blowing. New hope is stirring. Friends of freedom in other lands have found a new way to reach you. . . . Tyranny cannot control the winds, cannot enslave your hearts. Freedom will rise again." The backs of the leaflets listed wave lengths and schedules of RFE broadcasts to Czechoslovakia. In simultaneous broadcasts from Munich, RFE urged listeners to pick up the leaflets. When Czech officials filed a complaint with the UN, Stassen gloated, "We tore a big hole in the Iron Curtain."[29]

Another leaflet barrage in October 1951 informed Czechs of the daring defection of railroad engineer Jaroslav Konvalinka, who directed a train with 108 passengers aboard over the border at the German town of Selb. The leaflets, released in Selb, contained photographs of Konvalinka, the train, and 18 of the 31 Czechs who chose to defect along with him. (They settled in Canada). The leaflets also contained a message from Konvalinka dismissing propaganda that he and others had been "kidnapped by U.S. agents." The Crusade conducted another "Winds of Freedom" operation in 1953, floating some 10,000 balloons containing 13 million leaflets into Czechoslovakia and Poland. By the time the balloon program had been discontinued in October 1956, the FEC had floated some 600,000 balloons containing more than 300 million pieces of propaganda.[30]

CP authorities bitterly denounced the balloon leaflet initiative and sometimes responded with more than words. On one occasion, Red Army units in Austria opened fire on the floating propaganda with anti-aircraft guns. On May 24, 1954, the Czech government delivered an official protest over the balloon leafleting program to the U.S. embassy in Prague. It leveled more serious charges in 1956, blaming the crash of a Czech airliner that killed 22 persons on a propaganda balloon. RFE responded that the balloons, made of light plastic and weighing less than seven pounds, could not possibly have caused the accident, which it attributed to bad weather. The State Department investigated and dismissed the Czech government's version as "fiction." In February 1956, the USSR lodged an official protest against U.S. propaganda and photographic reconnaissance balloons over Soviet territory.[31]

While radio and leaflets created inroads behind the Iron Curtain, the FEC's Division of Exile Relations was less successful in efforts to create a unified exile force among the East European émigrés. The Division of Exile Relations sought "to promote political unity within the various exile organizations" and to help them "develop a dynamic, progressive platform of aims and principles." But the Jackson committee concluded that "efforts to form national councils composed of political leaders from the various emigrations have largely been frustrated by the bickerings and jealousies common to émigré politicians."[32]

The Jackson committee also lacked enthusiasm for yet another covert émigré program, the Free Europe University in Exile. Located in Strasbourg, France, the Free University offered an anti-communist education through seminars designed especially for émigré and East European youth. Operating on a large grant from the Ford Foundation, the Free University enrolled 5,500 students—40 percent of whom came from the Russian zone of Berlin. East German authorities prosecuted parents and imprisoned some of the students when they returned home for visits. The Jackson committee concluded that resources devoted to radio propaganda brought greater return than those provided by either the Free University or the Division of Exile Relations.[33]

Both the Truman administration and Eisenhower's Jackson committee concluded in late 1952 and early 1953 that radio was by far the most effective source of anti-communist propaganda. Although "some progress has been made in building up other capabilities for psychological activities," reported Truman's advisers, "radio broadcasting constitutes the major active element at our disposal." Despite Soviet jamming and the damage done by McCarthyism, the VOA maintained a persistent listenership in the USSR. RL complemented the Soviet effort, while in Eastern Europe RFE had made rapid strides. "Jamming by the Russian radio of our broadcasts continues to present a major problem," psychological warriors acknowledged. "There was, however, a perceptible increase in effectiveness of our radio resources in the last six months due to the inauguration of Radio Liberation and the stepped-up activity of Radio Free Europe."[34]

The Jackson committee gave priority to radio propaganda. It called for steps to "promote primary attention to RFE" and urged that "major attention should be concentrated on Radio Liberation." Radio propaganda offered the best means to achieve the overarching aim of doing "everything possible to aggravate internal conflicts in the hope that this will subsequently help to bring about a retraction of Kremlin control and influence."[35]

The stepped-up radio program was not the only psychological warfare initiative that sought to capitalize on the flood of anti-communist émigrés in Europe. In addition to employing émigrés in propaganda, even more provocative plans evolved for mobilizing the exiles into an armed liberation force. Rep. Charles J. Kersten (R-Wis.), a devout Catholic and ardent anti-communist, attached an amendment to the Mutual Security Act in October 1951 that allocated $100 million to organize East European escapees, or even those still "residing in" Eastern Europe, into "a legion of anti-communist exile peoples." Kersten argued that such a force would promote "potential resistance to the communist regime everywhere behind the Iron Curtain." The proposal envisioned legions of Czechs, Poles, and other Eastern European exiles being incorporated into NATO, although they would wear the traditional military uniforms of their countries.[36]

The Kersten Amendment aimed to convince East Europeans of Washington's commitment to their eventual liberation. Proponents hoped the amendment would encourage a mass exodus of refugees from the Soviet Empire. Another possibility, however, overlooked by zealous psychological warriors, was a crackdown on dissent by the CP dictatorships. Soviet Foreign Minister Andrei Y. Vishinsky suggested just that possibility in December, when he berated

Washington over the Kersten Amendment. Vishinsky charged the United States with funding "battle formations" that aimed to overthrow the regimes by force. Spokesmen for the East European regimes denounced Washington for an "aggressive act" through its promotion of "fascist refugees." The Soviets introduced a UN resolution condemning the Kersten Amendment, but the General Assembly rejected the measure.[37]

Supporters of the Kersten Amendment argued that it would advance the cause of liberation while simultaneously providing support and a sense of purpose to the estimated 18,000 Iron Curtain escapees in the West in 1952. Fully one-third of the refugees had escaped in that year alone, seemingly bolstering the argument that defection was an increasingly severe problem for the Soviets. Since no formal Western program had been initiated to aid the refugees, however, the State Department observed that "communist propagandists have exploited with telling effect the inadequate conditions and general neglect which greeted escapees upon their arrival in the West." The CP press could reasonably argue that despite the rhetoric of liberation, those who fled Eastern Europe could expect little help from the West. If, however, an assistance and resettlement program could be put into effect, and the volunteer armies formed as well, the refugees could serve as a model of Western compassion and a symbol of the sincerity of liberation.[38]

Since the Kersten Amendment had been proposed in Congress, rather than in the White House, the Truman administration came under criticism for inaction with regard to resettlement of the East European refugees. Advisers warned that the administration would continue to be "vigorously attacked unless it can demonstrate it has done something about this problem." Covert operations specialist Frank Wisner urged the administration to "do something to counter the beating it is receiving in connection with the Kersten Amendment." As a result, the State Department took responsibility for administering a program to aid and resettle escapees while exploiting their defection for propaganda purposes. The U.S. Escapee Program, established in 1952, coordinated the resettlement of some 25,000 escapees over the next three years.[39]

While the Truman administration thus acted to resettle anti-communist refugees, the proposal for a volunteer army of liberation awaited Eisenhower's arrival in the White House. By trumpeting "liberation" over mere containment, the Republican campaign put pressure on Eisenhower to pursue Kersten's proposal to form exile armies. After less than a month in office, Eisenhower ordered the NSC to study a proposed "Volunteer Freedom Corps" (VFC) to be "recruited from stateless, single, anti-communist young men, coming from the countries behind the Iron Curtain." Optimistic, the president declared that it ought to be possible, "with a zeal equal to need, to recruit up to 250,000 men" for the VFC.[40]

In contrast to the unanimous Republican campaign chorus for liberation, within the Eisenhower administration itself there was no small debate over the advisability of forming the VFC. Soviet expert Charles Bohlen, ambassador to Moscow, opposed the VFC as well as public advocacy of liberation, which he feared might spur violent but ultimately fruitless uprisings while committing the United States to overthrowing the CP regimes. General Omar Bradley voiced widespread military skepticism about the wisdom of the VFC, which might easily be infiltrated by spies posing as defectors. Bradley also observed that the program would require significant funding for administration and scores of interpreters of several different languages to achieve a disciplined force. In February 1953 the Joint Chiefs of Staff advocated "allowing the Kersten Amendment to lapse or at most leaving it on the books with no actual implementation."[41]

UN ambassador Henry Cabot Lodge and the ever enthusiastic psychological warrior C. D. Jackson were the chief proponents of the VFC. Referring to the Soviets, Lodge observed that the escapee program gets "under their skins" by calling attention to defections. Jackson complained that because of U.S. inactivity he had "watched the Kersten Amendment become a powerful propaganda weapon not for the U.S., but for the communists." The VFC, however, was "very merchandisable" in Eastern Europe and promised to "fit in with the overall program of taking the initiative in psychological warfare." Jackson strongly endorsed the VFC, arguing that "the sooner it was started, the better."[42]

Siding with proponents of the exile army, Eisenhower's NSC in May 1953 established the VFC "to provide additional combat manpower . . . in the world struggle against Soviet communism." According to NSC 143/2, initial efforts would be both "modest and austere," both for fiscal reasons and to avoid being unnecessarily provocative. The program would be kept secret until a time deemed "psychologically advantageous to announce the project." The NSC action designated the U.S. Army to operate the VFC, including recruitment and screening of its members, who would be eligible for U.S. citizenship after three years of service.[43]

Despite the opposition of Walter Bedell Smith, moved from CIA director to undersecretary of state by the new administration, Eisenhower flirted with the idea of an exile army based in West Germany and backed by U.S. funds. In a critical reference to U.S. troops abroad, Jackson added that a volunteer force would "not have to be surrounded by mobile breweries, ice cream factories, Coca Cola bottling plants, dependents" and other "expensive marginal trappings." Smith argued, however, that "German sponsorship of the VFC would inevitably be seized upon by Soviet propaganda as a move in the direction of a recreation of units such as were formed by the Nazis from Soviet prisoners of war in the latter stages of World War II."[44]

The outbreak of rioting in East Germany in June 1953—less than a month after the NSC action tentatively approving the VFC—contributed to a rethinking of the proposed volunteer exile army. "I fear that some of our friends will think that by our actions we are responsible for keeping the East-West temperature at a very high level," observed State Department counselor Douglas MacArthur II in the wake of the riots. Continuing incitement risked the possibility that "we will produce exactly the opposite psychological effect from the one we desire." George Kennan advised caution in dealing with "the ambitions of noisy, immature, and extremist exile figures" who might be "selling the U.S. Government a dangerous bill of goods." Key allies in London, Paris, and Bonn expressed concern over the provocative nature of the VFC. C. D. Jackson continued to press for the creation of an exile army, calling in October 1954 for the VFC to be "taken out of the ice box, unfrozen, and put on the front burner," but to no avail. The VFC concept lingered for two more years but by 1955, with the great power Geneva summit in progress, the proposed exile army struck allies and rivals alike as too provocative. Dulles and Eisenhower abandoned the proposal.[45]

By that time, Soviet actions had already demonstrated the futility of anti-communist uprisings in the Soviet sphere. The process began in the wake of Stalin's death on March 5, 1953, which had unleashed resistance to the pro-Soviet regimes he had placed in power across Eastern Europe. With demonstrations in Czechoslovakia and East Germany in 1953 seeming to suggest the tenuousness of the Kremlin empire, U.S. psychological warriors stepped up their activities. Wedded to liberation, they ruled out the possibility of negotiations or a gradualist strategy toward Eastern Europe.

Widespread unrest in the Soviet empire after Stalin's death first manifested itself in Czechoslovakia. The USSR had demonstrated its determination to maintain hegemony over the youngest of the Eastern European "people's democracies" by orchestrating a purge at the end of 1952. Eleven CP members were tried and executed for charges ranging from ideological deviation to sabotage of the economy. Undeterred by the terror, workers at the Skoda factory in Pilsen rioted outside party and government offices on June 1, 1953, in protest of the Czech government's new austerity program. The riots spread to other cities before the Czech police quelled the uprising.[46]

RFE exploited the unrest by encouraging the Czech people to continue their opposition to the regime, or to defect. RFE emphasized the weakness of the post-Stalin Soviet regime and encouraged the Czech armed forces to be loyal to the people instead of to the Prague government. On April 29, 1954, RFE launched Operation VETO, a propaganda campaign that declared a "People's Opposition" with a list of "Ten Demands" for greater economic and political freedom. VETO included "what is believed to be the first sustained campaign of coordinated radio-printed word operations directed across the Iron Curtain." The FEC timed the release of more than 20 million leaflets to coincide with the regime's May Day celebration. RFE's Voice of Free Czechoslovakia simultaneously altered its broadcast schedule to circumvent jamming and "ensure maximum impact for the first balloon drops."[47]

The radio and leaflet campaign of Operation VETO included political commentary and cultural appeals, such as the playing of popular songs. RFE encouraged Czechs to exercise their right to cross off regime-approved candidates on election ballots, while other programs discussed democratic parliaments in the West as opposed to the rubber-stamp Congress in Prague. Psychological warriors emphasized that VETO encouraged "specific, limited goals," such as agricultural and industrial economic reform. VETO did not "counsel the use of violent methods," although its appeals undoubtedly encouraged opposition to the regime. The Czech government responded with counterattacks on Western propaganda and issued warnings to farmers and workers.[48]

The violent opposition to Soviet authority in East Germany far exceeded the unrest in Czechoslovakia, in both scope and intensity. The riots erupted, ironically, less than a week after the East German government, on advice of the new Kremlin leadership, had relaxed accelerated production norms and other unpopular measures. The East German "New Course" served only to embolden, rather than mollify, the widespread opposition to the regime. At noon on June 16, workers at the Stalin Allee construction project went into revolt. Amid talk of a "people's uprising," the workers demanded free elections throughout Germany.[49]

An even larger demonstration materialized the next morning as the workers trumpeted a general strike. As the uprising quickly spread through more than 400 East German cities and towns, the Soviet High Command imposed a curfew and martial law. By June 19, Soviet troops made themselves conspicuous in all major East German cities. Some 20,000 Soviet troops and 350 tanks roamed Berlin alone. Resistance continued sporadically for weeks, but by June 21 the uprising had been suppressed. The CIA noted that the demonstrations had been "of sufficient magnitude to bring the entire nation under Soviet military control and to disrupt communications for several days." Soviet forces killed 125 men and women, injured hundreds, and arrested thousands more.[50]

At first, U.S. psychological warriors viewed the East German uprising with hopeful fascination. During an NSC meeting in the midst of the riots, John Foster Dulles reveled in the "evidence of the boundless discontent and dissension behind the Iron Curtain." He noted, however, that the crisis "posed a very tough problem for the United States to know how to handle." Hopeful that communism's "slaves" were in revolt, C. D. Jackson observed on June 18 that "the thing had developed past the riot stage, and was moving close to insurrection." As the Soviet troops intervened, Jackson fumed over rejection of a proposal under which the CIA would have provided weapons to the striking workers. Even in the event of a massive crackdown, Jackson argued, the "blood of martyrs" would have delivered a propaganda victory to the West.[51]

Eisenhower and Dulles concluded, however, that U.S. intervention would have precipitated war with the Soviets while sowing deep divisions in the Western alliance. The British, French, and West German governments did not share Washington's zeal for psychological warfare and certainly sought to avoid conflict with the Soviets. Eisenhower publicly ruled out military intervention in East Germany at a July 1 news conference.[52]

Powerless to prevent the repression in Berlin, the United States concentrated on reaping the propaganda benefits that flowed from Soviet intervention. Although it rejected the proposal to send arms, the Eisenhower administration did orchestrate a $15 million Berlin food relief program in July. In contrasting humanitarian aid through food relief with the brutal Soviet repression, Washington exploited an opportunity to make an "excellent impact on the Western German public." U.S. officials arranged for West German chancellor Konrad Adenauer to request the food relief. "I think it has generally been recognized as smart propaganda that we could say blandly that this was food 'distributed by Germans to Germans,'" counseled the American High Commissioner to Germany, James B. Conant.[53]

Eisenhower administration officials disagreed over the extent to which the United States should distance itself from the food relief program. Foster Dulles averred that there should be no doubt of U.S. sponsorship in order that the "maximum psychological benefits should be derived from the entire project." Conant argued, however, that the "best possible propaganda is food itself," hence Washington should abjure a blatant campaign. The High Commissioner explained that he had "talked with many East Zoners" who were "aware of the American origin of the food and are grateful for our assistance."[54]

As expected, Moscow refused a pro forma offer to cooperate in distribution of the food, but hundreds of thousands of East Germans flooded into the Western sectors of Berlin to receive their "Eisenhower packages." Under the program, more than three-fourths of the East Berlin population had received American food parcels. The American largesse, in contrast to the chronic East German food shortages, paid palpable propaganda benefits. The food relief program was having a "permanent effect upon the mass of East Zoners and upon their relationship with their communist masters," Conant advised. "The story will be carried by the most effective instrument of propaganda—word of mouth—throughout the East Zone and into the satellite countries as well."[55]

Itself aware of the propaganda implications, the Kremlin and its East German allies slapped travel restrictions on East Berliners and began meting out punishment to violators. The Soviets launched a rival aid program, but the East German population disdained it. By early fall the U.S. food relief program had begun to outlive its usefulness. Conant cabled Washington that the "profit from Berlin distribution is about to turn into loss" because "punitive measures against parcel recipients" were leading to resentment of the United States. Moreover, the High Commissioner warned, Soviet travel restrictions threatened to undermine the overarching goal of maintaining East German access to West Berlin. Dulles implemented Conant's recommendation to end the Berlin food distribution program in early October.[56]

The East German uprising and the popularity of the food relief campaign demonstrated the weakness of, and striking lack of popular support for, the Soviet-backed regime. The propaganda victory contributed to Konrad Adenauer's overwhelming electoral success in West Germany on September 6, 1953. The short-term propaganda victory ultimately backfired, however, as the demonstrations produced renewed determination on the part of the Kremlin to transform the East German regime into a rigid Soviet satellite. Measures included strengthening of state control, including reinforcement and expansion of the secret police.[57]

Although Washington had been unable to extend more than token support to the East Germans, the uprising offered compelling evidence of the influence of U.S. propaganda over Radio in the American Sector. Washington had launched RIAS at the end of the war as an alternative to the Berlin broadcasting station, over which the Soviets had established control in 1945, despite its location in the British occupation zone. Functioning at first with weak transmitters and inadequate technical equipment, RIAS did not become an important part of Western strategy until the 1948 Berlin Blockade and Airlift. As the Soviets sought to seal off Western access to the former Nazi capital, RIAS, under the direction of the High Commissioner's office, played a critical role in reassuring Berliners of Allied determination to resist the blockade. Having proven itself in the crisis, RIAS emerged in subsequent years as one of the larger radio stations in Western Europe, broadcasting over long, medium, and shortwave. RIAS established the model emulated by RFE and RL, of monitoring the CP press and radio stations, maintaining extensive files, and using the material to attack the East German regime.[58]

By the early 1950s, RIAS anchored the U.S. campaign of psychological warfare against the most vulnerable regime in the Soviet empire. The station could be heard throughout East Germany for more than 20 hours a day. Although financed and supervised by Washington, RIAS presented little American news. In addition to limited musical programming, RIAS featured 14 daily newscasts and a "telephone news service" that received some 1,800 calls daily. The station received as many as 400 letters a day. Some of the callers and letter-writers sought information; others provided it, as RIAS facilitated the "recruitment of covert sources and agents in the Soviet Zone." Five daily broadcasts targeted East German listeners, thousands of whom risked prosecution by contacting the station with suggestions, such as that broadcasts be quietly pitched and free of telltale sound effects (such as chiming bells) so that they might avoid being overheard while listening. The overwhelming majority of RIAS programming was locally produced.[59]

RIAS devoted its programming to efforts to destabilize Kremlin authority over the 18 million Soviet Zone residents. U.S. officials came to consider the station "the epitome of aggressive psychological warfare." They estimated that from 50 to 70 percent of Soviet Zone residents tuned in regularly to RIAS, which was the favorite station of 85 to 90 percent of those who listened. A large "eavesdropping" audience tuned in from West Germany and other East European regimes.[60]

Although RIAS did not instigate the June 1953 uprising, its programming encouraged the rebellion against Soviet authority. Special labor programs, initiated in 1950 but intensified in spring 1953, had focused on worker dissatisfaction with East German factories, which eventually provided the spark for the uprising. RIAS unrelentingly attacked the regime, citing countless examples of its corruption and perfidy. The station relied on "intimate contact with its listeners," many of whom visited RIAS offices in the Western Sector of Berlin. RIAS not only possessed a close relationship with its audience, but repeatedly confounded East German authorities with its extensive knowledge of their own activities. Through its awareness, RIAS developed "a curious, flexible, almost Gandhian strategy of constructive subversion, a technique of open conspiracy against which the communists seem to have no effective psychological defense."[61]

East German officials listened nervously at the end of each broadcast day, when RIAS presented "Berlin Speaks to the Zone," a program which often gave on the air the names of secret police agents, as identified by a former security official who had escaped to the West. The program relayed news and, when possible, warnings of impending actions by the East German government. Like RFE, RIAS adopted a "no holds barred" philosophy, including regular broadcasts on the sometimes scandalous private lives of party leaders. One program on RIAS featured "Comrade Otto Pieckewitz," a caricature of the East German head of state Wilhelm Pieck. In the radio skits, "Pieckewitz's" forte was "arguing communist ideology and party slogans to their illogical and absurd conclusions." He was canceled, then revived after "a flood of fan mail from Soviet zone listeners." In his regular Saturday night program, "Pieckewitz" satirized the "two hundred percent communist." "He has helped us remember how to laugh," one letter-writer observed.[62]

By the early 1950s, RIAS was contributing significantly to East German instability. When the Soviets sponsored a Berlin Communist Youth Festival, RIAS lured 13,000 young people to the Western Sector of the city by sponsoring and publicizing discussions, concerts, and tours. The Kremlin decided to act. Soviet propaganda lashed out at RIAS, which it called a "paid stinking news ulcer" that was "worse than poison gas." The *Atlantic* observed in 1951 that the "frenzy with which the communists are attacking" confirmed that RIAS was "dishing out some damaging stuff." With 8 Americans and some 600 Germans coordinating its operations, RIAS was "coming close to blanketing Germany." Although RIAS did not encourage permanent exile, preferring that citizens remain "at home to weaken the red regime," its broadcasts prompted scores of defectors on a daily basis. C. D. Jackson considered RIAS "one of the few really top-notch official American radio propaganda operations."[63]

Such praise notwithstanding, U.S. officials did not realize the extent of the popularity of RIAS until the 1953 uprising and its aftermath. "While we knew before June 16 that RIAS was an important factor in East German life," a State Department official observed, "it is now pretty clear that it played a major role in spreading demonstrations from East Berlin to the Zone." An internal East German analysis blamed RIAS for encouraging the zone-wide spread of the uprising. As the workers struck, RIAS provided on-the-spot reports and detailed accounts of the rioting, especially around the Brandenburg Gate and the Potsdammer Platz, key points of activity. RIAS reports also fed West German radio coverage.[64]

The outbreak of rioting confronted RIAS officials with hard choices that reflected the central dilemma of psychological warfare. When West German trade unions called for a general strike in the Soviet Zone on June 16, RIAS director Gordon Ewing, a former college English teacher, had to weigh the merits of broadcasting the appeal. Lacking guidelines from Washington on how to handle an uprising, Ewing sought to avoid a militant tone, which might create a war atmosphere, but knew he would be criticized for missing a rare opportunity if RIAS adopted a passive role. Ewing decided to air the call for a general strike, together with RIAS commentaries on the ineptitude of the East German police, with full knowledge that he "would be pouring gasoline on the flames." Ewing realized that eventually the revolt would be crushed, and that inevitably there would be many victims, but he felt "confident that the spirit of resistance in East Germany would be immeasurably strengthened by even a temporary victory over the communist regime."[65]

RIAS stopped short of openly encouraging armed resistance, but it attacked the East German regime and urged workers, peasants, youth, and others to challenge it. "Short of inciting violence," C. D. Jackson explained, "RIAS encouraged the continuation of demonstrations and gave moral support and highly complimentary treatment to actions of the East Zone populace." According to some reports, many East Germans expected RIAS to provide detailed guidance in support of the revolt. As even Jackson observed, however, "obviously this could not be done by RIAS" because, unlike the ostensibly private RFE, it was tied directly to the U.S. government. RIAS made no attempt to coordinate the insurrection once it began. As the Red Army suppressed the revolt, RIAS aired West German government calls for the rioters to desist. RIAS broadcasts bitterly condemned Soviet oppression as "a crime against the people."[66]

Although RIAS generated excitement and hope for change in East Germany, intrinsic opposition to the CP dictatorship, not the radio station, was the source of the uprising. RIAS did not directly incite the workers to riot, yet there can be little doubt that its in-depth coverage of the Berlin demonstrations encouraged outbreaks of resistance elsewhere in East Germany. "We struck in our town because of what the RIAS told us about the Berlin demonstrations," recalled one German worker who escaped to the West. "I am convinced that the uprising became zonewide only because of the broadcast reports from Berlin." A careful assessment, based on recently declassified documents, found that Western propaganda, and RIAS in particular, "was much more significant than has previously been realized."[67]

After reestablishing its authority, the Kremlin blamed Western propaganda for the uprising and launched a concerted campaign to jam RIAS. Radio and print sources, as well as a poster campaign, denounced RIAS and reported on court cases in which East Germans were forced to blame Western radio for their resistance in the uprising. RIAS director Ewing termed the jamming, which began in July, a "reprisal for the severe psychological defeats dealt them by the June 17 rebellion and the American free food campaign." The most intensive jamming occurred in the industrial region of Saxony, which had been the site of major strikes and continuing industrial unrest. In Dresden, residents informed RIAS that a large new jamming facility, which they dubbed *"Der wilde mann,"* had virtually blacked out the station's broadcasts.[68]

Germans representing all sectors of the occupied country left no doubt that they valued RIAS. Berlin mayor Ernst Reuter declared that RIAS was "inextricably entwined in every activity of our people." For the Soviet Zone residents, RIAS was a source of objective news as well as "a spiritual bridge that links them to their homeland." A German listener insisted, "I don't believe there is a house in Eastern Germany that doesn't hear RIAS. . . . RIAS is jammed but we listen to it in spite of the jamming." An East German worker reported that "our underground resistance is seriously worried about the threat of a radio blackout, for these broadcasts are our last link to the free world and our only chance to find out what goes on elsewhere, even in other German towns."[69]

Citing a "determined effort to jam" RIAS, the State Department moved to combat Soviet interference. The only alternative was to "let RIAS deteriorate with the interpretation that the United States is losing interest in Berlin and our friends behind the curtain in East Germany." Washington, accordingly, determined that increasing the number and quality of transmitters was both necessary and feasible.[70]

While the uprising revealed the influence of U.S. radio propaganda in the East Germany, the Soviet crackdown demonstrated that liberation remained a distant vision. The riots proved that psychological warfare could exploit instability behind the Iron Curtain, especially in East Germany because of direct Western access to Berlin. Nevertheless, as more sober observers had understood all along, the West could not prevent Soviet repression without a direct military conflict. Given this reality, the aborted uprising raised disturbing questions about the role of Western propaganda, which had encouraged the outbreak and spread of resistance to the East German regime through its inflammatory rhetoric. With Western radio broadcasting a drumbeat of liberation propaganda, the East Germans undoubtedly expected more tangible Western support for their cause than was forthcoming.

Repression in the Eastern European regimes pointed to the central contradiction of psychological warfare. Although committed to stirring unrest in the Soviet empire, the West also perceived that its propaganda could create false expectations that produced fruitless uprisings and loss of life. The Soviet crackdown demonstrated that Moscow had no intention of abandoning its hegemonic position. Accepting the inevitability of semipermanent spheres of influence, the USSR asserted East German "sovereignty" in March 1954.[71]

As Nikita S. Khrushchev gained ascendancy in the Kremlin, Soviet control tightened over Eastern Europe. Khrushchev compelled closer economic and military integration of the CP regimes, a process that culminated in the creation of the Warsaw Pact on May 14, 1955. That political and military alliance—the Kremlin's answer to West German integration into NATO—called for collective defense against external threats while guaranteeing nonintervention in members' internal affairs. Despite the "guarantee," the mutual security treaty provided a convenient pretext in the future for Soviet intervention to thwart liberation movements.

Those movements continued to arise in part due to the stunning impact of Khrushchev's "secret speech" at the Twentieth Party Congress on the night of February 24-25, 1956. For seven hours Khrushchev railed against Stalin and his legacy, calling special attention to the "cult of personality," Stalin's "despotic character," economic mismanagement, and violations of socialist legality.[72] News of the de-Stalinization campaign electrified Eastern Europe. In Washington, CIA director Allen Dulles concluded that the speech was "a most serious mistake" by Khrushchev, which provided "a great opportunity, both covertly and overtly, to exploit the situation to our advantage." After concerted efforts, the CIA obtained a copy of Khrushchev's speech through Israeli intelligence and leaked the document to the *New York Times*, which published it on June 4.[73]

Psychological warriors eagerly exploited Khrushchev's speech to a receptive Eastern European audience. As RFE, the VOA, balloon-borne leaflets, and other sources informed listeners about Khrushchev's speech, discontent rumbled across the Eastern European landscape. Ever optimistic, Foster Dulles told the Senate Foreign Relations Committee that because of opposition to Khrushchev's speech in the USSR itself, the Soviet leader was "on the ropes and, if we can keep the pressure up . . . there is going to occur a very great disintegration within the apparatus of the international communist organization."[74] RFE sources informed the CIA that "events were moving toward confrontation with the Soviets in Poland and Hungary."

The report proved to be accurate, as riots erupted in the Polish industrial city of Poznan on June 28. When Allen Dulles informed his brother of the news, the Secretary of State exulted that "when they crack, they can crack fast. We have to keep the pressure on." The Polish government responded swiftly to the workers attacks on government facilities, however, sending in armored units that quelled the revolt in three days. Scores of Poles were killed, wounded, and imprisoned. The Polish regime, described as "thoroughly shaken" by the riots, immediately attempted to win back popular support by promising higher wages, improved working conditions, more and better housing, consumer goods, amnesty for political offenses, and other measures. Western jurists monitored the subsequent trials of rioters, most of whom received light sentences.[75]

The political crisis remained tense into the fall of 1956, as deep tensions developed between Stalinists and reformers in the Polish CP. Seven divisions of Soviet troops, stationed in Poland and bolstered by tanks and artillery, prepared to move on Warsaw. In a bold speech on October 20, 1956, Wladyslaw Gomulka, the reform leader, denounced the cult of personality and "Beria-ism"—or secret police terror—declaring that "we are putting an end to it once and for all." Gomulka demanded that Khrushchev, who had arrived in Warsaw with much of the Soviet Politburo, call off the troop movements or face widespread resistance from workers, students, and the Polish militia. At the same time, Gomulka reminded Khrushchev that his emphasis on collective leadership and different roads to socialism converged with the Soviet leader's de-Stalinization campaign. Gomulka rejected Khrushchev's angry charge that the Poles sought to join the imperialist camp. The Polish reformer agreed that Soviet troops should remain in the country as long as NATO forces remained in Germany. Armed with these assurances—yet also mindful of almost certain popular resistance to Soviet military action—Khrushchev averted a bloodbath by calling off the Red Army advance. Having convinced Khrushchev that Poland would "not permit its independence to be taken away," Gomulka was left to restore order in Poland.[76]

Throughout the crisis Western propagandists demonstrated restraint. RFE warned Poles against mounting a reckless uprising and urged them to accept Gomulka's compromise rather than pressing for free elections and the withdrawal of Soviet troops. On October 23, 1956, the State Department recommended a restrained public response that "makes clear that while we welcome greater Polish independence we are not seeking to gain a position of special influence for ourselves in Poland." Both Eisenhower and Dulles issued public statements that reflected Washington's nonconfrontational approach. Dulles remained confident, observing that the "continuous sequence of concessions demonstrates the weaknesses of the communist regime and will ultimately lead to free elections."[77]

After the crisis had been averted, Western propagandists became more aggressive. As it had done in the wake of the East German riots, Washington offered food aid, but the Polish government promptly rejected the propaganda gambit. Meanwhile, USIA made "appropriate use" of eyewitness accounts of the Poznan riots, which were "exploited heavily by VOA." Psychological warriors emphasized that the grievances that led to the revolt in Poland "are widespread in the Soviet bloc, and that the demonstrations provide additional evidence that the peoples of the satellites are opposed to Moscow-dominated governments."[78]

Following resolution of the Polish crisis, attention focused on Hungary, where the combination of the New Course and Khrushchev's speech had devastated the Stalinist regime of Matyas Rakosi. On March 29, 1955, a U.S. intelligence estimate concluded that "Hungary has in recent years shown consistent evidence of political disharmony and economic dislocation, accompanied by popular unrest, and will probably continue to be the most troublesome of the East European satellites." The report noted that most Hungarians were anti-communist and possessed greater ethnic and cultural affinity for Germany than for Slavic Russia. While the New Course had sanctioned economic and political reforms, as well as increased religious freedom, such measures were "both limited and belated with resultant popular disillusion." Presciently, the intelligence estimate concluded that "the Kremlin will take all measures necessary to keep Hungary in the Bloc."[79]

Pressures for reform built in Hungary after the secret speech just as they had in Poland, leading to a similar split within the Hungarian CP. In response to reform leader Imre Nagy's pressure for sweeping changes under the New Course, Rakosi purged him from party membership for "deviationism" on April 18, 1955. That action only served to fuel an increasingly revolutionary situation. Trying to maintain authority in Hungary, the Kremlin on July 18 forced out Rakosi in favor of Erno Gero, who allowed Nagy to reassume his party membership. Emboldened by the reforms in Poland, thousands of Hungarian workers, students, and intellectuals pressed the revolution throughout the summer and early fall with calls for free elections and withdrawal of Soviet troops.[80]

Revolutionary sentiment climaxed on October 23, when demonstrators filled the streets of Budapest, tore red star insignias off buildings, and used trucks with winches to pull down a gigantic statue of Stalin. Secret police fired into crowds outside the broadcasting center and Soviet troops clashed with demonstrators. Gero attempted to placate the rebels by naming Nagy prime minister while simultaneously appealing for armed Soviet intervention. Two Soviet Politburo members rushed to Hungary, where they huddled with Ambassador Yuri Andropov to assess the situation. The Soviets forced Gero's resignation in favor of Janos Kadar, but the revolution could not be quelled. Nagy liberated from prison the popular Cardinal Jozsef Mindszenty, who immediately sought refuge in the U.S. embassy, from which he issued calls for independence, pluralism, and a mixed economy.[81]

Initially reluctant to intervene, Khrushchev saw no alternative after extensive meetings in the Kremlin on October 30-31. The Hungarian revolt was more clearly anti-Soviet and anti-communist than the Polish uprising had been. Khrushchev, concerned about falling dominoes of his own, would not allow the model of a breakaway CP regime. After gaining the sanction of the Czech and Rumanian communists—as well as Tito's reluctant endorsement—the Soviet leader ordered Defense Minister Marshal Georgi Zhukov to prepare a plan, "Operation Whirlwind," for decisive military intervention. After the Soviets provided Nagy with false assurances of nonintervention, a Red Army force of at least 60,000 troops marched on Budapest on November 4. Nagy responded by appealing to the UN and announcing Hungary's withdrawal from the Warsaw Pact, but it was too late to prevent the onslaught. Approximately

4,000 Hungarians and 669 Soviets died in the fighting. Some 300 Hungarian rebels, including Nagy, were later executed.[82]

The timing of the Hungarian revolt could not have been worse from Washington's perspective. The events not only unfolded in the last days of Eisenhower's reelection campaign, but they coincided with the Suez crisis, thus impeding the Administration's ability to devote its full attention to Eastern Europe. Ever hopeful that liberation was imminent, Dulles's initial reaction to the events in Budapest was that "the great monolith of communism is crumbling!" On October 25, after Soviet troops already in Hungary responded to the initial unrest, Eisenhower issued a statement deploring Kremlin intervention. The president pointed out that the Warsaw Pact pledged defense against outside aggression, whereas Soviet troops had intervened to "continue the occupation of Hungary."[83]

Harold Stassen urged the administration to do all it could to discourage all-out Soviet intervention by making it "clear that we are willing to have Hungary be established on the Austrian basis—and not affiliated with NATO." Eisenhower endorsed the proposal but Dulles rejected direct talks with the Kremlin. After considering the matter, Eisenhower decided that Dulles's upcoming speech before the Dallas Council on World Affairs provided the best opportunity to state the administration's position. In the October 27 speech, Dulles emphasized that Washington would welcome a Titoist, or national communist, solution in Hungary. Moreover, Dulles declaimed that the United States had no "ulterior purpose in desiring the independence of the satellite countries" and "did not look upon these nations as potential military allies." Dulles then charged Ambassador Bohlen with conveying to Khrushchev that Washington had no intent of luring Hungary into NATO. Not wishing to be seen as placating the communists, or selling out the "captive nations," Dulles advised Bohlen that it was "highly important that nothing done under this authorization should emerge publicly as a demarche attributable to Washington."[84]

On October 29, Israel invaded Egypt's Sinai peninsula, followed two days later by British and French aerial bombardment of Egyptian targets. Anglo-French ground troops followed, compelling the Eisenhower administration to divert its focus to the implications of a war launched by its closest allies without consultation with Washington. The Suez crisis could only have encouraged the Kremlin to intervene in Hungary. The example of European imperial aggression against a Third World nationalist regime could be exploited to divert attention from the propaganda damage that would flow from the repression in Budapest. In the midst of the Suez crisis, Eisenhower, still trying to avoid provoking the Soviets, excised a reference to the "irresistible" forces of "liberation" in an October 31 speech by John Foster Dulles.[85]

Decisive Soviet intervention precluded the spread of revolt to other regimes, thereby delivering a mortal blow to the elusive quest for liberation. Dulles, having entered the hospital for cancer treatments in the midst of the crisis, had to accept that his hopes for near-term liberation had proven illusory. For Eisenhower himself, Hungary was "indeed a bitter pill for us to swallow." Washington concentrated on making the most of what, in the absence of simultaneous Western intervention in the Mideast, would have been an unprecedented propaganda boon. USIA gave "heavy and effective play" to condemnation of the Soviet action, including film of Soviet tanks killing Hungarians in Budapest. Psychological warriors used all means at their disposal—broadcasts, leaflets, and protests before the UN and other international forums—to decry Soviet intervention. In 1957 the Congress for Cultural Freedom published *The White Book,* which documented Soviet repression. A broadcast directive limited coverage of Hungarian events to straight news, since the facts themselves were sufficiently damning. This directive left Munich's Radio Liberation "bitterly unhappy" about being compelled to exercise restraint in its commentary.[86]

While seeking to maximize the negative propaganda impact on the USSR, psychological warriors advised that the Hungarian intervention should not serve to "revive the Cold War on the scale of intensity of the late Stalin period." Eisenhower accepted advice to refrain from "drastic measures" such as blocking Soviet assets and intensifying trade embargoes.[87]

Undermining efforts to take maximum propaganda advantage of Soviet intervention were charges that Washington had incited the Hungarian revolt with its own psychological warfare campaign. It was to be expected that the Soviets, calling attention to RFE and the balloon-borne leaflets, would level such charges, but quite another for allies and the "captive peoples" themselves to lay the blame on Washington. Eisenhower was deeply disturbed by the widespread view that "our radio and balloon operations have led to belief that we would be prepared to do more" in the event of an uprising. Admitting that U.S. propaganda had undoubtedly encouraged the Hungarians to revolt, the president called for a maximum worldwide propaganda effort to head off charges that Washington would incite anti-communist rebels only to abandon them to the mercies of the Kremlin.[88]

Beyond question, Washington's propaganda encouraged the tragic events in Hungary. After all, fomenting opposition to Kremlin authority was the essence of U.S. propaganda in Eastern Europe. Radio propaganda—including RFE, the VOA, the BBC, Vatican Radio, and other stations—was more extensive than most Westerners realized. Millions of Hungarians listened.

Since its inception, the VOA's Hungarian station had condemned "Soviet methods by which human liberty was destroyed in Eastern Europe." In 1950 the station closely monitored émigré organizations dedicated to "the liberation of Eastern European peasants suffering under the Soviet yoke." The Hungarian Voice lashed "Soviet-Communist terror" against peasants, workers, students, and intellectuals. Hungarian VOA marked traditional religious and national celebrations, such as the October 6 "Hungarian National Day of Mourning" honoring the 1849 Hungarian independence struggle. Such occasions provided a convenient opportunity to link anti-communist Hungarians with historic struggles for freedom. "No torture could make Hungarians forget their national dignity, love of freedom and independence," VOA intoned. "Heroic resistance always opened the doors of life . . . as it is opening now." The station regularly broadcast Western support for Hungarian independence as when, in the midst of the 1952 presidential campaign, Adlai Stevenson's denunciation of the Soviet-backed government attested to bipartisan support in the United States.[89]

In line with a March 1953 policy directive, VOA broadcasts were "straightforward, factual, forceful." After the 1956 Soviet intervention, a USIA evaluation of VOA broadcasts found that the station had "neither encouraged nor discouraged the Hungarian freedom fighters." VOA reported extensively on the events in Budapest, as well as on Western reaction, but exercised "extreme caution . . . to avoid broadcasting back news which might prove inaccurate and inflammatory." VOA, whose headquarters had been moved from New York to Washington in 1955 to ensure close supervision, was functioning, in line with the Jackson committee's 1953 recommendation, as a straight news service modeled on the more popular BBC global network. While controversy swelled around RFE for encouraging the Hungarian uprising, the VOA's accurate and straightforward reporting on the event enhanced its credibility. New guidelines issued by Eisenhower on June 3, 1957, brought the VOA under still tighter control as a result of Washington's determination to "eliminate the 'propaganda' tone."[90]

While the VOA emerged unscathed from recriminations following the Hungarian repression, RFE's role proved far more controversial. However, because CIA funding and sponsorship of the station remained secret—or at least plausibly deniable—Washington was able to deflect some criticism for the station's role in inflaming the Hungarian uprising. RFE had long considered Hungary perhaps the most vulnerable regime and had targeted its audience accordingly. The station sought to stir unrest through appeals to religion, invidious comparisons with life in the West, and invocations of the tradition of nineteenth-century freedom fighter Louis Kossuth. RFE told the Hungarian people they were slaves, but promised that one day they would be free of their oppressors.

Just as it had done in Czechoslovakia with Operation VETO, RFE had launched a coordinated broadcast and balloon propaganda offensive, operation

FOCUS, against Hungary in 1954. FOCUS publicized the "Twelve Demands of the National Opposition Movement," including free elections and economic reform. Initial refugee reports indicated that "within a matter of hours the entire program was known in the remotest corner of Hungary." The FOCUS radio campaign progressed smoothly but the balloon effort required careful planning because of the long distance from the West German launching sites to Hungary. The operation succeeded, however, as within ten hours 1,880,000 leaflets—4,950 pounds of paper—were released from a single launching site. The Hungarian government protested the propaganda barrage in the fall of 1954, charging that the leaflets were "inciting anti-communist Hungarians to rebellion and subversion." The American legation denied involvement, explaining that "the activity in question was undertaken by the Crusade for Freedom and Radio Free Europe on their own initiative and responsibility."[91]

Recognizing the weakness of Rakosi's regime in the wake of Khrushchev's de-Stalinization campaign, Washington launched a "diplomatic offensive with coordinated propaganda exploitation" in the spring of 1956. Because of his Stalinist background, Rakosi was "an extremely vulnerable target" and there were "opportunities now open for exacerbating internal dissension and promoting already existing disaffection" from the regime. VOA also targeted Rakosi as part of longstanding VOA practice to miss no opportunity to remind listeners that "satellite regimes as a whole represent the interests of the Kremlin rather than those of local populations."[92]

As instability verged on revolution, RFE came perilously close to inciting its listeners to revolt. On October 24, the station emphasized "how great a confusion exists within the government itself. The government and its armed units are no more masters of the situation." RFE implored that "all those elements must be removed from the government which by their mere presence remind of the Stalinist past, as well as all those whose mere name is provocation to the nation." An RFE commentary rejected a negotiated settlement of the crisis, insisting that the goals of the revolution "cannot be allowed to dissolve at the conference table. . . . Instead of promises, however, and instead of words, action is needed." Another commentator exhorted that "there is no time—the victory must be realized." Hungarians were told that "this fight cannot be overpowered" and "under no conditions" would the Hungarian rebels "release from their hands that power which they possess in their arms and in their refusal to work." RFE encouraged Hungarian youth to accept Cardinal Mindszenty as the leader of the rebellion and called on them to fight "with all [their] strength on the streets to defend the Church."[93]

As charges, countercharges, and recriminations surfaced in the wake of Soviet repression in Hungary, the CIA conducted a secret analysis of RFE broadcasts. The agency report noted that a policy directive issued on December 12, 1951, had warned RFE broadcasters "not to yield to a natural impulse to bring hope to their compatriots by promising armed intervention by the West. . . . Such talks may not be broadcast on RFE." Following Khrushchev's speech, secret U.S. guidance for RFE broadcasts called for emphasis on evolutionary forces and "the progress of anti-Stalinism and the achievements of a degree of liberalization in the several captive nations."[94]

Interpreting RFE broadcasts in the most benign light possible, the CIA concluded that "no RFE broadcast to Hungary before the revolution could be considered as inciting to armed revolt." A review of scripts found that no broadcast implied promises of U.S. or NATO military intervention. Once the revolt began in late October, RFE immediately broadcast the news of the demonstrations in Budapest, but was cautioned to avoid tactical advice and intervention. The station described events, reported U.S. leaders' statements, and appealed to Soviet troops not to fire on Hungarians. "However, after the revolution was well under way," the CIA analysis noted, "a few of the scripts reviewed do indicate that RFE occasionally went beyond the authorized factual broadcasting . . . to provide tactical advice to the patriots as to the course the rebellion should take and the individuals best qualified to lead it. As soon as these deviations from policy were noted, steps were taken to insure rigid supervision of broadcasting content." The CIA concluded that "RFE did not incite the Hungarian people to revolution," which was instead the result of "ten years of Soviet repression."[95]

Hungarians, some 170,000 of whom escaped through a temporarily perforated border, offered a different perspective. The escapees agreed that Western propaganda did not *cause* rebellion, but most declared that they had been led to expect support from the West. "It will be hard to forget the unkept promises," one man explained. "Most of those who believed were bitterly disappointed." Explaining that he covered his radio with pillows to protect it as the fighting blew out the windows in his flat, the refugee described Western radio as "our source of hope, of connection with the outside world." He recalled that Hungarians listened and "cried with joy" in their belief that the West would come to their defense. "How can we ever believe anything again?"[96]

The testimony of hundreds of despondent refugees, together with the drumbeat of Soviet charges against Western propaganda, precipitated investigations by the UN and the West German government, which held formal responsibility for the Munich-based RFE. After the station turned over 250 hours of Hungarian broadcasts to the Bonn government, Adenauer, in a January 25, 1957, news conference, reported that the investigation concluded that RFE did not incite the Hungarian rebellion. The West German chancellor admitted,

however, that "remarks were made which were liable to cause misinterpreta-
tions." Discussion and personnel changes had resolved the issue and Bonn now
considered the matter closed. The UN Special Committee Report, released on
June 20, 1957, came to similar conclusions. Describing the Hungarian revolt
as a "spontaneous national uprising," the UN condemned Soviet intervention
while absolving the West of responsibility. The report, however, described
Western propaganda as "encouraging" the rebels as it sought "to exploit to the
maximum" the prospects of the anti-communist rebellion.[97]

In the final analysis, both RFE and the Hungarian rebels themselves
shared responsibility for the misperception that the West might lend tangible
support to the revolution. Once the uprising began, excited RFE broadcasters
went too far in encouraging the Hungarian rebels. But as one astute observer
explained, "the important propaganda fact is not what people hear, but rather
what they think they hear. To a certain extent the Hungarians believed they
heard what they wanted to hear. From the phrasing of RFE scripts the gap
between the actual promises and implied promises was easy to bridge for people
under the maximum of mental stress."[98]

The East German, Polish, and Hungarian uprisings, their repression by
the Soviets, and the controversy over RFE's role in them marked a turning point
in American strategy toward Eastern Europe. The Hungarian intervention
shattered optimistic projections of near-term liberation. Aggressive psychological warfare had not only failed to achieve liberation, but had invited Soviet
repression. As *The New Republic* put in the aftermath of the Hungarian crisis,
"for many years we have held aloft this torch of liberty. But at what point does
the torch become an incendiary weapon?"[99]

By the time of the Hungarian repression, a shift had already begun from
aggressive psychological warfare to an evolutionary strategy toward Eastern
Europe. Veteran State Department diplomat H. Freeman "Doc" Matthews
observed that the Eisenhower administration "came in [with] the idea you could
roll back communism by wishful thinking, or sending balloons over into
Czechoslovakia, that sort of thing. They had to learn and it took a while."[100]
The VOA, RFE, and other Western propaganda outlets would remain in force,
but there would be fewer balloons, more careful supervision of émigré broadcasts, and more creative—if gradualist—approaches to the ultimate goal of
breaching the Iron Curtain.

FOUR

From Revolution to Evolution: The Thaw in East–West Cultural Relations

Wedded to Cold War militarization and preoccupied with efforts to destabilize the Soviet empire through psychological warfare, Washington rejected opportunities during the Truman and Eisenhower years to seek a negotiated settlement of the Cold War. Given the antagonism inherent in the competing social systems, successful negotiations seemed unlikely. Soviet propaganda regularly scored U.S. imperialism in uncompromising terms. The bloody stalemate in Korea, coupled with McCarthyism, anchored equally hostile anti-Soviet perceptions in the West. With Stalin launching yet another internal purge of suspected counterrevolutionaries in 1952, accommodation seemed out of reach.

However, on March 10, 1952, Stalin issued a "Peace Note," in which he offered to negotiate a settlement of the German question. Anxious to head off full-scale integration of West Germany into the Western alliance, Stalin offered a basis for reviving the Potsdam formula aimed at German unification. The Soviet dictator proposed that all foreign troops be withdrawn within a year; that no military bases be permitted in Germany; that the former Reich be precluded from joining an alliance that included any of the World War II Allies; and that Germany be allowed limited armed forces, though it was to be free of all economic restraints.[1]

The United States and its allies—especially Konrad Adenauer—flatly rejected talks aimed at achieving a negotiated settlement. Adenauer, "extremely upset and nervous" about any proposal that would decouple Western Germany from the Washington-centered alliance, bitterly condemned the Soviet proposal. U.S. diplomats in Moscow dismissed the Stalin note as a "propaganda move" designed to impede Western rearmament. Secretary of State Dean Acheson concurred, rejecting the Soviet proposals as "intended solely to obstruct the building of the new Europe" rather than being "intended seriously to bring about German unification on the basis of freedom." A neutral Germany, he added, would "invite aggression and domination from the East."[2]

The Kremlin undoubtedly wished to exploit the propaganda benefit of posing as a peacemaker over Germany, but Stalin may well have been serious about achieving an agreement that would head off West German integration into NATO. "Although the public nature of the Soviet proposal lends itself to the propaganda interpretation," observed one student of the Stalin Note, "both the timing and the content of the Note indicate a serious Soviet initiative." No less an authority on diplomacy than Henry A. Kissinger concluded that "the tone and precision of Stalin's note suggested that his purpose transcended mere propaganda." Perhaps anticipating a long Cold War that his country could not win, Stalin "might have been willing to pay a significant price for a relaxation of tensions." The Truman administration, however, "scorned the Soviet overture," dismissed Stalin's initiative as propaganda, and continued to focus its sights on West German military and economic integration.[3]

Following the rejection of his Peace Note, Stalin abandoned any hope for compromise with the West. He urged East German leaders to "organize your own state," resumed a bitterly anti-Western stance, and launched a new purge of suspected counterrevolutionaries at home. Following the dictator's death on March 5, 1953, however, the prospects of a Cold War settlement reappeared. Stalin's death came six weeks after the Eisenhower administration had taken power and at a time when all the major powers sought a way to bring an end to the Korean War. In the USSR, Stalin's initial successor, Georgi Malenkov, advocated peaceful coexistence with the West in a speech at the dictator's funeral and stated publicly his willingness to negotiate on all outstanding European security issues.[4]

In high-level meetings called to discuss the impact of Stalin's death, Eisenhower expressed a view that ran "contrary to the views of many of our intelligence agencies," namely that the USSR had always been a government run by committee. Indeed, based on personal experience, "the President believed that had Stalin, at the end of the war, been able to do what he wanted with his colleagues in the Kremlin, Russia would have sought more peaceful and normal relations with the rest of the world."[5] While deeply flawed, the President's unorthodox interpretation of Soviet behavior might have led logically to the conclusion that Stalin's death would make less likely, rather than more likely, concessions on the part of the post-Stalin Kremlin. In any case, Eisenhower was to reject what may well have been a historic opportunity to reduce Cold War tensions.

George F. Kennan and C. D. Jackson, both staunch anti-communists, made the case for opening serious negotiations with the USSR. Jackson viewed Stalin's death as "the greatest opportunity presented to the United States in many years to seize the initiative." The extraordinary situation called for concerted efforts to "exploit Stalin's death to the limit of psychological usefulness." At the suggestion of Walt W. Rostow, Jackson had summoned Kennan—who had been forced out of the Foreign Service by John Foster Dulles—for a discussion of the consequences of Stalin's death. Kennan reiterated the position he had advocated since 1948, that Washington should open negotiations aimed at German neutralization and reunification. Such a settlement would establish a basis for Soviet and American disengagement from Central Europe, thus encouraging Moscow to tolerate liberalization and greater independence behind the Iron Curtain.[6]

Eisenhower and Dulles rejected negotiations and dismissed Soviet diplomatic initiatives as propaganda. As one preeminent Cold War historian has observed, "From the outset, the Eisenhower administration saw the Soviet Union as an adversary whose basic hostility and ultimate expansionist objectives were unchangeable." Focusing on worst-case scenarios of Soviet behavior, Washington rejected negotiations in favor of Cold War militarization.[7]

The Eisenhower administration responded to the Kremlin "peace offensive" with a series of propaganda campaigns. In fact, Stalin's death had rudely interrupted the timing of a U.S. propaganda offensive that had originated in the Princeton psychological warfare meeting called by C. D. Jackson on May 11-12, 1952. Anticipating a Republican victory, the Princeton group made plans to exploit Eisenhower's international prestige by launching a propaganda campaign through a presidential address circulated worldwide.[8]

Eisenhower's "Chance for Peace" speech had been planned for March 12, 1953, but the death of Stalin, dominating world news, forced a cancellation. Causing further delay was Malenkov's March 15 speech before the Supreme Soviet, in which he declared that disputes between Washington and Moscow could "be decided by peaceful means, on the basis of mutual understanding." Washington responded by advising overseas information personnel to play down the Soviet "peace offensive," which it dismissed as a disingenuous attempt to undermine the proposed European Defense Community. Dismissing the possibility that Stalin's death and Malenkov's overtures offered genuine opportunities for détente, the Eisenhower administration chafed over its inability to seize the initiative. As Eisenhower put it, "the question of when and how his speech was to be delivered was almost as important as its content."⁹

The administration finally seized the propaganda initiative on April 16, when Eisenhower delivered his "Chance for Peace" address before the American Society of Newspaper Editors in Washington. The speech, developed by Rostow and C. D. Jackson but put into final form by presidential speechwriter Emmett John Hughes, reflected a fundamental contradiction in Eisenhower's own thinking. The president embraced the Cold War ethos but abhorred the costs of the East-West struggle. He aspired to reduce defense spending in order to balance the budget and devote resources to improving people's lives. In a very real sense, the Cold War and its burden of armaments, offended his sensibilities.

Eisenhower was a fiscal conservative and a genuine humanitarian. Rather than focusing on the Korean negotiations and other thorny Cold War issues, the president decided that his speech should "concentrate instead on our determination to raise the general standard of living throughout the world." He would reiterate a pledge made in February of his willingness to hold a summit with the new Soviet leadership if "the basis for the meeting was honest and practical." The speech would focus, however, "on the common man's yearning for food, shelter, and a decent standard of living." The president hoped to make a direct appeal for peace to the Soviet people through a proposed exchange of radio and television time with the Kremlin leadership. Deferring to his advisers, Eisenhower allowed Hughes to delete both the proposed summit and the exchange of media time from the speech. The former, Hughes advised the President, smacked "too much of a publicity stunt." The offer to travel to meet the Soviet leaders was too conciliatory, the speechwriter added. As historian Blanche Wiesen Cook has noted, "It would not be the last time [Eisenhower's] own efforts at greater détente would be short-circuited by his staff."¹⁰

Eisenhower's speech was a well-conceived propaganda initiative, but the only "chance for peace" that it offered would have required Soviet capitulation to Western demands. The speech condemned the Cold War as "eight years of fear and force," a "wasting of strength" that undermined the quest for "true abundance and happiness for the peoples of this earth." Eisenhower declaimed that "every gun that is made, every warship launched, every rocket fired signifies, in the final sense, a theft from those who hunger and are not fed, those who are cold and are not clothed. . . . Is there no other way the world may live?" The president called for arms reductions and de-escalation that would free the world for "a new kind of war" on poverty and want.¹¹

Despite this eloquent plea, Eisenhower offered no concrete proposals that might have provided the basis for negotiations with Moscow. The president blamed the USSR solely for the Cold War, including the fighting in

Korea, and struck an uncompromising stance on Western military integration. The Kremlin was to sign the Austrian State Treaty, bring an end to the Korean War, end its hegemony over Eastern Europe, and ultimately abandon communist ideology. The United States, having done nothing to provoke the East-West conflict, as Eisenhower and Dulles saw it, offered no concessions or incentives to the Soviet leaders.

Eisenhower's speech, promoted worldwide in a maximum propaganda effort, compelled a Soviet response. As Ambassador Charles Bohlen reported from Moscow, *Pravda* carried an "unprecedented" full first page, six column article entitled "Regarding President Eisenhower's Speech." The CP newspaper reprinted the president's speech in full, uncensored form. The Soviets responded, however, that as long as the West remained opposed to German unification and committed to West German military integration under NATO, there could be no genuine drive for peace. The new Kremlin leadership would not simply capitulate to Western demands.[12]

The Soviet response suggested that UN recognition of China or U.S. willingness to reduce its own military presence around the world might provide the basis for mutual cooperation. The president's pledge that the United States would do its part to promote détente "was not strengthened in any way" by the absence of specific proposals, the Soviets noted. [The speech] "is actually lacking in this respect." By offering no specific concessions or initiatives of its own, Washington had done what it typically accused Moscow of doing: substituting rhetoric for action. Bohlen's interpretation was that the Kremlin response showed a desire to respond positively to Eisenhower's speech while rejecting his depiction of the Soviet Union as entirely at fault. Unlike Bohlen, however, a special intelligence estimate concluded that the Soviet reaction stemmed from propaganda motives and "gives no indication that they are prepared to make substantial concessions."[13]

In other capitals, including London, allies questioned the wisdom of Washington's refusal to consider German reunification as a means of reducing Cold War tensions. Despite his antipathy to communist ideology, Winston Churchill, serving once again as British prime minister, had undergone a change of heart and urged his Western colleagues in the spring of 1953 to drop all preconditions for a summit with the Soviets in order to achieve a Cold War settlement. When Churchill suggested a summit in the Soviet capital, Eisenhower expressed "a bit of astonishment that you think it appropriate to recommend Moscow to Molotov as a suitable meeting place." The president admonished "we should not rush things too much and should not permit feeling in our countries for a meeting between heads of states and governments to press us into precipitate initiatives." Provided a courtesy copy of the "Chance for Peace" address, Churchill urged Eisenhower to soften the tone of certain passages, which the President pledged to do "in order not to appear belligerent."[14]

Privately, Churchill complained that Eisenhower had been "weak and stupid" for declining an opportunity to pursue détente with the post-Stalin leadership of Russia. Speaking before the House of Commons on May 11, Churchill answered Eisenhower's "Chance for Peace" speech by advocating serious negotiations with the new Kremlin leaders, including "a meeting at the highest level of the leading world powers." Newspapers in London and Paris wondered aloud if Joseph McCarthy and John Foster Dulles, rather than Eisenhower, were in charge of U.S. foreign policy. Addressing U.S. newspaper editors only two days after Eisenhower's speech before the same group, Dulles had warned against succumbing to the "illusions of peace" emanating from Moscow. In Paris, Le Monde observed that the "conciliatory words and generosity of tone" of Eisenhower's speech had been followed by Dulles's "harangue" in which "intransigence competed with mock innocence."[15]

Even C. D. Jackson, the preeminent spokesman for psychological warfare, urged Dulles to consider negotiations with Moscow. The administration approach of demanding a Soviet capitulation to Western demands and conditions was "very much like 'unconditional surrender'" and offered the Kremlin "no room for the slightest maneuver. . . . I am all for complete, total, and crushing defeat if we really have the leverage to bring it about. But we haven't, and they know it." Jackson insisted that negotiations would enhance rather than undermine Western integration and that they offered a more hopeful course than simply continuing to "negatively oppose the USSR." The State Department rejected this view and "felt Mr. Jackson's initiative to be, simply, an uninformed gesture." Dulles agreed, declaring that negotiations with the Soviets would be futile.[16]

On August 17, 1953, NSC 160/1 pointed to the essence of the American position with the simple statement that "West Germany is far more important than East Germany." Integration of West Germany into the Western economic and military sphere was of far greater priority than entering into difficult and possibly hopeless negotiations on German reunification with the USSR. After all, West Germany was the greater prize, with a population three times larger and an industrial output five times greater than its eastern rival. Furthermore, U.S. and Western European officials, armed with vivid memories of German aggression in two world wars, were determined to prevent the emergence of a rearmed Germany unless it could be integrated into NATO. Pursuing a policy of "dual containment," Washington sought to ensure the emergence of a nonthreatening Germany while simultaneously checking Soviet power.[17]

Eisenhower's adherence to Cold War orthodoxy undermined his own genuine desire to be a man of peace. The president enjoyed enormous prestige and his Republican Party was far less vulnerable to charges of being soft on communism than Truman had been. But Eisenhower, architect of the Normandy invasion and NATO's first supreme commander, favored Western integration above all else, including pursuing a settlement with the Soviets over East-Central Europe. He embraced the advice of Dulles and Adenauer over the more uncertain course now advocated by Churchill, Jackson, and Kennan. Despite his own opposition to a diplomacy dominated by military considerations, Eisenhower declined to exploit his presidential "honeymoon" to pursue détente or cultural relations as an alternative paradigm. One historian concluded that "it is difficult to avoid the conclusion that the West missed a rare opportunity in the spring and summer of 1953 to renegotiate the division of Europe."[18]

At the time, U.S. national security elites rejected the possibility of negotiations because they still believed in the efficacy of psychological warfare. Despite Soviet repression of the East German uprising in June, Dulles viewed the unrest in Berlin as "a highly significant development," a reflection that the "present situation in satellite Europe causes the Soviets real difficulties." Less sanguine, Eisenhower observed privately that he "always thought Foster was a bit too optimistic" about the prospects of near-term liberation. Unable to win a quick victory over the CP regimes, psychological warriors would have to content themselves with efforts "to make the problem of Soviet control over the satellite people in the critical period which lies ahead as difficult as possible, without, however, inciting to revolt which might well lead to bloody reprisals."[19]

In fact, the East German riots reconfirmed the decision that there would be no negotiations on German reunification. Both Foster and Allen Dulles opposed conducting a great-power summit in the wake of the Soviet repression. Eisenhower himself seemed relieved that the "uprisings certainly had provided us with the strongest possible argument to give to Mr. Churchill against a four-power meeting." The president concluded that the only option was to proceed with integration and rearmament of Western Germany "just as rapidly as we could."[20]

On October 30, 1953, the NSC established the Eisenhower administration's "new basic concept" for national security policy in the wake of Soviet suppression of the East German uprising. NSC 162/2 concluded that "the detachment of any major European satellite from the Soviet bloc does not now appear feasible." NSC 174 reiterated this conclusion on December 23, yet called for a policy of "determined resistance to dominant Soviet influence," including political, economic, propaganda, and covert measures designed to "create and exploit troublesome problems for the USSR." Washington was to establish guidelines to exploit a future uprising such as the one in Berlin, but emphasized the need to avoid "incitement to premature revolt." Western propaganda would stir unrest by focusing on the themes of freedom of religion, nationalism, and the alternative model of Josip Broz Tito's independent CP regime in Yugoslavia.[21]

Washington still insisted on a virtual Soviet capitulation to Western demands as a basis for negotiations. NSC 174 recognized that the ongoing psychological warfare campaign might "preclude reaching any general accommodation with the Soviet Union in the foreseeable future." U.S. officials sought to create conditions that would induce the Soviet leadership to be "more receptive to negotiated settlements in line with U.S. objectives towards the satellites." A July 1954 progress report upheld NSC 174 as the guide to policy, but expected only "minor progress" toward liberation "under present conditions."[22]

Having rejected open-ended negotiations, Washington continued to emphasize propaganda. Following the "Chance for Peace" speech on April 16, Eisenhower's advisers urged "some initiative on our part . . . to counter arguments advanced in some quarters that the 'peace program' is just words for propaganda purposes and that the United States does not intend to press for its implementation." At the same time, Eisenhower himself sincerely desired to develop some means to rein in the arms race. The Kremlin's successful test of a hydrogen bomb in August 1953 demonstrated the escalatory action-reaction cycle of a perpetual nuclear arms race. Receiving little input from Dulles, who had no interest in arms control, and unhappy with the speech drafts, Eisenhower evolved his own concept, which he dubbed "Atoms for Peace."[23]

On December 8, 1953, the president unveiled "Atoms for Peace" in a speech to the UN General Assembly, which provided an ideal forum to maximize worldwide propaganda appeal. Eisenhower proposed that the United States and the USSR make joint contributions of fissionable material to an International Atomic Energy Agency, which would be established under UN aegis. The international agency would provide atomic power for electrification and other peaceful uses, thus demonstrating to the world that the great powers could dedicate "some of their strength to serve the needs rather than the fears of mankind."[24]

"Atoms for Peace" had obvious propaganda potential, which the Eisenhower administration immediately set out to exploit. The president's historic offer to cooperate with the Soviets in promoting the peaceful uses of atomic energy could be used to depict the United States as the champion of progress. By contributing to a joint stockpile, both Washington and Moscow would have less fissionable material to devote to bombs. Thus, the United States could also be depicted as a champion of arms control. The propaganda campaign emphasized Eisenhower's offer of cooperation with the Soviets, while stressing that "the speech under no circumstances should be interpreted [publicly] as 'psychological warfare.'"[25]

American propaganda fully exploited Soviet rejection of the Atoms for Peace initiative. The Soviets, running behind in the arms race, distrusted the proposal and refused to be limited by having to contribute fissionable material to an international agency. C. D. Jackson explained that "Atoms for Peace" had the Soviets over a "formidable barrel": they would have to "pony up some fissionable material, which they don't want to do (and maybe they haven't got so much of it), or they have got to stand revealed before the whole world as an enemy of mankind." By stressing Moscow's refusal to cooperate, Washington's propaganda "put the USSR on the defensive" and "gave the lie" to Soviet peace propaganda. From Moscow's perspective, the signals from Washington were mixed at best: Eisenhower's "New Look" emphasized greater reliance on nuclear weapons. Furthermore, only a month after Eisenhower's UN speech emphasizing "peaceful uses" of atomic energy, Dulles's trumpeted the prospect of "massive retaliation" against CP aggression in a widely publicized speech.[26]

Ephemeral propaganda victories satisfied the key figures in the Western alliance: Adenauer and Dulles. Both expressed relief that Eisenhower's "Chance for Peace" speech and the "Atoms for Peace" proposal had checked the momentum of the Soviet "peace offensive." Adenauer had achieved his main goal of warding off calls for reunification with the East. West German incorporation into NATO met the goal of Western military integration, simultaneously ruling out détente. By the time the administration succumbed to pressure for a great power meeting with the Soviets in Berlin in January and February 1954, the commitment to West German militarization within the NATO framework ruled out a settlement over East-Central Europe.[27]

Despite the Republican rhetoric about the immorality of mere containment and the urgent need for "liberation" of the "captive peoples" of Eastern Europe, the West declined to pursue avenues that carried any realistic prospect of an early achievement of that goal. With a few notable exceptions, such as Kennan and C. D. Jackson, U.S. officials made a genuine pursuit of liberation secondary to the broader strategy of West German integration. "I think it is pretty clear that if there is any conflict between our policy of reducing Soviet power in Soviet Occupied Germany (as well as the other satellites) and our policy of integrating the Federal Republic with the West, our policy of integration should be given priority," a State Department analysis concluded. The report noted that reunification of Germany on terms acceptable to the West was unlikely in the near term.[28]

On May 8, 1955, exactly a decade after Germany's unconditional surrender in World War II, the Western allies formally incorporated a remilitarized West Germany into the NATO alliance. C. D. Jackson worried that West German rearmament offered "perfect propaganda ammunition for the

Soviets in the satellite countries, principally Poland and Czechoslovakia." The Soviets could "now say with a straight face, 'Now you can see what your fine Western friends think of you and your eventual liberation. They are rearming the Germans to prepare for another war.... We may not be perfect, but the best way for you to protect yourselves from those Nazi beasts is to stick with us." Ambassador Bohlen judged the prospects of liberation now "extremely remote" in the absence of a general European settlement that included German reunification.[29]

The Eisenhower administration's intransigence helped empower orthodox Soviet cold warriors over reformist elements in the CPSU leadership. The lack of Western response to Malenkov's conciliatory diplomacy led him to recant his position in April 1954. Eight months later he resigned. One trenchant analysis of Soviet foreign policy concluded that Malenkov's fall was "a classic case in which a conciliatory strategy, under challenge at home by a more confrontational one, is undermined in the domestic debate by the competitive actions of another state."[30]

While emphasizing many orthodox perceptions of class struggle and Western imperialism, the new Soviet leadership under Nikita S. Khrushchev displayed diplomatic flexibility. In response to West German integration into NATO, the Kremlin created the Warsaw Pact alliance, further cementing the division of Europe. The day after the Warsaw Pact signing ceremony, the Soviets signed the Austrian State Treaty terminating the Four Power occupation of that country, which pledged to remain neutral in the Cold War. Less than two weeks later Khrushchev led a high-powered delegation to Belgrade, culminating a bid for rapprochement with Tito. The Soviet Union endorsed the Belgrade Declaration of June 2, 1955, which called for "non-interference in internal affairs, for whatever reason" and tolerance of "different forms of socialist development." Dissolution of the Cominform, a new trade agreement, and other forms of economic cooperation with Yugoslavia followed. In September the Soviets returned the Porkkala naval base to Finland in return for its pledge to maintain close economic ties.[31]

Consolidating his own power partly on the basis of diplomatic initiatives, Khrushchev invited Adenauer to Moscow, made plans to visit Great Britain, and called for "peaceful coexistence" with the West. Through these actions Khrushchev had met and exceeded Eisenhower's call in his "Chance for Peace" speech for "even a few . . . clear and specific acts" signaling Soviet efforts to reduce East-West tensions. Eisenhower and Dulles failed to respond to or to acknowledge the Soviet overtures as anything more than propaganda gambits.[32]

Despite the administration's intransigence, Khrushchev's diplomacy spurred renewed calls for a summit conference of world leaders, an idea urged once again by Churchill during a June 1954 visit to Washington. John Foster Dulles, still opposed to a summit with the Soviets, called for "delay until West Germany was in NATO." Once this had been achieved, Dulles reluctantly agreed to hold the meeting—as long as no substantive agreements emerged from it. The meeting would be held, he explained, "but on the terms that we should not seek answers but would seek new approaches toward the solution of our problems, perhaps thus infusing a new spirit."[33]

Interpreting the trip to Belgrade and the Austrian Treaty as signs of weakness and even desperation on the part of the new Soviet leaders, Dulles continued to reject negotiations with Moscow. Indeed, he anticipated that the Soviet leaders would soon be forced to offer unilateral concessions. "The present pace and vitality of the West has put too much strain on them," Dulles averred. Khrushchev and Soviet premier Nikolai Bulganin did not possess "the same personal strength as Lenin and Stalin. They cannot bear the burden of modern armaments on a 'long haul' basis. There are weaknesses in their industry. The strain of their aid to China and other areas is telling."[34]

On June 13, 1955, the same day the USSR accepted Geneva as the site of an impending great power summit, Dulles and Adenauer, conferring in Washington, agreed to offer no compromises to the Soviets. Already Ambassador James B. Conant had reported from Bonn that Adenauer remained "anything but enthusiastic" about détente with the Russians, believing that "the time is not yet ripe to push forward with real steps which will bring about German reunification and the creation of a more peaceful posture in middle Europe." In Washington, Adenauer told Dulles that he had postponed a trip to Moscow until after the summit, lamenting that "domestic considerations made it necessary that he should go to Moscow" at all. Dulles, reiterating the litany of weaknesses in the Soviet world position, was "anxious that we should not sell our strong position cheaply." He insisted that if the West remained "strong and resolute" it could achieve German reunification and an end to Soviet imperial domination on its own terms. Dulles observed that the major Soviet aim was a disarmament agreement to "relieve itself of the economic burden of the present arms race." Rather than negotiate arms reduction, the U.S. response was to escalate the arms race to place still greater strain on the Soviet economy.[35]

The report of a special panel of experts convened at Quantico, Virginia, June 5-10, 1955, encouraged Dulles's ongoing quest for liberation. The Quantico meeting originated with Republican internationalist Nelson Rockefeller, who had replaced C. D. Jackson as Eisenhower's psychological warfare adviser in December 1954.[36] Rockefeller charged the "Quantico Vulnerabilities Panel" with assessing Soviet weaknesses and possible U.S. initiatives at the upcoming Geneva Conference. MIT's Walt W. Rostow chaired the panel, comprised of

C. D. Jackson and ten academic and think tank specialists from MIT, RAND, and the Brookings Institution. The Quantico Panel concluded that the United States, operating "from a position of strength," should present the USSR "with heavy demands for major concessions." They concluded that "unusually rapid vacillations in Soviet policy" reflected a "transitory position of Soviet political vulnerability" which carried the prospect for "inflicting a diplomatic defeat upon the Soviet Union."[37]

The Quantico Panel rejected negotiations with Moscow, "however tempting the prospect of a relaxation of tensions may be." Instead, the panel unanimously agreed that the combination of Soviet vulnerabilities and Western strengths would allow the allies to "transcend the area of negotiations" to exact "genuine concessions." In addition to rejecting negotiations, the Quantico Panel urged continued German rearmament and maintenance of Western military superiority. Every policy should be directed toward "our constant goal, a rollback of Soviet power in Eastern and Central Europe and in Asia."[38]

While Dulles embraced the conclusions of the Quantico Panel, Bohlen, the administration's preeminent Soviet expert, doubted the wisdom of an approach to Geneva based on the notion that "the Soviets are under such overriding compulsions due to internal economic difficulties that they have lost their freedom of choice and must as a matter of necessity reach an accommodation with the West." Conceding that the Soviets faced economic problems and concerns about Tito as a model of independent national communism, as well as their own internal leadership struggle, Bohlen insisted that none of these concerns was so severe "as to force the Soviets to make concessions to the West which would either affect their existing security position or to give up at this time any areas they control as a result of World War II." Bohlen advised a willingness "to discuss certain substantive aspects of any of the major questions which may be raised by either side."[39]

Having decided to concede nothing, the West's negotiating posture at Geneva remained simply to demand unilateral Soviet concessions. Above all, the U.S. approach to the Geneva Conference, as codified in NSC 5534/1, was to reject the anticipated renewal of Soviet calls for German neutralization. Washington and its allies would not consider any proposal that envisioned "the withdrawal of all foreign forces from a united Germany." Consistent with national security policy since the onset of the Cold War, the West would reject any initiative that did not make "alignment of united Germany with NATO . . . virtually certain."[40]

On the eve of the conference, Dulles expressed profound anxiety—and little confidence—in Eisenhower's impending approach at the summit. Confiding in C. D. Jackson, Dulles explained that he was "terribly worried about this Geneva Conference." Although he had "nothing but admiration and respect" for Eisenhower, Dulles feared that because the president was so "humanly generous . . . that he might in a personal moment with the Russians accept a promise or proposition at face value and upset the apple cart." Dulles reiterated his conviction that Washington had "come a long way by being firm" and now had the Soviets on the ropes. He declared that he might have to "be the devil at Geneva, and I dread the prospect." Dulles's fear was that he would be confronted with either having to accept a U.S. approach that "could be described as appeasement" or resigning his position.[41]

While Dulles's perceptions of Eisenhower are revealing, he need not have worried about the president appeasing the Soviets. Eisenhower's main preoccupation at Geneva was another propaganda exercise rather than a concerted effort to come to terms with the new Kremlin leaders. At Geneva, Eisenhower unveiled "Open Skies," a sweeping proposal for mutual aerial inspection of each superpower's military installations. This propaganda gambit emerged from the Quantico meeting, in which Rostow's panel had called for an initiative at Geneva that would provide for "mutual inspection of military installations, forces, and armaments, without limitations" and "the right of aircraft of any nationality to fly over the territory of any country for peaceful purposes." It did so with full appreciation that the security-obsessed Soviets would reject the proposal. "After rejection of the plan," the Quantico report noted, Washington should "make every effort to win the arms race as the safest way of forcing the Soviet Union to accept a satisfactory arms convention." The thinking behind the Quantico report embodied the essence of Cold War militarization.[42]

Rockefeller embraced "Open Skies" as a means to seize the propaganda initiative from the Kremlin. Warning that the Soviets used conferences "more often to achieve psychological and propaganda advantage than to conduct serious diplomatic negotiations," Rockefeller wanted Washington to be armed with a campaign of its own. Harold Stassen, the former governor of Minnesota who was brought into the administration as a special assistant on disarmament, backed the proposal. Dulles, keenly sensitive to what he perceived as intrusions into his own private realm of diplomacy, clashed repeatedly with Rockefeller, Stassen, and military officials. Bowing to the president's obvious enthusiasm for "Open Skies," Dulles accepted the initiative as the focal point at Geneva. Military leaders also embraced the proposal, which, it was decided, would be launched with maximum fanfare by Eisenhower himself.[43]

In his speech on July 21, the fourth day of the Geneva Conference, Eisenhower delivered the unprecedented proposal for mutual aerial inspection of military facilities. "Open Skies" would have entailed each power providing the other with information about the location of military bases as well as access to airfields and facilities necessary to overfly and monitor activity on the bases. The idea, Eisenhower explained, was to build stability by removing the threat of a Pearl Harbor–like surprise attack. The proposal "had a reassuring heads-I-win, tails-you-lose quality," since U.S. military leaders agreed "that we would gain more information than would the Soviets." More likely, however, Moscow's almost certain rejection of the proposal would constitute the propaganda victory that Rockefeller and the Quantico Panel had been seeking. Eisenhower adviser Robert Bowie recalled that "Open Skies" was "a clever ploy but never in the least negotiable."[44]

Britain and France, Washington's allies at Geneva, enthusiastically endorsed "Open Skies," but as expected the Soviets, wedded to military secrecy and unwilling to reveal the extent of their strategic inferiority to the West, rejected the proposal. Bulganin at first expressed some interest, but Khrushchev told Eisenhower directly after his speech that "the idea was nothing more than a bald espionage plot against the USSR." This exchange revealed to Eisenhower that Khrushchev was "the real boss of the Soviet delegation." The United States, already engaged in covert aerial reconnaissance over Soviet airspace, had risked little and gained a propaganda victory with the "Open Skies" proposal. Stassen later reported that "Open Skies" had generated favorable world opinion and "done much to squelch the Soviet propaganda theme of 'Ban-the-Bomb.'"[45]

While "Open Skies" seized the spotlight, nothing substantive emerged from the initial discussions at Geneva on Germany and Soviet hegemony in Eastern Europe. Simply put, the West refused to negotiate on the former, the Soviets on the latter. Once again, Dulles interpreted Soviet intransigence on Eastern Europe as "evidence of weakness rather than of strength." At the end of meetings on these issues, Dulles declared that he was content to "keep pressing the German unification issue. He predicted, but did not wish to be held to his prediction, that we might get unification [on Western terms] in the next two years." Geneva had done nothing to deter the West from its ongoing efforts aimed at West German military integration into NATO. Noting that "we never wanted to go to Geneva, but the pressure of people of the world forced us to," Dulles was openly relieved at the preservation of the status quo.[46]

Eisenhower expressed disappointment at the failure of "Open Skies," which he, unlike his advisers, apparently considered a serious initiative. The president called the results of Geneva "a great blow to progress toward peace," yet he had done little, despite Dulles's pre-summit fears, to move events in the direction of détente. The world leaders had agreed in principal on the need for "freer contacts and exchanges," but had achieved no substantive understandings. The Soviets linked increased contacts with economic relations, calling for the removal of U.S. restrictions on trade with CP regimes as a condition for broadened cultural ties.

While expressing his disappointment in private, Eisenhower sought to perpetuate the "spirit of Geneva" in his public statements. The president reported in a radio and television address that increased contacts had been the source of the "greatest possible degree of agreement" in discussions with the Soviet leaders. Contradicting Eisenhower, Dulles declared that discussion of increased contacts and exchange programs had been "dealt with so briefly that it was not possible to discover how the Russians really felt about this issue." The world leaders concluded the East-West summit by agreeing to hold a follow-up conference among the foreign ministers to carry on further discussions on trade and communications barriers and on increased contacts and exchange programs.[47]

Despite Dulles's uncompromising attitude at Geneva, the administration's policy slowly began to shift. Incremental progress toward détente and cultural infiltration did not challenge the dominant paradigm of Cold War militarization, but it occurred nonetheless. In February 1956, Eisenhower's psychological warfare advisers urged "particular attention" be devoted to the prospect of making the Kremlin "more receptive to negotiated settlements." On July 18, Eisenhower approved NSC 5608/1, which directed the main lines of policy toward exploiting anti-communism, nationalism, and Titoism, the last as "a standing example of successful defiance of the Kremlin and a demonstration that the West is prepared to assist nationalistic communist leaders to assert their independence of Moscow." These same elements had been present in the now superseded NSC 174, but the shift in emphasis from revolution to evolution marked a critical transition.[48]

Having rejected negotiations and failed to achieve liberation, U.S. Cold War planners began to emphasize a gradualist approach over aggressive psychological warfare. In a series of policy papers, the NSC authorized an intensified yet gradualist approach to undermining Soviet and East European communism. On January 31, 1955, NSC 5505/1 determined that U.S. strategy toward the satellites should "stress evolutionary rather than revolutionary change." The policy paper called for U.S. information efforts to adopt "a forceful and direct approach, avoiding a propagandistic or strident tone." On March 15, 1956, NSC 5602/1 called for the foreign information program to be "materially strengthened" as part of a strategy to encourage "evolutionary change in the Soviet system" and in Eastern Europe.[49]

Eisenhower's own genuine enthusiasm for East-West exchange and increased cultural contact was partly responsible for the shift in U.S. policy. While the president opposed negotiations with the Soviets, his faith in propaganda and cultural initiatives eventually coalesced in a long term strategy to undermine internal support for the CP regimes. C. D. Jackson was equally committed to finding means to infiltrate American culture behind the Iron Curtain. Efforts to promote democracy and trumpet U.S. material success required "at least a fleeting exposure to be understood," Jackson explained. The problem was that "you have one hell of a lot of Russian population who know absolutely nothing about anything outside of their hermetically sealed setup." Without enough imagery and information to make a contrast between life in the East and West, it would be difficult to win hearts and minds and relatively easy for Soviet propaganda to convince people "that we are sinister liars." Jackson declared that Washington should "deluge Moscow with invitations for the Russian ballet, Russian symphony orchestra, choruses, scientists, engineers, journalists, etc., ad inf., to come here for conclaves." He predicted that 90 percent of Soviets who visited the United States would return "not necessarily convinced" about the superiority of the West, "but profoundly perturbed."[50]

Dramatic changes in the post-Stalinist USSR encouraged Eisenhower, Jackson, and others to explore the possibilities of cultural infiltration. Under the post-Stalinist leadership in Moscow, Soviet intellectuals, only recently cowed by Stalin's last campaign to purge the USSR of Western cultural influence, now condemned state restrictions on artistic expression while calling for increased exchange and greater contact with the West. Ilia Ehrenburg, whose novel *The Thaw* provided the metaphor for the era, and composer Dmitri Shostakovich were among those advocating normalization of East-West cultural relations. In April 1953, within weeks of Stalin's death, Americans applying for visas to enter the USSR received the surprising news that their requests would be granted. In subsequent weeks, journalists, editors, students, professors, athletes, chess players, and United States senators and representatives conducted wide-ranging discussions across the USSR.[51]

While the Soviets loosened restrictions on East-West travel, the Eisenhower administration failed to reciprocate in 1953. Still wedded to psychological warfare, Washington had not yet recognized the potential benefits of cultural exchange among individuals and delegations. Accordingly, only a handful of Soviets succeeded in touring the United States, reflecting the absence of a thaw in Washington. Typical was the fate of a Soviet chess team, which received visas in 1953 only to learn that team members would be strictly confined to New York City and thus forbidden to stay, as planned, at the Soviet UN delegation residence in Glen Cove, a mere 12 miles beyond the city limits. Denouncing the "intolerable measures violating all rules of hospitality and courtesy," the Soviet team canceled the visit.[52]

Admitting that Soviet initiatives seemed to be genuine attempts to forge closer cultural ties, State Department officials nevertheless refused to pursue opportunities because of their fear of political controversy. The 1952 Immigration and Nationality Act—one of two so-called McCarran Acts named after the staunchly anti-communist Nevada senator Patrick McCarran—plagued efforts to forge closer cultural ties with the USSR. Provisions of the 1952 law compelled unofficial visitors from the CP regimes to submit to fingerprinting upon their arrival in the United States. Rather than risking controversy by challenging the laws or exempting certain visitors from its provisions, the State Department concluded that "it would not be advisable for us, under present immigration restrictions, to push the question of cultural exchange with the USSR." In 1955, McCarran Act provisions led to the cancellation of a planned tour by a group of student editors, whose visit had been anxiously awaited and well-publicized. Protesting that fingerprinting equated the students with criminals, the Soviets canceled the visit when the State Department refused to waive the provision.[53]

The rejection of the Soviet visitors delighted propagandists in Moscow. On May 1, 1955, *Pravda* turned the tables on the Americans by featuring an editorial cartoon on U.S. cultural policy entitled "Behind the [American] Iron Curtain." Perhaps more unexpected was the criticism of Washington's policy by several U.S. newspapers and magazines. Western European allies, who had already forged closer cultural ties with Moscow, sided with the Soviets on the issue of cultural exchange. A State Department memorandum noted that Soviet trumpeting of "peaceful coexistence" with the West, coinciding with Washington's refusal to tear down cultural barriers, was "causing damage, and may cause further damage, to U.S. prestige" in the eyes of "otherwise friendly" nations.[54]

Harrison Salisbury, the *New York Times* correspondent in Moscow, told U.S. officials in 1955 that a noticeable change in atmosphere signaled a propitious opportunity to pursue cultural exchange with the USSR. Since Stalin's death, Soviet propaganda to Western Europe had been stressing "that they have the open door and we're the country with the Iron Curtain." In light of the Soviet propaganda, if Washington proposed a formal exchange program, "it would be extraordinarily difficult for them to refuse it." Like Jackson, Salisbury had little doubt that East-West exchange would redound to the benefit of the United States. Soviet visitors to American shores would return home and "spread the word of what we have in this country, what we have to offer." The *Times* correspondent admitted that returning Soviets would not "write letters to *Pravda*" praising life in the West, but they would talk about it among friends and associates. "It's surprising how much word gets around in a country where you have an Iron Curtain censorship." Already perceptions of life in the West "that circulate among people are favorable in general. We don't have as much of a propaganda barrier to break through as we are sometimes inclined to think."[55]

Eisenhower held the same views and continued to express a lively interest in exchange programs, often making "very expansive remarks" on their potential destabilizing impact on the CP regimes. "The exchange program and propaganda should be stepped up," the president told Dulles on May 24, 1955. "We have to get into it more intensively." Eisenhower declared that what "we have called psychological warfare for many years" was "an attack on the minds of men" and a means to promote "disaffection behind the Iron Curtain" as well as to win support for Western aims in the developing world. Dulles agreed that propaganda and exchange programs could enhance the prospects of achieving the "so-called 'liberation'" of Eastern Europe and the USSR itself.[56]

While the president, the American public, and even Dulles to a lesser extent expressed a growing desire for increased contacts, the Kremlin continued to take the lead in promoting exchange opportunities. Encouraged by the nation's postwar economic growth, the Kremlin leaders appeared less reluctant to offer Westerners a glimpse of life in the USSR. The Soviets remained willing to send their own delegates to the West. A breakthrough in East-West exchange came in the summer of 1955 when an Iowa newspaper responded to Khrushchev's call for increased corn production by inviting a Soviet agricultural delegation to visit the American corn belt "to see how we do it." Much to the newspaper editor's astonishment, the Soviet Agriculture Ministry accepted the invitation. As plans materialized for a reciprocal visit of Soviet and American farmers, the State Department wavered before announcing that it would consider the Soviet delegates as "official" visitors, thus exempting them from the McCarran Act's fingerprinting requirement. The reciprocal visits, carried out in the summer of 1955, elicited favorable publicity and much goodwill in both countries.[57]

By the time the second Geneva conference of foreign ministers convened in October, a consensus had begun to emerge in Washington to pursue increased cultural exchange with the Soviets. Aware of Eisenhower's personal enthusiasm for such projects, USIA director Theodore Streibert took the lead in advocating "a bold dramatic step to very substantially increase what we are doing in the whole area of overseas information and contacts—the exchange of ideas and people." Employing a wartime metaphor, Streibert declared that the "beachhead" established at the first Geneva meeting created "an opportunity to assume the initiative, and press for a breakthrough." USIA urged a doubling of the budget for information and cultural programs to $325 million.[58]

The Quantico panel, reconvened to assess the prospects of Geneva II, also embraced the shift from psychological warfare to a gradualist approach emphasizing cultural exchange. "'The Sprit of Geneva'" presented "a great psychological opportunity" to infiltrate the CP regimes with "an increased flow of peoples, ideas, books, magazines, newspapers, films, broadcasts, television, exhibits, cultural presentations, trade fair exhibitions, sports teams, technical groups, and delegations of all kinds—soldiers in the battle of ideas." Rather than tit-for-tat propaganda exchanges with the Soviets, Washington should adopt an approach emphasizing "the need for open-mindedness and for inter-cultural understanding." The Quantico panel endorsed Streibert's proposal that the "total U.S. effort in the information area should be at least double the present level."[59]

As was typically the case, the State Department was least enthusiastic and most threatened by the proposal to increase informational and cultural ties. Ever leery of USIA encroachments on policymaking, a State Department memorandum responded that Streibert's proposal "smacks too much of the shotgun, grandiose spending of money for spending's sake" and was a reflection of "our own lack of leadership and policy direction over USIA." State Department diplomats were "much less enthusiastic about cultural exchange with the Soviet Union than President Eisenhower," diplomat George V. Allen recalled. Dulles himself "was a good deal more skeptical about it and regarded President Eisenhower as rather naive in thinking that this kind of thing was really going to make much change in the world."[60]

While Eisenhower sought congressional funds for an expanded overseas program, he summoned his troubleshooter on information policy, William Jackson, to coordinate the administration's position at the Geneva Foreign Ministers conference. After assaying the situation, Jackson concluded that despite certain "risks"—notably, the likelihood of anti-communist disaffection within the CP regimes as a result of Washington's willingness to negotiate with Moscow—the United States should nevertheless proceed to "advance at Geneva a positive program for increasing East-West contacts." Another panel concluded that the prospects for some sort of agreement were good since the "Soviets continue to evince interest in a restricted increase in contacts and cultural exchange."[61]

Eisenhower pushed for a positive approach and warned against becoming "less aggressive in pursuing our objectives." For planning purposes, Jackson established two groups, one on East-West trade and another on increased contacts. Jackson endorsed Streibert's proposal to establish a USIA center in Moscow in return for a reciprocal Soviet facility in Washington. Dulles, however, countered that a Soviet center in Washington would be teeming with spies and opposed allowing a substantial number of Soviet students into the country. Eisenhower also expressed concern about the propaganda and domestic political implications of reciprocal information centers, which would allow the Kremlin to establish "a Soviet propaganda mill in the U.S." In response, Jackson stressed the reciprocal nature of the proposals, noting that "the more people the U.S. could place behind the Iron Curtain the greater would be our advantage."[62]

Despite a growing consensus in Washington on the benefits of cultural exchange, the Geneva Foreign Ministers conference, which convened on

October 27, achieved little more than the first meeting of the heads of state. Soviet foreign minister Molotov again linked broadened cultural ties with normalization of trade and economic relations, including, ultimately, most favored nation trade status. Washington refused to consider normalization of trade, especially on strategic items. Dulles flatly rejected Moscow's linkage of trade and cultural relations and countered by emphasizing the importance of the free flow of information and repeatedly condemning Soviet censorship and jamming of Western radio programming. A 17-point French proposal called for information centers, free distribution of books and publications, reduced restrictions on news gathering, increased tourism, direct air transport between Soviet and Western cities, and various forms of cultural exchange.[63]

After some 18 meetings by a committee of experts to whom the proposals of each side had been submitted, disputes over trade, the ruble exchange rate, and free flow of information remained unbridged. Joined by his British and French counterparts, Dulles accused the Soviets of refusing to compromise on the Western proposals. Molotov responded that those proposals interfered with Soviet internal affairs and that Moscow could not be expected to open its borders to anti-Soviet propaganda broadsides. The proposed information centers, whose counterparts had once served as "centers of intelligence activity" in the Eastern European countries, would obviously be "directed against the Soviet Government." While the Soviet side remained interested in "developing contacts in cultural, scientific, and economic fields, and also tourism," the "principal aspect" of the development of contacts should be in the realm of "economic and trade relations." Molotov criticized the Western powers for relegating trade issues to the back burner, insisting that cultural ties could not be expected to evolve in the absence of improved trade relations.[64]

The U.S. delegation concluded that the Kremlin "seemed to want exchanges supplying the Soviet Union with essential technical know-how without making corresponding concessions in the areas to which we attach importance." Dulles wired Eisenhower on November 14 that the Soviets were unwilling "to make any concessions in the way of freer flow of information through exchange of broadcasts, information centers and the like." Responding directly to Molotov, Dulles declared that Kremlin insecurities stemmed from their fears that the regime might "topple if perchance some contradictory ideas found their way into the Soviet Union." In virtually the only positive note in an otherwise acrimonious exchange, Dulles concluded that Washington would continue to pursue broadened East-West contacts.[65]

While each side blamed the other for the failure of the Geneva Foreign Ministers meeting, both had sought unilateral advantage rather than pursuing avenues of discussion leading to increased cultural contact. Dulles, however, still committed to achieving a near-term "liberation" and convinced of the inherent weakness of the Soviet system, seemed particularly anxious to avoid coming to terms with the detested regime. In his point-by-point attack on the Soviet position, Dulles skipped over Soviet proposals for increased exchange of artists, athletes, scholars, and scientists—proposals that Molotov had repeatedly declared the Soviets ready to move ahead with and that the French had endorsed. It was this type of exchange program that Streibert had been particularly keen to pursue, but Dulles had excluded the USIA director from the U.S. delegation at Geneva.[66]

Dulles clearly remained averse to both negotiations and cultural exchange with the USSR, a position that he clung to despite the implications of Khrushchev's de-Stalinization campaign. Khrushchev's stunning denunciation of Stalin at the CPSU Twentieth Party Congress in February 1956 seemed to offer a logical starting point for new thinking about East-West relations, but Dulles promptly rejected the prospect. The USSR remained a communist regime, he averred, and Khrushchev's purpose was "merely to persuade the subject peoples that the present dictatorship is good because it condemns the past dictatorship." The U.S. ambassador to Moscow, Charles Bohlen, disagreed. Calling attention to the sacking of first Malenkov and then the ultra-orthodox Molotov, Bohlen stressed that Khrushchev genuinely sought greater East-West cooperation. Bohlen also perceived a "greater frankness with which these people are now talking to foreigners."[67]

Khrushchev himself complained directly to Bohlen that he could not understand the attitude in Washington, "and particularly that of Mr. Dulles," whose speeches displayed unremitting hostility toward the USSR. Khrushchev "felt that the U.S. did not understand the depth and significance of changes which were taking place in the Soviet Union." Had he known Dulles's actual views, the Soviet leader would have been even more disturbed. Dulles considered Khrushchev "the most dangerous person to lead the Soviet Union since the October Revolution." Dulles believed that Khrushchev was "obviously intoxicated much of the time, and could be expected to commit irrational acts."[68]

Despite Dulles's palpable anti-Sovietism, cultural exchange was an irrepressible force as well as the engine of détente. The Soviet government and private American groups continued to pursue exchange opportunities, which official Washington remained reluctant to facilitate. Official opposition could not prevent an outpouring of enthusiasm for the American appearances of Soviet musicians Emil Gilels, David Oistrakh, and Mstislav Rostropovich in winter 1955 and spring 1956. In the same period, some 2,500 American musicians, educators, religious leaders, writers, and members of congress traveled to the USSR.[69]

While he often failed to ensure that action followed his words, Eisenhower continued at least to speak out in behalf of broadened East-West cultural contact. Accepting the Republican nomination for reelection in 1956, the president stressed his desire to "bridge the great chasm that separates us from the peoples under communist rule." Eisenhower soon had an opportunity to make an attempt to transform his rhetoric into reality. Continuing to take the lead in pursuing cultural exchange, the Soviets in January 1956 had proposed a 20-year treaty of friendship, which emphasized broadened artistic and scientific contacts. Moscow continued to lead in promoting individual contacts and called for a new film agreement as well. The Kremlin had already, in the wake of the Geneva Conference, established broader cultural ties with England, France, Belgium, and Japan. Vice President Richard Nixon admitted that extended U.S.-Soviet cultural contacts were there "for the asking."[70]

While Eisenhower periodically spoke out on the benefits of cultural exchange, he left the follow-through in the hands of Dulles, who remained wary. In part, Dulles opposed virtually any accord with the Soviets because such agreements implied respectability and permanence for a regime that he detested and believed had failed to prove itself as the ultimate master of Eastern Europe or even of the USSR itself. Accordingly, after Geneva the State Department placed roadblocks in the path of a second planned Soviet agricultural tour, infuriating a group of expectant Iowa farmers; opposed an exchange of the Bolshoi Ballet for an American symphony orchestra; and caused the cancellation of a planned visit by a Soviet track and field team. The State Department remained largely both disinterested in cultural exchange and anxious to avoid controversy over the fingerprinting law that would inevitably arise in the course of visits by a large contingent of Soviets.[71]

Confronted by evidence of mounting interest in East-West cultural exchange, Dulles finally began to reconsider his position. Aides reported the secretary of state "thinking intensively" on the subject. A few months removed from his acrimonious exchanges with Molotov at Geneva, Dulles eventually came to the conclusion that East-West contacts could provide a means to increase Soviet awareness of the "outer world," thus belying "communist fiction" about life in the West. In the spring of 1956, a State Department paper explored the potential of exchange programs to stimulate the Soviet public's "desire for consumer's goods by bringing them to realize how rich are the fruits of free labor." Still committed to liberation, Dulles and other State Department elites now hoped to "undermine the regime by exposing the people to Free World influences."[72]

With Dulles now urging the West to "take the offensive in the area of East-West contacts," an NSC policy paper called on Washington to pursue exchange programs "as a positive instrument of U.S. foreign policy." Promulgated on June 29, 1956, NSC 5607 formed the basis of U.S. policy on cultural exchange. Noting that the nation's approach to East-West contacts "had proved to be too passive and inert," NSC 5607 sought to undermine CP authority by "promoting a desire for greater individual freedom, well-being, and security within the satellites." In addition to endorsing the new NSC policy, Dulles now advocated eliminating the fingerprinting provision of the 1952 McCarran Act. He also rejected Department of Defense objections that East-West exchange would somehow undermine U.S. treaty obligations and create unacceptable internal security risks. A White House press release explained that the new policy would seek to promote "exchanges between the United States and the countries of Eastern Europe, including the USSR."[73]

Soviet repression of the Hungarian uprising in November 1956 posed a temporary setback to U.S. efforts to come to grips with a viable cultural strategy toward the CP regimes. In keeping with the new policy aimed at gradually increasing cultural ties, plans had been made for reciprocal visits and exchanges. In the wake of the repression of Hungary, however, Eisenhower suspended the nascent exchange program and canceled plans to send a U.S. representative to the annual celebration of the Bolshevik Revolution in Moscow. The State Department announced that as of November 13 the exchange program was in "temporary suspension pending clarification and a new evaluation of the situation."[74]

Despite the setback caused by events in Hungary, U.S. officials believed that "the cracks in the Iron Curtain have been widening perceptibly" and that "what was formerly a yearning for contact with the West is now a widespread demand, which has grown progressively as it has been fed." They drew encouragement from reports of sympathy with the Hungarian cause and a degree of unrest among youth and student groups in the USSR itself. In the summer before the Hungarian intervention, the Soviets had been on the verge of intervention against the independent-minded Gomulka regime in Poland. C. D. Jackson averred that "aggressive, imperial communism received a terrible blow in the one-two punches of Poland and Hungary."[75]

Following an initial reaction of outrage over Soviet intervention, the Eisenhower administration resumed its pursuit of broadened cultural ties. On February 28, 1957, only four months after the Soviet repression in Budapest, a survey of public opinion polls and newspaper editorials revealed that the U.S. and allied publics would look favorably upon a resumption of contacts with the USSR and Eastern Europe. One month later Dulles recommended that Eisenhower "resume gradually and carefully the series of officially sponsored exchanges with the USSR in pursuance of the objectives of NSC 5607. He added that such exchanges could also be exploited in pursuit of "our intelligence needs." With the president's concurrence, the State Department authorized "unobtrusive resumption" of the exchange program. Despite the putative desire to be unobtrusive, however, Dulles stated publicly that the United States would conduct exchange programs only because it believed they would help destroy the CP regimes.[76]

In the wake of the failure of liberation, Washington focused its attention in Eisenhower's second term on increasing cultural contacts with Eastern Europe. The United States operated missions in Poland, Czechoslovakia, Hungary, and Rumania, but had conducted little trade and cultural contact with those regimes since the end of the war. In the wake of the first Geneva Conference, administration officials had considered "precise and imaginative proposals for breaking down the isolation of the Eastern European people," many of whom had suffered a loss of morale as a result of the failure of the East-West summit to produce a meaningful change in their status. Cold War planners, reluctant to "confer respectability on puppet leaders" by entering into formal cultural agreements, nonetheless came to the conclusion that the West had more to gain from such exchanges than did the CP regimes. Psychological warriors declared that the policy goal was "gradually to build up pressure for a program of breaking down the isolation of the captive peoples from the West, by penetrating Eastern Europe with books, magazines, and newspapers, by exchange of personal visits, and by elimination of communist jamming of Western radio programs." Officials also believed that travel of Americans to Eastern Europe and reciprocal visits to the United States could become an effective means of "serving to remind the captive peoples of U.S. interest in their ultimate freedom, and correcting the distorted image of the West as mirrored in communist propaganda media."[77]

The shift from aggressive psychological warfare to a gradualist approach remained the consistent focus of policy throughout Eisenhower's second term. Policymakers believed widened contacts and cultural infiltration would eventually compel the CP regimes to grant increased internal freedom and independence from Soviet control. As a means to this end, NSC 5811/1, issued in May 1958, concluded that it would be necessary to pursue "more active U.S. relationships" with Eastern Europe. Washington would stop short of entering into agreements that would confer respectability on the regimes, thereby undermining morale among the "captive peoples." Nevertheless, officials now recognized that "popular revolts are unlikely" and that East European exiles, lacking any "significant following in their homelands," could not be expected "to return there to assume a role of political leadership." Accordingly, Washington would continue to denounce Soviet hegemony while bolstering informational and cultural activities, public and private, including radio programs, business ties, religious and cultural contacts, trade fairs and film festivals, and teacher and student exchanges.[78]

While direct Soviet intervention in Hungary ended the short-term prospects for fostering Titoism there, Washington viewed Poland as a model for other regimes to emulate in pursuing independence from Moscow. By the spring of 1957, U.S. policy sought to "expand, discreetly and gradually, the distribution of publications, wireless file material, documentary motion pictures, television films, radio broadcasting material, and approved books" in Poland. Plans called for a series of exhibits, an "American Book Store" with popular and scientific literature, and a U.S. library and reading room in Warsaw. Policymakers placed heavy emphasis on exchange programs involving technical experts, delegations of various federations and assemblies, academic, athletic, cultural, and literary contacts. Officials encouraged U.S. foundations to fund travel for groups and individuals between Poland and the United States. While the Polish government continued to proscribe certain activities, U.S. diplomats reported that "culture in practice in Poland offers a livelier fare than in any other eastern country."[79]

Efforts to lure Poland away from Soviet hegemony included millions of dollars of economic assistance. CIA director Allen Dulles believed loans and credits would provide tangible evidence of American support for Polish efforts gradually to reduce Soviet influence while strengthening Gomulka's position. The CIA anticipated Soviet hostility to the economic assistance, but believed the Kremlin would stop short of drastic countermeasures. Under the economic assistance plan, Washington granted Poland $95 million in American credits and orchestrated $80 million in loans from other countries. In keeping with the shift away from aggressive psychological warfare and toward a more subtle approach, the signing of the Polish economic agreement on June 7, 1957, was "treated in a matter-of-fact manner and its significance under-emphasized rather than stressed." Responding to Polish foreign minister Adam Rapacki's criticism of Radio Free Europe broadcasts that dealt "exclusively with questions of Polish internal politics," John Foster Dulles promised to "check into" the matter. The Polish station, considered the most successful of RFE operations, increasingly "veered away from the recommendations of the Polish government-in-exile" and offered "support of the Gomulka government."[80]

By fall 1957, Eisenhower's advisers reported "significant progress" in the effort to weaken Soviet control of Poland, an evolution it considered "far more significant than anywhere else in Eastern Europe, including Yugoslavia." The report cited the independence of the Catholic Church, growing freedom of personal expression, elimination of barriers of communication with the West, free market experimentation, and diminution of the role of the Polish secret police. The Polish economy remained weak, however, and despite the economic assistance program only small steps had been taken toward reorienting Polish trade toward the West.[81]

While strengthening economic and cultural ties with Poland, rigid adherence to Cold War militarization ensured Washington's rejection of an opportunity to pursue détente and arms control under a Polish initiative. The "Rapacki Plan," named for the Polish foreign minister, called for a nuclear-free zone comprised of Poland, Czechoslovakia, and both Germanys. The Poles made the proposal before the UN in the fall of 1957 in an effort to head off NATO plans to place medium-range nuclear missiles in Western Europe. The United States, already committed to West German rearmament and in the throes of panic in the wake of the Soviet launching of the first earth satellite, *Sputnik,* on October 4, 1957, summarily rejected the Rapacki Plan. Dulles called it "a highly dangerous proposal." Washington also rejected proposals by Khrushchev, George Kennan, and others for great-power military "disengagement" from Europe.[82]

Despite dismissing Polish calls for disengagement and denuclearization, Washington achieved broader cultural infiltration of Poland than of neighboring Czechoslovakia. Before the Hungarian intervention, Czechs were "beginning to encourage tourists from the United States" through publicity and bargain tours. The regime, however, had shown "no indication of a willingness to stop jamming or to permit the entry of Western publications." Still, Czechs had taken advantage of the Kremlin's emphasis on peaceful coexistence to display "a more friendly attitude toward the United States and things American." U.S. diplomats reported that ordinary citizens were "sick of the isolation" and "glad to come into the light of contacts and exchange with the West." More than a year later, in the wake of the Hungarian intervention, officials reported "little or no progress" in further efforts to reorient the Czech regime. American tourists still made their way into Czechoslovakia, but the Prague government canceled a planned visit by the Cleveland Orchestra, continued to jam Western broadcasts, and maintained close secret police supervision of citizens seeking contact with the West.[83]

Rumania had gone through a similar transition. Before the Hungarian intervention, U.S. officials described the Rumanian government as "making a sincere effort to normalize Rumanian-U.S. relations." Rumanian officials expressed a desire to establish commercial ties and increase technical and cultural exchanges. However, in part because the Soviets had used Rumania as a base of operations against Hungary, relations had deteriorated by fall 1957. The Rumanian government did allow the USIA to mount a "Built in USA" architectural exhibit and in 1960 Washington and Bucharest signed an agreement on exchanges of films, exhibits, and books. U.S. officials strongly supported continuing efforts to increase cultural exchange with Bucharest, out of their conviction that such events "redound overwhelmingly in favor of the West and should be encouraged and increased as much as possible."[84]

Eisenhower's advisers reported little progress in infiltrating American ideas and information into Bulgaria and Albania, whose communist regimes continued "to resist penetration by pro-Western or pro-American cultural influences." Jamming and restriction of U.S. publications were strictly enforced. Both Bulgaria and Albania, however, desired formal U.S. diplomatic recognition, which the NSC began to consider as a means of spurring cultural infiltration of the Balkan states. Overall, Eisenhower's advisers on cultural policy toward Eastern Europe concluded that progress was being made. They confronted a challenge, however, in their efforts to "straddle the contradiction between the traditional anticommunist posture of the United States and the interim NSC objective of encouraging the development of 'national communism'" and "change within Eastern Europe through evolutionary means."[85]

Nowhere was this contradiction more pronounced than in Hungary itself, where U.S. officials were reluctant to conduct diplomacy with the Soviet-backed, postrebellion regime led by Janos Kadar. After the intervention, Kadar ordered the U.S. legation staff cut and attacked Washington for granting refuge in the legation to Cardinal Jozsef Mindszenty. Despite the tensions in Budapest, U.S. diplomats advised in October 1957 that it would "be appropriate at the present time to review the question of cultural relations between the United States and Hungary." They reported that a "new phase has begun in the post-revolutionary government of Hungary" which might make feasible the prospect of increased cultural exchange. In Washington, the State Department gradually integrated Hungary into plans for East European exchange programs and cultural initiatives.[86]

Despite the limited results of these efforts, U.S. officials saw no alternative to the gradualist approach. An NSC progress report on NSC 5811/1 affirmed that "efforts to achieve U.S. policy objectives are based upon the concept of evolutionary development rather than the concept of liberation." Washington found it difficult, however, to deal with the CP regimes while insisting on the right to denounce them as illegitimate. "So far," the NSC concluded in the summer of 1959, "significant progress has not been made toward the expansion of direct contacts." Radio broadcasts remained "the primary means of circumventing regime controls aimed at excluding Western influence" behind the Iron Curtain.[87]

Ironically, the regime most open to Western cultural penetration proved to be the Soviet Union itself. In Moscow, as in Washington, contradictory impulses prevailed. The Soviet leadership pursued increased contacts primarily out of its desire to gain more ready access to Western scientific and technical knowledge and to gain legitimacy in the global community. However, because "deep interest in any information on life in the West" was "a dominant feature of present-day life in the Soviet Union," broadened cultural ties also underscored the regime's vulnerability. Embassy personnel, tourists, and other Westerners in Moscow received daily evidence, based on their contacts with Soviet citizens, of the growing appeal of Western ideas and information in the USSR. Many Soviets merely enjoyed the movies, music, and magazines, whereas others perceived the infiltration of Western culture as a means to achieve "the liberal evolution of Soviet society." Unlike their often skeptical brethren in Washington, U.S. diplomats stationed in Moscow were virtually unanimous in the view that even "the limited exchanges that have so far taken place" were having a major impact in the USSR. Despite official Kremlin support for renewed cultural ties, U.S. embassy personnel monitored evidence in the Soviet press of "increased sensitivity to the danger of ideological contamination."[88]

Radio remained central to efforts to infiltrate culture into the USSR. Increasingly aware that straight news and entertainment had greater effect than propaganda, the VOA made the shift from aggressive psychological warfare to the evolutionary approach. In 1955 a Soviet citizen delivered a letter for Eisenhower to the U.S. embassy in which he complained about the VOA's "antagonistic tone" and the "empty fuss" made in anti-Soviet diatribes. The citizen explained that while such broadcasts were dismissed as propaganda, "objective information" about American life was highly valued by "the majority of Soviet people." Another letter writer noted after the Geneva conference that the VOA's fare was "still too tendentious and sometimes inaccurate." He added, however, that Soviet audiences would pay careful attention to broadcasts on literary, artistic, and scientific developments. Gradually, the VOA began to respond to the tastes of its Soviet audience, which appeared more receptive to cultural programming than psychological warfare.[89]

The Soviets correlated the intensity of their jamming of signals to the level of propaganda of U.S. radio programming. In summer 1956, following "lengthy consideration," the State Department reached a decision to make an "informal approach" to the Soviets on cessation of jamming. Officials called the initiative "urgent" as a result of indications that VOA was losing audience to the rival BBC, whose straight news program was less often subjected to Soviet jamming. Officials hoped the Soviets might be willing to cease jamming because of "interference with their own internal communications and embarrassment to their policy position."[90]

Although the Soviets mounted continuous jamming of broadcasts in Russian—especially those over ostensibly private stations such as RFE and

RL—the Kremlin showed more toleration of VOA transmissions in English. In 1958 USIA director George V. Allen ordered English broadcasts around the clock on the assumption that they would be perceived as more credible than native language broadcasts. With use of English increasingly popular worldwide, the VOA instituted news in "special English," an approach that attracted thousands of listeners. By presenting the news at a slow pace, and with precise articulation, the radio network found a means to combine Western perspectives on world affairs with language instruction.[91]

While the VOA continued to transmit propaganda through commentaries, feature programs, and its selection of news, U.S. officials gradually perceived that music—and especially jazz—was the most powerful force in building new audiences behind the Iron Curtain. Following a suggestion from Ambassador Bohlen, the VOA launched "Music USA" in 1955 for "the purpose of reaching the youth of the Soviet Union." For the next 25 years the program was emceed by Willis Conover, a low-key, nonpolitical broadcaster from Buffalo, who "was to be the single most influential ambassador of American jazz in the USSR and Eastern Europe." The advent of "Music USA" brought clear evidence of the popular appeal of Western culture at the very time that the Eisenhower administration orchestrated the shift from psychological warfare to a gradualist approach.[92]

"Music USA" and other Western radio programs soon flooded the Soviet empire with jazz, prompting much consternation among CP officials. Despite repeated expressions of sympathy for the plight of "American Negroes" in official Soviet propaganda organs, the Kremlin resisted the infusion of jazz, a distinctly African-American art form. In the early postwar years, Soviet officials saw jazz as "in the vanguard of a Yankee [cultural] assault that had already brought Western Europe to its knees." Determined to resist the jazz craze, the Soviets jammed the initial VOA program, "Jazz Club USA," but stations such as Radio Iran and Radio Luxembourg continued to entertain Soviet audiences. Soviet police arrested jazz musicians, sending many to labor camps, particularly during the cultural repression of the late Stalin years.[93]

Suppression and censorship of jazz failed, however, as Soviet soldiers returned from Berlin and other Eastern European capitals armed with the latest recordings. Jazz groups flourished in provincial cities. Soviet dissident Vassily Aksyonov recalled spending hours during his youth in the provincial city of Kazan "fiddling with the dials on our bulky wireless receivers for even a snatch of jazz." Aksyonov explained that he and his friends relished jazz for "its refusal to be pinned down, its improvisational nature." The music represented release "from the structures of our minutely controlled everyday lives, of five-year plans, of historical materialism." For many Soviet citizens the music became "an ideology; or, rather, an anti-ideology." Jazz even flourished in the gulag, where prison camp administrators often turned out to be jazz fanatics who encouraged talented inmates to form bands. Some prisoners were given special privileges and allowed to tour.[94]

Under the thaw of the mid-fifties, enthusiasts mounted a public defense of jazz as a legitimate music form. Jazz influenced the so-called *stiliagi* ("style hunters"), mostly youth who preferred music to work, sought out foreign tourists, and wore long hair and zoot suits. Under the influence of American music and film, *stiliagi* employed slang words, such as "dudes," "chicks," and "grub," and referred to main thoroughfares in Soviet cities as "Broadway." *Stiliagi* "hung out," held cocktail hours, smoked Lucky Strikes and Camels, wore Western fashions, and listened to jazz. "What had begun as a fad among the children of the elite well before the death of Stalin," historian Frederick Starr has observed, "had burgeoned into a full-scale revolt by alienated Soviet youths." Despite stern lectures from the Komsomol (communist youth league) newspaper, jazz flourished as an outlet for rebellious youth and music lovers of all ages, while enhancing the image and prestige of the United States, its originator.[95]

By the early Khrushchev years, the Soviet repertoire of jazz, as well as offshoots such as bebop, closely followed that played on "Music USA." Well before Soviet dissidents made *samizdat*, or underground literature, widely known in the West, jazz enthusiasts developed homemade recordings out of X-ray sheets. They found that the emulsion on the surface of X-ray plates provided a useable surface for sound reproduction. The appearance of millions of these crude recordings of 7-inch discs, recorded at 78 RPM from radio, demonstrated the astonishing popularity of Western music. Some practitioners referred to the use of *Roentgenizdat* ("X-ray editions") as "recording on the bones." Unable to dissuade "new Soviet man" from tuning in to jazz, the Kremlin lifted its futile ban on listening to Western music at the end of 1955. The Soviets banned samizdat recordings in 1958, even dispatching roving bands of Komsomol "music patrols" to report on violators, yet the law was widely ignored.[96]

At first slow to understand the appeal of jazz—followed closely by rock 'n' roll—U.S. officials came to appreciate the potential of Western popular music as an agent of cultural infiltration. From Trieste in 1954, public affairs officers reported that jazz was proving itself "an effective instrument for positive American propaganda." Through their recognition of jazz as a distinctly American art form, "people who are exposed to it think about our country and this thinking, of course, leads to many further investigations and expressions of interest." The response to a recorded concert series, "From the American Jazz World," was "so great among the younger set of Trieste that soon a delegation approached the director of the Allied Reading Room" with a proposal to form a jazz club. Local music shops reported sharply increased sales of jazz records.[97]

According to USIA surveys, "Music USA" was heard by more Europeans than any other program. The same was true in Africa and the Far East. Mail received by the VOA revealed that "the most popular single feature is Willis Conover's show, 'Music USA.'" Such was the show's popularity that one historian has judged the VOA program "probably the most effective propaganda coup in [U.S.] history." A survey in Poland revealed that Conover was the "best-known living American." RFE boasted that "the communists don't know whether to ban [jazz] or boom it." The Polish government reversed its long-standing opposition to jazz by decreeing that the "building of socialism proceeds more lightly and more rhythmically to the accompaniment of jazz." Radio Warsaw began offering Benny Goodman, Duke Ellington, and other jazz artists. The Czech and Hungarian regimes, however, continued to label jazz a "decadent Western disease" that caused "hooliganism." A science student from Budapest, who escaped to the West, reported that "we listened to jazz late at night over Radio Free Europe in the common room of the University." Popular programs included Dixieland, Chicago, and New Orleans jazz, but also American popular music, musical comedy, swing, rock 'n' roll, and bebop.[98]

USIA and State Department diplomats recorded evidence of listenership to "Music USA," paying careful attention to the patterns of Soviet jamming. In 1958 the Moscow embassy reported that "Music USA continues to be an excellent program enjoying great popularity in the Soviet Union." The embassy prepared monthly statistical surveys, complete with long lists of frequencies and reports on audibility and jamming. Diplomats who traveled across the USSR monitored the VOA in different cities from the Baltic republics to Soviet Central Asia. Whenever possible, diplomats interviewed sources about VOA programming. For example, two Soviet youths told an embassy diplomat in 1959 that it was "permissible to listen to VOA and BBC music programs and not too risky to English-language broadcasts in general." They added, however, that it was "dangerous to be caught listening to any Russian-language broadcast abroad, particularly those of Radio Liberation and Radio Free Europe."[99]

The shift from psychological warfare to an evolutionary approach proved as effective with the printed word as it did with radio programming to the USSR. One of the few concrete results of the "spirit of Geneva" was a Soviet-American agreement, signed on October 9, 1956, for renewed circulation of slick magazines in the two countries. The Soviets authorized circulation of *Amerika,* whose publication had been suspended in 1952, in return for U.S. distribution of a like number of copies of the Soviet counterpart *USSR. Amerika* was an instant success and invariably sold out quickly, prompting Soviet officials once again to restrict its free circulation in violation of the agreement.[100]

Described as "polite propaganda," *Amerika* featured articles reprinted from popular magazines such as *Collier's, Life, Look, Popular Mechanics, Reader's Digest,* and *The Saturday Evening Post.* The first edition of the renewed version, appearing in Moscow in the summer and fall of 1956, informed Soviet readers that *Amerika* would be "a magazine about people of the United States: how they live, work, and play." Full-sized and abundantly illustrated, including high-quality photography, the first edition of *Amerika* featured articles on the American character, humor, a feature on hospital maternity wards, a profile of Benjamin Franklin, summer fashions, and, especially popular, "America's 1956 Model Automobiles."[101]

Subsequent issues featured articles on a range of subjects, including baseball, ballet, New York's Central Park, motorboating, breeds of cattle, corn production, church architecture, and jazz. The magazine profiled famous Americans, both past and present, as well as historical sites, individual states, and national holidays. *Amerika* featured a spread, accompanied by photographs, on the new federal highway system. The magazine trumpeted technological achievements, as in a feature entitled "The 320-mile Drink," which explained how water was pumped from the Colorado River over desert and mountains for use by California homeowners.

Stories solicited directly for publication in *Amerika*—as opposed to reprints—were those most likely to highlight a propaganda theme. Articles such as "The Role of the President" and "Labor and Management: A Partnership," betrayed obvious propaganda purposes, yet stopped short of hard-hitting psychological warfare. The editors of *Amerika* probably realized that features such as "Fashions Under Twenty Dollars," "Best Dressed College Girls," "Plastics Take Over," and "Television for the Millions," carried more appeal for their Soviet readers.

Amerika also provided a means to counter hostile Soviet propaganda on U.S. race relations. *Amerika* no. 27 featured African-American singer Marian Anderson, who recently had completed a tour of the USSR, on the cover and in a feature article. Washington attempted to counter Soviet propaganda more directly with articles such as "Facts About the U.S.: The Negro Today." The Soviets sometimes responded with propaganda counterblasts, demonstrating that *Amerika* was being read. In response to an *Amerika* feature on Abraham Lincoln and the Emancipation Proclamation, the Soviet newspaper *Muskovskii Komsomolets* devoted a full page to an attack on the history of U.S. race relations, replete with statistics, a feature on the Ku Klux Klan, atrocity drawings, and photographs of lynchings.[102]

U.S. officials interpreted such rejoinders as evidence of *Amerika's* popularity. In 1959 Moscow embassy diplomats reported that "with the exception of personal contacts, *Amerika* magazine has made the greatest contribution to better understanding of America by the Soviets and to provision of accurate information about the U.S., thus counteracting to some degree anti-American propaganda." Observations, interviews, and letters from Soviet readers suggested that *Amerika* "enjoys wide popularity" and was "accepted by readers as accurate, non-propagandistic information." The magazine spurred discussion among Soviet intellectuals, professionals, artists, working people and students. Because Soviet readers discussed various articles, and passed copies of the limited-circulation magazine along to family and friends, embassy diplomats believed that *Amerika* was having a "greater impact than [its] 50,000 circulation would imply." They noted that long lines invariably formed when the magazine went on sale, but that it also could be purchased on the black market at three times the regular five-ruble (about $1.25) selling price. U.S. officials carefully monitored *Amerika's* circulation, sometimes even following delivery trucks while themselves being shadowed by Soviet security police.[103]

As the popularity of programs such as "Music USA" and of *Amerika* magazine suggested, U.S. cultural infiltration was beginning to have an impact on popular perceptions of the United States inside the USSR during Eisenhower's second term. Having rejected negotiations with Moscow, and been forced to concede the failure of liberation in Eastern Europe, Washington adopted an evolutionary strategy that emphasized cultural exchange as a means of challenging CP authority. Policymakers in Washington acknowledged that gradual cultural infiltration could be a more effective weapon against the Soviet empire than aggressive psychological warfare. Driven by the activities of citizens on both sides, increased East-West cultural exchange seemed to offer the prospect of a thaw in the Cold War. Having succeeded in laying a foundation for cultural infiltration behind the Iron Curtain, U.S. propagandists turned their attention to burnishing the image of capitalism.

FIVE

"People's Capitalism": USIA, Race Relations, and Cultural Infiltration

In the mid-fifties, the United States Information Agency began to play a significant role in carrying out the nation's foreign policy. The Eisenhower administration employed USIA to counter "new and formidable propaganda problems" stemming from the Soviet de-Stalinization campaign and the emergence of the developing world as a focal point in the Cold War. Officials feared that Soviet premier Nikita S. Khrushchev's call for "peaceful coexistence" was "strengthening tendencies toward relaxation in Free World countries, and in reinforcing neutralist opinion." Moreover, as evidence of U.S. hostility to people of color, CP propaganda ruthlessly exploited abundant evidence of institutionalized racial inequality in the United States.[1]

Under the able leadership of Theodore Streibert, a former New York radio and television executive, USIA began to establish its role in the Cold War bureaucracy. Budget cuts and McCarthyist purges presented immediate challenges to Streibert and his equally capable deputy director, Abbott Washburn, a former General Mills executive and Eisenhower campaign official. In 1953, amid charges of inefficiency and communist subversion, Congress slashed personnel in the overseas program from 13,500 to 9,281. Streibert pledged to exercise "greater efficiency and economy" over the 217 overseas information posts in 76 countries, but the budget and personnel cuts had caused "amputation trauma," devastating USIA morale. McCarthy's investigatory antics had fostered a climate of "pure hysteria" within the new agency. An extensive interagency study of employee attitudes revealed "the kind of morale that dogs chased by wolves would presumably have," explained one propagandist. "We have had the kind of nervous breakdown that comes from rejection by the Congress and by the public."[2]

Recognizing the need to rebuild confidence in the overseas program, Eisenhower made a personal appearance before USIA's Washington staff on November 10, 1953. Stressing his "deep conviction" on the importance of overseas information, Eisenhower announced authorization for recruitment of additional personnel. Recruitment posed "a terrific problem," however, "because of McCarthy's activities . . . and the badgering which [USIA] and [the VOA] had taken." Yet, Abbott Washburn recalled, "the President wanted this to succeed. He believed in it." By mid-1954 the waning of McCarthyism and the bolstering of personnel had begun to restore agency morale.[3]

With the support of Eisenhower and the NSC, USIA found its niche by devising and carrying out anti-communist propaganda programs and cultural initiatives worldwide. The agency's three primary propaganda themes were to denounce communism, exalt the capitalist system, and promote democracy. "Every wire story, every feature article, photograph, exhibit, film and broadcast sponsored by the agency is now . . . closely related to these theme-approaches," an official declared in 1954. Efforts to promote democracy ranked last in priority and would be limited when there was a "general recognition that its pursuit may interfere with U.S. foreign policy . . . particularly in colonial areas." Consistent with the general character of U.S. Cold War diplomacy, undermining communism carried a higher priority than promoting democracy.[4]

USIA would challenge CP ideology by attacking it directly as well as by defending the United States against charges of racism and ruling-class domination. USIA would oppose efforts to portray Americans as "warlike and imperialistic" and as "barbarians without any culture." The agency trumpeted American religious freedom in contrast to the "anti-religious actions and statements of Soviet leaders." USIA would promote the three propaganda themes through both overt and covert means. Official information would be delivered in a non-strident, factual manner, but "where USIA output resembles the lurid style of communist propaganda it must be unattributed."[5]

While psychological warfare still had its place, USIA propaganda increasingly focused on developing a long-term evolutionary approach to undermining CP authority. In consultation with State and the NSC, USIA developed a country-by-country information strategy rather than a universal approach. Once propaganda themes had been agreed upon, the agency would commence its campaign through print communications, broadcast news, films, book displays, exhibitions, and exchange programs.[6]

USIA tirelessly promoted the Eisenhower administration's propaganda campaigns, especially the major disarmament initiatives "Atoms for Peace" and "Open Skies." Streibert described "Atoms for Peace" as a propaganda effort in which "the President went all out. This the agency backed fully around the world, and we kept on that theme of peaceful uses of atomic energy." While the United States promoted itself simultaneously as "the guardian of peace" and "foremost promoter of progress," only as an afterthought did the Quantico panel on psychological warfare express "grave doubt as to whether . . . it is to the interest of the United States to spread fissile material all around the globe."[7]

In somewhat Orwellian fashion, given the nuclear build-up under Eisenhower's "New Look," disarmament nonetheless provided USIA with a potent propaganda theme. Following Eisenhower's initiative at the 1955 Geneva Conference, the "Open Skies" proposal was "played to the hilt," despite a noticeable lack of enthusiasm on the part of Dulles and the State Department. "It had to be over their dead bodies, more or less," Washburn recalled. Whatever propaganda benefits Washington gleaned from these campaigns proved ephemeral, however, in the wake of the Soviet launch of *Sputnik* on October 4, 1957. Technologically rather crude, *Sputnik* carried little strategic significance, yet the launch stunned the American public and excited fears that the nation was in danger of losing its advantage in missile and space technology. Congress and the defense establishment soon sounded the alarm about a "missile gap," suggesting the United States, lagging behind the USSR, would be vulnerable to a first strike. Eisenhower knew such fears were nonsense, but he proved unable to seize control of the domestic debate. Internationally, the *Sputnik* launch had unquestionably delivered a "propaganda advantage to the Soviet Union," observed Dulles. "They are playing it for all it is worth at home and abroad."[8]

While loudly proclaiming its commitment to disarmament, USIA quietly went about the business of building overseas information facilities. McCarthy's spurious charges of widespread subversion plagued efforts to bolster overseas libraries, the shelves of which had been scoured for volumes written by leftist, or merely suspect, authors. USIA personnel resented the Wisconsin senator's roguish tactics, but continued his practice of censorship throughout the Eisenhower years. Among the books considered too subversive for overseas distribution were bestsellers such as *The Naked and the Dead* (1948), *From Here to Eternity* (1951), *The Invisible Man* (1952), and *The Ugly American* (1958). "We have drifted into a system," admitted one propagandist, "where anything that's in the least controversial is pushed aside."[9]

After the McCarthy-inspired controversy abated, USIA restocked the overseas libraries with materials promoting the agency's three key propaganda themes. By the end of the Eisenhower years, USIA operated libraries in 162 cities in all major countries of the world, with the exception of those with CP-dominated regimes, which "steadfastly refused" offers of facilities. Collectively, the overseas libraries stocked 2.28 million volumes and accommodated more than 80,000 visitors a day. George V. Allen, named director of USIA in 1957, expressed "astonishment at the amount of demand overseas for ordinary American textbooks." Although Dulles rarely supported USIA programs, Allen recalled that the secretary of state was "enthusiastic about sending books abroad."[10]

Beginning in the mid-fifties, U.S. officials paid particular attention to the role of overseas libraries in Third World countries. Concerned about CP propaganda in the developing world, Vice President Richard Nixon urged "that the U.S. compete more actively with the Soviets in the field of publications." In some Third World nations, the U.S. library became the most popular one in the city. Appreciated by many, the libraries were targets for others. Overseas libraries became "more often attacked, and more bitterly, than any other American installation abroad." In the late 1950s, mobs besieged libraries in Algiers, Athens, Baghdad, Beirut, Bogata, Calcutta, and Tapei.[11]

While books and magazines promoted the American image abroad, propagandists recognized that motion pictures represented a more powerful medium that could reach all classes of people, regardless of literacy. Gaining the "ready cooperation" of Hollywood, the Eisenhower administration received the rights and translations to distribute hundreds of films abroad. USIA showed Hollywood features as well as documentaries at overseas libraries, information centers, and in remote areas by means of 350 mobile units, including "boat-mobiles." "Life of President Eisenhower" was a popular USIA feature, shown to millions around the world. Other major themes were disarmament, U.S. economic assistance programs, and "hard-hitting anti-communist films" such as "My Latvia," "Poles Are a Stubborn People," and "Hungarian Fight for Freedom," which USIA distributed in 81 countries and in 27 languages in the wake of the 1956 Soviet intervention.[12]

Despite USIA's growing propaganda activities, the agency "lacked influence at the policy-making level." Dulles had little use for USIA and occasionally attacked its activities, such as opinion polling in foreign countries. Eisenhower himself, however, never wavered in his enthusiasm for the agency and its mission. Informed that other agencies were ignoring USIA, the president on at least one occasion ordered his Cabinet officers to consult more regularly with USIA propagandists.[13]

While Eisenhower could direct his Cabinet to cooperate with USIA, he found Congress far more intractable. Amid the McCarthy controversies, USIA's 1953-54 appropriation of $77 million represented a $20 million cut from the previous fiscal year and about half the budget of the overseas program at the height of Truman's Campaign of Truth. Eisenhower lobbied hard for USIA appropriations, which he described as "very close to his heart." The president insisted that the agency, now well-managed under Streibert, should be "stepped up to meet the needs of our foreign policy." Eisenhower added that he was "personally convinced that this is the cheapest money we can spend in the whole area of national security."[14]

Eisenhower sought steady increases in the USIA budget from the McCarthy era lowpoint, but encountered opposition at every step from Rep. John J. Rooney (D-New York), chairman of the House Appropriations Committee. During budget hearings in 1955, Rooney solicited testimony from Eugene Castle, the author of a sensational book, *Billions, Blunders, and Baloney,* which savaged USIA operations. Castle had traveled over 75,000 miles around the world to chronicle the alleged frauds and waste of taxpayer monies by USIA. Although the book was one-sided and contained several inaccuracies, Rooney exploited it to telling effect. House members condemned USIA for a variety of sins, including paying "Negro band leader Dizzy Gillespie . . . a salary higher than President Eisenhower's" for an agency-sponsored tour.[15]

Eisenhower contributed to USIA's budgetary problems through his disastrous choice of Arthur Larson to succeed Streibert, who returned to private business after the 1956 election. Larson, the author of the highly partisan *A Republican Looks at His Party* (1956), once declared that the New and Fair Deals represented "a somewhat alien philosophy, imported from Europe." An equally partisan Democrat, Senate Majority Leader Lyndon Johnson, primed himself for Larson's appearance before the Senate to appeal for restoration of House cuts of USIA funding in the 1958 budget. Dripping with sarcasm, Johnson thanked "the distinguished author and spokesman" for appearing "to enlighten us." Openly derisive of Larson's testimony, Johnson concluded that "this agency does not know what it is doing." Rather than restoring the House cuts, the Senate slashed USIA's budget further, to $96 million, $50 million less than Eisenhower had requested. Livid, the president denounced the "irresponsible diminution of an agency on the front line in the Cold War." USIA received stable funding around the $100 million mark for the remainder of Eisenhower's presidency.[16]

Before the Senate cuts had been enacted, Johnson offered to give the administration the money it requested if the president would agree to place overseas information under State Department authority, as the Jackson committee had originally recommended in 1953. Eisenhower initially supported the idea, but Dulles denounced the proposal as a "radical move." Once again bowing to Dulles's wishes, Eisenhower shelved the idea. The president attempted to rebuild congressional support by replacing Larson with George Allen, who had served as assistant secretary of state for overseas information under Truman. A 29-year Foreign Service officer, Allen had held numerous ambassadorships and was well respected in Congress and the State Department. Eisenhower enhanced the USIA director's role by inviting Allen to participate in NSC policy decisions. The president expected the career diplomat to forge a close working relationship with Dulles, but Allen recalled years later that the "main problem" for USIA remained "getting guidance from the State Department."[17]

Despite cuts in the USIA budget, concerns about the nation's overseas image—particularly in the developing world—continued to mount. From 1954 to 1956, the victory by the revolutionary Vietminh over the French in Indochina, the Bandung Conference of "non-aligned" nations, and the Suez crisis all suggested that the global balance of power would be determined in the "Third world." Armed with a body of Leninist theory on capitalist imperialism, the Soviet and Chinese CPs depicted themselves as liberators while savaging the Western powers in propaganda targeting Third World nations.[18] To counter Soviet propaganda and cultural efforts, the Eisenhower administration mobilized the resources of the USIA.

The American psyche, still reeling from Suez and *Sputnik*, received another blow from the sensation caused by publication of *The Ugly American* in 1958. Set in a fictional Southeast Asian country, the novel warned that "fat," "ostentatious," "loud," and "stupid" Americans were losing the Cold War through their inattention to the needs and desires of peasant peoples. The two authors, both former naval officers, concluded in a "factual epilogue" that the United States was losing the world struggle to communism "not only in Asia, but everywhere."[19]

Anxiety over the nation's standing in the developing world prompted a country-by-country assessment by USIA. Determined to counter perceived threats to U.S. hegemony over Latin America, USIA mounted efforts to promote cultural exchange as well as propaganda campaigns against CP activities. In 1957, concerned about the rebel movement against the U.S.-backed regime in Cuba, USIA bolstered agriculture, rural education, and exchange programs with the island. Cuban revolutionaries responded by publishing a pamphlet calling for struggle against the "imperialist penetration of Cuban education." U.S. propagandists planted stories in the Cuban press, offered English classes, and established a variety of programs facilitating cultural infiltration. Exploiting the new medium of television, USIA sent programs on "the dangers of Soviet imperialism" to Argentina, Brazil, Bolivia, Colombia, Ecuador, Guatemala, and Mexico. USIA authorized special initiatives to exploit opportunities that arose from political change in Latin America. For example, the fall of Juan Peron in Argentina in 1955 "opened up opportunities for extensive information activities in that country. . . . which were completely impossible under the Peron regime."[20]

Another propaganda drive accompanied the CIA-orchestrated overthrow of Guatemalan reformer Jacobo Arbenz in 1954. USIA arranged for "the publication of additional material on Guatemala, thereby completing the record on the action which led to the overthrow of the Communist-supported Arbenz regime." At the same time, the agency initiated a project in nearby Costa Rica aimed at "maintaining year-round contact with all Catholic priests for the purpose of combatting communism." U.S. propagandists perceived priests, held in high esteem by most citizens, as "perhaps our most natural allies in this struggle." After sending out letters and offering USIA materials, public affairs officers (PAO) received 27 letters as well as visits to their San Jose offices from "several padres" who requested publications and motion picture screenings. Several priests pledged to "deliver sermons exposing communism, based on our material."[21]

Mindful of "Asia-firsters" in the Republican Party, and of the shattering effects of the loss of China on domestic politics, the Eisenhower administration continued to pay careful attention to East Asia. In a review of information programs in 1956, officials reported "substantial progress" in enhancing Japanese opinion towards the United States. Similarly, the visit of Indonesian president Achmed Sukarno to the United States in May 1956 provided USIA with a propaganda opportunity that it capitalized on in "practically every village" in Indonesia. By arranging for the "widest possible dissemination" of newsreels, stories, pictures, pamphlets, and radio programs, USIA "took advantage of Sukarno's popularity and enhanced U.S. prestige." In South Korea, President Syngman Rhee was unpopular, prompting agency efforts to distance the United States from the leadership in Seoul, while using its various media as "a major channel of free and unbiased news to the Korean people over the heads of their government." U.S. standing was thought to be strong in Taiwan, Burma, Hong Kong, and the Philippines.[22]

The situation was different in Southeast Asia, where the legacy of Western colonialism was still keenly felt. After a tour of the region in 1954, Nixon concluded that Southeast Asian countries "have had long experience with colonialism, and relate us to colonialism." The vice president explained that U.S. propaganda failed to convince because the people of the region "are allergic to anything that comes from outside to tell them what to do or think." Despite these limitations, USIA attempted to bolster the American image through film, VOA broadcasts, leaflets, and printed materials such as the magazine *Free World*. In Cambodia, a traditionally anti-American newspaper warned of growing U.S. influence, noting that audiences had been "very impressed" by a USIA film on the peaceful uses of atomic energy. An American official also noted that "English-teaching programs have begun to take hold among Cambodian people."[23]

In Vietnam, Washington continued to mount efforts to bolster its role as the "protagonist" of the government of Ngo Dinh Diem in an ultimately futile search for mass support. USIA used films, road shows, and printed media in its efforts "to tell the story of communist oppression and terror in North Vietnam." In Laos, USIA propagandists claimed some of the credit for the success of non-communist candidates in the December 1955 parliamentary elections and "the consequent rebuff of the Vietminh-dominated Pathet Lao." In Thailand, USIA assisted anti-communist indoctrination programs in all provinces and distributed packaged program materials to provincial leaders.[24]

The twin evils of nationalism and neutralism posed the greatest challenge to U.S. propaganda efforts in South Asia and the Middle East. USIA expanded its programs in Afghanistan and Pakistan, but charged India's neutralist govern-ment with "interference" with informational campaigns. As a result, Washing-ton pursued propaganda projects in which "the originating hand of the U.S. government does not show." One such effort was publication of a booklet of Mahatma Gandhi's "Reflections on Democracy," in which "quietly implicit throughout" was the "mutuality of interests, concepts, and ideals between India and the United States."[25]

The "alarming emotional drive of Arab nationalism" presented a "note-worthy complex of propaganda problems" in the mid-Eisenhower years. Even before Gamel Abdul Nasser's nationalization of the Suez Canal in 1956, Washington mounted a major effort to discredit the Egyptian leader. Simulta-neously, the United States promoted the pro-Western Iraqi government as a model for the Arab world to emulate. USIA programs in Iraq sought to convince the rising middle class to support the current regime rather than to succumb to neutralism or Nasserism. Washington launched a propaganda offensive to bolster the 1955 Baghdad Pact, a military alliance that included Britain, Turkey, Pakistan, and Iran.[26]

The Suez crisis, in which Israel, Britain, and France attacked Egypt, brought war to the region, shattering U.S. propaganda efforts. The Kremlin exploited Western imperial intervention while posing as a defender of the Arab world. The USSR sought to capitalize on economic frustration and "underly-ing distrust of the white man" in the region. American propagandists found themselves hamstrung as their own allies' invasion of Egypt reinforced Soviet propaganda linking the West with imperialism. Moreover, an intensive Amer-ican propaganda campaign against the contemporaneous Soviet intervention in Hungary "had its edge dulled by the conflict which involved two of our leading allies in NATO."[27]

USIA strove to counter Soviet diplomatic efforts in the Mideast through both covert and overt propaganda. During a state visit to Syria by the Soviet foreign minister in 1957, for example, the USIA office in Damascus made "a strong effort to place anti-communist or pro-free world material in the press in an attempt to counter the pro-Soviet chorus greeting his arrival and activities." Although the majority of newspapers that picked up 24 American-authored stories were "anti-communist stand-bys," one "strongly pro-Soviet Damascus daily" printed two critical stories on Soviet foreign policy during the foreign minister's visit. While admitting that the press accounts made only a marginal impact, the PAO in Damascus noted that "the needling effect of such material was worthwhile."[28]

Clearly the propaganda problem in which Americans found themselves most vulnerable in the developing world was the issue of racism in the United States. Since the onset of the Cold War Soviet propaganda had regularly scored the United States for discrimination, low pay, unequal justice, and violence against African Americans. Psychological warriors identified race relations as an "Achilles heel," ruthlessly exploited by the Soviets among the peoples of the world, most of whom were themselves "colored." Propagandists recalled an occasion in 1946 when Truman's secretary of state, James F. Byrnes, found himself "stumped and defeated" when he attempted to protest Soviet denial of voting rights in the Balkans. The Soviets had replied that "the Negroes of Mr. Byrnes' own state of South Carolina were denied the same right" and that Byrnes "had better direct his attention to America's problems." The Soviet response was "a checkmate of the first order," as "everyone knew that in the Secretary's home state Negroes were at best second-class citizens."[29]

By the late Truman years psychological warriors sought a means to go on the offensive against "distortions," such as those which equated "a small number of negro lynchings [with] the millions who are enslaved in Soviet labor camps." Americans matched the Soviets distortion for distortion out of fears that if nothing were done the Kremlin would score "victory after victory" in the propaganda war. Washington could not afford to wait until the nation had solved its racial problems. By adhering to "the requirement that our hands be clean before we undertake propaganda, we tend to strike a defensive note in our discussion of race problems." Psychological warriors called for Washington to develop an approach—informed by "competent Negro guidance"—that would "defy any conceivable Red-inspired attempts to continue to make a mockery of our professions of democracy."[30]

In the early 1950s, propagandists confronted the race issue head-on by emphasizing that slow and steady progress was being made. Rather than an Achilles heel, race relations constituted "one of the proud achievements of

American democracy." Since the turn of the century, Polish listeners learned in a 1954 VOA broadcast, "literacy among Negroes rose from 56 percent to 94 percent." The 130,000 African Americans studying at U.S. universities represented a 25-fold increase over the black enrollment in 1930. Resorting to outright disinformation, the broadcast declared that, "in the economic field there have long been no restrictions or differences between the Negro and the white population." Similarly, Polish listeners heard that in the U.S. armed forces "there exists absolute equality in every respect at all levels."[31]

The 1954 Supreme Court decision in *Brown v. Board of Education of Topeka* called international attention to racial segregation, prompting U.S. propagandists to scramble for an effective response. Recently appointed Chief Justice Earl Warren wrote the majority opinion, declaring that "separate educational facilities are inherently unequal," thus reversing the 1896 precedent in *Plessy v. Ferguson.* The VOA reflected the confused and contradictory response of American propaganda. "The existence of segregation does not in the least mean worse schools for Negro children than for the non-Negro children," the VOA explained to Polish listeners in a broadcast on the *Brown* decision. Because schools, even though separate, had been organized on "an identical basis . . . the Negroes who came out of these schools were on an equal footing as regards level of education and preparation for work with all the non-Negroes." After offering a tortured and tendentious defense of segregation, the VOA intoned "nevertheless" that the *Brown* decision now meant that "the existence of separate schools cannot be reconciled with the constitutional ideals of American democracy" and that "there can be no return to the state of affairs of 1896."[32]

While the VOA responded tepidly, at least at first, others saw in the *Brown* decision an opportunity to emphasize the theme of steady racial progress in keeping with the organic character of democratic society. C. D. Jackson believed that the United States remained "much too defensive" on the issue of race relations. "Entirely aside from the Supreme Court decision on segregation," he advised the USIA, "the acceleration of economic, educational, and social opportunity for the Negro in the past ten years has been absolutely fantastic. It is time we stop explaining in terms of 'this dreadful blot on our scutcheon' and look the whole world in the eye, suggesting that they do at least as well as we have."[33]

The unfolding of the Civil Rights Movement, as reflected in two major stories emanating from Alabama in 1956, focused international attention on American race relations. Autherine Lucy's ultimately successful efforts to gain admission into the University of Alabama and the equally successful Montgomery bus boycott "furnished an opening for those who wanted to attack the U.S." The Alabama events sparked "prominent coverage" worldwide, including a renewal of intensive Soviet propaganda attacks after a lull in deference to the "spirit of Geneva." Following the Soviet lead in calling attention to U.S. racial discrimination were "the communist press and the intensely nationalistic and color conscious press in many parts of the world."[34]

Washington exercised damage control until the explosion over school desegregation in Little Rock, Arkansas, in the fall of 1957. The *Brown* decision, consistent with NAACP strategy, had unleashed a campaign of school desegregation across the country. In Little Rock, Arkansas governor Orville Faubus called out the National Guard to prevent the desegregation of Central High School. The mob scene at the high school, eagerly portrayed by Soviet propagandists, included spitting, the shouting of obscenities, and episodic violence. Eisenhower, who had refused to endorse the *Brown* decision, opposed on philosophical grounds the use of federal power to challenge the racial status quo. On this occasion, however, the president had no choice but to uphold the law in the face of Faubus's interposition. Eisenhower sent in some one thousand paratroopers to ensure that nine African-American children could enroll in the Arkansas high school.[35]

The Little Rock incident precipitated a crisis in U.S. propaganda. Dulles bemoaned that "this situation was ruining our foreign policy. The effect of this in Asia and Africa will be worse for us than Hungary was for the Russians." With pictures of visceral racial hatred circulating worldwide, USIA, somewhat pathetically, scoured its files in an effort to find "pictures of interracial activities to offset photographs and films of the mob scenes at Little Rock." American PAO, meeting in New Delhi, where the emotional response to U.S. racism ran high, had no doubt that "Little Rock makes it harder to talk about American equality, freedom, and justice."[36]

USIA "flash surveys" and opinion polls, broken down by nationality, age, and gender, attempted to measure the damage done by the Little Rock imbroglio. In Western Europe and Scandinavia, Little Rock received "major play" and "slanted headlines [of] disapproval." Many acknowledged that racial discrimination was not unique to the United States and that "the Negro's status in the U.S. has been improving over the past decade." The fact that a majority of the population of a country such as France believed there had been little or no progress, however, confirmed the view in USIA that more propaganda work needed to be done, particularly after Little Rock. On the other hand, the polls confirmed the presence of a "generally favorable image of America despite strongly negative opinion on U.S. race relations."[37]

As the storm abated in Little Rock, U.S. propagandists continued to press the theme of steady racial progress. Information packets sent worldwide included feature articles and photographs of well dressed, smiling "Negroes," often engaged in activities with whites. The exploits of African-American athletes, such as Wilt Chamberlain, Willie Mays, Floyd Patterson, and "Sugar" Ray Robinson received heavy play. Informational materials included features on the benevolent U.S. stewardship toward independence and economic prosperity of Puerto Rico and the Philippines.[38]

Propagandists strove, with limited success, to convince African students in the United States of the racial progress being made in the country. USIA sponsored programs for African students studying in the United States stressed that "we are moving toward a situation where no man's position will be determined by his color." USIA hoped that the African students would perpetuate the theme of steady U.S. racial progress when they returned to their home countries, but the message did not always convince. Most of the students expressed skepticism, with one noting acidly that "it is more important to us that one of our diplomats was refused service in a Virginia restaurant than any of this talk." Africa "tends to judge America by what you do not by what you say," added another.[39]

Despite palpable resentment of racial inequality in the United States, USIA marked some progress with African educators and elites, whom they regularly barraged with photographs and information stressing racial progress. A Central African editor reported that he had read with "keen interest" a feature on "The Contribution of Negroes to Cultural Life in the United States." Concerned about "irresponsible" reporting on U.S. race relations in the newspaper *The Voice of Ethiopia*, a PAO met with editors to emphasize that "federal law was on the side of the Negroes." After several meetings, the USIA official reported that "the talks and the specially supplied material had the desired effect" and that "sensational stories" had ceased to appear in the newspaper.[40]

Letters from African educators and elites attested to the impact of U.S. propaganda efforts. A school principal from Doula, Cameroon, for example, wrote to express his gratitude for a book on U.S. history as well as to "reaffirm my interest in receiving everything bearing upon the United States." Another educator wrote that, "above all the manual on the constitutional system of the United States impressed me." Still another educator expressed thanks for illustrated calendars, magazines, photographs, documents, and "the portrait of President Eisenhower, which will be highly valued when placed in my classroom." PAO received appreciative responses after sending such items as a packet on the life of Booker T. Washington and a Rand McNally guide to the United States, "which arrived today and has pleased me very much." Many Africans requested additional materials and made requests for information, such as "the opening hours of your Information Room."[41]

Despite the setbacks and anxieties fostered by Suez, *Sputnik,* and Little Rock, propagandists believed they had laid the foundation for a "more generous appreciation of American motives." Meeting in New Delhi in November 1957, a group of PAO concluded that the most effective propaganda would be positive in tone and keenly attuned to "local conditions and thinking." In keeping with the shift in strategy since the abandonment of aggressive psychological warfare, the PAO believed that "a straight presentation of facts about democracy and communism is more effective than the use of condescension, bombast, or superlative adjectives."[42]

Second only to race relations in creating anxiety among propagandists was the CP-inspired image of the United States under the domination of a capitalist ruling class. The Eisenhower administration feared that in the absence of a countervailing theme, the USSR and its allies would undermine the appeal of the Western liberal capitalist model, especially in the developing world. Needed, at a time when the "hidden persuaders" of Madison Avenue were fueling consumerism at home, was an attractive slogan that would appeal to allies, neutrals, and the "captive peoples."

The term "People's Capitalism," which originated with T.S. Repplier, a 14-year president of the Advertising Council and an adviser to Eisenhower, arose to fill the void. In August 1955, after completing a six-month tour evaluating USIA programs worldwide, Repplier reported that since Eisenhower took office U.S. propaganda abroad had become more professional and that "USIA morale was now good." He believed, however, that the nation would continue to "operate under a serious propaganda handicap until we can hold up for the world a counteracting inspirational concept. We cannot be merely against communism; we suffer from the lack of a *positive* crusade." Needed was "a moralistic idea with the power to stir men's imagination."[43]

As a propaganda theme, "People's Capitalism" was an attempt to trumpet U.S. material prosperity and individual opportunity to the world. The essence of Repplier's proposal, enthusiastically embraced by Eisenhower, was to emphasize "that an entirely new kind of capitalism has evolved in America." True believers rather than cynical propagandists, Eisenhower and his deputies sought to export the ideas they believed responsible for the nation's postwar prosperity. They believed that if only the truth could be made known to counteract CP propaganda, the American way would triumph in the "minds of men" worldwide. USIA exploited print, film, trade fairs, exhibitions, and exchange programs to nurture a benevolent image of capitalism while reassuring foreign audiences that the United States was working diligently to ameliorate its own social problems.[44]

In contrast to the CP-inspired dichotomy of oppressed workers and a vicious ruling class, "People's Capitalism" emphasized rising incomes and the growth of the American middle class. Avoiding theoretical concepts, USIA emphasized consumerism and opportunities for individual economic mobility. Increased savings and numbers of stockholders demonstrated that "ownership of capital is rapidly moving into the hands of more and more Americans." Under "People's Capitalism," propagandists asserted, the United States had evolved the highest standard of living in the world. Its accomplishments included automation and new businesses, social security, hospitalization benefits, labor unions, public education, and the finest university system in the world. "People's Capitalism" represented a social system in which all Americans could benefit from "the abundance of our land, the leisure to enjoy it, and the opportunity to grow intellectually and culturally."[45]

The propaganda campaign forcefully asserted that capitalism, far from collapsing from its own contradictions, as CP ideologues would have it, had demonstrated its superiority. In presenting the U.S. image abroad, "we need not and should not be foolishly apologetic for the fact that what we have in this country is capitalism," declared Sherman Adams, Eisenhower's chief of staff. Rather than try "to disguise it by calling it something it is not," Americans should present a "proud description of what our system in fact now is, namely a new 'People's Capitalism' which serves our nation in a way no other system has ever approached." Adams called on Washington to exploit every opportunity to offer the invidious comparison between "People's Capitalism" and "the wretched socialism of the Soviet, concealing behind its barbed wire and its low living standards, slave labor and cruel restrictions on personal freedom."[46]

Eisenhower himself expressed "complete agreement" with the new propaganda theme. The President urged "a good, long meeting" between administration propagandists to seek consensus on the best means to promote "People's Capitalism." C. D. Jackson—no longer formally part of the Administration but still an unofficial adviser to Eisenhower—endorsed the concept, but warned of the need for some subtlety in promoting it abroad. While it was important to condemn Stalinism and communism, Jackson recommended avoiding the term "socialism" in U.S. propaganda broadsides. "Once one leaves the shores of North America," he explained, "the word 'socialism' assumes a totally different significance and vitality." Jackson added that "considerable energetic, enthusiastic, and imaginative" efforts would be required to sell "People's Capitalism" to the Third World. The concept would not be convincing if promoted simply on the basis of issuing a pamphlet and stating, "'Here, you little brown bastard, read this:'"[47]

Despite Jackson's admonition, USIA authorized mass distribution of printed materials to promote "People's Capitalism." The agency distributed "feature packets," a package of press releases, speech and magazine reprints, and glossy photographs designed to extol the virtues of capitalist society. Sent to

PAO worldwide, the material focused on the U.S. economic system, labor, education, politics, women, cultural events, sports, Hollywood, and other subjects. The didactic propaganda cast these aspects of U.S. society in the favorable light of "People's Capitalism."

Feature packets promoting "People's Capitalism" included "America's New Economic Age," which trumpeted rising wages for workers; the role of the educational system in preparing a modern work force; and technological innovations. The printed material directly challenged Soviet propaganda emphasizing excessive military spending and the inevitability of depression in capitalist society. Articles within the economics feature packet included "Factors Which Make the U.S. Economy Depression-Proof"; "We Can Have Peace and Prosperity"; and "U.S. Economy Steadily Expanding, Survey Shows." The thrust of the economics feature packet was to stress "the weaknesses of communist economies and explain why the Soviet economy can never outperform America's economy."[48]

Feature packet propaganda challenged CP claims to represent the interests of labor by depicting the United States as a classless society. While workers prospered under "People's Capitalism," the USIA propaganda emphasized that the Soviet and Chinese systems were built upon the backs of "slave labor." Articles entitled "A Worker's Life in a 'Worker's State'" and "Communist China's Boast—Millions in Slavery" depicted working conditions in the worst possible light. By contrast, articles such as "Social Security in the United States," "The Guaranteed Wage," and "Better Living Through Productivity" countered CP propaganda about U.S. working conditions. Packets included feature stories on labor leaders such as John L. Lewis, George Meany, Walter Reuther, and Eisenhower's first labor secretary, Martin Durkin. A special Labor Day packet quoted Durkin describing the holiday as an occasion in which Americans "in white collars as well as those in overalls" joined with workers in other "free lands" in opposing "the ugly specters of dictatorship and communism."[49]

Articles, statistical tables, and photographs illustrated the valued role of women in capitalist society. While calling attention to increased numbers of women in the work force, one writer hastened to add that "women working are predominantly women whose children are of school age—not the mothers of very young children. . . . Traditionally the partner and helpmate of her husband, the working wife in the United States considers first the welfare of her family and then the contributions she makes to a better standard of living." Feature packets contained articles focusing on traditional female roles—for example, "What Makes a Good Home?" and "Women as Welcome Wagon Hostesses"—but also stressed women's roles in the workplace, in politics, and in the cultural realm. Articles included "Economic Status of American

Women," "Sixteen Women Serve in U.S. Congress," and features on prominent American women ranging from Eleanor Roosevelt to actress Shirley
Booth. U.S. propaganda called attention to low wages and harsh working
conditions of women under CP regimes.[50]
    Feature packets, including many targeted at youthful audiences, trum-
peted American popular culture. "The Hollywood Story," "Hollywood and
the Church," and "Hollywood: The Good Neighbor," emphasized the movie
industry's contributions to American society. Feature packets on sports carried
articles and photographs of popular athletes such as Bob Cousy, Mickey
Mantle, and Jim Thorpe. Features informed readers of "The Boston Mara-
thon," "Sport Fishing in the United States," and even "The Eisenhower Golf
Stroke," complete with a photograph of the smiling president with his golf
bag. Articles emphasized the role of U.S. athletes in promoting sport abroad,
while condemning regimented, state-directed athletic programs under CP
regimes. One feature, for example, contained interviews with Hungarian and
Rumanian athletes who had defected to the United States after the 1956
Olympic Games in Melbourne.[51]
    USIA expanded its efforts to promote "high culture" as well as popular
culture. Features on American art, music, and architecture circulated worldwide. Opera was a favored theme of American propagandists. A feature packet
on "Opera in the United States" offered a concise history of modern U.S. opera
composers. Articles included "Toward an American Opera," "The Young
Opera Composers," "The Operas of Gian-Carlo Menotti," and "The Story of
the Metropolitan Opera."[52]
    The stepped-up worldwide cultural effort reflected Eisenhower admin-
istration fears that the Kremlin had gained a distinct advantage through its
aggressive participation in international trade fairs and exhibitions. USIA
director Streibert called for a dramatically strengthened cultural program to
counter the Soviets, who were "spending vast sums of money in a 'cultural
offensive'" that included ballet, theater, and artistic tours abroad. "The recent
'soft' approach of communist propaganda with its emphasis . . .on 'peace' and
'culture' is especially dangerous," Streibert reported to the Cabinet in July
1955. By participating in ostensibly nonpolitical trade fairs and exhibitions,
the Soviets had found a means of "impressing thousands with communist
production." At the same time, the trade fairs and exhibits provided a forum
for staging elaborate peace rallies and campaigns while attacking the United
States for racism and warmongering. "These communist showpieces, like
communist offers of trade, economic aid and arms, demand strong American
counteraction," Collier's editorialized. "We have to put more punch in the
battle of ideas."[53]

By expanding dissemination of cultural information abroad, Washington hoped to counter Soviet propaganda that depicted the United States as "a nation of materialists interested primarily in mass production products." A concerted effort to demonstrate "cultural achievement and aspirations can influence political attitudes and actions," Streibert declared. In 1955 the USIA director created the position of cultural affairs adviser as part of "a cultural campaign to make the American way of life better understood."[54]

Convinced of the threat posed by the Soviet cultural offensive, Eisenhower requested "emergency" funding from Congress to enable the United States to step up its participation in international trade fairs and exhibitions. The president argued that overseas cultural efforts complemented the administration's quest to achieve "more bang for the buck"—an effective foreign policy coupled with fiscal responsibility. PAO posted abroad reported that educational and cultural exchange was "the No. 1 program in effectiveness in their country in terms of U.S. objectives, long and short term." From his position as UN ambassador, Henry Cabot Lodge advised that devoting increased attention to industrial, scientific, and medical exhibits, as well as musical programs, would increase the nation's prestige overseas. Despite the budget controversies over the overseas program in the mid-fifties, Congress responded to the emergency request and granted Eisenhower $5 million in July 1954. The President's Emergency Fund for International Affairs provided for more intensive participation in trade fairs as well as greater efforts to encourage artists, musicians, and theatrical troupes to take part in overseas cultural events.[55]

The stepped-up effort, which reflected the shift in U.S. policy from psychological warfare to gradual cultural infiltration, paid immediate dividends. An outpouring of enthusiasm for "Porgy and Bess," which played to capacity houses in an extended tour of Western Europe, attested to the benefits of presenting American culture abroad. Performed by the Everyman Opera Company, with a cast of 70 African Americans, the musical provided a means of representing race relations as intrinsic to the nation's culture while taking the edge off of hostile CP propaganda on discrimination against African Americans. After witnessing an electrifying performance of "Porgy and Bess" in Belgrade in December 1954, the *New York Times* reported that "with charm and grace, members of the cast created a new perspective here for a communist-led people sensitive to reports of American race prejudice and exploitation. The contributions which such presentations make toward a better understanding of America can scarcely be exaggerated." Funds under the emergency program also underwrote performances by the Philadelphia Orchestra, the New York City Ballet, the José Limon Dance Troupe, and other musical and artistic groups.[56]

Observers believed the president's emergency fund provided "a tremendous step forward" in presenting U.S. culture abroad. In addition to funding cultural presentations, Eisenhower formed a cabinet-level committee headed by Dulles "to provide coordination and guidance in the program and to increase U.S. participation in trade fairs overseas." The committee included secretary of commerce Sinclair Weeks, whose department would assume operating responsibility for trade fairs, while the State Department oversaw cultural exchange initiatives. Both were to act under USIA's overall supervision. The cabinet committee strove to secure "the maximum cooperation of American industry and cultural organizations." Always preferring to enhance the role of the private sector, Eisenhower hoped that the emergency funds would serve as seed money "to stimulate exhibition abroad by private firms or groups of the best this nation has to offer in industrial production and cultural achievement." The president directed Streibert and Weeks to lobby the National Association of Manufacturers, the Chamber of Commerce, and other business groups to participate in overseas trade fairs.[57]

The "basic objective" of the trade fair program was to show the world that the United States was "the greatest producer of peaceful goods for the service of mankind." Trade fairs and exhibitions would at the same time counter CP efforts to exploit international exhibitions to their sole benefit. Under the guidelines devised for U.S. participation, plans were made to "take on a greater degree of urgency when major Soviet bloc competition is present or threatened." Levels of participation and types of displays would vary, depending on the character of the audience and the political or ideological tendency of the host country. U.S. planners targeted countries perceived to be "in relatively great danger of communist infiltration or communist alignment."[58]

Washington put the emergency trade fair program into effect in December 1954 with U.S. participation in the Bangkok Constitution Fair. The American theme, "Fruits of Freedom," encompassed industrial exhibits with the "latest model automobiles and agricultural equipment, and a United States Army exhibit dispensing free American-made ice cream." Thais and international visitors cavorted before the "See Yourself on TV" exhibit as well as "Circarama," a 360-degree photographic display developed by Walt Disney that would become a popular standard at U.S. overseas exhibits. Washington planned to participate in eight additional fairs, before audiences of 12 to 15 million people. Reaching mass audiences would provide the opportunity to refute "as directly as possible the Soviet and anti-American propaganda line." As participation in overseas cultural events broadened, Congress provided regular funding through the International Cultural Exchange and Trade Fair Participation Act of 1956.[59]

Beginning in 1956, the Eisenhower administration initiated efforts to establish "People's Capitalism" as the central theme of all overseas trade fairs and exhibitions. USIA launched a pilot exhibition entitled "People's Capitalism—A New Way of Living" in Washington's Union Station in February 1956. If successful, the pilot exhibition was to represent a model for overseas efforts.[60]

Designed to "translate the principal facts of our economic life into popular terms," the exhibit featured as its centerpiece two American homes, one built in 1775, the other in 1956. The contrasts were meant to "highlight our economic achievement over the past 180 years" while demonstrating that "the people are the capitalists and the people share the benefits." The exhibition also featured new model automobiles, appliances, furnishings, road designs, art, libraries, books, and information about the salaries and benefits of American workers. A film traced advances that enhanced the lives of average consumers, such as the development of nylon with its "multiplicity of uses."[61]

Exhibits carried headlines such as "CLASS LINES BEGIN TO DISAPPEAR," "ALMOST EVERYBODY BECAME A CAPITALIST," "EDUCATION FOR ALL," and "MACHINES WERE INVENTED TO DO THE HARD WORK." The final, summary exhibit informed visitors than an "exciting and constantly changing new society has developed in America. It is truly and literally PEOPLE's CAPITALISM." Although the U.S. system was not perfect, it promised to "fulfill man's age old dream of a life free from want, with each individual free to develop to the fullest those talents and abilities given him by the Creator."[62]

Before the opening of the Washington pilot exhibition in February, Advertising Council consultants worried about "the degree of blatancy" required in setting forth the message of the exhibit. While not wanting to be so blatant as to repulse visitors, planners were determined to distinguish the main features of the U.S. exhibition "from those of its totalitarian competitors." At the same time, they wished to avoid leaving "a purely materialistic impression" that would divert attention from the "ideological battle front that is being fought."[63]

To test the effectiveness of the pilot exhibition, USIA contracted to conduct surveys and interviews with 105 foreign nationals and 44 foreign journalists. After the exhibition opened in February, USIA transported most of the foreign visitors from New York to Washington, where they received meals, lodging, and a tour of the exhibition. Seventy percent judged the exhibition "good" or "exceptionally good." They displayed particular enthusiasm for the modern house exhibit. Given a choice of responses on a checklist, 65 percent of the visitors selected either "The Capitalistic way of life has brought great benefits to most Americans" or "Most Americans belong to the great middle class, are neither very rich nor very poor." Interviews and questionnaires revealed that "the overall impression of the message conveyed by the exhibit largely corresponded to what was intended by the exhibitors."[64]

Encouraged by the favorable response to the "People's Capitalism" pilot exhibit, USIA launched similar exhibits at international trade fairs and exhibitions. The agency continued the practice first tested at the model exhibit in Washington of using interviews and surveys to test audience reaction to U.S. exhibitions. Streibert ordered PAO worldwide to consider whether "the term 'People's Capitalism,' or some variant of it, [is] one which would be productive in your area." USIA directed PAO to conduct personal interviews with local officials and any visitors to U.S. trade fairs and to submit reports on the "basic values and aspirations" of "key target audience groups." Field research and patterns of communication and information dissemination would enhance USIA's ability to measure the appeal of CP displays while designing an effective, credible propaganda campaign of its own.[65]

Visitor surveys taken in the wake of U.S. international exhibitions revealed that "the popularity of television continues unabated, especially with the advent of color TV." Exhibits based on Eisenhower's "Atoms for Peace" campaign remained "almost universally well-received," while operating models, industrial products, and machinery were also popular. Before and after surveys aided USIA in assessing the impact of changes in overseas exhibitions. For example, a survey of 800 visitors to the 1960 Berlin Industrial fair found that the efforts to counter "unfavorable stereotypes of American youth, such as lack of restraint, 'wildness,' over-enthusiasm for jazz, shallowness and laziness" had been successful. After exhibiting "actual American young people busy at serious pursuits," USIA found that foreign attitudes about American youth rose sharply and that there was a decrease in unfavorable stereotypes.[66]

While visitors often responded positively to American exhibits, the overall results of surveys based on 20 exhibitions revealed that "U.S. trade fair efforts have failed consistently to match Soviet and satellite efforts." Attendance at U.S. trade fair pavilions was high, but fell behind the Soviet and Chinese competition. At the 1958 International Trade fair in Zagreb, for example, a USIA survey of 802 visitors found that 81 percent of fair visitors had toured the U.S. pavilion. Although most visitors responded favorably to the exhibit, surveys showed that they considered the Czech and Soviet exhibits superior. Survey results indicated that the CP regimes were "engaged in an all-out effort at these international fairs, and anything less on our part threatens to leave us in the dust."[67]

In December 1958, Eisenhower lent his personal support by attending opening ceremonies of the first International Agricultural Exhibition in New Delhi. The president received an enthusiastic reception in an important neutral, developing country, where critical attitudes prevailed about U.S. racial practices. Taking note of the enthusiastic crowds greeting Eisenhower, Indian prime minister Jawaharal Nehru told the U.S. president that he had won "the heart of my millions." Indian leaders declared that the "Four F" theme of the president's major address—food, family, friendship, and freedom—earned the United States "concrete gains" that were evident "throughout the length and breadth of this land."[68]

The 1958 Brussels Universal and International Exhibition presented by far the most significant opportunity for the United States to use culture as an asset to the nation's foreign policy. Planning for the Brussels exhibition, the first world's fair of the postwar era, began under the Office of the U.S. Commissioner General for the Brussels Exposition (BRE), a division of the State Department. Edward Stone, architect of the new U.S. embassy in Delhi, was chosen to design the pavilion in Brussels. Howard Cullman, director of the Port Authority of New York, was Eisenhower's choice as commissioner general of the exhibition, a position he assumed on October 3, 1956. Planning for the exhibition centered in New York, with liaison offices in Washington and Brussels.[69]

In order to plan the pavilion in accordance with the Brussels theme, "A New Humanism," Eisenhower summoned leaders from business, labor, the media, and universities to collaborate on a design. After receiving suggestions from more than 50 consultants, BRE proposed three basic ideas to guide the exhibition. Although the panel abandoned the slogan "People's Capitalism" as too blatant, the essential theme that the United States was the most abundant and free land in the world would remain in force at Brussels. While stressing that Americans were a "people of plenty," the exhibition would at the same time admit that the nation confronted "unfinished business" in the form of social problems, including racial prejudice. The third conclusion offered by BRE was that the themes of the exhibition would be "put across by indirection" rather than "heavy, belabored" propaganda."[70]

After devising its basic approach, BRE turned to a familiar source—the Cold War intellectuals at MIT—for the "ideological glue" to hold the exhibition together. Having rejected "life, liberty, and the pursuit of happiness" as too "corny," BRE hoped that the MIT group could develop an effective central theme to dominate the exhibition. In a three-day symposium in March 1957, Walt W. Rostow, Jerome Weisner, and other psychological warfare veterans concluded that "the dominant theme should be, simply stated, that the United States constitutes a society in ferment." Americans were a dynamic, restless people engaged in a "continuous revolution" intended to produce a better way of life. Such an approach would allow Washington to trumpet its accomplishments, while at the same time admitting that "we Americans have problems which are germane to our society and that we are attempting to deal with them." Exhibits would focus on the land, everyday life, industry, science and technology, culture and performing arts, as well as the "unfinished business of the American community." While the CP leaders promised an ideal world, the United States was actually delivering it through the abundance of its "classless society."[71]

Abundance notwithstanding, a number of congressional representatives remained skeptical about allocating millions of dollars for participation in a European fair. In its initial deliberations in 1956, the House Foreign Affairs Committee envisioned a $15 million appropriation. By the spring of 1957, however, that figure had been trimmed by $4.5 million by the Appropriations subcommittee chaired by Rep. Rooney, an inveterate foe of the overseas program. The *Washington Post* reported that Rooney conducted only summary hearings and that his "pruning knife has been particularly active" in cutting appropriations for the Brussels fair. Since roughly $5 million had been earmarked for pavilion construction, the cuts meant that BRE would have only about half the funds it anticipated for exhibits.[72]

Commissioner General Cullman lobbied tirelessly in behalf of restoring congressional funding. Warning that budget cuts, when coupled with Belgian taxation and other unforeseen costs, would cripple the exhibition, Cullman urged the president to do what he could to make the Congress "conscious of the tremendous impact our country can make, particularly with the Iron Curtain countries, who will be fellow exhibitors." Cullman responded adroitly when the panic inspired by the Soviet launching of *Sputnik* in October threatened to divert all available resources to science, technology, and space exploration. Rather than cutting funds for Brussels, which would only reward the Soviets with a second propaganda coup to follow up the satellite launch, the United States should redouble its commitment to the world's fair. "With appropriate funds," Cullman insisted, "we can do a *Sputnik* culturally, intellectually, and spiritually."[73]

Encouraging Eisenhower to commit the administration's prestige in the budget battle, Cullman asserted that the CP regimes were dramatically outspending the United States in their preparation for Brussels. The U.S. appropriation was "embarrassing," not only in comparison with the $60 million the Soviets were investing, but when measured against the $10 million the Belgian Congo was spending and the $6 million appropriation of tiny Luxembourg. Citing both State Department inaction and congressional parsimony, Cullman declared himself mystified by "the passive reaction of our government in a most important enterprise." Cullman told Eisenhower he would "carry on" as commissioner general, but warned that without greater backing his would be "a most difficult assignment and one that will do this country no credit in a situation where we should, in my opinion, take the leadership."[74]

Responding to Cullman's insistent pleas, Eisenhower committed the administration's prestige to holding the line on cuts in the Brussels appropriation. The president received bipartisan support from influential politicians, such as Senator Hubert Humphrey (D-Minnesota), who declared that the public needed to realize "that the Soviet Union has declared war on us" and that the conflict was being fought on cultural ground. Two of the nation's most influential newspapers, the *New York Times* and the *Washington Post,* lent editorial support. The *Times* noted that there was no "evading the fact that the Brussels Fair will shape up as competition between East and West," and that "the Russians plan a big push at Brussels." The United States was building an expensive pavilion, complete with an auditorium, "but our commission lacks the funds to fill it with our performers" as a result of budget cuts. "When the fair is under way and the Russians are getting the best notices, it will be too late," the *Times* added. Under the headline, "We're Set to Be Shamed At Brussels," the *Post* declared that Rooney's obstructionism and "foot-dragging at the State Department" threatened to result in "a second-rate show for a first-rate nation." Fair coordinators also received a boost from entertainer Ed Sullivan, who devoted 15 minutes of one of his television shows to a feature on plans for the U.S. exhibition.[75]

The efforts of Cullman, Eisenhower, and their supporters succeeded in restoring some of the congressional cuts. The appropriation, considered barely adequate by Cullman, leveled off at about $12 million, $3 million less than the Foreign Affairs Committee had recommended in 1956. With the addition of various loans, grants, and donations, some of them sizable, the total investment in Brussels approached some $14 million. After receiving the final appropriation, construction moved ahead on the $5 million pavilion to be located between the Vatican and Soviet exhibits (or, as one wag put it, between heaven and hell). Consciously modeled on the Roman coliseum as a confident statement on the American imperium, the pavilion, one of the largest circular buildings of its time, was 85 feet high, 340 feet in diameter, and occupied a 7.4 acre site. A plastic roof spanning spoke-like steel cables enclosed several large trees, effecting an atmosphere "expressive of the American spirit, with a feeling of openness and naturalness." The U.S. pavilion finished a respectable fourth (the Czechs won), out of more than 50 entrants, in an architectural competition among the pavilions constructed at Brussels.[76]

After the six-month "show of the century" opened on schedule in Brussels on April 17, 1958, visitors began touring the U.S. pavilion. Stepping into the main entrance, they encountered the "Face of America" display beneath a 100-foot map of the United States. Juke boxes, a football uniform, automobile license plates, and other examples of Americana comprised the initial, impressionistic display. Following an obligatory "Atoms Serving the Community" exhibit, visitors encountered a display on the U.S. industrial revolution, featuring automation and technology, including an enormous IBM RAMAC computer which answered questions in ten languages. The exhibition included a model working television studio and color TVs, largely new to Europe at the time. Visitors could also select and play popular American music on a modern high-fidelity system. Those preferring live music or theater could attend performances in the auditorium.[77]

At Eisenhower's personal insistence, the pavilion featured a display of voting machines to emphasize the workings of democracy. Visitors using the machines to participate in straw polls named Abraham Lincoln the best president, Kim Novak their favorite American actress, and Louis Armstrong the greatest musician. USIA director George Allen reported to Eisenhower that the "voting machines are a great hit and are attracting much favorable notice." Disney's "Circarama," the 360-degree motion picture tour of the United States, which concluded with a choral rendition of "God Bless America," was one of the most popular features in the pavilion. Funded by a Ford Foundation grant, "Circarama" was "a winner from the start. As its fame spread, visitors had to queue for hours to get in for the 15-minute show."[78]

Americans emphasized that leisure and consumption were important aspects of their culture by providing lounge chairs around a reflecting pool in the center of the pavilion. Foot-weary visitors could relax around the pool while consuming hamburgers, hot dogs, chips, ice cream, and soft drinks. For their viewing pleasure, the Americans offered a popular fashion show on a platform overlooking the reflecting pool. Some critics wondered whether mink stoles and fountains in the open air of the pavilion would send a message of too much opulence, but Cullman doubted that any harm was being done. "It is quite true that too much emphasis from the visitors is spent watching the Vogue models and eating ice cream cones," he observed, "but I guess sex and gastronomy are here to stay."[79]

With the Soviet pavilion located next to the U.S. exhibition, "it is accepted that this is another propaganda battle in the Cold War." The two exhibitions offered a sharp contrast. The Soviets, ignoring the fair's theme of "a new humanism," filled their exhibition with machine tools, model hydroelectric dams, and statistics on industrial growth, as if to say "We are large, we are powerful, we have science and industry. We can make anything. . . . And we owe it all to communism." The U.S. pavilion, on the other hand, offered a spacious, uncluttered, and slower-paced exhibition that exuded a "quiet confidence." The Americans seemed to be saying, "We don't have to prove our industrial selves to anyone. You see our automobiles on all your streets. Relax a little and learn something of how we live." "Europeans I talked to found the Russian Pavilion stiff, old fashioned and dominated by machine tools," observed an American journalist who reported extensively from Brussels. He added, however, that the Soviets generated visitor enthusiasm with their timely display of three model satellites, whereas "the U.S. had not a single exhibit to show it was in the space race."[80]

American and Soviet intelligence agents toured one another's facility to record factory marks on exhibits and make additional observations. On the American side, FBI, CIA, NSA, Army Intelligence, and State Department investigators targeted not only the Soviets, but alleged U.S. subversives in Brussels. Most of this activity was senseless, such as the concern that Harry Belafonte, set to perform in the pavilion auditorium, might jeopardize U.S. interests since he was a "volatile" African American. As historian Robert Rydell has pointed out, the obsession with national security, while largely unseen, nevertheless became, unconsciously, part of the exhibition of U.S. culture in Brussels.[81]

The highlight of the exhibition came on the American "National Days" of July 2-4. Unable to attend the Brussels exhibition himself, Eisenhower dispatched a former president, Herbert Hoover, to preside over the holiday celebration at the U.S. pavilion. (Had Hoover declined, Eisenhower had been "thinking of asking the gentleman from Independence because of bipartisanship, etc.") Pleased with the progress in Brussels, Cullman declared that the exhibition was "creating tremendous goodwill and accolade among those we are trying to impress."[82]

Shortly after Cullman offered this roseate perspective, controversy exploded over the "Unfinished Work" exhibition acknowledging the existence of social problems, including racial discrimination. Named for a phrase from Lincoln's Gettysburg Address, the "Unfinished Work" exhibit reflected the decision of U.S. propagandists that the most effective approach to controversial issues was to acknowledge their existence while reassuring visitors that such problems were being addressed. This approach, judged successful in previous "People's Capitalism" exhibits, had been recommended for Brussels by Rostow and the MIT consultants. Rather than ignoring social problems, as the United States had done in exhibits at the 1939 New York World's Fair, propagandists concluded that international opinion would be favorable toward a frank acknowledgement of the existence of such issues as racial discrimination, as long as the exhibit emphasized that these problems were in the process of being solved as part of the continuous evolution of American society.

Three "Unfinished Work" exhibits—on race relations, urban renewal, and conservation—had been put in the U.S. pavilion. Each exhibit consisted of three cubicles: the first identifying the problem; the second explaining what was being done to address it; and the third an optimistic projection of the future. The exhibit on conservation issues, which focused on plans to address waste of natural resources and the erosion of farm land, attracted the least notice and little public criticism. The urban renewal exhibit, entitled "The Crowded City," called attention to the transition of the United States, in only two generations, from a predominantly rural nation to one in which three-fourths of Americans lived in cities. Such rapid urbanization caused "problems of congestion and of housing" which had not yet been brought into line with "the other standards of American life." Some American officials and visitors criticized the inclusion of photographs of slum dwellings, but defenders of the exhibit pointed out that those pictures were displayed alongside photographs of new apartment buildings, thus demonstrating the process of urban renewal. By acknowledging the existence of a social problem, but at the same time demonstrating that a solution was being put into place, the exhibit achieved the aim of the "unfinished work" concept."[83]

Far more controversial was "The American Negro," an exhibit which approached the neuralgic issue of race relations with unprecedented honesty and integrity. Informing visitors that "one American in ten descended from African slaves," the exhibit confessed that "these 17 million Negroes have yet to win all of the equal rights promised them by American democratic theory." After acknowledging that racial discrimination was part of the nation's history and culture, the exhibit stressed amelioration. One paragraph, appearing along-side a photograph of a black university professor, explained that the number of African Americans attending college had increased from 27,141 in 1930 to 196,000 in 1956. A chart traced the rise of African-American voter registration in the South, which it claimed had doubled since 1947. The photographic display included a portrait of the New York City Commission on Discrimina-tion. Another photograph showed "a Negro couple in a modern, upper middle class kitchen in a Little Rock home." The photograph appeared next to a chart on the rise of per capita black income. Another section explained the 1954 Supreme Court decision in *Brown v. Board of Education*. The final section of the exhibit, appearing alongside a photograph of black, white, and Asian-American children holding hands, pledged that "democracy's unfinished busi-ness, already partially mastered, will get done on a national scale." The goal that united Americans was "not utopia, but larger freedom, with more justice. Democracy is our method. Slowly, but surely, it works."[84]

"The American Negro" exhibit aroused enormous controversy in the United States. Southern segregationist politicians denounced the exhibit as unpatriotic and perhaps even a communist plot. Senator Olin Johnston of South Carolina declared that "this exhibit could not have been more designed to reflect against the American nation if it had been made in Moscow by the Kremlin." Another Southern congressman called it a "colossal and unimaginable stupidity." George Allen reported that USIA had received complaints from several politicians, mostly southerners who took "very vehement exception" to the display.[85]

Opposition to the Brussels exhibition on race was not confined, however, to the predictable reaction of racist politicians from the Deep South. Several USIA officials, not consulted initially, criticized a newspaper montage in the exhibition, which featured headline articles calling attention to police and mob violence against African Americans. They also expressed opposition to the photographs of "mixed-groups of school children at work and at play" as well as one of "a colored boy dancing with a white girl." USIA ordered the offending photographs taken down and posted a guard in front of the exhibit to prevent the press from witnessing the removal.[86]

As the controversy over the exhibition on race received play in the American press, Eisenhower sent Allen to Brussels to report directly on the display. The USIA director reported in June that the fair itself was a huge success, drawing an estimated 50 million visitors, about 15 million more than expected, and the vast majority of whom would tour the U.S. pavilion. Allen averred that the "major problem" was the race display, but noted the irony that European audiences, and especially the Belgian hosts, had defended the exhibit against its American detractors. Nevertheless, USIA made plans to shut down the "Unfinished Work" exhibit, prompting James Plaut, Cullman's deputy and director of the Boston Institute of Contemporary Art, to threaten to resign over the issue because he considered "the concept of showing our faults as basic to the exhibit."[87]

Plaut's threatened resignation, which would have ensured an even wider controversy, enraged Eisenhower, who displayed little sympathy for the "Unfinished Work" exhibition. "When we send our children up to receive their diplomas in high school, we have them put on their best clothes and do not show them in their jeans and sneakers," the president admonished. Eisenhower saw no reason "why we should not put our best foot forward in an exhibit such as this. Such is naturally only to be expected." The president also "objected very strongly to the 'finger-pointing' implicit in the setting up by a New Englander [Plaut] of an exhibit critical of the South on the racial problem." Secretary of State Christian Herter also sharply opposed the exhibit. Eisenhower ordered Allen to urge Cullman to "consider doing various things in the interest of making the exhibit better balanced and more broadly representative of America." Based on his review of the American guidebook and Allen's report, Eisenhower told the press that the "Unfinished Work" exhibit was "too narrowly based" and would be broadened to better reflect American life.[88]

Instead of "broadening" the "Unfinished Work" exhibit, Eisenhower closed it after ten weeks and replaced it with an exhibit on public health. The decision dismayed the young American guides at the exhibit, who wrote Eisenhower a long letter illuminating how effective the display had been, and thus by implication how ill conceived had been the president's action. The guides, predominantly college students from across the country, assumed the roles of courteous, multilingual ambassadors for their country. Described as "a pleasant surprise" to Europeans, the guides' role in explaining the meaning of exhibits was largely overlooked in press coverage that focused on quoting from the texts of U.S. displays. While accompanying groups of 5 to 25 persons through the "Unfinished Work" exhibit, the guides fielded scores of questions. "Throughout this exhibit, we try to be as honest as possible, admitting that many aspects of the present situation are unfortunate, but that recent changes justify optimism."[89]

The guides explained to Eisenhower how they had handled the perennial issue of the unrest in Little Rock. They reported that "all heads immediately nod in recognition" at the mention of the Arkansas city. "Without exception, every European and Asian is familiar with this incident and all too frequently, this is as far as his knowledge extends. We add, however, that while the headlines were filled with the violence of Little Rock, there were many other communities in the South which carried out integration in a quiet and orderly manner." After explaining U.S. racial issues in greater depth, the guides were convinced that "visitors are definitely and positively affected by this experience." The guides quoted visitors making comments such as "'It shows the democratic and free spirit of the United States,' or 'You are very courageous to do this,' or 'Only a great country can recognize its own faults.' Many who have only heard of Little Rock will say, 'We did not realize that the Negro had made so much progress.'"[90]

The guides told Eisenhower that visitors frequently commented favorably on the openness of the exhibition in contrast with the Soviet pavilion. "The most interested response, however, comes from peoples from Asiatic and communist countries. They have been told about our racial problems with more intensity and exaggeration than any other groups," the guides explained. "Many will start out with complete skepticism and leave with an indication of new respect." The United States was "the only country at the Brussel's World's Fair which is engaging in this type of open self-evaluation. What has been termed as 'hanging out our dirty linen' by critics of the exhibit in the United States, has, on the contrary, turned out to be a powerful type of inverse propaganda. It is a total contrast to the Russian Pavilion and provides a positive answer to their twisted propaganda about us." The guides concluded their letter by declaring that they "strongly believe that the proposed changes in 'Unfinished

Work' will diminish our prestige abroad and will open us up to new and severe criticism because we have been forced by domestic pressure to retreat from a courageous position." There is no evidence that the guides' response to the revision of the "Unfinished Work" exhibit had any influence on Eisenhower.[91]

Another source of controversy in the U.S. pavilion was the modern art exhibit, which traditionalists condemned as "abstract rubbish." A journalist recalled that "the controversy around the art section started on the opening day and was still raging when the fair closed." U.S. officials received myriad complaints over a representation of an old etching portraying a naked woman on a hammock. After receiving Allen's personal report on the situation in Brussels, Eisenhower, while not offended himself, concluded that the inclusion of the nude etching reflected poor judgment. Allen blamed Plaut, director of a modern art museum, for the controversy. Eisenhower, an amateur painter himself, responded that he "recognized that there is a place for the modernistic and impressionistic school but he doubted if this fair is the place to try to teach sophistication to the public of Europe or to American tourists." The president ordered a wider diversification of the art exhibit, which meant replacement of some of the offending pieces with more traditional art.[92]

The controversies over the "Unfinished Work" and modern art exhibits marred an otherwise creditable performance at Brussels. Domestic divisions and needless insecurity had undermined an honest and effective display on the "unfinished work" of race relations, the most sensitive issue that confronted propagandists in the late Eisenhower years. Not even the craven act of shutting down the display seems to have undermined the positive impression left with most visitors to the pavilion. There is some reason to doubt a confidential USIA assessment that the U.S. pavilion was "outranked in audience preference by several of its competitors and in particular by the presentation of the Soviet Union." This view reflected post-*Sputnik* anxieties about the nation's overseas image more than a balanced assessment of the American pavilion in Brussels. Most of the criticism at Brussels came from Americans, who were more sensitive about how their country was being portrayed abroad than foreign visitors. This criticism was "not shared by foreigners," noted the State Department post-mortem. As the young guides had observed, foreign visitors usually left with a favorable impression, even after being informed of the "unfinished business" of American society. As George Allen noted, Europeans often defended the U.S. exhibition against its detractors at home. Officials described foreign press coverage of the U.S. exhibit as highly favorable.[93]

Despite being embroiled in controversy over the modern art and "Unfinished Work" exhibits, both Cullman and Allen expressed satisfaction with the nation's performance in Brussels. Cullman believed that the "unique and unprecedented government project" had achieved its aims, while Allen declared that "the fair as a whole is highly successful." Most visitors praised the exhibit "as giving them a better conception of U.S. life than they had before."[94]

By the end of the Eisenhower years, Washington's campaign of propaganda and cultural infiltration had begun to prove itself as an important asset in both allied capitals and the developing world. Propagandists exploited material prosperity, popular and high culture, and the global appeal of the images and symbols of American life. U.S. propaganda either glossed over racial and class divisions or insisted that such "unfinished business" would soon be remedied. The ultimate test of the campaign of cultural infiltration would come as a result of an unexpected opportunity to exhibit American life in the Soviet Union itself.

SIX

From the Summit to the Model Kitchen: The Cultural Agreement and the Moscow Fair

On June 2, 1957, as five million Americans watched on television, Soviet premier Khrushchev declared in a CBS "Face the Nation" interview from Moscow that broadened trade and cultural ties were the keys to improved East-West relations. Blaming Washington for the impasse on cultural exchange, the Soviet leader called on Americans to "do away with your Iron Curtain." Four days after the CBS interview, the Soviets submitted a formal proposal for broad-scale exchange of technical, industrial, scientific, and artistic groups. Khrushchev continued to emphasize "peaceful coexistence," partly as a means to access Western science and technology.[1]

While the Eisenhower administration, apparently caught off guard by Khrushchev's public statements, said little in response, Senate majority leader Lyndon Johnson took the lead in urging a U.S. rejoinder. Calling for an "open curtain" that would allow Western ideas to "cleanse evil" inside the USSR, Johnson proposed specifically that Washington respond to Khrushchev by offering a reciprocal exchange of weekly radio and television broadcasts. The State Department embraced the idea, calling in July 1957 for a Soviet-American agreement "at an early date for regular exchange of uncensored radio and television broadcasts." Vice President Richard M. Nixon took the American counteroffensive a step further, condemning Khrushchev's Iron Curtain reference as "hypocritical double-talk" in view of continuing Soviet jamming, censorship, and travel restrictions.[2]

Responding in late July, the Soviets said they were willing to discuss the broadcast proposal, but only in conjunction with wider-ranging discussions of "contacts and ties in their entirety." Momentum toward renewed cultural contacts continued to mount on October 5, 1957, when John Foster Dulles and Andrei Gromyko met for four hours in New York, at Dulles's invitation, following the Soviet foreign minister's arrival for a meeting of the UN General Assembly. In addition to their discussion of Mideast geopolitics and disarmament issues, the two leaders focused on efforts to establish broadened East-West contacts. The final obstacle to negotiations aimed at achieving a new cultural agreement, the Soviets averred, was the odious fingerprinting provision of the 1952 Immigration and Nationality Act. If Washington intended to increase contacts, this remnant of McCarthyism would have to be removed. U.S. newspaper editorialists and various public figures, including the president and the secretary of state, joined the Soviets in condemning the law. In response, in October 1957, Congress amended the immigration law, removing the fingerprinting provision and with it the last barrier to resumption of full-scale negotiations on an East-West cultural agreement.[3]

High anxiety in the West over the October 4 *Sputnik* launch did not impede progress toward an East-West cultural accord. On October 28, only days after the congressional action removing the fingerprinting provision, a Soviet delegation headed by the ambassador to the United States, Georgi Zarubin, began discussions in Washington. Veteran diplomat William S. B. Lacy, head of a new State Department staff on East-West contacts, headed the U.S. delegation. In an opening statement, Lacy blamed Soviet censorship of news dispatches and systematic jamming for the failure at Geneva more than two years earlier. He commended the Soviets for new flexibility on the ruble exchange rate, thereby facilitating increased tourism in the USSR, but criticized Soviet laws confining travelers to specified areas. Noting that both countries had agreed to circulate the other's official magazine, Lacy charged the Soviets with a "less than satisfactory" follow-through in ensuring free distribution of *Amerika*.[4]

More positive and forward looking in his opening statement, Zarubin advocated a wide range of contacts and exchanges "to contribute to the normalization and improvement of Soviet-American relations." The Soviet diplomat offered concrete proposals for reciprocal exchanges, especially in industry, agriculture, and health, but also among writers, artists, musicians, filmmakers, journalists, professors, teachers, students, workers, and athletes. The Soviets also advocated staging reciprocal exhibitions and declared their readiness to come to terms on reciprocal direct air communication between major Soviet and American cities.[5]

Three months of detailed discussions culminated on January 27, 1958, with the signing of the 1958 cultural agreement. An executive agreement rather than a treaty, the cultural agreement did not require Senate ratification. During the negotiations, committees of the two delegations addressed the specific features of a broad-based cultural exchange agreement point-by-point. Dulles himself did not take part in the negotiations. In the final agreement, Soviet and American negotiators came to terms on reciprocal exchanges of radio and television broadcasts, feature and documentary films, students and professors, artists and writers, scientists and agricultural experts, athletes, youth, and civic groups. The exchanges of students, instructors, and professors would be the first of their kind during the Cold War.[6]

The two sides agreed "in principle" to establish direct air connections from New York to Moscow, although the details were to be worked out in subsequent negotiations. Similarly, both sides agreed "in principle to the usefulness of exhibits as an effective means of developing mutual understanding" and made specific plans for reciprocal atomic energy displays. In addition to agreeing to exchange publications in such fields as health and industry, both sides pledged to maintain circulation of *Amerika* and *USSR* "on the basis of reciprocity."[7]

What at first appeared as a victory for the Soviets actually may well have proven to be one of the most successful initiatives in the history of U.S. Cold War diplomacy. To be sure, negotiations toward the cultural agreement (as it became known) proceeded along lines laid down by the Kremlin. The USSR had achieved its main goal, an exchange program that would enhance Soviet capabilities in agriculture, industry, medical, and technical fields. Under terms of the final agreement, Zarubin successfully fended off Washington's efforts to reach the Soviet people through uncensored press, radio, and television broadcasts. Agreed-upon broadcast subjects were confined to science, technology, industry, agriculture, education, public health, and sports, as well as musical, literary, and theatrical productions. Broadcasts concerning "international political problems" were subject to further negotiations. In any case, the texts for such broadcasts would be exchanged in advance and programs could be canceled by either side on grounds—obviously subject to broad interpretation—that they would not "contribute to the betterment of relations."[8]

The cultural agreement provided the Kremlin with evidence to cite against Western charges that it maintained an Iron Curtain against the penetration of ideas. Moreover, the accord provided the Soviets with a sense of legitimacy, a recognition in the eyes of its arch rival that the USSR was a great power whose interests had to be acknowledged. Washington, appearing to have less to gain, could now say that it had not foreclosed all channels of negotiation with the

Soviets. But in the absence of widespread support for negotiations with the USSR, the State Department played the cultural agreement on a very low key.[9]

It was true, as critics pointed out, that Washington had failed to achieve its pre-summit goals of forcing an end to Soviet jamming. *Time* noted that when measured against "the U.S. government's original minimum conditions," the cultural agreement "left much to be desired." More apropos, however, was Lyndon Johnson's comment that the cultural agreement marked the "beginning of a beginning."[10] It was the first of a series of continuing two-year agreements that provided for the regular infiltration of American culture into the heart of the Soviet empire. From that point forward, despite a series of fits and starts, from crises to conferences, cultural exchange endured as one of the most stable elements of U.S.-Soviet relations.[11]

The cultural agreement—the first Soviet-American bilateral accord of the postwar era—provided tangible evidence of the shift in U.S. policy from aggressive psychological warfare to an evolutionary approach to undermine the Soviet empire. "Liberation" remained the end, but the means, as well as the timetable, had been adjusted in the wake of the failure of psychological warfare. By pursuing a gradualist agenda, Washington increased its ability to appeal to the peoples behind the Iron Curtain on the basis of the allure of Western ideas, symbols, and consumer culture.

The cultural agreement infused a new spirit of cooperation that led to a breakthrough in the long impasse on Soviet-American film exchange. The Eisenhower administration had long sought Hollywood's cooperation in efforts to revive a moribund film export program with the USSR. Hollywood films, highly popular among the Soviet people during World War II, had been barred from importation since the mid-1940s. In October 1953, psychological warriors had concluded that "the sale of motion pictures to the Soviets would make a contribution to U.S. foreign policy provided certain safeguards could be met." Harrison Salisbury, the *New York Times* Moscow correspondent, reported that U.S. films shown in the USSR offered "a good way to keep the picture of the American way of life alive in Russia." Classic films such as *Mr. Smith Goes to Washington* and the Tarzan stories were showing to "packed audiences" in the USSR, Salisbury reported. "They still show many, many older American pictures and I am a very strong advocate of our selling Hollywood pictures to Moscow under certain conditions."[12]

Charles Bohlen, the ambassador in Moscow, affirmed Salisbury's conclusions on the basis of embassy observations about the popularity of American films. Diplomats in Moscow reported that U.S. film clips appeared on Soviet television "more often than those of any other country." Among subjects favored most by Soviet audiences were "horse races, figure skaters, dolphins playing basketball at the Florida Marine studios, [and a] coed hoop-racing contest." Also popular were "get acquainted" clips on U.S. cities and regions, theater exhibits, sports and recreation, and fashion shows. The latter, reported a U.S. diplomat in Moscow, were "currently a lively topic in Moscow for the British have put on a fashion show with British models which has scored a great public relations success."[13]

As momentum built for an effort to resume sale of U.S. films to the Soviets, Hollywood responded with a noticeable lack of enthusiasm. Eric Johnston, president of the Motion Picture Association of America (MPAA), explained that studio executives anticipated more problems than profits in reopening the Soviet market. He added, however, that "if such sales were to be judged as an important contribution to American foreign policy, this would of course greatly influence our eventual decision." While urging the MPAA to pursue a new arrangement with Moscow, Eisenhower administration officials warned of the need for "a careful selection of pictures . . . bearing in mind that the subject matter should be of such a nature as to make it difficult for the Soviet Government to distort basic content or dialogue for propaganda purposes." The administration advised Johnston that Washington intended to "suggest criteria that might be used in the selection of specific films, furnish opinions on the probable effects of specific films, cooperate in the establishment and implementation of monitoring safeguards, and advise on the drawing up of contracts."[14]

On January 29, 1958, two days after the signing of the new cultural agreement, the State Department announced that Johnston had accepted its request to lead the film industry in negotiations for "the sale and purchase of U.S. and Soviet theatrical motion pictures." Discussions with *Sovietexportfilm* made progress at first, but by spring the negotiations "suddenly froze up," with the Soviets citing "the costs involved." The Kremlin complained that Washington's refusal to buy as many Soviet films as Americans were selling to Moscow reflected "disrespect for Russian films." After extensive follow-up discussions in Moscow in September and October, however, an agreement emerged under section VII of the cultural agreement on exchange of films. Johnston and the Soviets agreed on the sale and purchase of feature films, the exchange of documentaries, the holding film weeks and film premieres, and the joint production of features and documentaries. The Soviets agreed to begin distributing ten American films—*Roman Holiday, The Old Man and the Sea,* and *Oklahoma* among them—while Washington agreed to market seven Soviet films, including *The Idiot, Don Quixote,* and *Swan Lake.* Both sides pledged "maximum commercial distribution" and "wide publicity," including a premiere for the opening night of the first film in each country. Along with the agreement on feature films, Johnston and his Soviet counterparts agreed to exchange 15 documentaries and made plans to conduct ongoing negotiations through a standing committee on film distribution.[15]

While eager to view films and documentaries, Soviet citizens responded with even greater enthusiasm to performances by American artists. A talented young pianist from Texas, Van Cliburn, made the most dramatic impact when he mesmerized Soviet audiences in capturing the Tchaikovsky International Piano Competition in Moscow in April 1958. By allowing Cliburn to win the competition, CPSU officials—who had been known to influence the outcome of such events—offered a gesture of friendship and a signal of official receptivity to American culture. Cliburn had made a "tremendous impression on the Soviet public and officials," including Khrushchev, who attended the ceremonial concert. Drawing rave reviews, repeated standing ovations, and streams of shrieking followers, Cliburn had "done much to disabuse the Moscow public of the impression that the U.S. is backward culturally." *Time* gushed that Cliburn's triumph was nothing less than an "American sputnik."[16]

More than an appreciation of musical talent, Cliburn's reception was something of a cultural phenomenon in the USSR. The huge crowds, throngs of disappointed ticket seekers, and prolonged ovations were virtually unprecedented. Cliburn's appearance generated "a kind of mass hysteria," U.S. analysts reported, especially among "females between the ages of 15 and 65." The excited response of the Soviet women to the tall, slender Texan had "very little to do with Mr. Cliburn's considerable abilities as a pianist." An embassy diplomat explained that Cliburn could have played "Chopsticks" and the Soviet women would still have shrieked "Vania, Vania," thrown flowers, tugged at his clothes, and stood for hours in front of his hotel.[17]

U.S. officials worried that Cliburn would allow his popular acclaim in the USSR to "go to his head," turning a cultural triumph into a propaganda disaster. They displayed alarm when Cliburn expressed himself as "quite laudatory of his reception and stay in the Soviet Union," adding that he planned to return to Moscow for "a long vacation." The State Department advised diplomats in Moscow that Cliburn was "likely to make some very unwise statements if queried on political matters, about which he knows very little." Fearing that Cliburn may even have been "approached" by the Soviets, the State Department advised Ambassador Llewelyn Thompson to have a talk with the young musician about Soviet propaganda motives. After discussing the matter with Cliburn, Thompson offered reassurance, and Washington's exaggerated fears never materialized.[18]

U.S. officials were far more concerned about the socialist tendencies of Paul Robeson, the talented African-American performer who made repeated trips to the USSR. Robeson received a frenzied public welcome when he arrived in Moscow in August 1958. Enthusiastic, bouquet-throwing crowds greeted Robeson and his wife at each stop on their tour of Soviet Central Asia, the Caucusus, and the Crimea. Robeson's pro-Sovietism made him a target for FBI surveillance, State Department travel restrictions, and other forms of harassment that eventually contributed to his emotional instability.[19]

While crowds flocked to Robeson, far greater numbers of Soviets attended performances by nonpolitical purveyors of U.S. popular culture. "Holiday on Ice," Bob Hope, and the Harlem Globetrotters were among the more popular American shows in the USSR in 1959.

Less celebrated than these main events, but valued especially by Eisenhower, was a provision in the cultural agreement for a regular program of academic exchanges. Several U.S. academicians had been promoting the idea since the first Geneva conference. At that time, however, Livingston Merchant, assistant secretary of state, expressed "instinctive revulsion" against receiving Soviets "in one of our great universities in residence for a year when we know that they would be carefully selected . . . to represent a philosophy which is dedicated to our destruction." Despite the initial State Department opposition, academics and various university student organizations, as well as diplomats in the Moscow embassy, continued to press for educational exchange with the USSR.[20]

Eisenhower advocated East-West student exchange "in the interest of accelerating the awakening of Russia." The cultural agreement authorized student exchanges, but in 1958-59 only 20 students, representing Columbia, Harvard, Moscow, and Leningrad universities, participated. Eisenhower averred that he would be "happier if we could implement a program of getting some of these contacts based upon thousands rather than upon scores." The president favored a "massive" program and considered proposing to the Kremlin an annual exchange of 10,000 students. After discussing the issue in Washington in January 1959, Eisenhower and Khrushchev's deputy, Anastas Mikoyan, agreed that the annual student exchange should number "several hundred." However, Mikoyan declared that the exchanges would remain small as long as the USSR remained "suspicious" that they "would be used for other purposes than study. If they were real students this was all right but if they were agents it is another matter." At this point Eisenhower interrupted to assure Mikoyan that Washington would not "take an 18 year old student and make an intelligence agent out of him."[21]

The president's disclaimer notwithstanding, the CIA had in fact made spies, both foreign and domestic, out of 18-year olds in the National Students' Association. The CIA covertly funded the international activities of the student organization, which also happened to be one of the groups lobbying for increased U.S.-Soviet student exchanges. Although Mikoyan's concerns may have been well-grounded, both men probably knew that youthful spies would be included in a delegation of exchange students. In the end, Eisenhower and Mikoyan deferred discussion of an expanded student exchange program.[22]

Eisenhower confronted American as well as Soviet suspicions in his quest to increase the scope of East-West student exchange. Rather than pursuing his own inclinations to the end, the president decided to "put the idea out for consideration of his principal advisers and if they did not like it, he would just forget about it." Displaying little enthusiasm for the proposal, John Foster Dulles expressed concern about the security implications of hundreds of potential Soviets agents in the United States. Financial considerations were also at issue: because of the ruble exchange rate, Washington would pay roughly twice as much to support its students in the USSR as the Soviets would their students in the United States. FBI director J. Edgar Hoover told Eisenhower that a larger exchange program would require increased security measures, but that "it was well worth it" in view of the benefits of exposing Soviet students to American life. After running the proposal through the bureaucracy, Eisenhower found that "the comments that had reached him were about 50-50 in praise and criticism."[23]

A year later Eisenhower remained "quite excited at the possible effect of an American indoctrination of 10,000 young Russian students in any given year." In view of Mikoyan's reservations about accepting large numbers of U.S. students, the President considered making a unilateral offer to accept thousands of Soviet students. USIA director George Allen advised, however, that the program should remain reciprocal or the Soviets would dismiss it as a propaganda gambit. None of the nine advisers Eisenhower solicited in the spring of 1959 believed the Soviets would accept a stepped-up exchange program. At the same time, U.S. colleges and universities reported record enrollments, complicating any proposal to accept thousands of additional students. Despite his fervent desire to increase Soviet exposure to the West through sharply increased student exchange, Eisenhower abandoned the issue.[24]

While the number of U.S. students in the USSR remained small, the early pioneers established a precedent that would continue throughout the Cold War. The failure to increase the scope of the student exchange program revealed the limitations of the cultural agreement, yet it was beginning to make an impact nonetheless. In the first 18 months after the signing of the two-year agreement, 1,674 Americans in 107 delegations traveled to the USSR, while 1,637 Soviets involved in 100 projects came to the United States. The two powers conducted reciprocal exchanges in science, technology, education, athletics, film, and the performing arts. The Kremlin allowed relatively few Soviet tourists to visit the

United States, but American Express opened an office in Moscow to facilitate the increased flow of Americans to the USSR.[25]

Most Americans who visited the USSR on exchange programs received a warm Russian welcome, although several complained about restrictions on their movements, including refusals of requests to visit certain sites. Such restrictions occurred on both sides, however, as reflected in a protest by the President's Science Advisory Committee, which complained that restrictions placed on Soviet scientists were inimical to the spirit of the exchange program. While often critical of the Soviets for exercising state authority over the exchange programs, Washington made plans to brief U.S. participants on "the broader political purposes of the exchange." The State Department offered an "estimate the propaganda value" in deciding which groups and individuals would participate. For example, U.S. officials decided against sending a ballet troupe to the USSR "because American ballet is not up to the Soviet level." Instead, Washington selected the Philadelphia Orchestra, "which is far better than any the Russians have."[26]

Still slow to grasp the full potential of direct East-West contacts, Washington failed to capitalize fully on the opportunities presented by the sixth World Festival of Youth and Students, held in Moscow from July 28 to August 11, 1957. Some 30,000 young people in their twenties and thirties—including communists as well as the merely curious—converged in Moscow from all over the world. While they interacted with about twice that many Soviet youths, the recorded music of Louis Armstrong and Ella Fitzgerald blared over loudspeakers. At the officially sanctioned concert, featuring jazz and rock music, the crowd mobbed the stage, requiring the Soviets to summon dozens of police to maintain order.[27]

The Moscow youth festival marked a turning point in Soviet cultural history. After years of attempting to fight off just these sorts of cultural influences, the Kremlin welcomed 30,000 young people into the Soviet capital. The Soviet public received unprecedented exposure to Western youth, music, fashion, consumer goods, ideas, and political perspectives. The festival left a permanent cultural imprint, as Soviet and East European youth adopted Western expressions, such as "See ya later, alligator," sang "Love Potion Number 9," and called themselves *shtatniki*, for the States, or *bitniki* (beatniks).[28]

Oblivious to the Soviet hunger for contact with Western youth and the culture they represented, Dulles opposed American participation on grounds that the festival served as "an instrument of communist propaganda." That much was true: since 1947 CP front organizations had sponsored the biennial youth festivals. Employing traditional Cold War logic, the State Department reasoned that if the Soviets were spending more than $20 million to mount a successful festival, "it is obviously not in our interest to help them succeed." The State Department warned that it "frowned on" Americans attending the festival, but made no formal attempt to impede them. According to *New York Times* correspondent Max Frankel, some of the 160 Americans in Moscow displayed a sympathy for communism that ranged from "friendly to fervent," but most "were there simply because they could not resist a bargain-rate trip to Russia."[29]

What Dulles had failed to anticipate was that the American youths in Moscow would serve to combat Soviet propaganda while furthering the process of cultural infiltration. Taking advantage of a more relaxed atmosphere under Khrushchev, Soviet youth had already become accustomed to approaching Western tourists. Through the clothes they wore, the music they played and discussed, and the very language they spoke, the Americans attracted the attention of thousands of young people from the CP regimes who attended the festival. Several Americans recounted conversations in which crowds gathered as they challenged the Soviet interpretation of the Hungarian invasion. In the course of myriad "sidewalk seminars" and "bull sessions," the Americans also offered a more hopeful assessment of their country's racial progress than *Pravda* typically provided. Some of the American youths served as conduits, agreeing to carry letters out of the country for relatives abroad. Concluding that the Americans had made a lasting impression at the Moscow festival, Frankel wrote that "when the United States next complains about jamming of the Voice of America, it might well ask, 'Who jammed whom in Moscow?'"[30]

Two years later, Washington exploited the seventh biennial youth festival in Vienna to gather intelligence on the progress of the campaign of cultural infiltration. USIA officials perceived the festival as offering "a really exceptional opportunity to get some knowledge of radio listening and associated attitudes in communist countries and the hard-to-research underdeveloped countries." U.S. officials recruited several Americans who attended the Vienna festival to report on the attitudes of youth from the CP regimes, glean reactions to VOA broadcasts, and "talk with some real live Georgians, Armenians, Albanians, Chinese, maybe even Uzbeks and North Koreans."[31]

Although acclaimed by its organizers as a tremendous success, the Vienna festival was "torn with strife from the outset," the USIA reported. Various delegations, including the American, were riven with disputes between communist and non-communist factions. Thus, in contrast with the Moscow festival two years earlier, officials concluded that "the U.S. policy of not actively discouraging participation of individual American young persons contributed to lessening the impact of the festival."[32]

In the wake of the cultural agreement, both public and private activities expanded to facilitate greater East-West contact. On June 15, 1959, the State

Department established a Bureau of Intercultural Relations in recognition of the expanded role of cultural diplomacy. Washington also created a new position of counselor for cultural affairs at the U.S. embassy in Moscow. In 1959, 10,000 to 15,000 Americans visited the USSR, approximately twice the number who had toured the previous year. The Soviets facilitated the increased numbers of American tourists by processing visa requests with unprecedented efficiency.[33]

More attuned to the potential benefits of direct contacts than most of his subordinates, Eisenhower longed to stage something that would make a "spectacular" impact on Soviet society.[34] That opportunity came, after protracted negotiations, when the Soviets agreed to reciprocal exchange of national exhibitions, authorized by Article XIII of the cultural agreement. Under its provisions, the Soviets would stage an exhibition in New York in June and July 1959. Although well conceived and smoothly executed, the Soviet exhibition had little hope of fundamentally altering American mass perceptions of the USSR. The same could not be said of the American National Exhibition in Moscow later the same summer.

Soviet-American negotiations culminated on September 10, 1958, with a protocol agreement on reciprocal national exhibitions to be "devoted to the demonstration of the development of each of its science, technology, and culture." Details remained to be worked out. Shortly thereafter, the Soviets made a downpayment on the New York City Coliseum in midtown Manhattan. Negotiations aimed at securing a site and financial arrangements for the U.S. exhibition in Moscow proved far more challenging.[35]

While noting that negotiations with the Soviets would prove difficult, Eisenhower seized upon the opportunity to mount an exhibition of U.S. culture in the Soviet capital. Dulles, too, endorsed the initiative, observing that the Moscow exhibition might achieve "a breakthrough as regards U.S.-Russian people-to-people relationships." Eisenhower charged USIA director Allen with overall responsibility for the national exhibition. "It is a rare opportunity," the President told Allen and his deputy, Abbott Washburn, who worked full time on planning for the exhibition.

Eisenhower resolutely supported efforts to mount an impressive cultural display in Moscow. "There wasn't any question but what he saw immediately . . . an opportunity to tell several million average [Soviet] citizens directly the story of the United States, in a way that you could reach these people effectively," Washburn recalled. The president promised the USIA leaders that he would provide "all the help you need" and proved to be "as good as his word." Throughout the process of planning and staging the exhibition, Eisenhower "assisted us personally in getting the cooperation and liaison with all the other elements of government."[36]

Allen and Washburn shared the president's view that a U.S. exhibition in Moscow represented a unique opportunity to have a direct impact on the Soviet masses. Allen noted that widespread listening to Western radio, despite jamming, and the popularity of USIA's *Amerika* magazine reflected "the interest of the Russian people in things American—in anything foreign, but particularly in things American." An exhibition would be popular among the Soviet people while providing Washington with an opportunity to "try to correct the misunderstandings of the Russian people about the United States" through cultural interchange. Allen concluded that USIA possessed "abundant evidence—I don't think there can be any two views on the question—that there is a great eagerness on the part of the Russian people to find out about the United States."[37]

On the basis of a recommendation from Eisenhower, among others, Allen made his most important decision in planning for the Moscow fair by appointing businessman Harold Chadwick "Chad" McClellan as general manager of the exhibition. A World War I veteran, McClellan was chief executive of the Old Colony Paint and Chemical Co. of Los Angeles and a former president of the National Association of Manufacturers. He had been among a group of prominent southern California businessmen who had been instrumental in orchestrating the move of the Brooklyn Dodgers to Los Angeles in 1958. McClellan also had experience in government, having served as assistant secretary of commerce, a role that found him promoting U.S. exhibits in CP regimes. With a rare combination of extensive business experience, government connections, negotiating skills, and tireless devotion to the project, McClellan proved a brilliant choice to spearhead the exhibition.[38]

Diplomats in Moscow shared the enthusiasm of Eisenhower, McClellan, and the USIA leadership for the American exhibition. The embassy staff had already observed "intense interest on the part of all of our Soviet contacts." Ambassador Llewellyn "Tommy" Thompson, who postponed a home leave to remain in Moscow for the opening of the exhibition, declared that "nothing we have ever done will have the impact on Soviet developments that this exhibition will have if we do it right." Thompson told Allen that he was "much impressed with the way McClellan and his team have tackled the negotiations" in Moscow.[39]

Sent to Moscow to secure an agreement on the U.S. exhibition, McClellan soon began to think he would never leave the Soviet capital. He had expected to stay in Moscow a few days to sign the agreement, but remained for three weeks instead. "Negotiations have been very difficult," McClellan reported from Moscow. "I've been in many tough negotiations—and the moments put in by the Soviet team match the best. I think we'll get a deal," he added, "but it's still touch and go."[40]

The initial stumbling block proved to be the site of the exhibition. The United States accepted the Soviet offer of Gorkii Park in the September protocol agreement, but later learned the park was to be occupied until 30 days before the exhibition. Upon visiting the site, the Americans also concluded that its physical structures failed to meet the needs of the exhibition. McClellan rejected Gorkii Park and the next two sites offered by the Soviets as well. "They first tried to put us over in left field, and then in right field, and then over the back fence," McClellan recalled. Finally, however, the two sides agreed on Sokolniki Park, a 1,500-acre wooded recreational park 15 minutes by subway from the center of Moscow. Negotiations continued concerning structures the United States planned to build on the 400,000-square-foot site allotted for the exhibition. After much wrangling, the Soviets agreed that at the close of the exhibition they would purchase the 30,000-square-foot geodesic dome that would be the centerpiece of the exhibition. On November 9 McClellan announced that a tentative agreement had been concluded.[41]

In explaining terms at the White House upon his return to Washington, McClellan expressed pride in the agreement on the exchange of exhibitions. "If you can find another document between the United States and the Soviets since 1917 which has as its premise mutual trust, confidence, and cooperation, without censorship of film or written line, I would like to see it."[42] McClellan's optimism proved short lived, however. When Soviet officials arrived in Washington to discuss details and conclude a formal contract, sharp disagreements surfaced. Astonished to find "how far we still were from agreement," McClellan prepared for another round of tedious negotiations.

In almost daily meetings from December 12 to 24, U.S. and Soviet negotiators discussed virtually every aspect of planning for the reciprocal exhibitions. The meetings, often punctuated by "vigorous disagreement," sometimes lasted well into the night. While Washington generally accommodated plans for the New York exhibition, the Soviets mounted a point-by-point challenge to American plans. "The smallest detail was time and again the cause for long discussion," reported an exasperated McClellan. Even before they took on the major displays, the Soviets challenged plans for the distribution of souvenirs, samples, pamphlets and exhibit literature, the operations of concessions, proposed operating hours, and the days the exhibition would be held. According to McClellan, the Soviets reversed their positions on these issues, which had been tentatively agreed upon in Moscow.[43]

The shift in the Soviet negotiating posture may have reflected rising East-West tensions as a result of Khrushchev's "Berlin ultimatum." On November 10, the Soviet leader had announced plans to sign a peace treaty with East Germany, granting the CP regime the right to cut off Western access to Berlin.

Although he had consolidated his power over the "Anti-Party Group" led by Malenkov and Molotov, Khrushchev confronted continuing opposition to his policy of "peaceful coexistence" with the West. The NATO decision to place medium-range nuclear missiles in Western Europe had only served to encourage Soviet and Chinese hardliners. Khrushchev's Berlin ultimatum, immediately rejected by the West, may have been the product of political debate in the socialist camp, as well as a sincere desire to resolve the anomalous status of the former German capital. Whatever the rationale, the Berlin ultimatum ranks as one of Khrushchev's most serious mistakes. The ultimatum created a war scare in the West, whose leaders were already jittery over the *Sputnik* launch. Khrushchev's action empowered the very forces in the West that he most wanted to contain: proponents of the mythical "missile gap," which held that the Soviet nuclear arsenal was outpacing the West's. In reality, the opposite was true.[44]

East-West tensions over Berlin and the nuclear arms race may have led to some degree of reconsideration in Moscow over the wisdom of allowing an American cultural display in the Soviet capital. U.S. and Soviet negotiators found themselves far apart on central issues such as plans for performing arts, motion picture and slide displays, and even the purchase of buildings at Sokolniki, all of which McClellan thought previously had been agreed upon in Moscow. "It seemed almost impossible to find a meeting of minds on these issues," McClellan recalled. In the midst of sometimes heated exchanges, both sides accused the other of changing positions. When Soviet negotiators demanded that the United States abandon plans to present performing artists and film and slide shows, McClellan responded with an ultimatum. Reminding the Soviets that "this is supposed to be a cultural as well as scientific and techno- logical exhibition," he threatened to pull out unless these two "essentials" remained. "My government may overrule me," he averred, "but I doubt it." As the Soviets conferred among themselves, it appeared that both exhibitions might well be canceled. On December 29, however, five days after McClellan issued his ultimatum, the Soviets accepted his terms and signed in the State Depart- ment the final agreement on the exchange of exhibitions.[45]

Under the agreement both sides pledged to consult one another and to employ "flexibility and discretion" in mounting their exhibitions in the rival capital. The Americans won the right to show slides and motion pictures with the provision that they be "cultural and non political in character." The agreement sanctioned reciprocal performances authorized under the cultural agreement, or as "mutually agreed" upon by both sides. The Soviets agreed to purchase the buildings constructed at Sokolniki Park as well as to provide the necessary landscaping, site preparation, utility hook-ups, fencing, and gates. Each side would charge admission and had the right to distribute programs and publications pertaining to the exhibition. A buffet or cafeteria featuring typical national foods would be established at each exhibition.[46]

The practical nature of the reciprocal exchange, rather than the "high degree of trust and cooperation" to which the agreement referred, would ensure that its terms were followed. As the State Department's William Lacy put it, "they understand that any monkey shines played on our people, in Sokolniki, will undoubtedly result in funny things happening at the coliseum" in New York. Although both sides understood that the reciprocal exhibitions would serve as a battleground in the Cold War, they reached a mutual understanding on the need for restraint. The Soviets abandoned formal provisions for censorship but only on the basis of "a gentleman's agreement that neither side will get into anything political."[47]

The Soviets surprised George Allen, among others, with their willingness to enter into an agreement at all. The USIA director concluded that the Kremlin was feeling confident in the wake of a successful exhibition in Brussels, but McClellan discerned a more telling motive. Based on his stay in the USSR "and having talked with these fellows, and having had a drink or two with them, and having them as my guests at my own home," McClellan concluded that the Kremlin leaders hoped to use the example of the American exhibition to spur economic progress in the USSR. "They want us to serve, out of what we exhibit, as catalysts to their own Russian people, to produce things in Russia which they need and do not now enjoy," McClellan explained. "This was a shocking surprise to me. They want to push them a bit, to show it can be done." A second overarching Soviet motive, McClellan believed, was to use the reciprocal exhibitions to "open up travel and trade patterns" with the West. "The Russians want to trade with us. . . . There is a real interest in trying to find a way to do business."[48]

While the Soviets hoped that the rival exhibition would spur their own economic development, Washington sought to exploit an unprecedented opportunity for propaganda and cultural infiltration of the USSR. The primary motive on the U.S. side, according to a classified policy guidance document, was to "increase the knowledge of the Soviet people about the United States" to counter "communist fiction." The primary theme to carry out this objective was "freedom of choice and expression." The U.S. exhibition would emphasize "the unimpeded flow of diverse goods and ideas" as the "sources of American cultural and economic achievements." The United States would portray itself as "progressive" and "dynamic," "free" and "creative," "peace-loving" and "well-rounded." As it had done in the Brussels World's Fair the previous year, Washington planned to present examples of deficiencies in American society with evidence of progress and amelioration. The Moscow exhibition

The President and Secretary of State John Foster Dulles flank Llewellyn "Tommy" Thompson, U.S. ambassador to Moscow from 1957 to 1962. Dulles lacked the President's enthusiasm for propaganda and cultural initiatives. After Dulles's death, Thompson played a prominent role in staging the American National Exhibition in Moscow in the summer of 1959. (Courtesy Wide World Photos, Inc.)

represented "the best opportunity it has yet had to reach a highly important target audience, including the politically alert and potentially most influential citizens of the Soviet Union."[49]

The confidential policy guidelines called for caution in cultivating support from the American public. "No propaganda operation of the U.S. government since the war will be under as intense a spotlight of press, public, and congressional attention as will this exhibit," the policy statement averred. Accordingly, it would be prudent "to take into account the advice and suggestions of leading American groups and individuals in planning the contents of the Exhibit." Plans called for keeping the American public fully informed about plans for the exhibition, but only "to the extent that this does not jeopardize the carrying out of the policy."[50]

Responding to the proposed guidelines from Moscow, Ambassador Thompson warned that "propaganda objectives" should remain submerged lest they undermine the "explosive effect" and "incalculable benefit" he anticipated would result from the exhibition. For Thompson, the primary focus of the exhibition should be to "endeavor to make the Soviet people dissatisfied with the share of the Russian pie which they now receive and make them realize that the slight improvements projected in their standard of living are only a drop in the bucket to what they could and should have." He advised caution in promoting freedom of choice and expression, explaining that if carried too far this theme "would constitute a direct attack upon the Soviet system." Thompson urged careful handling of plans to exhibit the flaws of American society, as this was "not a technique to which the Soviet people are accustomed and could have the effect of merely confirming charges made about the U.S. by Soviet propaganda."[51]

Moscow embassy diplomats familiar with Soviet life agreed with Thompson that an emphasis on consumerism would prove most effective. The Soviet public would display intense interest in items such as American shoes, clothing, reading material, and records, all of which sold for high prices on the black market. Also effective would be a food display that would "dramatically present American food purchasing methods and packaging, variety of prepared and ready to eat products (not dreamed of here), and attention to consumer wants." Washington should supply "as many Sears Roebuck, Montgomery Ward, and other catalogs as possible," allow them to "disappear," and replenish stocks with additional supplies. One diplomat reported that Sears and Roebuck catalogs were being sold on the black market for 75 rubles—almost $20, a vast sum in the USSR at the time. Above all, the Moscow diplomats advised, Washington should "avoid ethnocentric attitudes" that might "offend mass sensibilities . . . while still making it clear that a free society has great advantages over a non-free one."[52]

The Moscow diplomats' recommendations, most of which McClellan embraced, included providing "reaction books" where fair-goers could record their comments on the exhibition. The diplomats endorsed plans to set up voting booths, which Eisenhower himself had ordered included in the Brussels exhibition, as well as a music section with several jukeboxes featuring "the latest (but non-extremist) records." The travel section would make a strong impression if it "emphasized the freedom of movement in the U.S." Finally, the embassy officers advised that the Soviets, known for doting on their children, would respond to a display of children's clothes and a model playground.[53]

To coordinate planning, McClellan established the Office of the American National Exhibition in Moscow in Washington. Working closely with

McClellan were USIA's Washburn and, representing the State Department, Lacy and assistant secretary of state Andrew Berding. Thompson and the Moscow embassy diplomats continued to advise the group, which reported periodically to a presidential advisory committee. By quickly winning virtually everyone's confidence, McClellan gained "wide latitude" as the unquestioned leader of the U.S. effort. One official referred to the "general agreement that Mr. McClellan was doing a good job under a very tough time schedule."[54]

The high level of cooperation achieved between Eisenhower, McClellan, USIA, and the State and Commerce departments reflected the growing consensus behind cultural initiatives in the late Eisenhower years. The national security bureaucracy united behind the effort to put forth a favorable image of the United States in the Soviet capital. Absent from the deliberations were the bureaucratic and jurisdictional disputes that had sometimes plagued previous efforts to exhibit U.S. culture abroad. Both Eisenhower's strong support, and perhaps the absence of Dulles as well, encouraged the high level of bureaucratic cooperation. Although he had endorsed the idea of the exhibition, Dulles had always been determined to ensure State Department primacy in the national security bureaucracy, an attitude that may well have impeded a cooperative effort on the Moscow fair. Stricken with cancer, Dulles took a leave of absence in February 1959 and played no role in the planning of the exhibition.

Congress remained parsimonious, authorizing only $3.6 million, all but $300,000 in Mutual Security Administration funds, for the unprecedented overseas exhibit in the Soviet capital. Given the funding limitations, McClellan concluded that the success of the exhibition depended on generating the rapid and enthusiastic support of private business and industry. U.S. officials would have to appeal to businessmen on patriotic grounds, since they were unlikely to realize a profit from their participation in the Moscow exhibition.[55]

Eisenhower, McClellan, and his deputies launched their appeal at a White House luncheon for a newly appointed advisory committee of 51 leaders of industry, science, education, and the arts. The exhibition planners appealed to the corporate executives on the basis of the rare opportunity to encourage the progressive evolution of Soviet society by appealing directly to the people. By displaying U.S. productivity in Moscow, Washington could increase respect for the West as well promote "a greater demand on the part of the Soviet citizens for products" available only to Western consumers. Increased Soviet demand for consumer goods would "lower the possibility of production for either heavy industry or, and more particularly, for war purposes." While the potential impact on Soviet society could be far-reaching, success or failure of the effort depended to a significant degree on the willingness of business and industry to underwrite the costs of the exhibition by donating facilities and equipment.

"We are not just here to have you tell us we are doing a good job," McClellan told the group. "We are running scared."[56]

More than any other initiative in the Eisenhower years, the Moscow exhibition made a reality of the president's vision of harnessing business and industry to complement the nation's overseas cultural policy.[57] As talks continued at the White House after the luncheon, it became "obvious that the whole exhibition idea appealed to the advisory committee members and that their cooperation would be forthcoming in generous measure thereafter." The business community offered suggestions, samples of their products, pamphlets, and brochures. More substantially, some major manufacturers agreed to supply exhibits and to pay the freight to Moscow as well.[58]

Taken as a whole, the response of the business community was unprecedented. Following a trip to Detroit, McClellan and Washburn secured a complete underwriting of an automobile show in Moscow, including seven staff cars for their own use and transportation both ways for equipment and service personnel. RCA agreed to assume half the costs for installation and operation of "a complete color television studio." American Express underwrote a travel exhibit. General Mills, General Foods, Grand Union, and other companies signed on to provide food displays and demonstrations. Outjockeying the competition from its Atlanta-based rival, Pepsi-Cola offered free soft drinks, installations, transportation, and personnel. Dixie Cup Co. agreed to provide "several million" paper cups in which to serve the soft drinks.

A substantial contribution came from IBM, which donated its RAMAC "electronic brain" computer as it had done for the Brussels exhibition. Publisher McGraw-Hill agreed to supply more than 20,000 books. Other significant contributions included a model home and designs for the fashion show. When it became clear that the number of exhibitions planned could not be made to fit into the two principal buildings at Sokolniki, McClellan and Washburn summoned 25 representatives from the plastics industry to the White House, at which time Eisenhower appeared with a request for a minimum $125,000 pledge to support construction of canopies. All but one plastics supplier acceded to the president's request. Other donations included contributions ranging from $5,000 to tens of thousands of dollars from companies such as Sears, Kaiser, Whirlpool, Macy's, Singer, Kodak, and DuPont. In all, some 450 companies contributed to the effort in Moscow. The president's son, John S. Eisenhower, observed that "the generosity and cooperation provided by American business in support of this exhibition is, in my judgment, without precedent."[59]

Gratified by the response of corporate America, McClellan and his deputies still confronted a "cruel" timetable. "We had about six months to mount an extremely complex and large exhibition," Washburn recalled, "and it seemed like an almost foolhardy thing to try to do in the time available." Quickly abandoning visions of a gala July 4 unveiling of the exhibition, U.S. officials struggled to arrange an opening night before the August 2 deadline established under the protocol agreement. Building construction in Sokolniki began in December, but progress depended on the arrival of prefabricated structures from Helsinki, Finland. "This is a show, my friends, which we will not know whether or not will be opened until it is opened," McClellan observed.[60]

Following a visit to Sokolniki in February, a relieved McClellan found Soviet cooperation "at a very high point." Workers had cleared the site, begun construction, and displayed full cooperation. Planning and construction reached a feverish stage by late spring, with a July 24 opening now firmly established. McClellan had assumed almost total authority over the exhibition and continued to win praise from virtually all concerned. Typical was a report to the State Department, which noted that McClellan had "done an extraordinarily competent job of organizing, expediting, and arranging for the construction of what promises to be an extremely impressive and important exhibition."[61]

As the Americans continued to implement plans for Sokolniki, the Soviets prepared to open their own exhibition—their first on U.S. soil since the 1939 New York World's Fair. CPSU directives charged the Soviet Ministry of Foreign Trade to "make sure the exhibition opens on time and is conducted at a high standard." The Soviets publicized the fair, which featured some 10,000 exhibits on science, technology, and culture, in Western magazines and over Radio Moscow. Eisenhower became the first American in the door and spent more than an hour touring all three floors of displays of Soviet achievements in science, industrial and consumer production, education, and the arts. The president spent most of his time admiring paintings in the arts section. Soviet deputy premier Frol Kozlov escorted Eisenhower and later attended a speech by Nixon marking the opening of the Soviet exhibition. Throughout his stay in the United States, Kozlov emphasized the Kremlin's desire for increased trade and "peaceful coexistence" with the West.[62]

Unlike the U.S. exhibition, which would attempt to wow the masses with consumer goods, the Soviet display emphasized machinery, science, and technology. Computers, farm machinery, and televisions were featured. Playing the October 1957 *Sputnik* launch for its maximum propaganda value, the Soviets suspended several model satellites from the ceiling of the coliseum. "Even though the inferiority of some of the consumer goods to ours is all too obvious," observed Christian Herter, Dulles's replacement as secretary of state, "it remains a fascinating and convincing show. Those sputniks suspended from the ceiling alone would carry the message of progress and achievement."[63]

As the Soviet exhibition opened in New York, 75 young Americans underwent the final stages of a briefing to prepare them for the crucial role they would play as guides at the Moscow fair. The guides—27 women and 48 men, including 4 African Americans—were all fluent in Russian. They were chosen from more than 1,000 applicants after taking language tests and interviewing in Washington, Chicago, and San Francisco before a panel affiliated with the Foreign Service Institute. The selection criteria stipulated that guides be "between the ages of 20 and 35, fluent in the Russian language, well adjusted, well educated, and of good appearance." Unsalaried, the guides received free transportation to and from Moscow as well as a $16 per diem.[64]

Training focused on preparing the guides on ways to respond to questions that Soviet visitors were likely to ask. The panel asked prospective guides how they would handle questions about school desegregation in the wake of the highly publicized clash in Little Rock in 1957. In addition to receiving a thorough briefing on race relations, guides received tutoring on how to respond to provocative questions about unemployment and class divisions. Preparers tested the guides on "their ability to reply in a calm, objective manner." While it was impossible to anticipate all the questions they might be asked in their six weeks at Sokolniki, the guides received briefings on American culture, traditions, economy, political structure, and social life. It is likely that some of them were trained to gather intelligence during the course of their stay in Moscow.[65]

Aware of the crucial role the guides would play as direct representatives of American society, Eisenhower summoned the young people for a personal meeting before they departed for Moscow. The president's desire to meet with the guides stemmed in no small part "because he was so curious as to why four Negroes should have studied Russian well enough to act as interpreters." Eisenhower could not have been oblivious to the fact that should any one of the African-American youths emerge as a critic of the United States while in Moscow, the action would deliver the Russians a propaganda bonanza. "I just would like to ask a question first of the four Negroes here," he ventured at the June 15 White House meeting. "How did you happen to get interested in Russian?" Apparently satisfied by their responses, Eisenhower told the group as a whole that they were proceeding into "the heart of the Iron Curtain" and into "a country where the human being is nothing but a creature of the State." After concluding his talk, the president posed with the guides for photographs and wished them good luck.[66]

Despite efforts to plan for all contingencies, inevitable domestic controversies erupted both before and after the official opening of the fair on July 24. Showing that depictions of U.S. race relations before foreign audiences remained a neuralgic issue, Southerners decried a planned sequence in the fashion show displaying white and black couples mingling together at wedding and barbecue scenes. In one scene, an African-American couple, who were in fact engaged to be married, went through a mock ceremony attended by white couples. On July 16, South Carolina Senator Strom Thurmond protested "fashion shows which misrepresent life in the homes of typical American families." Forty-one fashion editors signed a petition protesting the mixed race scene as well as a rock 'n' roll display featuring leather jacketed performers. In a reprise of the fiasco over the "Unfinished Business" exhibit in Brussels, U.S. officials cut the African-American wedding scene from the planned fashion show, lamely explaining that it was removed because of time constraints rather than as a result of segregationist protests.[67]

In another parallel with Brussels, the proposed art exhibition at Sokolniki aroused a storm of controversy. The selection of paintings to be exhibited, chosen by a committee of distinguished artists and museum directors, included examples of modern art, which many Americans found objectionable and unrepresentative of popular tastes. Among the committee's selections for display in Moscow was Jack Levine's "Welcome Home," which depicted a corpulent U.S. Army major general and a group of obviously wealthy friends stuffing themselves at a banquet table. Interpreted as a satire on military and class snobbery, Levine's work elicited praise from the CP's *Daily Worker,* but outrage from several American critics.[68]

Not only the art, but the artists themselves aroused the ire of American conservatives, who decried the painters' alleged leftist sympathies. Strom Thurmond, again, protested taxpayer financed displays of art by "pro-communists," but it was Rep. Francis E. Walter, chairman of the House Committee on Un-American Activities (HCUA), who launched an investigation into the matter. Walter asserted that half of the artists whose works would be shown in Moscow "have records of affiliation with communist fronts and causes."[69]

On June 25, Walter demanded that USIA's George Allen forward transcripts of all meetings of the art selection committee to HCUA "as expeditiously as possible." Allen refused, explaining that the selection committee had been assured its deliberations would remain private in order to ensure an uninhibited evaluation of the paintings under consideration. Walter criticized USIA and the State Department and summoned some of the artists whose works had been chosen to appear before the House committee. The representatives grilled some of the witnesses about organizations to which they had belonged, and statements they had once made, while others refused to testify.[70]

Various officials, including Nixon, suggested withdrawing the art exhibit entirely from the Moscow fair. Secretary of State Christian Herter replied that while he was "very unhappy about this art exhibit" Washington wished to avoid any comparison with the Soviets, who had drawn international criticism for banning works such as Boris Pasternak's *Doctor Zhivago*. In order to avoid being victimized by "the Pasternak thing in reverse," Herter advised Nixon to respond to administration critics by saying that "we had put the selection of art in the hands of a competent panel of art experts and that the government is not in the business of censoring art." The administration would "just have to live with this."[71]

Herter's advice reflected Eisenhower's own decision. The president, who displayed skills of his own as a portrait painter, declared that the paintings chosen for Moscow "represented an extreme form of modernism." He found many of the works "unintelligible to the average eye" and declared that the committee who selected them "represented a thin stratus of artists" who were "apparently not much interested in public taste." Eisenhower attempted to put an end to the controversy a week before the opening of the exhibition. "I have considered this matter fully and, as previously stated, am of the firm opinion that to remove works of art in this case would be inappropriate and detrimental," he wrote in a letter to Walter. To censor the art exhibit "would invite consequences considered more likely to impair the effectiveness of the exhibition."[72]

Although the Museum of Modern Art commended the administration for standing by the selection process, the praise was not entirely justified. Rather than remove any of the offending paintings, Allen added to the size of the collection to be displayed in order to further marginalize the abstract art, which had comprised only about 10 percent of the original selections. In early July the USIA director began seeking "some good examples of nineteenth century art to round out" the Moscow exhibit. The additional paintings helped mollify critics on the eve of the opening of the exhibition.[73]

The art controversy left a bad taste in Eisenhower's mouth, especially when one of the defenders of the original selections noted that "some people thought the president's paintings were not so good either." Eisenhower had quietly consented to McClellan's request that he be allowed to hang the president's portrait of his grandson, David, in the exhibition director's office in Moscow. Word about the Eisenhower portrait leaked in Moscow, prompting "two or three hundred Soviet requests to view it." After hearing the criticism of his own work, Eisenhower exploded at Abbott Washburn and was "adamant" that his portrait of David be removed from McClellan's office and returned to Washington.[74]

Critics protested not only against those controversial displays, such as the art exhibit, that were being included in the exhibition, but that some were being left out as well. U.S. Senator Barry Goldwater of Arizona was among those who criticized fair officials for omitting the nation's "religious heritage" from the exhibition. McClellan, Allen, and Thompson argued that the emphasis on

The official model for the American National Exhibition in Moscow's Sokolniki Park. From the main gate (far left) visitors entered the geodesic dome (center) before passing through to the main pavilion, outdoor exhibits, and the smaller dome (right). Officially, 2.7 million visitors attended the six-week exhibition, but tens of thousands of gate-crashers made the actual number of visitors much higher. (Courtesy U.S. Information Agency)

consumerism would be more effective than displays on religion or the blessings of democratic government, which would repulse Soviet visitors as overtly propagandistic. Allen sought to mollify critics by arguing that religion was "a continuing theme running all through the American exhibits." He noted that copies of the Bible, printed in several languages, were to be available in the book display. Once the fair opened, Soviet visitors showed a high degree of interest in American religion, peppering the guides with questions on the subject and pilfering scores of Bibles. While a religious display undoubtedly would have irritated the Soviet government, masses of visitors may well have responded favorably to it.[75]

As the controversies simmered, U.S. officials put the finishing touches on the "corner of America" that they had feverishly erected amid the lofty pines of the former tsarist preserve at Sokolniki. Coming into the main entrance, the visitor would be confronted by the dominant structure of the exhibit, the 78-foot-high, gold-anodized geodesic dome that served as the information center for the exhibition. Inside the 200-foot-wide dome, giant slides displayed color pictures of American life accompanied by a musical score and a voiceover commentary in Russian. Flashing across seven 20- to 30-foot-high screens suspended from the dome's interior, the slides depicted scenes of U.S. highways, supermarkets, cities, and college campuses.

After gazing at the colorful slide show, which *Time* called "the smash hit of the fair," Soviet visitors could tour the scientific and technical exhibits housed in the dome. The most popular of these was the IBM computer, offering answers in Russian to thousands of questions about American life. Eight exhibits around the dome's interior perimeter focused on labor, agriculture, public health and medicine, education, space research, peaceful atomic research, plastics, and basic scientific research. Planners counted on moving 5,000 persons an hour through the dome.[76]

Directly behind the dome, visitors encountered the centerpiece of the exhibition: the sprawling, 50,000-square-foot, see-through glass pavilion. On display in the pavilion were the items that the American planners knew that Soviet consumers were aware of, and intensely curious about, but could not hope to possess themselves. Featured were colorful displays of food, clothing, toys, sporting goods, travel information, art, books, newspapers, musical instruments, stereo equipment, a model kitchen, and a color television studio. The focus was on "the great abundance of the goods and things which come to the American family and the American people as a result of our free society, our consumer-oriented society, this tremendous freedom of choice that exists in this country," McClellan explained. "It is almost like a great bazaar of the conveniences that the American family enjoys."[77]

The third major structure at the exhibition was the 360-degree Circarama, transported to Moscow for an encore performance after its favorable reception at the 1958 Brussels World's Fair. Visitors could view the Walt Disney production, "Trip Across the U.S.," revised and equipped with a sound track in Russian. Other exhibits scattered across the grounds included a model American home; gleaming new 1959 automobiles; trucks and trailers; farm and lawn and garden machinery and equipment; sports boats anchored in a specially constructed pond; camping gear; and a 150-ton "Jungle Jim" playground for children. Other popular displays included the voting machines, another holdover from Brussels, and the "Family of Man" photographic essay representing more than 300 countries. Throughout the exhibition grounds, Americans dispensed information, publications, and, especially popular, free samples of Pepsi-Cola.

With the exhibitions in place, McClellan, his deputies, and the Soviet labor crews worked desperately to complete preparations on the eve of the formal July 24 opening ceremonies. "Nobody was holding back now," McClellan recalled, noting that some labor crews worked 24 hours straight in advance of the opening. The effort paid off, as "many visitors who had been to the site two or three weeks earlier, or even a few days before we opened, reported to me that they could not understand how so much had been done so quickly. It truly did seem a miracle." Khrushchev himself interrupted the last minute preparations during a second site visit, prompting Soviet and American workers to drop their tools and follow the official party on its tour. "We lost hours of needed last minute preparation as a result," McClellan grumbled, adding that the race to beat the clock before the opening was "a photo finish." On the night before the opening ceremonies, Washburn recalled that he, Thompson, and the embassy staff "were out there putting on the last splashes of paint and cleaning up the last amount of rubble from here and there, and there was an awful lot of stuff swept under the rug that night, I can tell you." At last, less than 24 hours before opening ceremonies took place, workers poured cement on the spot where Nixon and Khrushchev were slated to speak.[78]

Plans for the historic meeting at the exhibition site between Nixon and Khrushchev had been under way for months. Long eager to tour the Soviet Union, Nixon first proposed to visit Moscow in an April meeting with Dulles, only a month before the latter's death from cancer. Despite his aversion to "personal diplomacy" with communists, Dulles told Nixon he would "have no objection to the vice president's raising the matter with the President." From Moscow, Thompson wired that "VP visit particularly in connection with exhibit would be most useful not only in improving general relations but particularly in promoting the exchange program which I consider very much to our advantage." After receiving the endorsement of Christian Herter, as well as Chad McClellan, Eisenhower authorized Nixon's appearance at the opening ceremonies in Moscow.[79]

Approached by Thompson on the proposed Nixon visit, Khrushchev declared that he would "welcome" the vice president's appearance despite his frequent "uncomplimentary remarks" about communism. After inviting Khrushchev to attend opening ceremonies with Nixon, Thompson reported that the Soviet leader "evaded any answer about being present." Khrushchev was upbeat, however, during a tour of the Sokolniki construction site in May. He expressed keen interest in the geodesic dome designed by Buckminster Fuller and surprised Thompson by observing that he had "read about such buildings in *Amerika* magazine." Later, Khrushchev agreed not only to attend the opening ceremonies with Nixon, but to grant the U.S. vice president television time to address the Soviet people, a courtesy previously accorded to his own deputies, Anastas Mikoyan and Frol Kozlov, during their visits to the United States.[80]

All the preparations were complete for the "kitchen debate"—the dramatic encounter between Nixon and Khrushchev at the opening of the Moscow exhibition. The often contentious exchanges between the two men seemed to take the world by surprise, but they were not as spontaneous as they appeared. East-West tensions remained high over Soviet demands for a resolution of the anomalous status of the Western enclave in Berlin, as well as the ongoing, post-*Sputnik* nuclear arms race. Both Khrushchev and Nixon were highly ideological, ambitious, and aggressive politicians accustomed to engaging in political gutter fights and coming out on top. Each held the rival social system that the other represented in complete contempt. Both men had been thoroughly briefed and, befitting their personalities, merely awaited an opportunity to go on the offensive. A tour of the glittering and provocative U.S. exhibition, explicitly designed to challenge the communist system, could hardly have failed to provoke the sort of exchanges that emerged between Nixon and Khrushchev. Already the Kremlin had signaled its mounting anxiety about the U.S. exhibition by launching a sweeping propaganda campaign against the display (see Chapter 7).

Washington encouraged Soviet hostility with an ill-timed and self-serving "Captive Nations" declaration, issued only a week before Nixon's arrival in Moscow. Confronted with the congressional resolution calling for a week of prayer for the "enslaved peoples" of Eastern Europe, Eisenhower duly issued the proclamation, though he lamented its timing, if not its spirit. Traveling in Poland at the time, an irate Khrushchev condemned the resolution as aggressive and even suggested that perhaps Nixon should reconsider his proposed visit. Undaunted, Nixon not only remained eager to go through with his visit, but told Eisenhower of "his intention of debating with Khrushchev and countering his points." Nixon believed he had "an excellent chance to probe and cause some blurting out of Khrushchev's real feelings." Eisenhower encouraged Nixon to take a tough stance with the Soviet leader.[81]

In Moscow, however, Ambassador Thompson warned that a confrontational approach in the first high-level meeting between Soviet and American leaders since the Geneva conferences might be ill timed and counterproductive. On April 8, Thompson declared that as long as Khrushchev remained receptive to "increased exchange of information," Washington should avoid risking a reversal "by making remarks too objectionable to the Soviets." A better approach would be to respond positively by emphasizing the Soviet call for peaceful coexistence, increased contacts, and more exhibits. Thompson advised Nixon to avoid contentious issues and even to compliment the Soviets on their success with the sputniks. "With their inferiority complex," the American ambassador advised, "the Soviets are suckers for flattery."[82]

A subtle approach to the Soviets carried little appeal for Nixon, who longed to confront Khrushchev in order to defend what he perceived as U.S. interests and to enhance his own prestige in anticipation of the 1960 presidential campaign. In preparation of the meeting in Moscow, Nixon pored over State Department, CIA, NSC, and military assessments of Khrushchev and the USSR. To round out the briefing, he sought out politicians, diplomats,

A tense Khrushchev joined Vice President Richard M. Nixon for the official opening of the American National Exhibition on July 24, 1959. Their "kitchen debate" that day reflected Khrushchev's anxieties over the potential impact of the display of American consumer culture in the Soviet capital. Harold "Chad" McClellan, pictured between Nixon and Khrushchev, was the driving force behind the American exhibition. George V. Allen, director of the United States Information Agency, appears on Khrushchev's right. (Courtesy U.S. Information Agency)

foreign leaders, and journalists who had served in Moscow. Close to Dulles in his Cold War perceptions, Nixon joined the dying statesman at his hospital bedside for a final conversation about the proposed trip to Moscow. Finally, Nixon summoned VOA translators to "give him a few appropriate Russian phrases," which he soon mastered. As Nixon later wrote in his own account of the encounter with Khrushchev—depicted as one of the "six crises" of his early career—"I had never been better prepared for a meeting in which I was to participate."[83]

Time described what followed as "peacetime diplomacy's most amazing 24 hours." After arriving in Moscow on the evening of July 23, Nixon arose early the next morning after a fitful sleep and visited a market, where he received a warm reception from the stunned Soviet citizens. Nixon tactlessly offered one man a 100-ruble note on the mistaken assumption that he lacked the money to attend the U.S. exhibition. Muscovites actually suffered from the unavailability, not the cost, of exhibition tickets, which sold for one ruble, or 25 cents. Exploiting Nixon's faux pas, the Soviet press seized on the vice president's "bribe" as a degrading capitalist affront to an honest citizen.[84]

After arriving at the Kremlin that same morning, Nixon found Khrushchev in a "testy mood." The Soviet leader's demeanor grew progressively worse as he denounced the Captive Nations "provocation," engaged his penchant for pounding his fist on the tabletop, and uttered a series of expletives. "This resolution stinks!" Khrushchev roared. Nixon rode out the storm and assumed Khrushchev would display more restraint following their arrival at Sokolniki shortly before noon to preview the exhibition before hordes of news reporters.[85]

The display of U.S. culture at Sokolniki seemed only to shorten Khrushchev's fuse, however. Once again, the Soviet leader attacked Nixon on the Captive Nations Resolution as the two men tested new equipment at the color television exhibit. Khrushchev implicitly acknowledged the superiority of Western technology by vowing that "in another seven years we will be on the same level as America." The Soviet leader also betrayed his own class anxieties during the encounter with Nixon, warning that even though he had been a coal miner, while Nixon had been trained as an attorney, he would hold his own in any argument. Responding that there was need for greater communication, Nixon tweaked Khrushchev by declaring that he "should not be afraid of ideas. ... After all, you don't know everything." "If I don't know everything, you don't know anything about communism—except fear of it," Khrushchev shot back, as the television cameras rolled, shutters snapped, and reporters scrawled furiously in their notebooks.[86]

After this tense engagement, the two men moved on to the Pepsi-Cola booth, where Khrushchev took an approving sip of the soft drink—which he soon allowed to be marketed in the USSR on a continuing basis. The next stop was the six-room model ranch house, which the Soviet press had already ridiculed as more opulent than average American homes. While Nixon insisted that a "typical" U.S. worker could indeed purchase the $14,000 home, the two men leaned over a railing at the "gadget-stocked" model kitchen, complete with a range, dishwasher, upright refrigerator, and other appliances. "You Americans think the Russian people will be astonished to see these things. The fact is," Khrushchev dissembled, "that all our new houses have this kind of equipment."

As "tense and wide-eyed" newsmen and Soviet and American officials looked on, the two leaders spent the next few minutes engaged in the finger-wagging, chest-tapping "kitchen debate" on the relative merits of the rival social systems. Before the exchange was over, Nixon had warned Khrushchev about threatening the West with its rockets over Berlin. Citing the Soviet leader's repeated interruptions, Nixon compared him to a U.S.

senator engaged in a filibuster. Khrushchev raised his voice and warned Nixon about potential "very bad consequences" to uttering threats against the USSR. The Soviet leader calmed himself, however, and declared "we want peace with all other nations, especially America." Nixon accepted the overture, putting his arm on Khrushchev's shoulder and admitting, "I'm afraid I haven't been a good host." Khrushchev turned and quipped to the shocked American guide, "Thank you for letting us use [your] kitchen for our argument." The kitchen debate was over.[87]

The two leaders continued their ideological jousting later in the evening in speeches that marked the formal opening of the exhibition. The kitchen debate in the morning followed by the official opening ceremonies in the evening had provided a dramatic culmination to the weeks of feverish preparation for the unprecedented event. "It was a thrilling moment when the two national anthems were played and the flags were raised," McClellan recalled.[88]

In his official welcoming statement, Khrushchev commended the U.S. exhibition, acknowledging that he felt a "certain envy" while touring the cultural display. He quickly added, however, that before long the Soviet Union would "overtake our American partners in peaceful economic competition." In his official opening statement, Nixon stressed the inevitability of material progress under the American system and rebuked the Soviets for depicting the Moscow fair as an unrepresentative propaganda display. The vice president read a conciliatory statement from Eisenhower, who invoked fond memories of the wartime alliance and declared that the Cold War had "saddened me greatly" because the break in relations had been "so unnecessary." Eisenhower wrote that he had "greatly enjoyed" the Soviet exhibition in New York, which demonstrated the "strides taken in science and industry." The president concluded by declaring his "hope that this exchange of exhibitions will be a first step toward a restoration of the trust and unity that we felt during the recent war."[89]

At the conclusion of the speechmaking, Nixon once again escorted Khrushchev on a tour of the displays he had not seen that morning. The two leaders avoided a reprise of the confrontation that had erupted earlier in the day, but tensions remained palpable. Khrushchev rejected efforts to steer him toward the voting booth display, which would have offered Nixon an ideal opportunity to challenge the Soviet leader on the absence of democratic elections under CP regimes. "I have no interest in that," Khrushchev bluntly declared. He also dismissed the IBM computer by noting that the Soviets had machines "just as complicated" to "shoot off rockets." Stopping at the wine-tasting booth, Khrushchev tried a propaganda gambit of his own, proposing a toast to the "elimination of all military bases on foreign lands." Nixon kept a smile on his face, but had no intention of raising his glass to *that* toast.[90]

After spending the next day meeting with officials and touring a massive new Soviet agricultural and economic exhibition, Nixon met privately with Khrushchev for the last time on Sunday, July 26. Before proceeding by boat from Khrushchev's dacha down the Moscow River, the two issued a joint statement declaring that the "kitchen debate" had merely been a "frank" rather than a "belligerent" exchange, as characterized in press reports. During the boat trip, Khrushchev continued to needle Nixon by stopping along the river and asking the bathers whether they considered themselves "captive peoples." The crowds shouted "nyet, nyet," but also cheered Nixon and his wife, Pat, with enthusiasm.[91]

After the riverboat trip Nixon and Khrushchev conducted their most substantive talks over the course of a five-hour traditional Russian meal. They made no progress on the impasse over Berlin, the subject of stalled foreign ministers' talks in Geneva, but remained cordial throughout the discussion. Nixon reiterated Eisenhower's desire for Khrushchev to tour the United States, a visit that the president hoped to follow up with his own tour of the USSR. Nixon wired Eisenhower with details of his "extraordinary" encounters with Khrushchev before departing on a strenuous 5,000-mile tour, first to Leningrad, then to Sverdlovsk in the Urals, and finally to Novosibirsk, in Siberia. Nixon encountered enthusiastic crowds as well as teams of orchestrated hecklers, who reminded him derisively of the Captive Nations Resolution at every stop. Growing irate over the heckling as well as the occasional police manhandling of Soviet citizens who displayed enthusiasm for Nixon and his entourage, the vice president warned his Soviet handlers that if the boorish behavior continued, "I am going to blast the whole bunch of you publicly in a way you'll never forget."[92]

After relieving himself of tensions that "had been building up to the exploding point," Nixon concluded his exhausting ten-day tour with an un-precedented nationwide radio and television address delivered to the Soviet people from Moscow on August 1. Working closely with Ambassador Thompson, Nixon carefully crafted the speech in two all-night sessions. After thanking the Soviet people for their hospitality, Nixon insisted, in contrast to Soviet propaganda, that U.S. military forces were maintained worldwide for defensive rather than aggressive purposes. The vice president called for "sharply expanded" exchange programs, an end to all jamming, and "regular radio and television broadcasts" by Soviet and American leaders.[93]

While the speech may have seemed tepid to Western audiences, Nixon struck a balance by stressing an American desire for peace and increased contacts while avoiding provocative assertions that might have risked alienating his Soviet audience. This nonpolemical approach stood the best chance of making a strong impression on the Soviet people. *New York Times* reporter James Reston noted the "almost unanimous agreement" of the 56 reporters who accompanied

Nixon that his mission had been a foreign policy success for the United States. Moreover, the image of Nixon, cool and smiling, yet determined to defend his country under Khrushchev's attack, all but sealed the 1960 Republican presidential nomination. Reston wrote that Nixon had found "a new and perfect way to launch a campaign for the American presidency. Instead of throwing his hat into the ring, he is throwing Nikita S. Khrushchev."[94]

Denied by the Soviets in his request to return home via Alaska through the Soviet Far East, Nixon retaliated by stopping in Poland for a three-day visit following his departure to the West. The Poles greeted the vice president and his entourage with an outpouring of enthusiasm, as tens of thousands lined the streets of Warsaw to cheer and throw flowers before the motorcade. During subsequent talks with Polish CP leader Wladyslaw Gomulka, both Nixon and the president's brother, Milton Eisenhower, president of Johns Hopkins University, who accompanied Nixon and his wife throughout their tour, advocated increased exchange of persons. Receptive to the idea, Gomulka made it clear that while he maintained a friendly relationship with Khrushchev, the Poles were determined to press their independence from Moscow.[95]

Gomulka, however, sharply condemned Radio Free Europe propaganda and rejected Nixon's and Eisenhower's lame attempts to dismiss the network as a private station over which Washington had no control. The bottom line to Gomulka was that RFE was a "U.S. government-financed" station "pouring out hours of abuse daily into Poland." Following his return to Washington, Milton Eisenhower told the President that RFE broadcasts were "strengthening the hands of Poland's communist leaders, rather than weakening them." RFE broadcasts on the corruption and sex lives of Polish CP members smacked of "yellow journalism" and were "degrading to our government" since most Poles viewed RFE as an official voice of the U.S. Government. The comments of both Milton Eisenhower and Gomulka reflected the declining effectiveness of aggressive psychological warfare, in contrast to the popular reception of Nixon and his entourage, which demonstrated the appeal of direct diplomacy and cultural exchange.[96]

Perhaps belatedly, given his decision to confront Khrushchev in Moscow, Nixon acknowledged that an evolutionary approach offered the most hopeful means of encouraging change in Moscow. "The only long-range answer" to the CP regimes, Nixon reported to Eisenhower shortly after arriving in Washington, was "a gradual opening of the door through contacts." Nixon stressed the popular reception he had received throughout his tours of the USSR and Poland. The enthusiastic response in Warsaw, as well as Gomulka's professions of independence, revealed Poland as "the true Achilles heel of the Soviet system." Confirming Nixon's view, U.S. Embassy diplomats in Warsaw reported that the vice presidential visit had provided a "tremendous morale lift, dramatically rekindling sentimental ties" between the Polish and American peoples.[97] Nixon's tour, coinciding with the opening of the American exhibition in Moscow, marked dramatic progress in the campaign of cultural infiltration of the Soviet empire. While the exhausted vice president returned home to further his political ambitions, the U.S. exhibition had six more weeks to leave its imprint on the Soviet imagination.

SEVEN

Six Weeks at Sokolniki: Soviet Responses to the American Exhibition

During the summer of 1959, the United States and the Soviet Union waged an epic propaganda battle at the site of the American National Exhibition in Sokolniki Park. While the Americans mounted a massive exhibition of consumer capitalism, the Soviets mobilized a counterattack against the Western cultural invasion. The Soviet Communist Party (CPSU), backed by various affiliated committees, employed a variety of means to discredit the exhibition. The Kremlin's counterattack—reflecting profound insecurities about the impact of Western consumer culture—failed to undermine the appeal of the American exhibition.

The decision to mount a massive propaganda campaign to counteract the potential appeal of the American National Exhibition emanated from the highest levels of the CPSU. Foreign Minister Andrei Gromyko and Georgi A. Zhukov, head of the ministry of cultural affairs, participated in planning for the Soviet campaign of counterpropaganda and agitation. In the weeks before the opening of the Sokolniki exhibition, the CPSU Central Committee issued a set of decrees to counter "the transparent intention of the United States Government to use [the Moscow exhibition] for a wide-ranging propaganda of the American way of life." Realizing that the Americans would appeal to visitors on the basis of their advanced consumer culture, CPSU authorities sought to discredit the exhibition. The Kremlin's approach would be to step up activities glorifying Soviet achievements while depicting the exhibition as a blatant propaganda display that bore little relation to the realities of everyday life of the average U.S. citizen.[1]

By early spring, Soviet officials had gleaned an accurate assessment of U.S. plans for the national exhibition. The CPSU Central Committee noted that Washington had solicited the cooperation of hundreds of private businesses to bolster the central thrust of the exhibition, which was to "portray the United States as a country of freedom and of prosperous economy." The CPSU anticipated exhibitions calling attention to the construction of millions of single-family homes, schools, churches, and synagogues. Even more threatening were plans to "demonstrate various conveniences of everyday life so as to make the Soviet people believe in the allegedly high standard of living of the 'average' American and to distract the visitor's attention from the real vices of capitalism with its mass unemployment and impoverishment of the broad masses of the working people, race discrimination, etc."[2]

A CPSU Central Committee report reflected detailed knowledge of plans for exhibits at the Sokolniki fair. "Special attention will be paid to the demonstration of domestic appliances: electric kitchens, vacuum cleaners, refrigerators, air conditioners, etc." The Soviets knew that exhibits would display "how American housewives prepare dinner" and that visitors would be "treated to the cooked dishes." The Central Committee report noted that "the American side attaches great importance to the exhibition of books, magazines, and newspapers." CPSU officials expressed even greater concern about plans to make "use for propaganda purposes television and the cinema." Color television, still unavailable in the USSR, and the Circarama movie show were sure to make a strong impression on Soviet visitors. The Americans could also be expected to screen popular films and hand out tens of thousands of souvenirs, including lapel pins, model cars, plastic cups used to dispense ice cream, and "a soft drink Pepsi-Cola."[3]

In anticipation of the American cultural invasion, the Central Committee approved a resolution authorizing a propaganda campaign against the exhibition. Countermeasures would be launched in an effort to dissuade masses of people from descending upon the Sokolniki site and delivering a propaganda victory to the West. The first decree called for CPSU organizations to conduct "explanatory work" among the population to discourage mass gatherings of visitors at the exhibition site "and in particular to prevent inordinate admiration on the part of certain individuals that might infringe on the dignity of Soviet man." The Soviets would attempt to discourage visitors by exposing efforts to present the everyday life of U.S. workers and farmers "in a distorted and glossed-over form." In contrast to the favorable images portrayed at Sokolniki,

Soviet counterpropaganda would emphasize the weaknesses of capitalist society: the "multi-million army of unemployed," millions living below the poverty line, indebtedness, a heavy tax burden to finance the arms race, "chronic stagnation," "increasing bankruptcies of the farmers," and "the lack of rights for ethnic minorities, especially negroes."[4]

While criticizing the United States on the above themes, the Central Committee mounted a propaganda campaign to trumpet the achievements of the Soviet economy, science and culture, improved living standards, and "the glorious perspectives of the development of the USSR." Especially concerned about the potentially favorable impact of the Sokolniki exhibition on Soviet youth, the CPSU ordered secret planning sessions within the Komsomol (Communist youth organization) "for the purpose of discussing measures which could distract young people from displaying too much interest in the American exhibition."[5]

The second CPSU Central Committee decree issued in the weeks leading up to the opening of the exhibition focused on varieties of media to be mobilized for the counterpropaganda campaign. The CPSU directed the editors of national and Moscow newspapers as well as the State Committee for Radio and Television to mount a propaganda campaign to "expose the bourgeois legend about 'prosperity' in the capitalist world." In addition to newspaper, radio and television, the CPSU called for strengthening of "visual propaganda," including billboards, sides of buses, and posters in parks, gardens, and public places. The Central Committee also directed the Ministry of Culture "to screen on Moscow television new Soviet and foreign films and to start television broadcasts earlier than usual." Party elites hoped the additional entertainment offered by the new films and expanded television programming would divert attention from the U.S. exhibition.[6]

Along the same lines, the third CPSU Central Committee decree directed various ministries to collaborate on "planning of additional cultural events (shows, festivals, exhibitions, public festivities, carnivals, and amateur art shows)" to be staged in Moscow at the same time as the U.S. national exhibition. The Exhibition of the People's Economic Achievement—the VDNKh—a permanent exhibition opened in February 1959, was "to conduct additional mass events to attract visitors in July and August." Finally, the CPSU called on ministries "to organize in July and August in a region of Moscow a trade fair featuring the sale of goods which are in particularly great demand." The decree directed the Soviet Ministry of Foreign Trade to organize a Czech exhibition of artistic glass and china to be held in Moscow coinciding with the American exhibition. Similarly, the Soviets would ask the Polish foreign trade ministry to stage an industrial exhibition in Moscow. The CPSU called for special sporting events, including a "'Spartakiad' of the Peoples of the USSR" in August.[7]

Acting under the decrees of the party Central Committee, myriad groups collaborated in a massive Soviet counteroffensive against the U.S. exhibition. Beginning the first week of June 1959, the Bureau of the Moscow City Committee of the CPSU launched a campaign of "mass political, cultural, and educational work for the summer period" to counteract the anticipated impact of the exhibition. The Moscow committee mobilized CPSU elites, Komsomol officials, trade union organizations, managers of enterprises, and editors of factory newspapers to deliver thousands of lectures throughout the city emphasizing the achievements of the USSR and "the prospects for communist construction." While calling attention to Soviet accomplishments, lectures on the "internal situation and external policy of the United States" strove to counter the themes of the exhibition in Sokolniki Park.[8]

The Society for the Propagation of Political and Scientific Knowledge, a national lecture society, conducted conferences and seminars offering data, financial assistance, and sponsorship of lectures. The Society arranged some 10,000 lectures to anchor the propaganda counteroffensive against the exhibition. Both the Society and "The House of Political Enlightenment," a nationwide CPSU affiliate, distributed lectures and information provided by Soviet research institutes and think tanks. For example, the House of Political Enlightenment circulated a paper entitled, "United States Economy and the Situation of the American Working Class," prepared by researchers at the Institute of World Economy and International Relations of the prestigious Soviet Academy of Sciences.[9]

The Soviet campaign to counteract the exhibition soon became evident to U.S. officials. Stepped up activities at the VDNKh included a copycat Circarama display in a transparent effort to detract from the novelty of the Disney feature at Sokolniki. Other Soviet actions, including plans for an international film festival, struck U.S. officials as "part of a growing effort to weaken and undermine the impact which the American National Exhibition may be expected to have on its Soviet and foreign visitors." The Americans hoped that Soviet actions would backfire by drawing into Moscow increased numbers of visitors, who might then make their way to Sokolniki Park.[10]

With the CPSU bureaucracy mobilized to counteract the American exhibition, the propaganda campaign began in the Soviet press on April 10. *Pravda*, the official CPSU newspaper, under the headline "Is This Typical?" charged that the U.S. exhibition would feature homes, cars, appliances, and conveniences in an attempt to convey the false impression that such items could be possessed by the typical American consumer. Focusing particularly on the model homes, which contrasted sharply with the small apartments in Moscow's high rises, *Pravda* charged that "such a house can be called a typical home of an American laborer with no more right than, say, the Taj Mahal is a typical house of a Bombay textile worker or Buckingham Palace the typical home of an English miner." Prior to the *Pravda* attack, noted U.S. embassy diplomats, Soviet press coverage of plans for the exhibition had been "only favorable."[11]

In addition to planning diversions and launching a propaganda offensive against the exhibition, the Soviets challenged U.S. plans for various facilities and promotions at Sokolniki. Even more threatening to the Soviets than the model homes were plans, recommended by embassy diplomats, to construct "a large, really up-to-date, color-tiled restroom for exhibit visitors with all the modern gadgets such as hot hand blowers, ultra-violet sanitation, [and] rapid flush toilets." Such facilities, nonexistent in the USSR, would have astonished the Soviet public. In a typically successful lobbying effort with U.S. corporations, Chad McClellan and Abbott Washburn had persuaded the American Radiator and Standard Sanitary Corporation to provide, free of charge, 150 toilets, 50 urinals, and 50 wash basins. Soviet officials flatly rejected the plans, however, and insisted on installing their own restroom facilities in Sokolniki Park.[12]

CPSU authorities also squelched U.S. plans to appeal to Soviet women by giving away free cosmetic samples. Soviet officials informed McClellan on May 25 that they would not allow handouts of the cosmetics, or of toy models of GM cars, or of free samples of Pepsi-Cola. Furious, McClellan engaged Soviet officials in three days of "vigorous discussion," after which "Pepsi Cola was back in, but we couldn't do a thing" about the Soviet veto of plans to dispense cosmetics and toy cars. Soviet officials insisted that "there might be a stampede on the pavilion that would be dangerous to life and limb" if plans for the cosmetics giveaway had been allowed to proceed. The exaggeration may have been only slight, but it was also true, as one American noted, that Soviet officials "do not want Russian women to have the chance to compare Russian cosmetic products with American cosmetics." As a result of the Soviet veto, Coty Cosmetics had to withdraw $150,000 worth of free samples as well as nine Russian-speaking American women who had been hired to hand out the make-up. GM faced a recall of thousands of plastic toy cars. Thanks to Chad McClellan, Pepsi narrowly survived an effort to veto its ultimately successful efforts to break into the Soviet soft drink market.[13]

The cycle of Soviet veto, American resistance, and eventual accommodation characterized other aspects of planning for Moscow. Citing concerns about crowd control, Soviet authorities flatly rejected plans to include a jazz band at the exhibition. Nothing the Americans could do would change this decision.[14]

U.S. officials fought back against Soviet protests over the circulation of American newspapers, magazines, and books from kiosks outside the exhibition. McClellan confronted the choice of challenging Soviet censorship or facing the wrath of the American press. While Coty Cosmetics and GM officials had agreed to remain silent about the Soviet rejection of their products, the newspaper industry could hardly be expected to do so. McClellan countered Soviet charges that the newspaper headlines would serve to "further the Cold War" by pointing out that the Soviets had displayed newspaper headlines at their own exhibition in New York. During the discussion McClellan "emphasized that total elimination of this display could not be kept out of press" and that the resultant publicity "would be bad for both sides." McClellan reached a compromise with the Soviets by agreeing that newspapers would be displayed under plexiglass along a wall inside the glass pavilion. The American general manager agreed to screen the newspapers to ensure that there would be "no headlines or articles in view which the Soviets were likely to deem offensive."[15]

The Soviets continued to monitor closely all printed materials that the United States sought to dispense at Sokolniki. The CPSU Central Committee countermeasures against the exhibition included an order "to strictly examine the lists and contents of the American literature to be displayed and of the documentary films, posters, diagrams, photographic shows, etc." Books displayed at Sokolniki had been selected to reflect the "breadth of American intellectual and cultural development and our interest in the cultures of other societies." U.S. officials had agreed to exclude "any materials which might be considered provocative from the Russian point of view," a provision the Soviets meant to enforce. After reviewing the list of books in early July, CPSU officials issued a sharp protest over efforts to include those published in the Russian language by the New York-based Chekhov Publishers. They read out a long list of anti-Soviet quotations taken from some of the books, insisting that the offensive texts "violated both the spirit and the letter of the agreement on the exchange of exhibitions." Soviet officials threatened "unspecified measures" unless the offending works were removed.[16]

After agreeing to remove all books sent by Chekhov Publishers, McClellan confronted new Soviet demands for the removal of texts deemed offensive. On the opening day of the exhibition, McClellan removed more than 100 books from the display and sent to Washington a list of titles that the Soviets found offensive. Among them were works by prominent U.S. statesman that directly focused on the Cold War. These included Dean Acheson's *Power and Diplomacy* (1958), Herbert Hoover's *The Ordeal of Woodrow Wilson* (1958), Adlai Stevenson's *Friends and Enemies* (1959), and *Prerequisites for Peace* (1959) by Norman Thomas. The Soviets also objected to some works on religion, including *Great Ages and Ideas of the Jewish People* (1956) by Leo Schwarz, whose removal by McClellan brought an angry charge of American kowtowing to "communist tyrants" by the American Jewish League Against Communism. While McClellan consented to the removal of works on political and religious themes, he rejected the Soviet request to remove the *1959 World Almanac,* a compilation of facts and figures that might call into question official Soviet statistical claims on a variety of issues.[17]

Defending his decision to comply with Soviet censorship, McClellan insisted that he did not "intend to lose sight of the main objective of the exhibition and get into trouble over a small thing." Grilled by reporters about his decision, McClellan asked rhetorically, "Do you think I should insist on showing the books if it means closing the fair?" Soviet officials "could cause a lot of trouble and I don't want any more than I have." Neither Ambassador Tommy Thompson nor officials in Washington challenged the decision of McClellan, who maintained wide authority to conduct the American exhibition as he saw fit. Thompson noted that the "favorable effect of the great number of books" that would reach the Soviet public should not "be jeopardized by intransigence" over the relatively few books that were removed.[18]

McClellan's decision to remove the offending titles did not end controversy over the book display. After the opening of the exhibition on July 24, Soviet visitors made off with hundreds of books from the display shelves. On the first day alone, Soviet visitors exited with some 600 books, including 14 Bibles. The Americans had both foreseen and invited the pilferage, as evidenced by the reserve stocks accumulated to replace the missing books. Irate Soviet officials summoned McClellan and demanded that the books be placed under plexiglass or the book display would be shut down. McClellan insisted that the books remain accessible to the public, so that they could be held and appreciated. Anything else, he insisted, would be "contrary to the understanding between us from the beginning." In yet another compromise solution, McClellan agreed to place some of the books under plexiglass, attach others to chains, and to reorganize the book display for closer monitoring so that there was only one entrance and one exit. He also acceded to Soviet requests that signs be posted warning that books were only to be perused, and not taken. These steps reduced, but did not altogether stop, the pilferage. A week into the exhibition, a U.S. diplomat reported that "the book corner is a favorite area, as evidenced by the number of items which have been disappearing."[19]

In the ensuing weeks of the exhibition Soviet officials remained "extremely sensitive" about the book display, raising protests when they discovered material deemed offensive. They demanded removal of a book comparing Soviet and American economic development as well as a text on archeology, which they termed "slanderous." The overwhelming majority of books remained on display, however. By the end of the six-week exhibition, several volumes were so well thumbed by the Soviet visitors that their covers fell off and the spines turned to mush.[20] Despite the CPSU propaganda barrage against the exhibition, Soviet citizens displayed enthusiasm for the spectacle from the. moment the gates opened. U.S. diplomats reported that Muscovites had been buzzing about the exhibition since plans were announced months before. Neither the propaganda countermeasures nor intimidation by CPSU agitators and secret police agents would deter masses of people from touring the exhibition.

In addition to the propaganda barrage, the Soviets exercised control over the distribution of admission tickets. McClellan had planned on selling 100,000 tickets a day outside the gates at Sokolniki. The Soviets agreed on the low admission price of one ruble (about 25 cents), even less for children, servicemen, and senior citizens, but rejected the plan to sell all the tickets at the gate. Soviet authorities explained that "riots resulting in pandemonium around the park" would be the result of exclusively on-site ticket distribution. Aware of mounting enthusiasm for the exhibition among Muscovites, McClellan concluded that the Soviets might be right. He agreed to limit the number of tickets sold daily to 50,000 as well as to their distribution from kiosks and tourist hotels in downtown Moscow.[21]

Considering the limited amount of time, the formidable logistical challenges, and the unending series of disputes with the Soviets, McClellan and his colleagues viewed the opening of the exhibition, as planned, on July 24 as little short of miraculous. On the opening weekend, from Friday to Sunday evening, 140,000 persons surged through the exhibition. In the first two weeks especially, Soviet control over ticket distribution ensured that crowds were heavily represented by CPSU members and agitators associated with the Party-directed campaign of countermeasures. With Soviet sources controlling the distribution of tickets, U.S. diplomats took note of an "intense desire for tickets, unavailable to the average citizen."[22]

Ambassador Thompson advised Washington that the various restrictions and countermeasures revealed "Soviet anxiety over the potential impact of Sokolniki and a continuing Soviet propaganda effort to provide ideological prophylaxis against its message." Embassy diplomats monitored the propaganda campaign, calling attention to the "constant official agitation against the basic themes of the fair." U.S. officials also noted that Soviet stores appeared better stocked than usual with consumer goods.[23]

CPSU documents confirm that "from the very moment of the opening of the American exhibition" a campaign had been conducted to expose "the falsehoods of bourgeois propaganda extolling the so-called American way of life."[24] "Hundreds" of CPSU propagandists and Komsomol activists "were delegated daily to conduct explanatory work among the people on the territory of the United States exhibition." The agitators, many of them young people, loudly criticized the exhibits, engaged the American guides in debate, and intimidated unofficial Soviet visitors. U.S. officials could not know the extent of efforts to disrupt the exhibition, but noted that the number of agitators "would appear to be considerable, involving mobilization of substantial numbers of individuals." Embassy diplomats on the scene witnessed arrests and the taking down of names of individuals "for being too friendly with exhibitors." One diplomat judged police intimidation "a more serious problem than agitation."[25]

Soviet agitation and harassment took a variety of forms. Police, ostensibly sent to Sokolniki to maintain order among the crowds outside the exhibition gates, often took the opportunity to intimidate would-be fair-goers to discourage their attendance. Similarly, agitators urged people waiting for available tickets to attend the rival Soviet exhibitions in the city. "Why bother with the American exhibit?" they asked. "Go to our own 300 meters away. . . . We've got better things to see and you don't need a ticket."[26]

While striving to discourage and intimidate citizens, CPSU officials thoroughly toured the exhibition themselves and reported to their superiors on what they found. On one occasion, a group of 20 Party members divided themselves into pairs, drew up a schedule, and carefully observed activities at the exhibition for three hours. Reporting in mid-August, they averred that Soviet propaganda was having its intended effect in that "the attitude of most visitors is healthy and somewhat skeptical." Such reporting, designed to reassure CPSU superiors, was not an accurate assessment of the typical response.

Agitators did admit that Soviet visitors reacted excitedly to various exhibits. Among the more "unpleasant scenes" they witnessed was "a ridiculous commotion" near the fashion show when one of the American guides offered to take snapshots of some of the visitors. "People began begging, 'Please, take a picture of me,' etc." The CPSU monitors also condemned visitors for their eagerness to "carry away dirty Pepsi-Cola cups, some of them full. Others pleaded for souvenir plastic cups with the Pepsi logo from the automatic dispenser."[27]

The CPSU report went on to describe other incidents of what the agitators perceived as excessive displays of enthusiasm, adding that "in all of these cases our comrades tried to interfere." One CPSU official, describing the "Family of Man" photographic exhibit as a "disguised weapon of American monopolistic imperialism," called for swift countermeasures. The focus of the exhibit on the equality and brotherhood of humanity masked "materialist realities" and sought

Pepsi-Cola outmaneuvered Coca-Cola to break into the Soviet market by giving out free samples on the grounds of the American National Exhibition. "Several million" Dixie cups were required to meet the demand of the Soviet audiences. Khrushchev complimented the taste of Pepsi and authorized marketing of the American soft drink in the USSR on a continuing basis. (Courtesy New York Times Pictures)

to "distort class struggle," the CPSU member declared. He added that "this dangerous influence on the thinking of the people . . . should be opposed by explaining Marxist-Leninist tenets."[28]

Any hope that agitation would succeed in undermining the appeal of the exhibition depended on a successful challenge of the American guides. It quickly became obvious that the young Russian-speaking guides—articulate, attractive, and thoroughly briefed for their mission—were having a positive impact on the Soviet visitors. They appeared as representatives of a more materially advanced culture, yet spoke the language of their audience. The guides, some the children of Soviet émigré families, appeared to embody the American dream.

Adopting a "soft sell" approach, the guides fielded endless questions, parried criticisms, and served as effective ambassadors for their country. Rather than attacking Soviet society directly, the guides concentrated on presenting a positive image of American life. Guide Tania Akhonin, the 22 year-old daughter of Russian parents, called the "soft sell" approach "the most important part of our job. The Russians have a great feeling of inferiority and it is not in our interests to intensify this feeling." Rather than trying to sell the Soviets on capitalism, she concentrated on correcting some of the "fantastic misconceptions" her audience reflected about American life. After fielding hundreds of questions and charges about U.S. poverty and unemployment, the young guide claimed that Soviet propaganda had structured an image of the United States "based on 1930 depression concepts." The Soviet image of widespread poverty was not merely a throwback to the Depression, however, as evidenced by President Lyndon Johnson's call for an American "war on poverty" in 1964.[29]

Although trained to parry Soviet criticisms, the guides did sometimes acknowledge the weaknesses of American society. Stressing the importance of maintaining composure at all times, guide Vera Garthoff explained that when her Soviet critics "strike something that is weak in our system, I don't try to hide it but admit, for example, that our private medical service is expensive. But we have medical insurance and clinics for the poor."[30]

While avoiding overt displays on race relations—including the craven decision to remove the African-American couple from the fashion show wedding scene—U.S. guides could scarcely ignore the issue of civil rights. Consistent with their pre-exhibition briefing in Washington, the guides admitted that the United States had yet to afford equality to African Americans, while stressing that progress was being made and would continue. The approach was the same as the "unfinished business" exhibit at Brussels, but guides conveyed the message in response to questions from their Soviet audience rather than through a more provocative formal exhibit. White America will "become wiser (on racial matters) over time," one guide explained. The African-American guides "were naturally objects of much interest" and something of a curiosity for the Soviets. Peppered with questions about segregation, slums, and poverty, they acknowledged the existence of discrimination while adding that amelioration was the hallmark of American democracy.[31]

With the exception of the organized CPSU agitators, relatively few Soviets bothered the guides with questions about controversial political subjects. A typical discourse might begin with a question or two about a particular exhibit. The questions would then quickly evolve into a wide-ranging discussion of all aspects of American society. "You get one or two questions about the exhibit you happen to be standing by and then 99 questions about America," noted Herb Miller, an African-American guide from New York. "They know that somehow we have it better in America, but they want to know how we live and they ask each guide about it." Russian émigré Igor Kosin, an agriculture professor, declared that "about 10 percent of my time is devoted to explaining American agriculture. Most of the time I find myself answering questions about everything under the sun, with accent on the American education system, the problem of racial discrimination, and comparative wage scales."[32]

Based on his discussions with the guides, USIA's Abbott Washburn estimated that "95 percent of the questions were asked out of pure intense curiosity." Guides fielded hundreds of questions a day about American homes, automobiles, televisions, wages and prices, schools, sports, and entertainment. Throngs of Soviet visitors perpetually hovered around the automobile and model home displays, prodding the guides with questions about availability and cost. Soviet audiences displayed intense curiosity about prices and frequently stopped to convert the dollar amounts into ruble prices in order to assess what items they might be able to afford on their own salaries.[33]

Most of the Soviet visitors responded warmly to the guides, thanking them for the information they had provided about life in the United States. Some confided their feelings and dissatisfactions about Soviet life. One elderly man, speaking in a hushed voice, inquired as to the whereabouts of Alexander Kerensky, head of the Provisional Government before the Bolshevik Revolution. Informed that Kerensky worked at the Hoover Institution on the campus of Stanford University in California, the elderly Russian whispered, "Give him my greetings and tell him that one of his defenders is still alive and prays for him."[34]

Other Soviet visitors slipped notes to the guides, "the most salient feature of [which] is their outspoken hostility to communism." Guides received notes of gushing praise about the U.S. exhibition. "If the Exhibition represents the American way of life," one declared, "then it is the American way of life we should overtake." "The American Exhibition convincingly shows that private enterprise produces more and in stupendous quantities the very best goods in the world," wrote another. "Greetings and best wishes to the clever American people." Other Soviet visitors surreptitiously handed the guides letters intended for friends and relatives in the West.[35] Whatever the popularity of the consumer items exhibited at Sokolniki, U.S. observers agreed that, as McClellan put it, "beyond the slightest doubt, the best exhibits we had were the American guides, who performed magnificently." "They would stand there answering questions hour after hour," Abbott Washburn recalled, "and they in themselves were the best exhibit the United States could have." "There is no doubt at all that the guides were the hit of the fair," declared Katherine G. Howard, an American visitor who had also attended the Brussels Fair. "For the Russian people to be able to freely talk with Americans and question them on any subject whatsoever was an astounding fact to them and one they appreciated to the fullest."[36]

Quickly recognizing the appeal of the guides, CPSU officials attached "great importance to conducting effective counterpropaganda" by directly challenging the young Americans. In one case, the CPSU delegated 20 agitators from the Office of Literary Censorship *(Glavlit)* "to carry out special work to expose the mendacious claims of the American guides." The agitators first monitored the presentations of individual American guides in order to prepare rebuttals, counterarguments, and challenging questions. The Soviet agitators interrupted guides to demand explanations for the incidence of unemployment, expensive health care, lack of concern for the mentally ill, segregation and race discrimination, the arms race, U.S. imperialism, and myriad additional criticisms of capitalist society. Unemployment and race relations received the most attention in Soviet counterpropaganda.[37]

Contemptuous of the "impudent" guides, "well trained by their bosses," the Soviet agitators were on a mission to counter the "mendacious and brazen propaganda . . . that jars one's ears." In their reports to CPSU superiors, the agitators claimed victory. While it appears they often did score propaganda points, and caught some of the guides unawares, the agitators were not above exaggerating their own effectiveness. One report boasted that a U.S. guide had been left "totally demoralized by the irrefutability of the arguments put forward" by the agitators on race relations, treatment of Indians, and incidence of mental illness in American society. The agitators claimed that their performance showed "how effective our counter-propaganda is and how single-minded were the Soviet people in their attitudes to the vices of the capitalist system."[38]

In the main pavilion, CPSU activists again rendered the U.S. guides "crushed by the arguments put forward by our communists concerning the essence of the vices of the American health service and race discrimination existing in the United States." The "helplessness of the guides" became evident, as they "evaded questions concerning the internal political situation in the United States, particularly the persecution of the Communist Party." At the "Family of Man" photographic exhibit, agitators countered the guides' attempts to "gloss over class contradictions and to conceal the differences between the exploited and the exploiters. Our communists gave appropriate and competent explanations to the visitors in place of that missing from the American guides' presentation." The agitators claimed they "exposed the myth of democracy in the United States in view of the existence of race discrimination and the lynch law."[39]

Armed with statistics, the CPSU counterpropagandists attempted to force guides to admit facts such as the rate of unemployment, health care costs, and the percentage of income earmarked for rent and tax payments. Day after day they grilled guides about race relations, the topic on which the Soviets correctly perceived the Americans as most vulnerable. The CPSU agitators boasted that under their questioning a guide "had to admit that the situation of negroes in the southern states was difficult, although he tried to prove that Soviet citizens had one-sided information." Similarly, agitators expressed satisfaction when one African-American guide was allegedly "taken aback by questions of marriages between the negroes and the whites." The black guide "evaded the question," yet admitted that while "everybody is equal before the law, this is only in theory."[40]

While most agitators trumpeted the effectiveness of the CPSU counterpropaganda campaign, others admitted to shortcomings. "The preparation of certain comrades is insufficient," noted one CPSU activist. For example, one agitator, obviously inadequately briefed, or simply in over his head, had demanded an explanation about the problems of racketeering in America. When the guide asked for a clarification of the question, it became clear that the Party activist had "asked about racketeers, without actually knowing what the term meant." Agitators also displayed bad timing on several occasions. In the midst of an American guide's explanation about how to operate the model motor boat, a comrade "suddenly asked about the lynch law, which produced a negative reaction" on the part of a public clearly more interested in motor boats.[41]

CPSU reports criticized the caliber of questions, noting that many had become "monotonous" and the guides had "long ago learned how to reply to them and to counter them, sometimes skillfully." The Party activist recommended determining in advance "the most vulnerable points in the guides' explanations and to find out which of them should be asked what particular questions. This would permit making our work more effective." Reports cautioned agitators about guides who had shown themselves to be particularly effective in countering the counterpropagandists. One report called attention to an older guide who was "very talkative and rather skillfully goes into attacks" on the USSR. One of the guide's favorite ploys was to tell his Soviet audience that he did not "understand why you should manufacture the luxurious Chaika [a limousine reserved for high government officials] while most people don't even own a Volga." The guide insisted that most American adults had an opportunity to own their own automobile.[42]

Despite the boasts of the CPSU agitators, the popularity of the guides and the reports of American observers suggest that the agitators made relatively little impact and were sometimes even counterproductive. "In every crowd every day there would be professional agitators, but as a rule the majority of the Russian audience would turn on the hecklers and tell them to be quiet," Katherine G. Howard recalled. "They wanted to hear what the American [guides] had to say." A U.S. newspaper editor reported that the Soviets "went to absurd lengths" to try to discredit the exhibition. "In the groups crowding around American exhibits there are obviously party-trained hecklers," the editor reported. "You can pick them out by the way they never wait for answers before asking other questions. The tactic often backfired with the heckler being told by the Russian spectators to shut up."[43]

Despite the best efforts of the agitators, the guides could not be dismissed as mere propaganda agents. "Their ability to be honest, plus their long seasoning in the art of intellectual give-and-take, gave them a depth and a flexibility in debate that made them much more than a match for the Soviet agitators who came up against them," a USIA official concluded. The guides appeared as "sincere persons who were trying to see the world fairly and truly. Could anything be more subversive, in a spot like Moscow?" Despite years of intense anti-American propaganda, Americans were struck by "the friendly attitude of most of the Soviet visitors toward America and Americans" in contrast to "the indifference of most Americans toward the Russian people." A common reaction was that of a Moscow man, who wrote, "Best of all I liked conversation with the American lads. We had a straightforward, frank talk. It seems to me that such contacts, such meetings are very useful."[44]

Unable to win the propaganda battle with the American guides, CPSU agitators, sometimes aided by the police, intimidated Soviet visitors who displayed "excessive" enthusiasm for the U.S. exhibition. "We had to remonstrate with one visitor who almost begged the guide to sell the exhibited cars," noted one report. The CPSU monitors shadowed a young woman involved in "an intimate conversation with a guide for an hour. She was flirting with him." Whenever possible, Party activists responded to such behavior by taking the Soviet citizen aside for a stern rebuke. In this case, however, the American guide perceived that "his conversation with the girl was attracting everybody's attention, [so] he took her to another pavilion." Counterpropagandists reported another occasion when a group of five or six people, in the presence of a guide, "obsequiously praised all the exhibited American products. The remonstration of our comrades concerning their conversation with the guides resulted in the visitors quickly leaving the pavilion."[45]

Counterpropagandists paid "special attention" to the visitor's remarks book, which the Americans placed near the exit of the exhibition. "We have an impression that it is the people who are full of admiration for the exhibition (and they constitute a tiny minority) who write in that book," CPSU activists reported. "We recommend being more active writing remarks with the correct evaluation of the situation." While most visitors prudently refrained from writing in the reaction book, a few brave dissidents and unhappy ethnic minorities used the comment books to vent their spleens. "We are Lithuanians and we can write and say only what the Government orders us," read one entry. "We are unhappy and impatiently are awaiting the time when we can be our own masters.[46]

Such comments were few, however, as CPSU officials monitored activity around the remarks books and practiced intimidation and censorship against those who attempted to write favorable comments. "When we approached the visitor's book we saw a middle-aged woman, fairly well dressed, obviously an office worker," one group of CPSU monitors reported.

> She was writing the following: "I really enjoyed the exhibition. We can see that your living standard is higher than ours and the people live better than we do." We asked her, "How was it possible for her to conclude that Americans live better?" Maybe she was so impressed by all kinds of little pots and pans that she was unable to see anything else. She started covering up what she had written with her hand and we told her that people cover up what they have written only when they are ashamed of it. In short, our presence made her finish her remarks somewhat differently than she had intended. She wrote the following: "But our government is also taking care of its people and is trying to make our life better."[47]

On another occasion the Party monitors overheard an elderly man, "a Jew," invite one of the American guides to his flat. They followed "the old geezer" *(starik)* to the visitor's book, where he wrote: "I'm 64 and an old-age pensioner. I am very happy to have survived to the day when I, with my own eyes, was able to see the American National Exhibition." He declared that "all the pavilions are beautiful" and thanked "from the bottom of my heart the people who made this exhibition possible. Thank you for the wonderful drink Pepsi Cola!" The CPSU officials confronted and criticized the elderly man before writing their own comments, under assumed names, in the visitor's books.

"This frivolity is not to our liking," they scrawled. "Do not try to hoist your way of life onto us."[48]

While the roaming packs of agitators could bully individual citizens, the CPSU failed in its larger quest to stem the popularity of the exhibition with the Soviet public. Despite the campaign of propaganda and intimidation, crowds of curious Soviets swarmed Sokolniki Park. From the opening day "the Soviet public evidenced tremendous interest in the Exhibition," McClellan reported. On Saturday morning, the day after the opening ceremonies, a throng of more than 20,000, kept in check by militiamen toting loudspeakers, waited outside the park entrance for the 11 a.m. opening. The same scene was repeated every day for the remainder of the exhibition. Shortly after the fair closed each night at 10 p.m., a huge line would begin to form outside the gates to buy tickets for the next day. McClellan recalled that the lines formed "regardless of weather. Frequently after a night of rain we would arrive at the site in the morning to find a wet crowd outside, still waiting a chance to get in."[49]

After the first week of operations, daily attendance ranged from 55,000 to 77,000—well in excess of the 50,000 tickets officially sold. For the six-week exhibition as a whole, attendance averaged 64,000 a day, for a total of more than 2.7 million. "There was a chronic ticket shortage and long lines formed as early as one o-clock in the morning to snap up the quota of tickets released by the Soviet authorities for the day," McClellan noted. "Easily twice as many tickets could have been sold had the exhibition site been able to accommodate the masses of Soviet citizens who wanted to see the American display." One entry in the remarks book, typical of many, alluded to "the great number of people who would like to visit it but are prevented from doing so by the limited number of tickets." Tickets for the exhibition, officially costing 1 ruble (25 cents), went for as much as 50 rubles on the black market. Black market ticket prices rose as the fair progressed and as its end loomed.[50]

Having personally observed "a good bit of gate crashing and fence climbing," McClellan noted that actual attendance of the exhibition substantially exceeded the official figure of 2.7 million. "They came in over the fence and under the fence. On one crowded day I checked what seemed to me as high as 20 percent pushing their way in with no tickets at all, simply because the guards and ticket takers at the gate were unable to restrain them." Ticket holders were supposed to arrive at 11 a.m., 2 p.m., or 5 p.m. and to depart after three hours, although such stipulations were widely ignored. Under the typically cumbersome Soviet procedure, fair-goers had to stand in three lines—one to take a number a second to receive a ticket, and a third to file into the exhibition. Those too impatient to wait, especially young people, found a way over the fences or simply bullied their way through. One U.S. diplomat reported that

Soviet citizens crowd around the exhibit of Detroit's latest model automobiles. The auto display was one of the more popular exhibits at the American National Exhibition. (Courtesy New York Times Pictures)

two boys, lacking tickets but "full of interest and questions in regard to the exhibit," asked him for details on the height of the fence since for them it had "become necessary to gain entrance by climbing it."[51]

As the Soviet propaganda campaign fizzled, the once highly visible agitators toned down their criticism and increasingly gave way to teeming crowds of ordinary citizens. In fact, as one U.S. diplomat reported, the remaining agitators themselves became "rapt with attention at U.S. displays and only hypocritically went about their tasks." With one or two exceptions, the U.S. exhibits proved well conceived and highly popular among the Soviet visitors. One Soviet, describing the exhibition as "excitingly beautiful" and making "the deepest impression," declared that he was coming back "for the third time with pleasure."[52]

According to the USIA's official analysis of the fair and its impact, the "Family of Man" photographic exhibition, the automobile display, the Circarama slide show, and the color television displays were the four most popular exhibits. Despite the threat of CPSU and police intimidation, the percentage of favorable comments in the remarks book rose from 59 percent early in the fair, when the agitators were most active, to 68 percent by the end of the fair.

No one could say what percentage of the unfavorable comments were still being written by the agitators.[53]

With the exception of the guides themselves, the automobile display may have been the single most popular exhibit at Sokolniki. Crowds, mostly men, gazed ceaselessly at 21 different new makes and models from Detroit's assembly lines. The Soviets nodded their heads in approval, muttering *"ochen khorosho"* ("very good") as they moved from car to car. A U.S. diplomat, touring the exhibition with a 28-year-old Soviet, noted that the young man had masked his emotions early in the tour, but "the automobile display completely broke down his reserve and his praises were unstinted." Visitors peppered the guides with questions about the cost, availability, and maintenance of the new automobiles. As with the auto display, "a severe crowd control problem in the glass pavilion became evident when the Lionel electric train was put into operation."[54]

While the auto exhibit was "getting a big play from men," Soviet women flocked to the Helena Rubinstein beauty salon to watch beauticians performing facial and hair treatments. Barred by Soviet authorities from receiving cosmetics samples, the women had to be content with watching the application of makeup and mascara in the model beauty salon. After contemplating the latest in beauty aids, women surveyed the most modern household appliances. Ambassador Thompson observed that "women as well as men were curious about American refrigerators and deep freezes. Such makes as Philco, Westinghouse, and General Electric Kelvinator attract considerable attention."[55]

As U.S. officials had anticipated, the model home display proved effective with Soviet audiences plagued by housing shortages and cramped apartments often occupied by multiple families. "At the first opportunity I would buy such a house," commented one Soviet visitor. "Meanwhile I have no house and live in a rented apartment and pay 300 rubles. I earn 700 rubles a month."[56]

Soviet visitors had an opportunity to see 16,208 pounds of frozen food prepared in the "miracle kitchen." The most common reaction to the Birds Eye Foods products, preparer Barbara Sampson reported, "is astonishment at their bright color, delicious aroma and, most of all, their great variety. Seeing us prepare in a few minutes four appetizing kinds of potatoes—mashed, crumble cut, french fried, and puffs—brings exclamations of delighted surprise." Convenience foods, relatively new even in the United States at the time, fascinated the predominantly female Soviet audiences. The women shook their heads in wonder at the demonstrations of appliances such as the Sunbeam mixer and a pyrex double boiler.[57]

Not every device and demonstration met the approval of the Soviet audience. Most of the visitors—unable to obtain fruit on a regular basis in any event—had little use for the orange juice squeezer on display. The Soviets, most of whom enjoyed a supply of fresher, higher quality bread than most American consumers, wondered aloud at the absurdity of cooking bread in a small metal box. The toaster was a "stupid" device, one of them declared. "After all, bread is already cooked! Why cook it again?"[58]

Disappointments were rare, however, as the Soviets strolled among the exhibits. They marveled at Walt Disney's Circarama, with its gigantic movie screens flashing pictures, beginning with the Statue of Liberty and followed by panoramic shots of American cities, highways, supermarkets, churches, national parks, and bucolic agricultural scenes. One U.S. diplomat, touring the exhibition with a Soviet acquaintance, observed that "the overall impact of the Circarama show was to sharpen his longing to visit the United States and see its wonders for himself." Almost as popular, despite the countermeasures of the CPSU activists, was the "Family of Man" photographic exhibit representing people from more than 300 countries.[59]

The IBM RAMAC 305 computer, programmed to answer 4,000 questions in ten languages spoken in the USSR, never failed to attract a large crowd. After 16 days the "electronic brain" had answered 15,381 questions about the United States. The 20 most often asked questions ranged from mundane concerns such as "How much do U.S. cigarettes cost?," to weightier issues such as "What is meant by the American dream?" Questions focusing on American jazz and economic issues were those asked most frequently. The 20 most-asked questions, including the two cited above, were the following: "Origins of American Jazz?" "What is the Present Direction in the Development of American Jazz?" "Most Popular U.S. Jazz Band?" "How Old Is Louis Armstrong?" "What Is American Rock and Roll Music?" "What Is the Liberty Bell?" "What Is the Average Family Income of the U.S. Family?" "Division of Budget Planning Between Husband and Wife?" "What Is Minimum Wage in the U.S.?" "Costs and Earnings in the U.S.?" "Assistance Which U.S. Renders to International Agency for Atomic Energy?" "Commercial and Technical Research in Food Products?" "How Many Negroes Have Been Lynched in the U.S. Since 1950?" "Reasons for Abstract Paintings?" "Miniature Radio Receivers in the U.S.?" "Achievements in Chemistry?" "Favorite Recreational Activities in the U.S.?" "Number of Unmarried Men and Women in the U.S.?"[60]

Those preferring image to information could leave the IBM computer behind for a short trek to the fashion show, with its parade of brightly clad models. Controversy over the desegregated mock wedding scene preoccupied mainly Americans—it was the models and the clothes they wore that captivated Soviet audiences. Eschewing glamorous attire, the fashion show—using children, teens, grandparents, and whole families as models—emphasized everyday wear. Rather than a parade of evening gowns, tuxedos, and the trappings of

The nude sculpture by Lachaise became one of the more notorious examples of modern art at the U.S. exhibition. Soviet leader Nikita S. Khrushchev targeted the modern art display for criticism and declared of this sculpture: "only a homosexual could have done such a statue since he obviously didn't think much of womanhood." (Coutesy New York Times Pictues)

high fashion, the fashion show attempted to convey the high quality of mass produced clothing. The aim was to emphasize "the fact that the American man, woman, and child can purchase directly, or by mail, a well fitting wardrobe within any budget."[61]

A total of 47 models depicted scenes ranging from the mock wedding ceremony to a rock 'n' roll dance. "We love the way you show your clothes—it's like going to the theater," one Soviet commented after witnessing the show. "You American models seem so happy on the stage," noted another visitor. "You smile naturally, from your whole soul." Crowds of Soviets admired and photographed the models, some of whom received chocolates and bottles of vodka. One smitten Soviet man even offered his Soviet medal, the prestigious Order of Lenin. Soviet women complimented the trim shape and fair skin of the older female models. "You remind us of Catherine the Great," offered one Soviet woman, "but you have a better figure!"[62]

As in virtually every exhibit, the Soviets launched a plethora of questions. "How do you stay so thin?" they asked the models. "Do you have to diet all the time?" "Do you really dress this way?" "Is this the way Americans really look?" Some even waited until the show was over to catch a glimpse of the models once they had changed clothes in an effort to see how they "really dressed." Soviet women asked numerous questions about cosmetics, nylons, underwear, and false eyelashes ("Can you wear them in sleep?"). The most often asked questions, however, focused on the costs and availability of the clothes being modeled. The Soviets would plead, "Please, *tovarish* (comrade), where can we buy it?"[63]

Despite Soviet propaganda targeting "decadent" capitalist entertainments, the rock 'n' roll scene in the fashion show was popular with most audiences. "Although some of the older generation say they don't like it, most of the young Soviet citizens seem intrigued by the Elvis Presley record and the American dance," U.S. observers noted. "We always heard that rock 'n' roll was a wild dance—for hoodlums—but you all look like you're having such fun!" one teen exclaimed. The cathedral wedding scene provoked a "most enthusiastic response" from the Soviet audience. The fashion show sometimes became the scene of interactive entertainment between the audience and the models. On one occasion, when rain prompted cancellation of the show, a crowd of disappointed Soviets remained standing. The American models quickly donned raingear and returned to the stage to lead the Soviets in a chorus of "Singin' in the Rain."[64]

A musical presentation of decidedly higher quality, held in conjunction with the U.S. exhibition, "took Moscow by storm," declared *Time*. Leonard Bernstein, conductor of the New York Philharmonic Orchestra, presented 18 concerts across the USSR under the auspices of the president's special international program. Stopping to lecture and entertain his audiences, Bernstein generated unbridled enthusiasm in five Moscow concerts coinciding with the Sokolniki fair. "I have never seen greater appreciation for fine music demonstrated nor a more hearty welcome afforded to a man because of his humility of spirit and generosity with his talents," McClellan declared. Overall, the tour was "tremendously successful. The orchestra and its talented director were acclaimed by standing ovations night after night."[65]

Variety show host Ed Sullivan also evoked a popular response by hosting a 14-act program in conjunction with the American exhibition. Warned to "keep in mind the extreme prudery of the Soviet public," Sullivan presented a tame but popular show. The Soviet audience of 14,000 responded with "waves of thunderous applause," threw flowers onto the stage, and mobbed the performers at the end of the show. Sullivan taped the show, which later played on U.S. television.[66]

While the popularity of the shows and exhibits attested to the success of the American effort in Moscow, Soviet visitors did express disappointment at the absence of technological and industrial displays. "Is it possible that you think our mental outlook is restricted to everyday living only?" read one comment in the remarks book. "There is too little technology. Where is your industry?" "We expected that the American exhibition would show something grandiose, something similar to Soviet sputniks . . . and you Americans want to surprise us with the glitter of your kitchen pans and the fashions which do not appeal to us at all."[67]

Although such comments may well have been written by CPSU agitators, U.S. guides confirmed that the most common of the negative comments concerned an absence of displays of the "marvels of American technology." Other complaints included an unrequited desire to see more examples of a life of luxury. Clearly, many Soviets came for a glimpse of the capitalist decadence that CPSU propagandists so often made the focus of their attacks. "How well this portrays the manner in which the average American lives," one Soviet woman observed, but she lamented the absence of displays on the lives of the fabulously wealthy. While the Americans stressed that the goods on display could be purchased by the average consumer, Soviets longed to know "how a genuine millionaire lives."[68]

In response to repeated Soviet pleas for an opportunity to purchase display items—as well as the challenges and expense of striking and shipping the exhibition—the Commerce Department announced on August 25 that it would offer some 1,800 items for sale to Soviet buyers at the closing of the exhibition. The model kitchen, home furnishings, tools, sporting goods, office equipment, automobiles and photographic equipment were among the items to be offered for sale. The heart-lung machine and a few other items would be donated to the USSR. Commerce Department officials declared that by offering the display items for sale, Washington hoped to make a "sincere gesture of good will to the Soviet people" and to establish a precedent of Soviet and American business transactions.[69]

The Kremlin, however, responded in "sharp and highly critical" fashion to the offer, immediately denouncing the proposed sale as a "propaganda gimmick." U.S. diplomats reported that "resultant Soviet ill-feeling risks complicating the process of striking the exhibition and the financial settlement connected with it." U.S. officials responded by issuing a clarification and reducing the number of items offered for sale to the Soviets.[70]

Only days after the announcement of the proposed sale, Soviet premier Nikita S. Khrushchev arrived for a final, unscheduled tour of the exhibition. Making his third visit to the exhibition site on its second to last day of operation,

September 3, Khrushchev offered a characteristic display of contradictory behavior that ranged from crude and boisterous criticism to quiet praise. The Soviet leader criticized the absence of evidence of technological achievement and attempted to dismiss the display of consumer goods as frivolous. At one point he declared—in defiance of the crowds of enthusiastic Soviets milling around Sokolniki—that "our people are not really interested in your exhibition." Only minutes later, however, the Soviet leader told McClellan he was impressed by the exhibition and that "the exchange of exhibits was a good thing and more should be scheduled in the future."[71]

Khrushchev's unscheduled visit provided the occasion for more theatrics. Throughout his visit, U.S. diplomats reported, Khrushchev "was surrounded by a great number of KGB functionaries" and "lesser goons," who "behaved in a most amateurish way and seemed to enjoy acting like toughs and mauling whomever they could lay their hands on." U.S. diplomats noted that when a huge, appreciative crowd swarmed around Khrushchev the "crush to see him was so tremendous that it got out of hand on several occasions. Exhibit structures were dangerously threatened by the press of humanity at several spots."[72]

Although accompanied by McClellan, Khrushchev made it clear that he would tour only those exhibits that he had already decided he wanted to see. The Soviet leader rejected McClellan's suggestion that he view the "Family of Man" and Circarama exhibits, making his way instead to the art exhibition. The Soviet leader's purpose at once became clear. The art exhibit had been the least popular display—with Soviet audiences as well as among the Americans themselves. Controversy had swirled in press accounts in both nation's capitals about the examples of modern art chosen for display in Moscow. Soviet critics condemned the "filthy and revolting abstract art," which they advised Americans to "keep at home and use it on ranches to scare off crows." Evidence gathered by USIA, however, suggested that a substantial number of Soviet artists and intellectuals were "intensely interested in our abstract art and began to look at it with open minds."[73]

Anxious to score points against the most vulnerable display, Khrushchev unleashed a tirade of invective as he viewed the canvasses of modern art. "I was struck by Mr. Khrushchev's obvious delight in making disparaging remarks about the paintings he saw," noted a U.S. diplomat. The Soviet leader's remarks were unquestionably "strong and, in some cases, very crude." Touring beside Khrushchev was Richard McClanathan, curator of the U.S. art exhibit, who explained that artist John Marin's seascape "isn't just a seascape: the subject is movement—sea and sky, and the artist has painted it . . . in such a way that you can be looking at it and share his feelings for the beauty of nature." Khrushchev responded to this sympathetic interpretation by turning to his entourage and bellowing, "It reminds me of a little boy making a puddle on the floor!" Turning to the next canvass, the Soviet leader declared that "it looks like tripe to me." "That's terrible, too," he averred in front of the next painting. "What is it? . . . People who paint like that are obviously crazy, but people who think it's art are crazier still."

Punching, back-slapping, and exclaiming "O.K." throughout his tour, Khrushchev bore no resemblance to the tense, defiant opponent of Nixon in the kitchen debate during his last visit to Sokolniki. Continuing his tour outside the pavilion, Khrushchev stopped before a nude sculpture by Lachaise and made a "remark to the effect that only a homosexual could have done such a statue since he obviously didn't think much of womanhood."[74]

The Soviet crowds responded enthusiastically to Khrushchev's appearance at Sokolniki, but at the same time he did nothing to dampen their enthusiasm for the exhibition. Indeed, a record crowd of 130,000 people surged through the gates on the final day of the fair. Just after 9 p.m. on September 4, the exhibition closed after 42 days. "The visitors did not want to go," a U.S. diplomat recalled. "They hung back as much as they could, begging a last look at the Sears, Roebuck catalog, trying for one more conversation, one more question, one more contact, one more glimpse."[75]

Khrushchev's visit marked the last propaganda offensive against the exhibition—it ceased to exist in the Soviet press the day of its closure. Soviet memories, bolstered by memorabilia, remained, however, and spread across the USSR by word of mouth. The "universality and urgency" of visitors' desires for souvenirs impressed their U.S. hosts. Crowds grappled for red, white, and blue fair buttons, auto brochures, plastic cups and many other "tangible trophies" from the exhibition. "Some near riots occurred when these things were distributed," noted the USIA.[76]

Other popular souvenirs included the 20-page color guidebook, 2.5 million of which had been handed out, pamphlets, and corporate handouts. Soviet visitors took home one million *znachki* (lapel pins) commemorating the exhibition, yet the demand for them was still only partially met. Weeks after the exhibition's close, commemorative lapel pins and automobile pamphlets "still passing from hand to hand all over the country indicate that the public remembers, whether the press does or not." Soviet visitors took home tens of thousands of plastic ashtrays stamped with the exhibition's emblem. Others cherished snapshots of themselves from the Polaroid "pictures in a minute" exhibit. Untold numbers of Soviet visitors had pleaded successfully with Americans at Sokolniki for the sale or exchange of items of clothing and various paraphernalia.[77]

The popular appeal of the U.S. exhibition gratified the Americans who were responsible for it. McClellan, Washburn, and those most familiar with the exhibition considered it an unambiguous success. Ambassador Thompson and the Moscow embassy diplomats betrayed none of the traditional State Department suspicions and prejudices against cultural initiatives. One embassy officer spoke of "the impression I have received from dozens of conversations with Russians that they admire the American living standard, are eager for friendship and have a remarkably ready credulity for favorable information about the United States." Before the exhibition, noted Katherine Howard, "many Russians, affected by propaganda, had pictured America as a nation with a few capitalists, and masses of downtrodden people." After viewing the products available to American consumers, and speaking at length with the impressive young guides, their view of the United States had been irrevocably altered.[78]

The American press, which like the State Department often had been congenitally dubious about overseas cultural initiatives, heaped praise upon the U.S. exhibition. *Time* declared that the Sokolniki exhibit had "wowed" the Soviets; the *New York Herald-Tribune* judged the fair "a smash hit." Typical newspaper headlines attested to the favorable press coverage and perceptions of U.S. success in Moscow: "Ivan Appears to Like the Way Joneses Live"; "Muscovites Marvel at Kitchen Show"; "American Ideas Leap Curtain"; "Iron Curtain is Breached"; "Main Street Goes to Moscow"; "70,000 See U.S. Exhibit Daily"; "Controversial Art Draws Throngs"; and "Russians Eager to Know U.S."[79]

The USIA concluded that the Moscow exhibition was "the largest and probably the most productive single psychological effort ever launched by the U.S. in any communist country." Noting that the Sokolniki fair outdrew the Soviet exhibition in New York by a ratio of almost three to one, officials concluded the United States had "won" the battle of the exhibitions. The Sokolniki fair had served to communicate ideas about American culture and life and, especially through the activities of the guides, had achieved "a humanizing of [the Soviet] image of America."[80]

Despite the praise, USIA itself was more equivocal than most sources in its overall evaluation. While attendance at Sokolniki had been gratifying, especially given the difficulty in obtaining tickets, the USIA report on the fair noted that simple curiosity and the dearth of entertainment opportunities in the USSR might have accounted for much of it. Analysis of written and oral evidence indicated that most Soviets left with a favorable impression, yet others had been disappointed, primarily as a result of "exaggerated, unrealistic expectations" about the United States. The USIA report declared that the "preoccupation with consumer goods was somewhat too great, with too little on either actual living in America . . . or on the essentials of democracy." The United States had accomplished its aim of convincing the Soviet visitors that most Americans had an opportunity to live well, but had presented "too little about the life and spirit of America." The USIA report also concluded that a "really massive and spectacular technical exhibit" in Moscow would "create wonderment and admiration in even the most skeptical Soviet mind. If we've learned any one thing about the Soviet public it is that they *want* to be amazed and impressed by the technically best things we have."[81]

In Washington, a group of governors who had visited the exhibition criticized the focus on consumerism, complaining to the president that "we stress nail polish and cosmetics too much." Vice President Nixon disagreed, telling Eisenhower that the governors failed to "realize the drabness of life in the Soviet Union," and thus underestimated the appeal of the exhibition. McClellan, too, rejected the criticisms, declaring that "it is my view and the view of the staff that the mass of visitors who came to the park, while interested in machines and production, were even more interested in consumer items, in furnishings, kitchens, toys, and clothing." He noted that "the Soviets, over and over again, asked the guides how they lived, what they earned, what clothes cost, how they were educated, as well as something about their freedoms."[82]

Soviet actions in the wake of the American exhibition bolstered McClellan's argument that the focus on consumerism appealed to average citizens, while putting pressure on the Kremlin leaders. Throughout the exhibition, Soviet citizens had demonstrated their desire to purchase American products. Eager to be consumers, they revealed frustration with the dearth of available goods in their own stores. The demand for more consumer goods was "a natural result" of the American exhibition, noted a U.S. diplomat in Moscow. "Official recognition of this development has already been evident in the attention given to so-called display sales of better quality merchandise around Moscow. Khrushchev is in fact under a self-compulsion to demonstrate that his system can provide in quantity goods similar to those put on display by the leading capitalist power."[83]

Within six months of the closing of the exhibition, a USIA study reported, the Soviet consumer "has witnessed an unusual number of announcements, decrees, and official actions designed to assure the citizen that his material existence is improving." More processed foods, medicine, and medical supplies began to appear in stores. Soviet officials bolstered retail services. The Sokolniki exhibit had exercised a "direct influence" in the changes. U.S. officials noted "conscious imitation in several fields—ranging from blond streaks in the hair-dos of fashion models, to clothing styles, to the projected modernization of refrigerator and washing machine design." Following the Sokolniki fair, GUM, the mammoth state department store in Moscow, offered brighter colors and new styles patterned on those worn by American models in the fashion show. Installment credit, explained to Soviet consumers by U.S. guides, spread across the Russian republic in the wake of the exhibition. Analysis revealed an "increase in official acknowledgement that drastic improvements must be made in the quality and variety of goods and in consumer services." Khrushchev himself had offered such acknowledgement after being questioned, sometimes sharply, on the availability and cost of consumer goods during his travels around the USSR.[84]

Thus, in real and tangible, as well as in subtle and symbolic ways, the 1959 American National Exhibition in Moscow was a highly successful initiative. For its cost—$3.6 million in federal appropriations—the exhibition arguably offered a greater return than any single Cold War initiative since the Marshall Plan. One Soviet expert "believed that the exchange of national exhibits between the U.S. and the USSR possesses a potential efficacy that is unlikely to be matched by any other conceivable East-West feature." The exhibition had reached a wide audience—both directly and through word of mouth—and had provided "the opportunity to seek modifications, however small and possibly temporary they may be, in the attitudes, policies, regulations, etc., of the Soviet Government." The relatively few weaknesses identified could have been remedied with better funding. The USIA final report concluded that "a doubled budget is a minimum" in the event of a future exhibition of similar magnitude in the USSR. No doubt in part because of the success of 1959 exhibition, no comparable U.S. display was again staged during the Cold War.[85]

Given the resources available, and the daunting challenges he confronted, Chad McClellan had performed an astonishing feat. Only after the exhibition closed were U.S. officials "in a position to savor the magnitude and quality of his achievement." Through a combination of intelligence and persistence, McClellan had seen his vision come to life. "It was a crash operation from the beginning," Abbott Washburn recalled, "and one that could only have been achieved by this kind of combined effort and driving wonderful leadership of an executive like Chad McClellan." Gratified, McClellan mused that he would savor vivid memories of the extravaganza, especially at night, when it was "most beautiful, when all the lights were on and the crowds could be seen about the grounds, under the translucent plastic parasols, and in the glass pavilion."[86]

Confronted with the undeniable popularity of the Sokolniki fair—and the futility of their own, often pathetic, propaganda counteroffensives—the Kremlin leaders must have questioned their decision to agree to the staging of the U.S. exhibition. The Americans themselves had no doubt that the United States had "gained much more from this opening of doors than the Soviet Union did, or could, in presenting a similar show here. . . . Through the guides and through other direct contacts the exhibition opened doors that for the first time permitted extensive, two-way communication between this country's representatives and Soviet citizens."[87]

The Sokolniki exhibition had provided the United States an ideal forum to respond to Khrushchev's claim that the Soviet system would overtake and "bury" the capitalist West. The teeming crowds at Sokolniki now knew, from first hand experience, that their country lagged well behind the United States in the quality of life that it could provide to consumers. The images and symbols of American life had made a profound impression. Most Soviets, it seemed, were still willing to be patient and give the socialist system the time it needed to catch up with the West. Thirty years later, their patience would come to an end.

EIGHT

Conclusions: Militarization, Cultural Infiltration, and the Cold War

Despite the tensions evident at the Sokolniki fair, the prospects appeared good for continuing amelioration of Soviet-American relations in the wake of the U.S. exhibition. Overcoming opposition in Moscow and Beijing, Khrushchev had placed his own prestige behind the campaign of "peaceful coexistence" with the West. The Soviet leader hoped to calm international disputes and achieve agreements over Berlin and arms control in order to focus attention on domestic economic development. Khrushchev anxiously pursued a summit with Eisenhower in an effort to achieve the aims of his peaceful coexistence policy.[1]

For months Khrushchev expressed his desire to visit the United States, but John Foster Dulles remained adamantly opposed. Receiving the Kremlin leader would serve only to enhance Soviet prestige while sowing divisions in the allied coalition, Dulles insisted. Typically reluctant to overrule his secretary of state, Eisenhower waited until two months after Dulles's death from cancer on May 24, 1959, before extending an invitation to Khrushchev. At a news conference on August 3, Eisenhower announced that he and Khrushchev had agreed on reciprocal visits, beginning with the Soviet leader's tour of the United States the following month.[2]

On September 15, 1959, Khrushchev embarked on a historic visit to the United States, the first ever by a Soviet leader. The tour illuminated both the promise and the perils of Soviet-American relations. Khrushchev betrayed sharp anxieties, brought to the surface by the Sokolniki exhibition and reinforced during his tour, about the superiority of American material society. These anxieties, compounded by unresolved Cold War conflicts over Berlin, the nuclear arms race, and competition in the Third World, placed limits on what could be achieved during Khrushchev's visit.[3]

After arriving at Andrews Air Force base near Washington on September 15, Khrushchev spent two days conducting talks, attending formal dinners, and touring the capital. Exchanges between the two world leaders were friendly, except when Khrushchev berated Eisenhower over the Captive Nations Resolution. Pointed exchanges followed over the Berlin question and nuclear weapons. As the two leaders, meeting first in Washington, attempted to set an agenda for subsequent talks at the presidential retreat in Camp David, Maryland, Eisenhower stressed "trade and especially the development of tourist exchanges." When the president expressed satisfaction that the two sides had cooperated on the staging of national exhibitions, Khrushchev made a point of appearing unimpressed. The Soviet leader "interrupted at this point to say that as concerns exhibits, he could say in a friendly way that the United States exhibit could have been much better than it was."[4]

Before returning to Camp David for talks, Khrushchev embarked on a cross-country tour of the United States that left him alternatively impressed and irritable. The Soviet leader complained repeatedly of disrespect, as evidenced by hostile political speeches, chanting anti-Soviet crowds, and denial of his requests to visit sites ranging from Harlem to Disneyland. The low point came in Los Angeles, where he not only received a cool reception but endured what even his hosts admitted was "a really vulgar, even obscene show" by the cast of *Can Can* during his tour of a Hollywood studio. When the studio's publicity staff attempted to arrange pictures of Khrushchev surrounded by the scantily clad dancers, he was "quite obviously offended at this treatment of the Premier of Russia." After threatening to cancel the tour and return to the USSR, Khrushchev recovered his equilibrium in San Francisco, which he judged a beautiful city.[5]

Throughout his stay in the United States, Khrushchev insisted that "nothing had impressed him particularly because he had been familiar with the United States previously by watching movies, reading books, and studying reports." Just the opposite was true, according to Henry Cabot Lodge, who had acted as Khrushchev's shepherd during the tour. Lodge declared that the Soviet leader had been "deeply impressed by much that he has seen—the condition and attitudes of our people, our roads, automobiles, factories, etc. He was really struck by the vitality of our people. He probably does not really think the Soviets

Eisenhower and Khrushchev were all smiles at the Camp David summit in September 1959. Less than a year later, the U-2 incident destroyed the "spirit of Camp David" and Eisenhower's hopes of achieving some accomodation with the Soviets during his presidency. (Courtesy Dwight D. Eisenhower Library)

are likely to surpass us, at least anytime soon." Despite his determination to act unimpressed, Khrushchev did admit that he "had never denied that the United States had the highest standard of life and the most efficient methods of production."[6]

After returning to Washington on September 25, Khrushchev and Eisenhower took a helicopter to Camp David for two days of talks. Khrushchev continued to insist that American prosperity did not impress him. He complained of the wastefulness of so many private automobiles and single-family homes as opposed to Soviet multifamily apartment buildings. Speaking "in a rather irritated and excited manner" at a luncheon on September 26, Khrushchev "again referred to the attempt by the United States to impress the Soviet people with gadgets displayed at the Moscow exhibit." He added that the effort at Sokolniki had "completely failed" because the Soviets "had a high standard of living of their own, and that any attempt to lure them toward capitalism would fail." U.S. analysts concluded that "the compulsive (and often counterproductive) way in which he reacted to all criticism" illustrated that Khrushchev possessed "to an extraordinary degree the feelings of inferiority characteristic of his countrymen and their resultant drive for self-assertion."[7]

Despite such anxieties, Khrushchev and Eisenhower made progress at Camp David. The two leaders put aside the dispute over Berlin and Khrushchev quietly abandoned any mention of a deadline or ultimatum. They made plans to meet again in May 1960 at a summit in Paris. With both powers observing a moratorium on nuclear weapons tests, the stage was set for signing a nuclear test ban treaty at the Paris summit.[8] Perhaps more significantly, however, the two leaders mused about the pressures placed upon both of them by their respective military establishments to approve of new weapons systems and thus fuel the Cold War. In his memoirs, Khrushchev made it clear that he sought to check Soviet militarization as a means of improving living standards in the USSR. Moreover, Soviet arms reductions could reduce the appeal of U.S. militarists and the "wealthy aggressive capitalistic circles" that guided them.[9]

The Camp David summit served to further the spirit of goodwill first established through cultural exchange programs. The Soviets set the tone by announcing on the day of Khrushchev's arrival in the United States that they were suspending all jamming of VOA broadcasts. "We are ready to establish altogether normal relations in radio," Georgi A. Zhukov, head of the ministry of cultural affairs, told USIA director George Allen. The Soviets also pledged to allow broader circulation of *Amerika* magazine in the USSR and to consider the establishment of permanent libraries and information centers in New York and Moscow. "If the American side was ready to normalize relations in the field of exchanges of information," Zhukov declared, the Soviet side was "willing to go very far."[10]

Washington responded positively, reinforcing guidelines that ensured that the VOA continued to function as a tame informational network rather than reverting to its original mission of psychological warfare. In response to the Soviet suspension of jamming, Allen issued instructions to the VOA "to be particularly careful and not be provocative," especially in its Russian language broadcasts. The State Department directed the USIA to "continue to treat Soviet activities in reasoned, moderate tones and avoid Cold War vocabulary." All USIA media were to "avoid any plausible pretext for Soviet resumption of full jamming or blatant anti-American propaganda."[11]

The Camp David discussions on informational and cultural exchange "went very well," as cultural issues remained the one area most conducive to détente. Both leaders reaffirmed their support of expanded scientific, technical, and cultural exchanges, paving the way for renewal of the 1958 agreement. Eisenhower and Khrushchev parted on amiable terms and looked forward to their meeting in Paris in May. The joint communique on the Camp David talks reported "substantial progress" in discussions on exchange programs, adding that "certain agreements will be reached in the near future."[12]

The forecast proved accurate less than two months later with the announcement of the signing of a new cultural agreement. The agreement included a provision for increased circulation of the magazines *Amerika* and *USSR* in the respective countries. There would be no grand displays on the scale of Sokolniki under the new agreement, but each side would present three smaller exhibitions over the next two years. The themes of the three U.S. exhibitions would be medicine and medical services, plastics, and transportation. Finally, both sides agreed "to do everything possible to promote the development of tourism," including renewed negotiations on reciprocal direct air links.[13]

Eisenhower hoped to advance the spirit of cooperation through his own tour of the Soviet Union, slated for June 10-19, 1960. The president was widely admired in the USSR as an Allied war hero, and his reciprocal visit was to serve as a prelude to the Paris summit. The proposed tour across the USSR, returning home through Alaska, would have been the first by an American leader. Eisenhower himself believed the visit "might have been quite a significant one." If nothing else, he told an aide, "I'm like any other American, I'd like to see the damned place."[14]

The shootdown of an American U-2 spyplane over Soviet airspace on May 1, 1960, ended not only planning for Eisenhower's tour but the prospects of East-West détente as well. U.S. spyplanes had been conducting aerial reconnaissance missions over Soviet airspace—in violation of international law—since the early years of the Cold War. Several planes had been shot down. Eisenhower encouraged and expanded overflights to gather intelligence on Soviet military capabilities. The lightweight Lockheed U-2 spyplanes had been conducting reconnaissance overflights, under CIA oversight, since 1956. The Soviets had lodged protests against penetrations of their airspace, but had been unable to impede the high-flying U-2 until the May 1 shootdown.[15]

Eisenhower personally approved all U-2 overflights, but often with serious, even haunting, reservations. The president feared "undue provocation" of the Soviets, noting that "nothing would make him request authority to declare war more quickly than violation of our air space by Soviet aircraft." Eisenhower expressed anxiety about exacerbating world tensions through "our pursuit of a program of extensive reconnaissance flights" over Soviet territory. The CIA and Joint Chiefs of Staff continued to press Eisenhower to approve overflights, however, assuring the president that a shootdown of the high altitude U-2 was impossible. In any case, Eisenhower's advisers assured him, the pilot would perish in such an incident, allowing Washington enough maneuverability to deny responsibility.[16]

Having established a hopeful "spirit of Camp David" with Khrushchev, Eisenhower expressed "considerable reservations" about the risks associated with additional U-2 overflights. The president saw "no hope for the future unless we can make some progress in negotiation" with the Soviets. An airplane incident would undermine the impending Paris summit and bring down "the revulsion of world opinion" on the United States. The president's aide Andrew Goodpaster recalled Eisenhower's concern "over the terrible propaganda impact that would be occasioned if a reconnaissance plane were to fail." The President did not want to do anything to disrupt plans for further discussions with Khrushchev in Paris, especially as it appeared "the Soviets really want a summit meeting." Despite his reservations, and awareness that the Soviets had improved the capability of surface-to-air missiles, Eisenhower authorized U-2 flights on April 9 as well as the final U-2 overflight on May 1. Eisenhower caved in to his military and intelligence advisers despite his own belief, confirmed by previous reconnaissance flights, that Khrushchev had provided him with an accurate evaluation of Soviet missile capability at Camp David.[17]

The President's worst fears materialized when a Soviet missile shot the U-2 out of the sky. Assuming that the pilot had perished, Washington denied Soviet charges of an espionage overflight, thus falling into a Kremlin trap. The Soviets soon produced abundant evidence of Washington's culpability. Hauled before a Soviet court, the U-2 pilot, Gary Powers, who had parachuted to safety, confessed that his mission was part of a broad and long-standing aerial espionage campaign. Unable to deny responsibility, Eisenhower publicly admitted that he had approved the mission, but justified it as a means of discerning Soviet capabilities and ensuring against surprise attack.[18]

Despite Khrushchev's triumphant exposure of American culpability for the overflight, the U-2 incident was an unmitigated disaster for the Soviet leader. Khrushchev had overcome domestic and Chinese opposition to gain approval of his "peaceful coexistence" policy. On January 14, 1960, he had cut Soviet troop strength by 1.2 million men, arguing that such action served to encourage moderation in the West and free up resources for domestic economic growth. Having backed off on the Berlin ultimatum in deference to the West, Khrushchev needed to deliver results from the Paris summit—either a test ban agreement, which Eisenhower also wanted, or an understanding over Berlin.[19]

Following his return from Washington, Khrushchev had expressed his personal trust and confidence in Eisenhower in a cross-country speaking tour. Both the U-2 incident, occurring on the Soviet May Day holiday, and Eisenhower's subsequent dishonesty about American responsibility shattered Khrushchev's depiction of the president as a reliable negotiating partner. Soviet defense minister Rodion Malinovsky, who had opposed the cuts in troop strength, declared that the lesson of Camp David, contrary to Khrushchev's peaceful coexistence policy, was that "One should not trust the words of the imperialists." Years later Khrushchev admitted that "From the time Gary Powers was shot down in a U-2 over the Soviet Union I was no longer in full control."[20]

Even though Soviet officials had been aware of the overflights for years, the shootdown of the U-2 was a galvanizing event that changed the Soviet posture toward the United States. Under pressure from Soviet hardliners as well as the Chinese CP, Khrushchev abandoned the quest for détente. The Soviet leader confided to Llewelyn Thompson, the ambassador in Moscow, that "he had been obliged to use all of his authority to persuade the Soviet military" to accept cuts in the armed forces as well as the policy of peaceful coexistence with the West. Khrushchev emphasized to Thompson "the great importance he attached to the fact that U-2 flights were made after his visit to the U.S. and especially his friendly conversations with the president. He has thus indicated that not only was Soviet military prestige an important factor but also his own personal prestige in view of favorable remarks he made about the president after his return to the Soviet Union."

Thompson, who had established a close relationship with Khrushchev, found the Soviet leader genuinely "offended and angry" by the U-2 overflights. Using terms befitting his peasant upbringing, Khrushchev explained that he canceled plans for Eisenhower's tour of the USSR because when "someone comes to visit you and you catch him redhanded throwing a dead cat over your fence, you could not respect yourself if you received him as an honored guest."

In addition to alienating Khrushchev and undermining détente, Thompson reported, the U-2 incident had wrecked a favorable image of Eisenhower with the Soviet public, which had been a "great asset" to the United States.[21]

When the Paris summit convened on May 14, Khrushchev denounced the United States for the U-2 overflight and demanded both a public apology and promises against similar espionage missions in the future. When Eisenhower, backed by his British and French allies, refused to comply with these demands, Khrushchev and the Soviet delegation walked out. Khrushchev privately informed Thompson that there was "no possibility of resolving our problems during the rest of the current Administration." The abortive summit in Paris ended any prospect of the two powers signing a test ban treaty. Noting that Eisenhower failed to act decisively on the issue for two years, a careful student of the test ban negotiations concluded that Eisenhower's "own lack of leadership" was responsible for the failure to achieve an accord.[22]

With only eight months remaining in his term, Eisenhower realized that he would fail in his quest to achieve a breakthrough in the Cold War. As a result of "the stupid U-2 mess," he told one of his advisers, "there was nothing left worthwhile for him to do now until the end of his presidency." As for Khrushchev, with peaceful coexistence discredited, the Soviet leader had no choice but to gravitate toward the hardline "anti-imperialist" approach of his critics if he hoped to retain his authority. Khrushchev grew increasingly aggressive and reckless, practicing brinkmanship in Berlin and Cuba in 1961 and 1962.[23]

Immediately after the U-2 incident, the Soviets reinstituted massive jamming of the VOA, but it tapered off into more selective interference by the end of May. Otherwise, the increased tensions did not lead to a disruption in East-West cultural ties. U.S. musicians and performing arts groups continued with their itineraries as the U-2 incident unfolded. Soviet audiences reacted "enthusiastically and genuinely" to the performances. Embassy diplomats in Moscow noted that, with the breakdown of summit diplomacy, "continuation and intensification" of the cultural program was more important than ever. They called for greater efforts to encourage private tours by artists and performers to supplement "the occasional spectacular presentation which the government is able to afford only rarely."[24]

Christian Herter emphasized that the U-2 incident would not deter the State Department from proceeding with cultural exchange programs. The U-2 incident and the abortive Paris summit did not result in a substantial reduction of exchanges of cultural, scientific, and technical groups. U.S. exhibitions on medicine, plastics, and transportation proceeded as planned under terms of the renewed cultural agreement. *Amerika* magazine "continued to enjoy the improved distribution progressively achieved over the last two years." In the same month the U-2 was shot down, American movies were being shown by 63 of Moscow's 102 movie houses.[25] Although successful in laying a foundation, Washington remained ill prepared to pursue opportunities for expanded cultural infiltration of the USSR. "The success of the Moscow exhibition has been recognized and extolled in our government," reported a presidential commission on information programs in 1960, "but there seems to be little effort to follow through on it." Although the Soviets and the East European regimes were more open than ever to Western cultural infiltration, the commission found that "present budgets for this purpose seem totally inadequate."[26]

Despite the achievements of the cultural agreement and the Sokolniki fair, progress in the cultural Cold War would remain halting because of budgetary constraints and the persistent inability of the U.S. foreign affairs bureaucracy to grasp its potential benefits. Nonetheless, through USIA activities and NSC actions, the national security bureaucracy had begun to recognize the importance of cultural interaction. The Sokolniki exhibition offered abundant evidence of the appeal of American culture—even among those conditioned to expect the worst—and a symbolic culmination to the first generation of efforts.

By the end of the Eisenhower years, a foundation had been established for cultural infiltration of Eastern Europe and the USSR. Building on that foundation, cultural infiltration would increase over the next thirty years and eventually play a major, perhaps even decisive, role in the collapse of the Soviet and East European regimes.

Despite their success in laying a foundation, U.S. national security planners failed to realize the potential of cultural infiltration during the Truman and Eisenhower years. From the outset of the Cold War, an excessive preoccupation with "liberation" undermined efforts to effect a viable cultural strategy. By conducting aggressive psychological warfare, Washington sought to capitalize on widespread dissatisfaction with Soviet hegemony in Eastern Europe. The weapons of psychological warfare, including radio propaganda, leaflets, émigré activities, and various covert operations, did not lead to the disintegration of Soviet power. Psychological warfare unnerved the Kremlin, and often achieved the desired effect of spurring unrest behind the Iron Curtain. While difficult to gauge, evidence of the effectiveness of radio warfare came in the form of intensified Soviet counterpropaganda, approving letters sent to the West, interviews with émigrés and refugees, and persistent Soviet jamming, despite the expense and negative propaganda implications that interference with radio signals entailed.

Although effective in contributing to destabilization of the East European regimes, psychological warfare failed to achieve its aim: liberation. Determined to cling to its postwar sphere of influence, the Kremlin showed it would use whatever means necessary, including military force, to maintain hegemony. After employing the Red Army to maintain authority in East Germany in 1953, the Soviets achieved a *modus vivendi* with Gomulka to avoid direct intervention in Poland in 1956. The Hungarian intervention that same year, however, clearly revealed the limitations of psychological warfare. U.S. radio broadcasts, particularly over Radio Free Europe, encouraged unrest but ultimately delivered disillusion rather than liberation. Psychological warfare had proven itself as an auxiliary weapon during World War II, but failed to achieve its aims in the Cold War.

Although Eastern Europe was indeed the Achilles heel of the Soviet empire, liberation failed because it put Soviet prestige squarely on the line. Had the Kremlin allowed the Eastern European states to gain independence, the result would have been to expose Soviet borders to a Europe united behind liberal capitalism and wedded to American military power. The Soviets would use all means at their disposal to avoid such a potentially devastating loss of credibility, one that may well have spurred disintegration of the USSR itself. Washington's aggressive campaign against communism succeeded only in ensuring an even more rigid Soviet domination of Eastern Europe.

Only an evolutionary strategy, combining restraint, détente, and increased cultural exchange, could promote a gradual weakening of Soviet hegemony. Understanding the threat posed by Western cultural infiltration, Joseph Stalin shut down Western contacts in the context of rising Cold War tensions. Yet even during Stalin's reign, repeated opportunities materialized for a negotiated settlement in Europe. Whether such negotiations could have succeeded, leading to a more relaxed approach to cultural exchange, cannot be known because Washington and some of its key allies rejected talks in deference to Western political, economic, and military integration.

On several occasions, perhaps most notably in Poland, the Kremlin had shown a willingness to tolerate change as long as reformers did not denounce outright communist ideology and threaten to join the capitalist camp. With the greater part of Germany integrated into a hostile military alliance, and U.S. propaganda sounding the drumbeat of liberation, the Kremlin placed definite limits on East European liberalization. The West's commitment to Cold War militarization, and its refusal to negotiate with the Soviet regime, impeded the course of liberalization in Eastern Europe.

Although Eisenhower left office bitterly disappointed over having failed to achieve a breakthrough in the Cold War, his own lack of leadership accounts in large measure for the inability to achieve a wider détente. This assessment calls into question some of the main arguments of "Eisenhower revisionism." By understanding better than most the potential benefits of U.S. cultural initiatives, Eisenhower revealed a degree of perspicacity that belies traditional criticism questioning the president's intelligence and command of his own administration. Nevertheless, Eisenhower often failed to provide the necessary leadership to follow through on his perceptions, which he often compromised in deference to his secretary of state, John Foster Dulles. These findings echo one of the central tenets of the traditional view of Eisenhower, that he deferred too willingly to others, especially the arch cold warrior Dulles.[27]

While the "loss" of China, the Korean War, and McCarthyism overwhelmed Truman's efforts to devise an effective cultural strategy, Eisenhower enjoyed greater flexibility. Furthermore, his military career had provided him with the opportunity to perceive the appeal of American culture abroad. Impressed by the effectiveness of propaganda in World War II, Eisenhower understood better than most that the essence of the Cold War was a psychological struggle for the support of world public opinion—a battle for hearts and minds. The president signaled his commitment to propaganda and cultural infiltration by authorizing and implementing the Jackson committee recommendations in 1953.

Eisenhower was no less committed to liberation than John Foster Dulles, but he possessed keener insight into the role cultural initiatives might play in encouraging change in Eastern Europe and the USSR itself. Adopting the conventional State Department geopolitical perspective, Dulles dismissed cultural diplomacy as insignificant. Eisenhower repeatedly compromised his own inclinations in deference to Dulles's point of view. He allowed Dulles to veto proposals to incorporate the overseas program in the State Department, a decision that left information and cultural initiatives on the margins, in USIA, rather than at the center of U.S. diplomacy. The President also allowed aides to water down his "Chance for Peace" speech, which may have represented an opportunity to pursue détente and increased cultural contact with the new Kremlin leaders early in the Eisenhower presidency. At the 1955 Geneva Conference, Eisenhower declined to pursue meaningful negotiations, which Dulles equated with appeasement.

Like Dulles, C. D. Jackson, and other advisers, Eisenhower gave priority to psychological warfare over détente and cultural infiltration until late in his first term. Eventually, the president's conviction that Western ideas could make a difference did lead to the implementation of an effective cultural policy by the end of his second term. Blessed with common sense and often the right inclinations, Eisenhower could have moved earlier and more decisively to translate his own inclinations into action.

Nowhere was the absence of presidential follow-through more apparent than in the limitations of Eisenhower's rhetoric against the militarization of

American diplomacy. From the outset of his presidency, Eisenhower displayed his determination "to limit, though not reverse, the course of militarization." He issued repeated warnings of the threat of a "garrison state" that would result in economic ruin, corporate domination, and loss of "the very values we were trying to defend."

Despite his desire to contain militarization, Eisenhower's Cold War perceptions perpetuated the "garrison state" that he claimed to abhor. Implacably hostile perceptions of the USSR and communist ideology encouraged militarization, in which planning was based on worst-case scenarios of Soviet behavior. Under the Eisenhower-Dulles New Look, Washington continued to take the lead in fueling the nuclear arms race. Until late in his second term, by which time it was too late, Eisenhower declined opportunities to pursue détente.[28]

In both real and symbolic terms, the U-2 incident represented an appropriate culmination to a presidency dominated by militarization. Eisenhower repeatedly warned of the potentially disastrous consequences of the U.S. overflights of Soviet airspace, yet authorized them anyway. Had Eisenhower followed his own inclinations, instead of deferring to advisers, he would have canceled the U-2 overflights after the Camp David summit. A test ban treaty might well then have emerged from the Paris summit. Instead, in the wake of the U-2 incident, Khrushchev abandoned his discredited policy of peaceful coexistence for an aggressive campaign against the imperialist camp. Eisenhower and Khrushchev were tragic figures in that both sincerely desired to overcome the obstacles posed by militarization in their respective countries, yet neither succeeded.

While Eisenhower's own inconsistencies gave a hollow ring to his condemnation of militarization, the president remained more rational in his Cold War assessments than most national security elites, politicians, and the public. While others overreacted to the *Sputnik* launch, and encouraged the myth of a "missile gap," Eisenhower maintained his equilibrium. In the wake of *Sputnik,* however, the momentum of militarization accelerated well beyond the president's control.

Eisenhower mounted one final assault against militarization in the famous warning in his Farewell Address against "the acquisition of unwarranted influence . . . by the military-industrial complex."[29] Eisenhower had hoped to contain militarization because he had long viewed the Cold War as a psychological struggle in which ideas, symbols, and core values—in a word, culture—would play a more decisive role than military hardware. Cultural initiatives such as a massive exchange of students with the USSR would pay greater dividends than "vast military expenditures," which weakened the economy. At one point Eisenhower called attention to "the irony inherent in the fact that we had invested some $6 billion in the B-47, now obsolete—while the House had chopped $12 million from the Educational Exchange Program, which is of demonstrated worth." The example of skewed priorities, he added, "was just criminal."[30]

Such comments reveal Eisenhower's grasp of the potential of cultural initiatives, and the need for rethinking priorities in Cold War strategy, yet he proved unable to persuade Congress or even his own subordinates to undertake the effort. On myriad occasions the president complained about lack of congressional support, declaring "I am personally convinced that this is the cheapest money we can spend in the whole area of national security." Despite Eisenhower's convictions, midway through his presidency the United States was spending under $1 million on overseas information activities—less than *one four-hundredth* of the U.S. military budget at the time. At the end of the Eisenhower years, a presidential commission reported that "informational activities broadly defined constitute slightly more than one percent of the approximate total of $50 billion spend annually for national security."[31]

Despite the preoccupation with militarization, a more hopeful, albeit longer term, strategy emerged to challenge Soviet hegemony. The "evolutionary concept" focused on increasing East-West contacts to lay a foundation for gradual cultural infiltration of the Soviet empire. U.S. officials discovered through letters and interviews with émigrés that straight news enjoyed greater credibility than strident anti-Soviet propaganda. The popularity of jazz, heard over the VOA's "Music USA" program, signaled the growing appeal of Western popular culture in Eastern Europe and the USSR. USIA monitoring revealed that the Soviets were far less inclined to jam straight news, English-language broadcasts, and entertainment programming than they were anti-Soviet propaganda barrages.

The shift to the gradualist approach, which began in the months before the Soviet intervention in Hungary, soon paid off through increased cultural exchange. The significance of the 1958 cultural agreement—the first U.S.-Soviet accord of the Cold War—was not readily apparent at the time, nor has it been properly appreciated by historians since. The 1958 agreement marked the triumph of the gradualist approach and dramatically increased U.S. cultural infiltration of the USSR. Under its terms, students, professors, scientists, artists, athletes, tourists, and others began to have a direct impact through their contact with the Soviet people. Over the next 40 years, the steady flow and growing appeal of Western influence in the USSR would play a role in undermining CPSU authority. Viewed over the long term, the 1958 cultural agreement was one of the most successful initiatives in the history of American Cold War diplomacy.

The American National Exhibition in Moscow culminated efforts to establish a foundation for cultural infiltration of the USSR. Here, Eisenhower was at his best as an unstinting supporter of the exhibition. Despite constraints of time, logistics, and political controversy, the exhibition—the first ever staged by the United States in the USSR—achieved its aims. The unprecedented display of material progress and consumer goods, transported into the heart of the Soviet world, made a favorable impression on the 2.7 million visitors and countless others who heard about it through word of mouth. Despite extensive CPSU agitation and propaganda, the exhibition became increasingly popular over the course of its six-week run. Based on what they saw and heard from the impressive young American guides, the Soviet visitors perceived that the capitalist system offered more consumer goods and choices of lifestyle than their own system.

The six-week display of American life in Sokolniki could not shake the foundations of the Soviet regime, yet the response that it provoked was a harbinger of the mounting appeal of Western culture. The enthusiasm of the Soviet audiences revealed the growing desire to access consumer goods, benefit from technological progress, and attain middle class status and individual freedom. The Soviet public admired American single-family homes, automobiles, kitchen appliances, convenience foods, open-shelf libraries, fashion accessories, and Pepsi-Cola. Over the years, radio, film, students, tourists, and literature would continue to circulate the images and symbols of Western culture throughout the Soviet empire. Blue jeans, rock 'n' roll, McDonald's, "Dallas," and CNN would follow in the path blazed by *Amerika* magazine and VOA jazz programs.

At the time of the Sokolniki exhibition, the USSR was achieving economic growth, creating jobs, building comfortable apartments, and providing social welfare. Despite the ravages of Stalinism, the aura of victory in World War II and the appeal of communist ideology to victims of Western imperialism in the developing world were sources of strength to the regime. The *Sputnik* launch, although of more symbolic than real significance, nonetheless bolstered confidence in the Soviet system. While many remained embittered toward the Soviet regime, others could find credence in Khrushchev's pledge that, eventually, socialism would "bury" capitalism.

Back-to-back comments in the visitors' remarks book at the Sokolniki exhibition attested to the tensions in Soviet society at the time. "Bravo Yanks," wrote the first, "but we Russians are going to pass you by very soon." Below, however, the next entry read, "Please let me off in the United States as you go by."[32] While some were willing to give the CPSU time to catch up with the West, others stood ready to embrace the rival social system. After the passage of 30 more years, support for the Soviet regime dwindled, while opposition reached a critical mass.

Afterword

Cultural contact weathered most of the Cold War's storms to endure as a source of stability and reassurance among global rivals in the nuclear age. Soviet and American negotiators continued the practice of renewing the cultural agreement every two years. The détente of the 1970s included expanded East-West trade, cultural exchange, and joint scientific and technical projects. Tourism between the United States and the Soviet and East European regimes increased sharply, though far more Americans traveled east than residents of the CP regimes came west. Direct air links were established in 1968, terminated by Washington in 1981, and resumed in 1986.

Psychological warfare and radio propaganda remained a part of American strategy until the end of the Cold War. The Soviets ceased jamming VOA signals in 1963, resumed the practice after the Red Army intervention in Czechoslovakia in 1968, halted jamming again during détente in 1973, and resumed interference again in 1980 in the wake of the Soviet invasion of Afghanistan. Radio Liberty (formerly Radio Liberation), Radio Free Europe, and Radio in the American Sector were jammed continuously throughout the postwar era. In 1981 CP-backed terrorists damaged facilities in a bombing attack on the Munich headquarters of RFE and RL. By the mid-1990s, RFE and RL, no longer subjected to jamming, were being reorganized under a new board of governors, while RIAS operated under authority of the German government. With the Cold War over, *Amerika* magazine ceased publication in 1994.[1]

How and why did the Cold War end? This question looms over the work of the Cold War historian in the same way that historians of the American South must explain secession, or colonial historians grapple with the causes of the

American Revolution. Definitive explanations are still premature. At present, the event is too recent, too much remains uncertain, and classification of important documents remains too much the standard procedure in both East and West. Despite these constraints, and the limitations imposed by my own focus on only the first generation of the Cold War, some broad conclusions merit consideration.

Clearly the collapse of the CP regimes, including the USSR, from 1989 to 1991 stemmed from profound economic and social decay. Stagnation gave rise to reform, first in Poland under the Solidarity movement of the early eighties, and later in the USSR itself under Mikhail Gorbachev's perestroika. So sweeping was the economic and social malaise by the late eighties, however, that reform proved unable to arrest the momentum of disintegration. Ultimately, the people of Eastern Europe and the USSR overthrew CP authoritarianism for political pluralism.

While the Soviet empire collapsed primarily from internal causes, it did not exist in a vacuum. The implications of the collapse of the Soviet system, followed by the embrace of a Western pluralist model of political development, are obviously significant. Clearly the Cold War played a critical role in the revolutionary changes in the former Soviet empire. Beyond question the costs of the Soviet Union's half-century pretension as a global superpower contributed to its ultimate weakness and collapse. Just as clearly, the United States, as the Soviet empire's persistent enemy, played a significant role in its ultimate destruction. But how did the dynamics of the Cold War affect the CP regimes? In what *ways* and by what *means* did the United States and its allies contribute to the process of disintegration in the former Soviet empire?

I believe one key to answering such questions will be found in analyzing the role of cultural infiltration. Recognizing the potentially corrosive impact of Western culture, Stalin erected an Iron Curtain aimed at sealing off the Soviet empire. Ironically, however, what ensued was precisely the opposite of the Orwellian nightmare of a closed totalitarian state employing modern communications technology to dupe the masses. Modern communications, especially radio, television, and film, provided residents of the Soviet empire with the ability to access Western culture in spite of restrictions on travel and East-West contacts. Increased awareness of a more modern, consumer-driven culture could raise expectations and undermine the authority of the CP regimes.

The revolutionary events of 1989-91 found Soviets and East Europeans embracing Western models such as market economics, parliamentary democracy, and political pluralism. But the peoples of those states were in pursuit of something deeper (or perhaps shallower).[2] They sought to become part of the modern, consumer-driven, mass-mediated society associated with the West. They longed for affluence, consumerism, middle-class status, individual freedom, and technological progress. In a very real sense they wanted their own slice of what we call "the American dream."

As the American exhibition in Moscow suggested, residents of the Soviet empire wanted consumer goods and the trappings of a better life that they could glimpse to the West. In 1958 Todor Zhikov, head of the Bulgarian CP, complained that his people's "necks have been twisted from looking toward the West." Rather than developing a socialist consciousness, he bemoaned, many Bulgarians believed "the American way of life remains the best example to follow." Stalin's own daughter, Svetlana Alliluyeva, wrote in 1963 after her defection to the United States: "People want to be happy. They want bright colors, fireworks, noise, excitement." Soviets would "eagerly adopt everything from abroad," she explained, as a result of "being walled off from the rest of the world."[3]

After his ouster from power in 1964, Khrushchev wrote in his secret memoirs about the Soviet public's growing obsession with Western consumer goods. "The best proof of this is how some of our own Soviet citizens love fancy goods or any kind of innovation," he explained. "They hang around foreign delegations and tourists and con them out of these kinds of items or simply buy them outright. In our market we cannot hope to compete. It's too bad; it's shameful, but it is a fact that can't be denied."[4]

Instead of devoting substantial resources to bolstering the consumer sector, the Soviets, though limited by a much weaker economy, remained as obsessed with Cold War militarization as their Western rivals. Cynicism, corruption, and inefficiency, rather than progress and socialist construction, became the hallmarks of CPSU authority, particularly in the era of stagnation under Khrushchev's successor, Leonid Brezhnev. As the Soviet system crumbled, the images and symbols of the West filtered through at an ever increasing pace. The same scenario, exacerbated by deep-seated resentment of Soviet hegemony, rendered the Eastern European regimes even more vulnerable to collapse.

The argument sketched out above should not be confused with the crude and parochial Western triumphalist perspective on the end of the Cold War. Indeed, the Western "victory" may prove ephemeral. Residents of both Eastern Europe and the USSR have discovered that liberal capitalism offers no panacea for solving their social and economic problems. Ideology quickly became irrelevant in the former Yugoslavia, where "ethnic cleansing" replaced CP authority. The United States itself, in part because it devoted so much effort and vast resources to Cold war militarization, confronts serious social and economic problems, challenges that can no longer be shunted aside in deference to girding against the "communist threat." All of this suggests that the West achieved a Pyrrhic victory in the Cold War.

The masses of people in Eastern Europe and the USSR were the ultimate arbiters of the Cold War. The impact of Western culture upon their consciousness was substantial, and perhaps decisive. The extent to which they based their decisions on a realistic assessment of capitalist society, however, is subject to debate. The ultimate course that these states will take also remains open to question. The possibility exists that disillusion, and perhaps reaction, will emerge when realities fail to measure up to expectations and aspirations.

If cultural infiltration indeed played a central role in "winning" the Cold War, the implications are mixed, at best, in assessing the effectiveness of postwar American foreign policy. While the United States rediscovered "realist" geopolitics, investing heavily in Cold War militarization, classical "idealist" diplomacy ultimately proved more effective in combating the Soviet empire. Proponents of classical diplomacy, dating back to the Revolutionary era, viewed the ascendance of the United States as "manifest destiny"—the inevitable product of the nation serving as a model of material success and democratic values. Reflecting a "decent respect for the opinions of mankind," the Declaration of Independence confidently called for the facts to be "submitted to a candid world." By serving as a "city on a hill," the United States was destined to lead.

Revolutionary advances in global communications, especially in the twentieth century, provided expanded opportunities to disseminate American culture. Radio, film, television, transcontinental air travel—and ultimately satellite dishes and computer chips—offered unprecedented opportunities to submit facts, and convey culture, to a "candid world." Communications technology revolutionized modern life and transformed diplomacy. The essence of that transformation was that foreign policy was no longer conducted primarily between diplomats, states, and governments but increasingly through dissemination of information and culture to masses of people.

The Cold War stood Clausewitz on his head: in an age of mutual assured destruction, war was no longer a viable means to solve political conflict among superpowers. The men who conducted the Cold War, in both Washington and Moscow, failed to grasp the essence of the struggle. Unable to enjoy the luxury of hindsight, they lived in the shadow of World War II and its legacy—the vivid memories, yet all too simple lessons, of Munich, Barbarossa, Pearl Harbor, and Hiroshima. Obsessed with military preparations, Washington squandered enormous energies and resources in preparation for a conventional "hot" war.

Equally excessive Soviet militarization, coupled with vows to preside over the liquidation of capitalism, only served to encourage the worst-case scenarios that fueled militarization. It seems likely that militarization did more to increase than to "contain" the threat of war.

If the Cold War was, at its core, a battle for public opinion—a struggle for hearts and minds—its outcome could only be decided on cultural ground.

NOTES

Introduction

1. See, for example, Stephen F. Whitfield, *The Culture of the Cold War* (Baltimore: Johns Hopkins University Press, 1991); Lary May, *Recasting America: Culture and Politics in the Age of the Cold War* (Chicago: University of Chicago Press, 1989); Elaine Tyler May, *Homeward Bound: American Families in the Cold War Era* (New York: Basic Books, 1988); Paul Boyer, *By the Bomb's Early Light: American Thought and Culture at the Dawn of the Atomic Age* (New York: Pantheon, 1985).

2. Stephen L. Vaughn, *Holding Fast the Inner Lines: Democracy, Nationalism and the Committee on Public Information* (Chapel Hill: University of North Carolina Press, 1980); Allan M. Winkler, *The Politics of Propaganda: The Office of War Information, 1942-1945* (New Haven, Ct.: Yale University Press, 1978); Holly Cowan Shulman, *The Voice of America: Propaganda and Democracy, 1941-1945* (Madison: University of Wisconsin Press, 1990); Emily S. Rosenberg, *Spreading the American Dream: American Economic and Cultural Expansion, 1890-1945* (New York: Hill and Wang, 1982); Frank Costigliola, *Awkward Dominion: American Political, Economic, and Cultural Relations with Europe, 1919-1933* (Ithaca, N.Y.: Cornell University Press, 1984).

3. See, for example, Edward W. Barrett, *Truth Is Our Weapon* (New York: Funk and Wagnalls, 1953); Hans J. Tuch, *Communicating with the World: U.S. Public Diplomacy Overseas* (New York: St. Martin's Press, 1990); Thomas C. Sorensen, *The Word War: The Story of American Propaganda* (New York: Harper and Row, 1968); Sig Mickelson, *America's Other Voice: The Story of Radio Free Europe and Radio Liberty* (New York: Praeger Publishers, 1983); James Critchlow, *Radio Hole-in-the-Head: Radio Liberty* (Washington, D.C.: The American University Press, 1995); Randolph Wieck, *Ignorance Abroad: American Educational and Cultural Foreign Policy* (Westport, Ct.: Praeger Publishers, 1992).

4. Raymond Williams, quoted in John Tomlinson, *Cultural Imperialism: A Critical Introduction* (London: Pinter Publishers, 1991), 4.

5. Lawrence Levine, *Highbrow/Lowbrow: The Emergence of Cultural Hierarchy in America* (Cambridge, Mass.: Harvard University Press, 1988); Clifford Geertz,

"Thick Description: Toward an Interpretive Theory of Culture," in *The Interpretation of Cultures: Selected Essays* (New York: Basic Books, 1973); Tomlinson, *Cultural Imperialism,* 4-5.

6. For an excellent, succinct overview of the applicability of the cultural approach to foreign relations, see Akira Iriye, "Culture and International History," in Michael J. Hogan and Thomas G. Paterson, eds., *Explaining the History of American Foreign Relations* (Cambridge: Cambridge University Press, 1991), 214-25.

7. Ibid., 223.

8. Emily S. Rosenberg, "Cultural Interactions," in Stanley Kutler, ed., *Encyclopedia of the United States in the Twentieth Century* (New York: Scribner's, 1996), 695-717.

9. See the stimulating essays in Rob Kroes, Robert Rydell, and D.F. Bosscher, eds., *Cultural Transmissions and Receptions: American Mass Culture in Europe* (Amsterdam: VU University Press, 1993); on the tensions associated with the reception of U.S. culture, see Richard Kuisel, *Seducing the French: The Dilemma of Americanization* (Berkeley: University of California Press, 1993); and Petra Godde, "Reeducating Germany: American Fraternization with the German Population After World War II" (Ph.D. diss., Northwestern University, 1995); see also Ariel Dorfman, *The Empire's Old Clothes: What the Lone Ranger, Babar, and Other Innocent Heroes Do to Our Minds* (New York: Pantheon, 1983) and Orville Schell, *Discos and Democracy: China in the Throes of Reform* (New York: Pantheon, 1988).

10. Reinhold Wagnleitner, *Coco-Colonization: The Cultural Mission of the United States in Austria After the Second World War* (Chapel Hill, N.C.: University of North Carolina Pres, 1994), xii, 278.

11. Relatively little work has been done on the dissemination and reception of Western culture in the former Soviet empire. More attention has been paid to Western cultural influence in the USSR than in Eastern Europe. Useful studies include Richard Stites, *Russian Popular Culture: Entertainment and Society Since 1900* (Cambridge: Cambridge University Press, 1992); Frederick Starr, *Red and Hot: The Fate of Jazz in the Soviet Union, 1917-1980* (New York: Oxford University Press, 1983); Timothy W. Ryback, *Rock Around the Bloc: A History of Rock Music in Eastern Europe and the Soviet Union* (New York: Oxford University Press, 1990); John Bushnell, *Moscow Graffiti: Language and Subculture* (Boston: Unwin Hyman, 1990); and Scott Shane, *Dismantling Utopia: How Information Ended the Soviet Union* (Chicago: Ivan R. Dee, 1994); see also Vasily Aksyonov, *In Search of Melancholy Baby* (New York: Random House, 1985); Ludmilla Alexeyeva and Paul Goldberg, *The Thaw Generation: Coming of Age in the Post-Stalin Era* (Boston: Little, Brown and

Co., 1990); by far the best work on U.S.-Soviet cultural relations is J. D. Parks, *Culture, Conflict, and Coexistence: American-Soviet Cultural Relations, 1917-1958* (Jefferson, N.C.: McFarland, 1983).

12. Among the best guides to a voluminous historiography are Stephen G. Rabe, "Eisenhower Revisionism: A Decade of Scholarship," *Diplomatic History* 17 (Winter 1993): 97-115; and John Robert Greene, "Eisenhower Revisionism, 1952-1992, A Reappraisal," in Shirley Anne Warshaw, ed., *Reexamining the Eisenhower Presidency* (Westport, Ct.: Greenwood Press, 1993).

13. For a more extended discussion of the concept of militarization and its pervasive impact on American society, see Michael S. Sherry, *In the Shadow of War: The United States Since the 1930s* (New Haven, Ct.: Yale University Press, 1995), especially 123-87.

14. I offer more elaboration on this point in "Reassessing Kennan After the Fall of the Soviet Union: The Vindication of 'X'?" *The Historian* 59 (Summer 1997).

15. Among the best works on the end of the Cold War are Raymond L. Garthoff, *The Great Transition: American-Soviet Relations and the End of the Cold War* (Washington: The Brookings Institution, 1994); Michael J. Hogan, ed., *The End of the Cold War: Its Meaning and Implications* (Cambridge: Cambridge University Press, 1992); Richard Ned Lebow and Janice Gross Stein, *We All Lost the Cold War* (Princeton: Princeton University Press, 1994); Daniel Deudney and G. John Ikenberry, "Who Won the Cold War?" *Foreign Policy* 87 (Summer 1992): 123-38; Thomas G. Paterson, "Toward a Post-Cold War Order," in his *On Every Front: The Making and Unmaking of the Cold War* (New York: Norton, rev. ed., 1992), 221-31; and H. W. Brands, *The Devil We Knew: Americans and the Cold War* (New York: Oxford University Press, 1993).

16. Walter L. Hixson, *Witness to Disintegration: Provincial Life in the Last Year of the USSR* (Hanover, N.H.: University Press of New England, 1993).

Chapter 1

1. Stephen Vaughn, *Holding Fast the Inner Lines: Democracy, Nationalism, and the Committee on Public Information* (Chapel Hill, N.C.: The University of North Carolina Press, 1980), deals primarily with the CPI's domestic activities. Gregg Wolper, "The Origins of Public Diplomacy: Woodrow Wilson, George Creel, and the Committee on Public Information" (Ph.D. diss., University of Chicago, 1991), focuses on the Committee's overseas efforts. The quote is from Wolper, 362.

2. Martin Ebon, *The Soviet Propaganda Machine* (New York: McGraw-Hill, 1987), 7-10; David Welch, *The Third Reich: Politics and Propaganda* (London and New York: Routledge, 1993), 6, 8-16; see also Jay Baird, *The Mythical*

World of Nazi War Propaganda, 1939-45 (Minneapolis: University of Minnesota Press, 1974); Harold D. Lasswell, *Propaganda Technique in the World War* (New York: Alfred A. Knopf, 1927), 222.

3. Clayton R. Koppes and Gregory D. Black, *Hollywood Goes to War: How Politics, Profits, and Propaganda Shaped World War II Movies* (New York: Free Press, 1987), 141; John W. Henderson, *The United States Information Agency* (New York: Prager Publishers, 1969), 31-32.

4. Henderson, *U.S. Information Agency*, 34. On this point, see chapter 2.

5. On the perceptions of U.S. diplomats, see Robert D. Schulzinger, *The Making of the Diplomatic Mind: The Training, Outlook, and Style of the United States Foreign Service Officers, 1908-1931* (Middletown, Ct.: Wesleyan University Press, 1975) and Hugh DeSantis, *The Diplomacy of Silence: The American Foreign Service, the Soviet Union, and the Cold War, 1933-1947* (Chicago: University of Chicago Press, 1979); on OWI, see Allen Winkler, *Politics of Propaganda: The Office of War Information, 1942-1945* (New Haven, Ct.: Yale University Press, 1978), 84.

6. Richard Dunlop, *Donovan: America's Master Spy* (New York: Rand McNally, 1982), 421.

7. Robert Dallek, *Franklin D. Roosevelt and American Foreign Policy, 1932-1945* (New York: Oxford University Press, 1979), 364-65.

8. Robert T. Holt and Robert W. van de Velde, *Strategic Psychological Operations and American Foreign Policy* (University of Chicago Press, 1960), 123-58.

9. Wallace Carroll, *Persuade or Perish* (Boston: Houghton Mifflin, 1948), 113-25.

10. Winkler, *Politics of Propaganda*, 137-47.

11. Henderson, *U.S. Information Agency*, 36-39.

12. "Statement by the President," Aug. 31, 1945, Box 166, White House Central File: Official File, Papers of Harry S. Truman, Harry S. Truman Library Institute (HSTL); see also, Arthur McMahon, "Memorandum on the Postwar International Information program of the United States," July 5, 1945, Box 8, Papers of Charles Hulten, HSTL.

13. Frank A. Ninkovich, *The Diplomacy of Ideas: U.S. Foreign Policy and Cultural Relations, 1938-1950* (Cambridge: Cambridge University Press, 1981), 119-20; Henderson, *U.S. Information Agency*, 38.

14. Benton to Marshall, Nov. 1, 1946, Box 166, White House Central File: Official File, Truman Papers, HSTL.

15. Ninkovich, *Diplomacy of Ideas*, 160.

16. J. D. Parks, *Culture, Conflict, and Coexistence: American-Soviet Cultural Relations, 1917-1958* (Jefferson, N.C.: McFarland, 1983), 47-62.

17. Ibid., 69-70.

18. Ibid., 79-85.
19. Ibid., 90-103; Ninkovich, *Diplomacy of Ideas*, 108.
20. Parks, *Culture, Conflict, and Coexistence*, 104-115.
21. Ibid., 116-33.
22. "The Scope and Nature of Communist Propaganda," Feb. 23, 1953, Box 2, Miscellaneous Reports and Studies, 1952-53; U.S. International Information and Educational Exchange Program, July 1951, Box 29, Records of the Psychological Strategy Board (PSB Records), HSTL; Foreign Relations Series of the United States (FRUS) 1952-1954, II, 2: 1847, 1849.
23. *New York Times*, Dec. 4, 1951.
24. Randolph Wieck, *Ignorance Abroad: American Educational and Cultural Foreign Policy and the Office of Assistant Secretary of State* (New York: Prager, 1992), 14; Randall Bennett Woods, *Fulbright: A Biography* (Cambridge University Press, 1995), 129-36.
25. "Swords Into Plowshares," International Educational Exchange Service, State Department, undated, BCN 57: 741, Fulbright Papers (FP), University of Arkansas; *Newsweek*, Aug. 19, 1946; Randall Bennett Woods, *Fulbright: A Biography* (Cambridge University Press, 1995), 130-36; Ninkovich, *Diplomacy of Ideas*, 141.
26. Ninkovich, *Diplomacy of Ideas*, 149; William Preston, Jr., Edward S. Herman, and Herbert I. Schiller, *Hope and Folly: The United States and UNESCO, 1945-1985* (Minneapolis: University of Minnesota Press, 1989), 60; William Benton to George C. Marshall, Sept. 3, 1947, Box 6, Papers of Howland Sargeant, HSTL; Benton speech before U.S. National Commission for UNESCO, April 13, 1950, Box 6, Papers of Howland Sargeant Papers, HSTL.
27. Ninkovich, *Diplomacy of Ideas*, 146-47; Mark S. Steinitz, "The U.S. Propaganda Effort in Czechoslovakia, 1945-1948," *Diplomatic History* 6 (Fall 1982): 359-85.
28. CIA report, "Soviet-Satellite Drive Against Western Influence in Eastern Europe," June 2, 1950, President's Secretary's Files: Intelligence Files, CIA Reports, 1949-1950, Box 257, HSTL; see also FRUS 1950, IV: 290-92.
29. CIA report, "Soviet-Satellite Drive Against Western Influence in Eastern Europe."
30. Ibid.
31. Henderson, *U.S. Information Agency*, 40.
32. Hans N. Tuch, *Communicating with the World: U.S. Public Diplomacy Overseas* (New York: St. Martin's Press, 1990), 17; Wieck, *Ignorance Abroad*, 15; *Department of State Bulletin*, Nov. 28, 1948, 672-76.
33. Henderson, *U.S. Information Agency*, 42-43; Parks, *Culture, Conflict, and Coexistence*, 124-25.

34. George F. Kennan, "Sources of Soviet Conduct," 576, 580; George F. Kennan, "Russia's International Position at the Close of the War with Germany," 535, both in Kennan, *Memoirs, 1925-1950;* for an analysis of Kennan's perceptions, see my "Reassessing Kennan After the Fall of the Soviet Union: The Vindication of 'X'?" *The Historian* 59 (Summer 1997).

35. Rhodri Jeffreys-Jones, *The CIA and American Democracy* (New Haven, Ct.: Yale University Press, 1989), 24-41.

36. Memorandum for the Director, "CIA Authority to Perform Propaganda and Commando Type Functions," Sept. 25, 1947, CIA, FOIA request.

37. James Edward Miller, *The United States and Italy, 1940-1950: The Politics and Diplomacy of Stabilization* (Chapel Hill, N.C.: University of North Carolina Press, 1986), 213-71; FRUS 1948, III: 848-49.

38. Peter Grose, *Gentleman Spy: The Life of Allen Dulles* (Boston: Houghton Mifflin Co., 1994), 285; Edward W. Barrett testimony, Exec. Sess., "Voice of America," July 27, 1950, U.S. Senate, Committee on Foreign Relations, Subcommittee on Public Affairs, SFRC Selected Documents, Box 10, HSTL.

39. Jones, *CIA and American Democracy*, 42-62; Church Committee (U.S. Senate) Final Report, Book IV, Supplementary Detailed Staff Reports on Foreign and Military Intelligence, 29.

40. NSC 59/1, March 9, 1950, Records of the NSC, Box 18, HSTL; FRUS 1950, IV: 297, 305-06.

41. Dec. 12, 1949, Memoranda of Conversation, Papers of Dean Acheson, Secretary of State, 1949-53, Box 64, HSTL.

42. FRUS 1950, IV: 272-82; 86-90.

43. FRUS 1950, IV: 276; Edward W. Barrett, *Truth Is Our Weapon* (New York: Funk and Wagnalls, 1953), 73; FRUS 1950, IV: 304; *Department of State Bulletin,* May 1, 1950, 669-672.

44. Quoted in Ernest R. May, ed., *American Cold War Strategy: Interpreting NSC 68* (New York: Bedford Books of St. Martin's Press, 1993), 9; NSC 68 appears at Ibid., 21-82. When approved by the President, NSC's numbered papers became U.S. policy.

45. Edward W. Barrett testimony, "Voice of America," July 27, 1950, U.S. Senate, Committee on Foreign Relations, Subcommittee on Public Affairs, exec. sess., SFRC Selected Documents, Box 10, HSTL; Melvyn P. Leffler, *A Preponderance of Power: National Security, the Truman Administration, and the Cold War* (Stanford, CA.: Stanford University Press, 1992).

46. Barrett testimony, SFRC; FRUS 1950, IV: 311-13.

47. Edward W. Barrett, Oral History Interview by Richard D. McKinzie, New York, July 9, 1974, HSTL.

48. FRUS 1950, IV: 316; Benton speech before U.S. National Commission for UNESCO, April 13, 1950, Box 6, Sargeant Papers, HSTL.

49. Acheson statement before U.S. Senate Appropriations Committee, Aug. 31, 1950, Box 72, Acheson Papers, Secretary of State, HSTL; Truman aide Mark F. Etheridge recalled that Acheson, reflecting the traditional State Department view, lacked enthusiasm for the overseas program. "He didn't think information ought to be mixed with policy." Mark F. Etheridge, Oral History Interview by Richard D. McKinzie, Moncure, N.C., June 4, 1974; see also Barrett interview; Henderson, *U.S. Information Agency,* 45; FRUS 1950, IV: 316-17.

50. Barrett testimony, SFRC; on Korea, see the recent information from Soviet archives, as discussed in *Cold War International History Bulletin* 3 (Fall 1993), 1, 14-18 and *Cold War International History Bulletin* 4 (Fall 1994), 21; the classic work is Bruce Cumings, *The Origins of the Korean War, Vol. 2, The Roaring of the Cataract* (Princeton, N.J.: Princeton University Press, 1990).

51. Edward P. Lilly, "Organizational Developments and Delineation of Psychological Warfare Responsibilities Since World War II," 1952, Box 22, PSB Records, HSTL.

52. Allan A. Needell, "'Truth Is Our Weapon'": Project TROY, Political Warfare, and Government-Academic Relations in the National Security State," *Diplomatic History* 17 (Summer 1993), 405-6.

53. Ibid., 400, 413-25; James E. Webb, Sept. 24, 1951, "Psychological Operations Coordinating Committee, Report to the NSC," Box 26, PSB Papers, HSTL.

54. Needell, "'Truth Is Our Weapon,'" 409, 411, 413; Edmond Taylor, "The Field and Role of Psychological Strategy in Cold War Planning," Dec. 30, 1952, PSB Files, Box 15, Truman Papers, HSTL.

55. *New York Times,* March 22, 1951; April 2, 1951; Truman executive order, April 4, 1951, Box 25, PSB Papers, HSTL; FRUS 1951, I: 58-60; 178-80; CIA Paper, "Definition of Psychological Operations," Box 14, PSB Papers, HSTL.

56. "Background Notes on the Psychological Strategy Board," Jan. 3, 1952, Box 25, PSB Papers, HSTL; FRUS 1951, I: 959.

57. Wallace Carroll to Gordon Gray, Sept. 20, 1951, PSB Papers, Box 14, HSTL; Webb, "Psychological Operations Coordinating Committee, Report to the NSC"; "Background Notes on the Psychological Strategy Board."

58. Wallace Carroll, "Principal Elements of a Cold War Strategy Plan," Oct. 12, 1951, Box 34, PSB Papers, HSTL.

59. FRUS 1951, I: 127-48; 942-54.

60. Ibid., 922-33.

61. "Status Report on the National Psychological Effort and First Progress Report of the Psychological Strategy Board," Aug. 1, 1952; "Status Report on the Psychological Effort as of December 31, 1952," Jan. 5, 1953, both Box 22, PSB Papers, HSTL.

62. Undersecretary of Defense John Magruder to Gordon Gray, July 19, 1951, Box 31, PSB Papers, HSTL; "Report on the Organization of Psychological Strategy Board," June 5, 1952; Walter Bedell Smith to Harry S. Truman, May 19, 1952, both in Box 18, Records of the NSC, HST Papers, HSTL.

63. FRUS 1951, I: 902-12.

64. FRUS 1952-54, II: 1591-1600.

65. Ibid., 1646.

66. FRUS 1952-54, II: 1627; Subcommittee Draft Report, BCN 90: 718, FP, University of Arkansas; Subcommittee Report No. 406, 83rd Cong., 1st sess., June 15, 1953.

67. Henderson, U.S. Information Agency, 48; "Benton speech before U.S. National Commission for UNESCO."

68. FRUS 1952-54, II, 2: 1644-45.

69. Department of State Bulletin, Feb. 18, 1952, 252; FRUS 1951, I: 957, 959.

70. Bennett Kovrig, Of Walls and Bridges: The United States and Eastern Europe (New York: New York University Press, 1991), 46; James Burnham, Containment or Liberation? An Inquiry Into the Aims of United States Foreign Policy (New York, John Day, 1952).

71. Abbott Washburn, Oral History Interview, Washington, D.C., April 20, 1967, by Ed Edwin, DDEL; Barrett interview by Richard D.McKinzie, July 9, 1974, HSTL; Theodore Streibert, Oral History Interview, Columbia University, Dec. 10, 1970, by Don North, DDEL.

72. FRUS 1952-1954, II, 1: 267-68.

73. Carroll, Persuade or Perish, 12; Blanche Weisen Cook, The Declassified Eisenhower: A Divided Legacy of Peace and Political Warfare (New York: Penguin Books, 1981), 13-15.

74. Cook, Declassified Eisenhower, 13-15.

75. Washburn interview.

76. Cook, Declassified Eisenhower, 126; C. D. Jackson to Tony Biddle, March 17, 1952, Box 28, Jackson Papers, Dwight D. Eisenhower Presidential Library (DDEL), Abilene, Kansas.

77. C. D. Jackson to Tony Biddle, March 17, 1952, Box 28, Jackson Papers, DDEL; for an excellent assessment of C. D. Jackson and psychological warfare, see James Jensen, "'Singing a Beautiful Hymn:' The Psychological Warfare Option in U.S. Foreign Policy During the Early Cold War" (M.A. thesis, University of Akron, 1995).

78. Abbott Washburn to Eisenhower [1952], Box 69; "Princeton Meeting on Political Warfare," May 10-11, 1952, Box 69, both in Jackson Papers, DDEL.

79. Eisenhower to C. D. Jackson, May 8, 1952; Eisenhower to C. D. Jackson, Aug. 22, 1952, both in Box 69, Jackson Papers, DDEL.

80. Henderson, *U.S. Information Agency*, 48; "Remarks of the President to the Staff of the USIA," Nov. 10, 1953, Box 5, Papers of Dwight D. Eisenhower (Ann Whitman File), Speech series, DDEL.

81. FRUS 1952-1954, II, 2: 1867.

82. William H. Jackson, "The Fourth Area of the National Effort in Foreign Affairs," 1956, Box 4, White House Office of Staff Secretary: Subject Series, White House Subseries, DDEL; Interview with Gordon Gray, January 23, 1967.

83. Jackson, "The Fourth Area of the National Effort"; FRUS 1952-1954, II, 2: 1797, 1812.

84. "The Scope and Nature of Communist Propaganda," Feb. 23, 1953, Box 2, Miscellaneous Reports and Studies, 1952-53, DDEL.

85. FRUS 1952-1954, II, 2: 1854-57; the OCB was formally established by Eisenhower's Executive Order 10483, Sept. 2, 1953, Box 5, C. D. Jackson Records, DDEL; *Department of State Bulletin*, Sept. 28, 1953, 420-21.

86. FRUS 1952-1954, II, 2: 1691-92; Robert E. Elder, *The Information Machine: The United States Information Agency and American Foreign Policy* (Syracuse, N.Y.: Syracuse University Press, 1968), 39.

87. FRUS 1952-1954, II, 2: 1863; Streibert interview.

88. Thomas C. Sorensen, *The Word War: The Story of American Propaganda* (New York: Harper and Row, 1968), 46.

89. FRUS 1952-1954, II, 2: 1710-11, 1724-26; *Department of State Bulletin*, June 15, 1953, 853; Shawn J. Parry-Giles, "The Eisenhower Administration's Conceptualization of the USIA: The Development of Overt and Covert Propaganda Strategies," *Presidential Studies Quarterly* 24 (Spring 1994): 263-76.

Chapter 2

1. Holly Cowan Shulman, *The Voice of America: Propaganda and Democracy, 1941-1945* (Madison: University of Wisconsin Press, 1990); John W. Henderson, *United States Information Agency* (New York: Praeger, 1969), 34.

2. Shulman, *Voice of America*, 93-113; Henderson, *U.S. Information Agency*, 34.

3. Shulman, *Voice of America*, 93-113; James P. Warburg, "The 'Moronic Little King' Incident," in William E. Daugherty, ed., *A Psychological Warfare Casebook* (Baltimore, Md.: Johns Hopkins Press, 1958), 300-303.

4. Robert W. Pirsein, "The Voice of America: A History of the International Broadcasting Activities of the United States Government, 1940-1962"(Ph.D. diss., Northwestern University, 1970).

5. *Washington Post*, Dec. 27, 1951; see also *Reader's Digest*, August 1953, 41-43.

6. Pirsein, "Voice of America," 122-23.

7. U.S. Cong., Exec. Sess., "Investigation of 'Voice of America' and 'Know North America' Series of Broadcasts," June 16, 1948, U.S. Senate, Subcommittee of Committee on Foreign Relations (SFRC), SFRC Selected Documents, Box 4, Harry S. Truman Library Institute (HSTL).

8. Ibid.

9. "Draft Outline of Procedures for Russian Language Broadcasts," undated [1946], Box 5, Papers of Charles W. Thayer, HSTL; "Draft Press Release," undated [February 1947]; Thayer to Kenneth Fry, Box 5, Thayer Papers, HSTL.

10. "Memorandum to Members of Advisory Committee, Russian Language Broadcasts," January 17, 1947; "Draft Opening Statement for First Week of the Russian Broadcasts," undated, both in Box 5, Thayer Papers.

11. Foy Kohler to Wilson Compton, Feb. 12, 1952, Box 5, Papers of Howland Sargeant, HSTL.

12. "Voice of America Effectiveness," undated [1949], Box 5, Thayer Papers. Neither the VOA nor the U.S. Information Agency preserved letters received by VOA from foreign listeners. Spokespersons for the agencies told the author they presume the letters have been destroyed.

13. "Indications of VOA Penetration of Soviet Jamming," May 15, 1950, Box 16, Papers of Charles Hulten, HSTL.

14. *Time,* May 23, 1949, 58.

15. Ibid.

16. *New Yorker,* June 4, 1949, 22.

17. Victor Franzusoff, telephone interview by Walter L. Hixson, March 29, 1996.

18. Ibid.; "United States Policy and the USSR," May 1949, Box 188, President's Secretary's Files, Subject File, HSTL.

19. "Soviet Reactions to the Voice of America," Report No. 2, Aug. 1, 1949 to Oct. 31, 1949, Feb, 28, 1950, Box 15, Hulten Papers, HSTL.

20. *Department of State Bulletin,* May 15, 1949, 638; "United States Policy and the USSR."

21. *New Yorker,* June 4, 1949, 22.

22. *Department of State Bulletin,* April 7, 1952, 22; *New Yorker,* June 4, 1949, 22; *Time* May 29, 1950, 59-60.

23. "Historical Developments in the Jamming of the VOA by the USSR," undated, Box 257, President's Secretary's Files: Intelligence Files, CIA Reports, 1949-1950, HSTL; *New Yorker*, June 4, 1949, 22.

24. *Department of State Bulletin*, Nov. 28, 1949, 310; Pirsein, "Voice of America," 176; Franzusoff interview.

25. Allan A. Needell, "'Truth Is Our Weapon': Project TROY, Political Warfare, and Government-Academic Relations in the National Security State," *Diplomatic History* 17 (Summer 1993): 399-420; Foreign Relations Series of the United States (FRUS) 1950, IV: 279-82; 286-90, 297; Pirsein, "Voice of America," 175-79; Dean Acheson, "Statement before Appropriations Committee," Aug. 31, 1950, Box 72, Papers of Dean Acheson, Secretary of State, HSTL; "Suggested Electronic Countermeasures Against Soviet Jamming of the British and American Shortwave Radio Broadcasting Stations," Sept. 7, 1949, Box 5, Sargeant Papers, HSTL.

26. *Department of State Bulletin*, Sept. 12, 1949, 403; Pirsein, "Voice of America," 170-74.

27. Russian broadcast, July 2, 1950, Box 5, Voice of America, Records of the U.S. Information Agency, Record Group 306 (RG 306), National Archives, College Park, Md.

28. Edward P. Lilly, "The Development of American Psychological Operations, 1945-1951," Dec. 19, 1951, Box 22, Papers of the Psychological Strategy Board, HSTL.

29. Pirsein, "Voice of America," 207-11; *Department of State Bulletin*, Sept. 12, 1949, 403.

30. "International Broadcasting of All Nations," Feb. 15, 1953, Box 20, Hulten Papers, HSTL; *Department of State Bulletin*, July 16, 1951, 102

31. FRUS 1952-1954, II, 2: 1845.

32. Quoted in Oshinsky, *A Conspiracy So Immense*, 267.

33. *New Yorker*, June 4, 1949, 22; "Analysis of the 'Voice' Broadcasts to Russia, Poland, Germany and Italy, March 26-May 13, 1950," November 1950, Box 1, International Broadcasting Division, State Department, Miscellaneous Reports and Studies, 1949-53, HSTL.

34. Alex Inkeles (Russian Research Center, Harvard University), "Soviet Reactions to the Voice of America," January 1950, Box 16, Hulten Papers.

35. Alex Inkeles, "Soviet Reactions to the Voice of America, 1947-1951," May 1952, Reports and Related Studies, 1948-1953, Box 40, RG 306, USIA.

36. Polish broadcast, Aug. 20, 1951, Box 25, VOA Papers, RG 306, USIA.

37. Edward W. Barrett, Oral History Interview, by Richard D. McKinzie, New York, July 9, 1974, HSTL; Streibert to Robert Gray, Oct. 5, 1956, FOIA

request, Box 99, Subject Series, Papers of Dwight D. Eisenhower, Dwight D. Eisenhower Presidential Library (DDEL), Abilene, Kansas.

38. Polish broadcast, May 22, 1954, Box 73, VOA Papers, RG 306, USIA.

39. Lithuanian broadcast, Oct. 17, 1951, Box 28, VOA Papers, RG 306, USIA.

40. Czech broadcast, Nov. 21, 1952, Box 57, VOA Papers, RG 306, USIA; Polish broadcast, July 22, 1954, Box 74, VOA Papers, RG 306, USIA; Albanian broadcast, March 2, 1952, Box 36, VOA Papers, RG 306, USIA.

41. Polish broadcast, Aug. 23, 1952, Box 50, VOA Papers, RG 306, USIA; Albanian broadcast, March 2, 1952, Box 36, VOA Papers, RG 306, USIA; Czech broadcast, Nov. 21, 1952, Box 57, VOA Papers, RG 306, USIA; Thomas G. Paterson, "Red Facism: The American Image of Aggressive Totalitarianism," in his *Meeting the Communist Threat: Truman to Reagan* (New York: Oxford University Press, 1988): 3-17.

42. Pirsein, "Voice of America," 203; *Time,* May 1, 1950, 23.

43. Czech broadcast, June 7, 1950, Box 3, VOA Papers, RG 306, USIA.

44. "Religion and the Voice of America," *Department of State Bulletin,* Nov. 10, 1952, 727-28; Hungarian broadcast, Oct. 5, 1952, Box 57, VOA Papers, RG 306, USIA.

45. Estonian broadcast, Dec. 24, 1951, Box 33, VOA Papers, RG 306, USIA.

46. Russian broadcast, May 17, 1954, Box 73, VOA Papers, RG 306, USIA.

47. Russian broadcast, Aug. 3, 1951, Box 24, VOA Papers, RG 306, USIA; Estonian broadcast, Nov. 11, 1953, Box 57, VOA Papers, RG 306, USIA.

48. Russian service, March 15, 1950 Box 3, VOA Papers, RG 306, USIA.

49. Rumanian broadcast, Aug. 26, 1952, Box 50, VOA Papers, RG 306, USIA.

50. Russian broadcast, Aug. 3, 1951, Box 24, VOA Papers, RG 306, USIA; *Time,* May 1, 1950, 23.

51. Czech service, Aug. 20, 1952, Box 49, VOA Papers, RG 306, USIA; Russian broadcast, June 13, 1950, Box 4, VOA Papers, RG 306, USIA.

52. Russian broadcast, June 13, 1950, Box 4, VOA Papers, RG 306, USIA; Russian broadcast, May 17, 1954, Box 73 VOA Papers, RG 306, USIA.

53. Russian broadcast, Aug. 3, 1951, Box 24, VOA Papers, RG 306, USIA.

54. *Time,* May 1, 1950, 23.

55. Albanian broadcast, undated, Box 73, VOA Papers, RG 306, USIA.

56. Latvian broadcast, Aug. 23, 1952, Box 50, VOA Papers, RG 306, USIA.

57. "Broadcasts to Soviet Russia in the 'Cold War' and Korean War Periods," New York University study, July 1951, Box 17, Hulten Papers, HSTL.

58. Russian broadcast, July 2, 1950, Box 5, VOA Papers, RG 306, USIA; Russian broadcast, May 15, 1950, Box 3, VOA Papers, RG 306, USIA.

59. *FRUS* 1952-54, II, Part 2: 1731-32, 1743-50.

60. *Department of State Bulletin,* Dec. 4, 1950, 897.

61. *Department of State Bulletin,* Sept. 18, 1950, 449; Ibid., May 14, 1951, 783.

62. FRUS 1950, IV: 318-19; "Indications of VOA Penetration of Soviet Jamming," May 15, 1950, Miscellaneous Reports and Studies, 1949-1953, Box 1, VOA Papers, RG 306, USIA.

63. *Time,* May 1, 1950, 23; "Indications of VOA Penetration of Soviet Jamming"; *Department of State Bulletin,* Sept. 11, 1950, 416; Pirsein, "Voice of America," 212; see footnote 12, this chapter.

64. *Department of State Bulletin,* Dec. 4, 1950, 898.

65. "Indications of VOA Penetration of Soviet Jamming"; "A "Comparison of Responses to Voice of America Programs Directed to Three Soviet Bloc Countries," February 1954, Box 14, Multi-Country Project Files, 1952-1963, VOA Records, RG 306.

66. "Indications of VOA Penetration of Soviet Jamming"; Interview with Dr. Leonid Sidorov, Kazan State University (Russia), by the author, Akron, Oh., May 14, 1994.

67. "Examples of VOA Effectiveness," April 1, 1952, Miscellaneous Reports and Studies, 1952-53, Box 2, VOA Papers, RG 306, USIA.

68. Ibid.

69. Wilson Compton, "The Campaign of Truth," May 7, 1952, address, Box 5, Thayer Papers, HSTL; *Time,* Oct. 8, 1951, 37.

70. *Time,* May 1, 1950, 23.

71. "The Opinions of Satellite Refugees on Western Broadcasts," July 1951, Box 17, Hulten Papers, HSTL.

72. *Department of State Bulletin,* Dec. 4, 1950, 897; "Indications of VOA Penetration of Soviet Jamming."

73. "Iron Curtain Radio Comment on VOA," Report No. 49, April 21, 1950, Box 16, Hulten papers, HSTL.

74. Ibid.

75. "The Scope and Nature of Communist Propaganda," Feb. 23, 1953, Misc. Reports and Studies, 1952-53, Box 2, VOA Papers, USIA.

76. "Examples of VOA Effectiveness."

77. "The Scope and Nature of Communist Propaganda."

78. Franzusoff interview.

79. Inkeles, "Soviet Reactions to the Voice of America," January 1950, Box 16, Hulten Papers.

80. *Chicago Tribune,* Feb. 13, 1950.

81. FRUS 1952-54, II, Part 2: 1671-72; *Time,* March 2, 1953, 15-16; David M. Oshinsky, *A Conspiracy So Immense: The World of Joe McCarthy* (New York: The Free Press, 1983), 262-67; *Newsweek,* March 2, 1953, 35; Jeff Broadwater,

Eisenhower and the Anti-Communist Crusade (Chapel Hill, N.C.: University of North Carolina Press, 1992), 69-76.

82. *Time,* March 2, 1953, 15-16; Oshinsky, *A Conspiracy So Immense,* 271-72.

83. Oshinsky, *A Conspiracy So Immense,* 271-72.

84. *Newsweek,* March 9, 1953, 20; *Newsweek,* March 23, 1953, 28.

85. Oshinsky, *A Conspiracy So Immense,* 275-76.

86. *New York Times,* Feb. 19, 1953; Oshinsky, *A Conspiracy So Immense,* 270-71; Charles Bohlen, *Witness to History, 1929-1969* (New York: W.W. Norton, 1973), 323.

87. Oshinsky, *A Conspiracy So Immense,* 270-71; FRUS 1952-1954, II, 2: 1675-77.

88. FRUS 1952-1954, II, 2: 1847, 1890.

89. FRUS 1952-54, II, 2: 1825-26.

Chapter 3

1. C. D. Jackson to Eisenhower, April 2, 1953, Box 41, Papers of C. D. Jackson, Dwight D. Eisenhower Presidential Library (DDEL); Rhodri Jefferys-Jones, *The CIA and American Democracy* (New Haven: Yale University Press, 1989), 89-92.

2. The Office of Policy Coordination, brought under administrative control of the CIA in the fall of 1950, actually conducted some of these operations under the direction of Frank Wisner; the quotation is from the *Boston Pilot,* April 10, 1954, Box 21, Papers of Charles Hulten Papers, Harry S. Truman Presidential Library (HSTL).

3. Coleman, *The Liberal Conspiracy: The Congress for Cultural Freedom and the Struggle for the Mind of Postwar Europe* (New York: The Free Press, 1989), 1-57; Jones, *CIA and American Democracy,* 69, 87.

4. Sig Mickelson, *America's Other Voice: The Story of Radio Free Europe and Radio Liberty* (New York: Praeger, 1983), 14; DeWitt C. Poole to John C. Hughes, June 9, 1950, CIA Records, FOIA request.

5. Lawrence C. Soley and John S. Nichols, *Clandestine Radio Broadcasting: A Study in Revolutionary and Counterrevolutionary Electronic Communication* (New York: Praeger, 1987), 42-43; Donald R. Browne, *International Radio Broadcasting: The Limits of the Limitless Medium* (New York: Praeger, 1982), 132-33.

6. Mickelson, *America's Other Voice,* 26.

7. Ibid., 58; Jones, *CIA and American Democracy,* 60.

8. Mickelson, *America's Other Voice,* 30-32.

9. Ibid., 37; *Radio Free Europe: Policy Handbook* (November 1951), CIA Records, FOIA.

10. *Time,* July 17, 1950, 68.
11. *RFE Handbook.*
12. Ibid.
13. Ibid.; Pamphlet, "National Committee for a Free Europe," undated [1953], Box 22, Hulten Papers, HSTL; *Reader's Digest,* February 1954, 48-51.
14. *Newsweek,* Sept. 19, 1955, 107-110; *Reader's Digest,* February 1954, 48-51.
15. Peter Grose, *Gentleman Spy: The Life of Allen Dulles* (New York: Houghton Mifflin Co., 1994), 322; *Newsweek,* Sept. 17, 1951, 25.
16. Radio Free Europe, "The Swiatlo Disclosures," Box 21, Hulten Papers, HSTL.
17. *Life,* March 10, 1952, 154-55; John Foster Dulles to Henry Ford II, March 25, 1954, Box 7, John Foster Dulles Chronological Series, DDEL.
18. *Newsweek,* Sept. 19, 1955, 107; Pamphlet, "National Committee for a Free Europe," undated [1953], Box 22, Hulten Papers, HSTL.
19. FRUS 1952-1954, II, 2: 1832.
20. Ibid.; *Reader's Digest,* February 1954, 48-51.
21. Mickelson, *America's Other Voice,* 59-83; James Critchlow, *Radio Hole-in-the-Head: Radio Liberty* (Washington, D.C.: The American University Press, 1995), 90-93.
22. FRUS 1952-1954, II, 2: 1829; Critchlow, *Radio Hole-in-the-Head,* 31-34.
23. *Commonweal,* Dec. 21, 1956, 303-6; Critchlow, *Radio Hole-in-the-Head,* 123.
24. Critchlow, *Radio Hole-in-the-Head,* 99.
25. Mickelson, *America's Other Voice,* 75-76.
26. Critchlow, *Radio Hole-in-the-Head,* 56-57, 93, 108-9.
27. "Status Report on the Psychological Effort as of December 31, 1952," Psychological Strategy Board Report, Jan. 5, 1953, Box 22, PSB Records, HSTL.
28. Pamphlet, "National Committee for a Free Europe," undated [1953], Box 22, Hulten Papers, HSTL.
29. *Time,* Aug. 27, 1951, 27; Mickelson, *America's Other Voice,* 56-57.
30. *Time,* Oct. 8, 1951, 37-38 and Jan. 3, 1955, 22; *Boston Pilot,* April 10, 1954, Box 21, Hulten Papers; Pamphlet, "National Committee for a Free Europe," undated [1953], Box 22, Hulten Papers, HSTL.
31. *Time,* Jan. 3, 1955, 22 and Mar. 5, 1956; *Department of State Bulletin,* June 7, 1954, 881-82 and Feb. 20, 1956, 295.
32. Pamphlet, "National Committee for a Free Europe," undated [1953], Box 22, Hulten Papers, HSTL; FRUS 1952-1954, II, 2: 1832.
33. FRUS 1952-1954, II, 2: 1832, 1898-99; *The Atlantic,* October 1951, 16.
34. "Status Report on the Psychological Effort as of December 31, 1952," PSB Report, Jan. 5, 1953, Box 22, PSB Records, HSTL; PSB, 13th meeting, June 12, 1952, Box 27, PSB Records; "The Psychological Program," PSB Report, undated [1953], Box 4, White House Office, NSC Series, Status of Projects.

35. FRUS 1952-1954, II, 2: 1831; "Status Report on the Psychological Effort as of December 31, 1952," PSB Report, Jan. 5, 1953, Box 22, PSB Papers.

36. U.S. Congress, House, Committee on Foreign Affairs, *The Mutual Security Program: Hearings*, 82nd Cong., 1st sess, 1951, 1106-9; Kersten Resolution, Aug. 15, 1951, Box 35, PSB Papers; Charles Byler, "Trouble for Joe Stalin in his Own Backyard: The Kersten Amendment and the Debate Over American Policy in Eastern Europe," paper delivered at Society for Historians of American Foreign Policy, Summer Conference, June 24, 1995.

37. Ibid.; *New York Times*, Dec. 20, 1951; Byler, "Trouble for Joe Stalin in his Own Backyard."

38. FRUS 1952-1954, VIII: 161, 185.

39. Ibid., 167-69; C. Tracy Barnes to Gordon Gray, Dec. 20, 1951, Box 9, PSB Papers; Bennett Kovrig, *Of Walls and Bridges: The United States and Eastern Europe* (New York: New York University Press, 1991), 65.

40. FRUS 1952-1954, VIII: 181.

41. Ibid., 184; Kovrig, *Of Walls and Bridges*, 63.

42. FRUS 1952-1954, VIII: 199-208.

43. Ibid.; "Statement of Policy by the National Security Council on a Volunteer Freedom Corps" (NSC 143/2), May 20, 1953, Jackson Records, DDEL.

44. FRUS 1952-1954, VIII: 225-29.

45. Ibid., 221-26; 236-37; FRUS 1955-1957, XXV: 79-80, 160; George Kennan to C. D. Jackson, Sept. 15, 1953, Box 4, Jackson Records, DDEL; C. D. Jackson to Cutler, Box 90, C. D. Jackson Papers, DDEL; Byler, "Trouble for Joe Stalin in his Own Backyard."

46. Robert T. Holt and Robert W. Van de Velde, *Strategic Psychological Operations and American Foreign Policy* (Chicago: University of Chicago Press, 1960), 207-8.

47. Holt and Van de Velde, *Strategic Psychological Operations*, 206-32.

48. Ibid.; "A New Weapon," Free Europe Press pamphlet, undated [1955], Box 22, Hulten Papers, HSTL.

49. Two articles by Christian F. Ostermann, based on recently declassified sources, offer the most complete account to date of the East German uprising: "The United States, the East German Uprising of 1953, and the Limits of Rollback," Working Paper No. 11, Cold War International History Project, Woodrow Wilson International Center for Scholars; and "'Keeping the Pot Simmering:' The United States and the East German Uprising of 1953," *German Studies Review* 19 (February 1996): 61-89.

50. FRUS 1952-1954, VII, Part 2: 1584-85; Kovrig, *Of Walls and Bridges*, 59; CIA report, undated, Box 5, C. D. Jackson Records, DDEL; Ostermann, "The United States, the East German Uprising of 1953, and the Limits of Rollback."

51. FRUS 1952-1954, VII, Part 2: 1587; Kovrig, *Of Walls and Bridges*, 59; Grose, *Gentleman Spy*, 356-57.

52. *New York Times*, July 2, 1953.

53. FRUS 1952-1954, VII, Part 2: 1639; Ostermann, "'Keeping the Pot Simmering.'"

54. FRUS 1952-1954, VII, 2: 1631-35.

55. Ibid., 1609-24, 1635; Ostermann, "The United States, the East German Uprising of 1953, and the Limits of Rollback."

56. Ibid., 1655; Ostermann, "'Keeping the Pot Simmering.'"

57. Ostermann, "The United States, the East German Uprising of 1953, and the Limits of Rollback"; Valur Ingimundarson, "The Eisenhower Administration, the Adenauer Government, and the Political Uses of the East German Uprising in 1953," *Diplomatic History* 20 (Summer 1996): 381-409.

58. Browne, *International Radio Broadcasting*, 132-33; Edmond Taylor, "RIAS: The Story of an American Psywar Outpost," in Daugherty and Janowitz, *Psychological Warfare Casebook*, 145-50.

59. Browne, *International Radio Broadcasting*, 134; Taylor, "RIAS," 145-50; Ostermann, "The United States, the East German Uprising of 1953, and the Limits of Rollback."

60. Taylor, "RIAS," 145-50; Ostermann, "The United States, the East German Uprising of 1953, and the Limits of Rollback."

61. Taylor, "RIAS," 149.

62. *Department of State Bulletin*, Dec. 4, 1950, 895.

63. *Life*, Dec. 3, 1951; *The Atlantic*, October 1951, 16; *Department of State Bulletin*, Feb. 16, 1953; Jackson to Rep. John Taber, July 22, 1953, Box 5, Jackson Records, DDEL.

64. FRUS 1952-1954, VII, Part 2: 1665; Ostermann, "The United States, the East German Uprising of 1953, and the Limits of Rollback."

65. Taylor, "RIAS," 148.

66. Jackson to Rep. John Taber, July 22, 1953, Box 5, Jackson Records, DDEL; FRUS 1952-1954, VII, Part 2: 1637-38; Ostermann, "The United States, the East German Uprising of 1953, and the Limits of Rollback."

67. FRUS 1952-1954, VII, 2: 1575-78; Ostermann, "The United States, the East German Uprising of 1953, and the Limits of Rollback."

68. Frank Wisner to Allen Dulles, July 10, 1953; reports from Germany, Aug. 10, 1953, both in Box 5, Jackson Records, DDEL.

69. Frank Wisner to Allen Dulles, July 10, 1953, Box 5, Jackson Records, DDEL; FRUS 1952-54, VII, 2: 1576-77, 1829.

70. FRUS 1952-1954, VII, 2: 1575-78; Frank Wisner to C. D. Jackson, July 2, 1953, Box 5, Jackson Records, DDEL.

71. FRUS 1952-1954, VII, 2:1675-96; Ostermann, "'Keeping the Pot Simmering.'"

72. Nikita S. Khrushchev, *Khrushchev Remembers* (Boston: Little, Brown and Co., 1970), 346-50; Bohlen, *Witness to History*, 397-98.

73. Khrushchev, *Khrushchev Remembers*, 346-50; Bohlen, *Witness to History*, 397-98; FRUS 1955-1957, XXIV: 74.

74. NSC 5611, Part II, "Status of U.S. National Security Programs on June 30, 1956," Box 7, White House Office, Office of the Special Assistant for National Security Affairs: Records, 1952-61, NSC Series, Status of Projects Subseries; Kovrig, *Of Walls and Bridges*, 78-79.

75. FRUS 1955-1957, XXV: 181, 244-47.

76. FRUS 1955-1957, XXV: 258, 331; L. W. Gluchowski, "Poland, 1956: Khrushchev, Gomulka, and the Polish October," *Cold War International History Project Bulletin*, Issue 5 (Spring 1995), Woodrow Wilson Center for Scholars, Washington, D.C.

77. Kovrig, *Of Walls and Bridges*, 82-84; FRUS 1955-1957, XXV: 260.

78. FRUS 1955-1957, XXV: 269, 222; NSC 5611, Part II, "Status of U.S. National Security Programs on June 30, 1956," Box 7, White House Office, Office of the Special Assistant for National Security Affairs: Records, 1952-61, NSC Series, Status of Projects Subseries, DDEL.

79. FRUS 1955-1957, XXV: 16-23.

80. FRUS 1955-1957, XXV: 25-33.

81. FRUS 1955-1957, XXV: 342.

82. Khrushchev, *Khrushchev Remembers*, 417; Csaba Békés, "New Findings on the 1956 Hungarian Revolution," *Cold War International History Project Bulletin* (Fall 1992), Woodrow Wilson International Center for Scholars, Washington, D.C.

83. *Department of State Bulletin*, Nov. 5, 1956, 700.

84. FRUS 1955-1957, XXV: 305-6, 318, 321, 328.

85. Emmet John Hughes, *The Ordeal of Power: A Political Memoir of the Eisenhower Years* (New York: Atheneum, 1963), 219-20.

86. FRUS 1955-1957, XXV: 419, 310, 401, 343.

87. Ibid., 416-18.

88. FRUS 1955-1957, XXV: 430, 425, 435, 509-14.

89. Hungarian VOA broadcasts, May 9, 1950, and Oct. 5, 1952, both in Box 2, Papers of the Voice of America, Record Group 306, United States Information Agency (USIA).

90. FRUS 1955-1957, XXV: 471; FRUS 1955-1957, IX: 590-98; Arthur Larson, "Guidelines on VOA Objective, Content, and Tone," July 22, 1957, with John Foster Dulles's "Memorandum for the President," Aug. 9, 1957, Box 9,

Papers of Dwight D. Eisenhower (Ann Whitman File), Dulles-Herter Series, DDEL.

91. "A New Weapon," Free Europe Press pamphlet, undated [1955], Box 22, Hulten Papers, HSTL; Holt, *Strategic Psychological Warfare,* 225-32; *Time,* Jan. 3, 1955, 22; "U.S. Reply to Hungary Concerning Balloon Leaflets," undated press release, Box 21, Hulten Papers, HSTL.

92. FRUS 1955-1957, XXV: 147-48, 15.

93. *The New Republic,* Dec. 17, 1956, 13, and Nov. 26, 1956, 4-5; Report by Walter Ridder, Box 21, Hulten Papers, HSTL.

94. "Radio Free Europe," Nov. 20, 1956, memorandum, CIA Records, FOIA.

95. Ibid.

96. "Radio Free Europe," 71.

97. *U.S. News and World Report,* Dec. 21, 1956, 18; "Memorandum for Allen Dulles," undated, RFE Records, CIA, FOIA; *New York Times,* Jan. 25, 1957; FRUS 1955-1957, XXV: 637-38, 652; Jones, *CIA and American Democracy,* 94.

98. Report by Walter Ridder, Box 21, Hulten Papers, HSTL.

99. *The New Republic,* Nov. 26, 1956, 5.

100. H. Freeman Matthews, Oral History Interview by Richard D. McKinzie, June 7, 1973, Washington D.C., HSTL.

Chapter 4

1. U.S. Department of State, *Documents on Germany, 1944-1985* (Washington: Government Printing Office, 1986), 361-64.

2. FRUS 1952-1954, VII: 287, 178, 204. See also additional pertinent documents scattered throughout this volume as well as Thomas A. Schwartz, *America's Germany: John J. McCloy and the Federal Republic of Germany* (Cambridge, Mass.: Harvard University Press, 1991), 260-69.

3. Schwartz, *America's Germany,* 263; Henry A. Kissinger, *Diplomacy* (New York: Simon and Schuster, 1994), 498; Melvyn Leffler, *A Preponderance of Power: National Security, the Truman Administration, and the Cold War* (Stanford, Ca.: Stanford University Press, 1994), 457-58; for references to literature on Stalin's Peace Note, the subject of no small debate, see "Stalin and the SED Leadership, 7 April 1952," *Cold War International History Project Bulletin,* Woodrow Wilson International Center for Scholars (Fall 1994): 34-35, 48, 96.

4. Bennett Kovrig, *Of Walls and Bridges: The United States and Eastern Europe* (New York: New York University Press, 1991), 51-53; "Stalin and the SED Leadership, 7 April 1952."

5. FRUS 1952-1954, VIII: 1118.

6. Ibid., 1118-19, 1179; Walter L. Hixson, *George F. Kennan: Cold War Iconoclast* (New York: Columbia University Press, 1989), 73-98.

7. Raymond L. Garthoff, *Assessing the Adversary: Estimates by the Eisenhower Administration of Soviet Intentions and Capabilities* (Washington, D.C.: The Brookings Institution, 1991), 5; the best work on militarization is Michael S. Sherry, *In the Shadow of War: the United States since the 1930s* (New Haven, Ct.: Yale University Press, 1995), especially 123-87.

8. FRUS 1952-1954, VIII: 1173.

9. Stephen E. Ambrose, *Eisenhower: Soldier and President* (New York: Simon and Schuster, 1990), 323; FRUS 1952-1954, VIII: 1124, 1130, 1135-39, 1181 1183; FRUS 1952-1954, II, 2: 1699-1706.

10. FRUS 1952-1954, VIII: 1122-23; Blanche Weisen Cook, *The Declassified Eisenhower: A Divided Legacy of Peace and Political Warfare* (New York: Penguin, 1981), 179.

11. FRUS 1952-1954, VIII: 1147-55.

12. Ibid., 1162-63.

13. Ibid., 1163-69.

14. Ibid., 1115-16, 1143; Peter G. Boyle, ed., *The Churchill-Eisenhower Correspondence, 1953-1955* (Chapel Hill, N.C.: University of North Carolina Press, 1990), 48-51.

15. Kovrig, *Of Walls and Bridges,* 53; FRUS 1952-1954, VIII: 1183; *Department of State Bulletin,* April 27, 1953, 603-8; Burton Kaufman, *Korean War: Challenges in Crisis, Credibility, and Command* (New York: Knopf, 1986), 313-15.

16. FRUS 1952-1954, VII, 1: 611-14; FRUS 1952-1954, VIII: 1182.

17. FRUS 1952-1954, VII, 1: 510-12; James G. Hershberg, "'Explosion in the Offing:' German Rearmament and American Diplomacy, 1953-1955," *Diplomatic History* 16 (Fall 1992): 511-49; Schwartz, *America's Germany,* 299.

18. Kovrig, *Of Walls and Bridges,* 53.

19. FRUS 1952-1954, VIII: 77; FRUS 1952-1954, II, 2: 1726-31; Kovrig, *Of Walls and Bridges,* 50.

20. FRUS 1952-1954, VII, 2: 1588.

21. FRUS 1952-1954, II, 1: 577-96; FRUS 1952-1954, VIII: 110-27.

22. FRUS 1952-1954, VIII: 110-36.

23. FRUS 1952-1954, II: 1198-99; 1170-74, 1759.

24. Ambrose, *Eisenhower,* 343.

25. Ibid., 343-45; FRUS 1952-1954, II, 2: 1759.

26. John Newhouse, *War and Peace in the Nuclear Age* (New York: Vintage Books, 1988), 107-9; Ambrose, *Eisenhower,* 343-57; H. W. Brands, *Cold Warriors: Eisenhower's Generation and American Foreign Policy* (New York: Columbia

University Press, 1988), 129; FRUS 1952-1954, II, Part 2: 1411; "The Atoms for Peace Program," Quantico report, November 1955, Box 73, C. D. Jackson Papers, Dwight D. Eisenhower Presidential Library (DDEL).

27. FRUS 1952-1954, II: 1205-6, 1215-33; *Department of State Bulletin*, Mar. 8, 1954, 343-47.

28. FRUS 1952-1954, VII, 2: 1666.

29. C. D. Jackson to Dillon Anderson, April 19, 1955, Box 90, C. D. Jackson Papers, DDEL; FRUS 1955-1957, XXV: 541.

30. James G. Richter, *Khrushchev's Double Bind: International Pressures and Domestic Coalition Politics* (Baltimore, Md.: The Johns Hopkins University Press, 1994), 30-52.

31. Robert T. Holt and Robert W. van de Velde, *Strategic Psychological Operations and American Foreign Policy* (Chicago: University of Chicago Press, 1960), 226; FRUS 1955-1957, X, 1: 58-60, 366.

32. Garthoff, *Assessing the Adversary*, 7-8.

33. FRUS 1955-1957, V: 307.

34. Ibid., 147, 215, 224-27, 239, 248.

35. Ibid.

36. FRUS 1955-1957, XXIV, 5, 32.

37. "Report of the Quantico Vulnerabilities Panel," White House Office, Box 17, National Security Council Staff Papers, 1948-61; NSC Registry Series 1947-1967, DDEL.

38. FRUS 1955-1957, V: 219; "Summary of Recommendations: Quantico Vulnerabilities Panel," Box 17, NSC Registry Series, DDEL.

39. FRUS 1955-1957, V: 283-85.

40. FRUS 1955-1957, V: 293, 239-85.

41. FRUS 1955-1957, V: 301-4.

42. Ibid., 219.

43. FRUS 1955-1957, V: 298, 225-27, 434; White House News Conference, Dec. 16, 1954, Box 6, John Foster Dulles Subject Series, DDEL.

44. FRUS 1955-1957, V: 450-53, 434; Newhouse, *War and Peace in the Nuclear Age*, 115.

45. Dwight D. Eisenhower, *Mandate for Change, 1953-1956* (Garden City, N.Y.: Doubleday, 1963), 521; FRUS 1955-1957, V: 619.

46. FRUS 1955-1957, V: 804-5, 531, 535.

47. FRUS 1955-1957, XXIV: 211; FRUS 1955-1957, V: 528, 533; *Department of State Bulletin*, Aug. 1, 1955, 171-76.

48. FRUS 1955-1957, XXV: 121-30, 212-21.

49. FRUS 1955-1957, XXIV: 21; FRUS 1955-1957, IX: 534-35; FRUS 1955-1957, XIX, 254.

50. C. D. Jackson to John Osborne, May 26, 1949, Box 66, C.D. Jackson Papers, DDEL.

51. J. D. Parks, *Culture, Conflict, and Coexistence: American-Soviet Cultural Relations, 1917-1958* (Jefferson, N.C.: McFarland, 1983), 134-37.

52. Ibid., 138.

53. FRUS 1952-1954, VIII: 1217; Parks, *Culture, Conflict, and Coexistence,* 138-40.

54. FRUS 1955-1957, XXIV: 201.

55. Salisbury comments, plenary session, "Report on the National Conference on Exchange of Persons," Institute for International Education, New York, Feb. 25, 1955, BCN 57, 753, Fulbright Papers, University of Arkansas.

56. George V. Allen, Oral History Interview; May 24, 1955, phone call with John Foster Dulles, Box 10, John Foster Dulles Telephone Calls Series, DDEL.

57. Frederick C. Barghoorn, *The Soviet Cultural Offensive: The Role of Cultural Diplomacy in Soviet Foreign Policy* (Princeton: Princeton University Press, 1960), 63; Parks, *Culture, Conflict, and Coexistence,* 141-45.

58. Theodore Streibert, "Memorandum for the President," Sept. 4, 1955, General Correspondence and Memoranda Series, Box 3, John Foster Dulles Papers, DDEL; FRUS 1955-1957, IX: 556-58.

59. "Psychological Aspects of United States Strategy," Panel Report from Quantico Meetings, November 1955, Box 73, C. D. Jackson Papers, DDEL.

60. FRUS 1955-1957, IX: 559; Allen interview.

61. *Department of State Bulletin,* Oct. 3, 1955, 529; FRUS 1955-1957, V: 603-4.

62. FRUS 1955-1957, V: 606, 608; FRUS 1955-1957, XXIV: 212.

63. Parks, *Culture, Conflict, and Coexistence,* 146-51; FRUS 1955-1957, V: 537-38.

64. FRUS 1955-1957, V: 68-85.

65. Ibid., 762-85; Parks, *Culture, Conflict, and Coexistence,* 146-55.

66. Parks, *Culture, Conflict, and Coexistence,* 146-55.

67. *Department of State Bulletin,* June 25, 1956, 1064; FRUS 1955-1957, XXIV: 70.

68. FRUS 1955-1957, XXIV: 113-14, 119-20.

69. Parks, *Culture, Conflict, and Coexistence,* 153-71.

70. Ibid.

71. Ibid., 156-63.

72. FRUS 1955-1957, XXIV: 216-22.

73. FRUS 1955-1957, XXIV: 226-46; Telephone call to William H. Jackson, June 29, 1956, Box 11, JFD Telephone Calls, DDEL.

74. FRUS 1955-1957, XXIV: 253-55.

75. "Proposed European Advisory Committee," Free Europe Committee, Nov. 1, 1958, Box 44, Jackson Papers, DDEL; FRUS 1955-1957, XXIV: 141; C. D. Jackson to William Jackson, Nov. 17, 1956, Box 52, C. D. Jackson Papers, DDEL.

76. FRUS 1955-1957, XXIV: 256-59; Parks, *Culture, Conflict, and Coexistence,* 165.

77. FRUS 1955-1957, XXV: 74-78, 209; FRUS 1955-1957, IX: 550-55.

78. FRUS 1958-1960, X, I: 5-6, 18-31, 79-94.

79. FRUS 1955-1957, XXV: 628-30; FRUS 1958-1960, X, II: 22-35.

80. FRUS 1955-1957, XXV: 610, 694-95; *Harper's,* April 1957, 70-74.

81. FRUS 1955-1957, XXV: 611-12, 671-75.

82. *Department of State Bulletin,* Jan. 27, 1958, 122-30; FRUS 1958-1960, X, I: 1-4, 52-53; Richter, *Khrushchev's Double Bind,* 111-14; Hixson, *George F. Kennan,* 171-94.

83. FRUS 1955-1957, XXV: 176-80.

84. FRUS 1955-1957, XXV: 174-75; 564; *Department of State Bulletin,* Dec. 26, 1960, 968-72.

85. FRUS 1955-1957, XXV: 690-98.

86. FRUS 1955-1957, XXV: 669-96.

87. FRUS 1958-1960, X, I: 95-98.

88. John C. Guthrie, "Soviet Sensitivity to Possible Contaminating Effects of East-West Cultural Ties," Jan. 8, 1957, Box 42, Dwight D. Eisenhower Diary Series, DDEL.

89. General Records of the Department of State, RG 59, 511.614/10-1455.

90. RG 59, 511.614/7-456, 511.614/7-1156.

91. Theodore Streibert to Donald Durham, Aug. 20, 1954, Box 1, Foreign Service Dispatches, Records of the U.S. Information Agency, RG 306; *New York Herald-Tribune,* Aug. 4, 1963, Box 4, Papers of George V. Allen, Duke University, Durham, N.C.; Thomas C. Sorensen, *The Word War: The Story of American Propaganda* (New York: Harper and Row, 1967), 107.

92. "Status of U.S. National Security Programs on June 30, 1956," NSC 5611, Part II, Box 7, White House Office, Office of the Special Assistant for National Security Affairs: Records, 1952-61, NSC Series, Status of Projects Subseries, DDEL; S. Frederick Starr, *Red and Hot: The Fate of Jazz in the Soviet Union, 1917-1980,* 243-44; see *New York Times,* Aug. 6, 1955.

93. Starr, *Red and Hot,* 204-34; Timothy W. Ryback, *Rock Around the Bloc: A History of Rock Music in Eastern Europe and the Soviet Union* (New York: Oxford University Press, 1990), 12-17.

94. Vassily Aksyonov, *In Search of Melancholy Baby* (New York: Random House, 1985), 12, 203.

95. Starr, *Red and Hot,* 235-60; Ryback, *Rock Around the Bloc,* 10-12.
96. Starr, *Red and Hot,* 235-60; Ryback, *Rock Around the Bloc,* 19-34.
97. "Evidence of Effectiveness of USIS Projects," Oct. 5, 1954; "Effective USIS Projects," July 26, 1954, both in Box 1, Foreign Service Dispatches, RG 306.
98. "Mail Survey of Listeners to the Voice of America World Wide English Service," June 1961, Box 2, Program and Media Studies, 1956-62, RG 306; Reinhold Wagnleitner, *Coca-Colonization and the Cold War: The Cultural Mission of the United States in Austria after the Second World War* (Chapel Hill, N.C.: University of North Carolina Press, 1994), 211; USIA Newsletter, November 1959, Box 1, Monthly Employee Newsletters, RG 306; "News from Radio Free Europe," press release, undated [1956], Box 22, Papers of Charles W. Hulten, Harry S. Truman Library Institute.
99. FRUS 1955-1957, IX: 509-10; RG 59, 961.40/6-1559, 961.40/12-858, 961.40/3-659, 961.40/10-1058, 961.40/12-858, 761.00/2-959; "Status of U.S. National Security Programs on June 30, 1956."
100. RG 59, 511.612/10-1256; George V. Allen, "The Impact of the Printed Word," May 2, 1958, speech, Box 4, Allen Papers; FRUS 1955-1957, XXIV: 216; FRUS 1955-1957, V: 761.
101. *Amerika,* No. 1 [1956], and all subsequent issues through 1994, when the magazine was discontinued, can be found (in Russian) in the Office of Historical Collections, United States Information Agency, Washington, D.C.
102. RG 59, 511.612/2-2059, 511.612/2-1959.
103. RG 59, 511.612/3-259, 511.612/4-2059, 511.612/5-2359, 511.612/10-2959, 511.612/12-2859.

Chapter 5

1. NSC 5611, Part II, "Status of U.S. National Security Programs on June 30, 1956," Box 7, White House Office, Office of the Special Assistant for National Security Affairs: Records, 1952-1961, NSC Series, Status of Projects Subseries, Dwight D. Eisenhower Presidential Library (DDEL); FRUS 1955-1957, IX: 507.
2. Leo Bogart, *Premises for Propaganda: The United States Information Agency's Operating Assumptions in the Cold War* (New York: The Free Press, 1974), 26-28.
3. Thomas C. Sorenson, *The Word War: The Story of American Propaganda* (New York: Harper and Row, 1968), 52; Abbott Washburn, Oral History Interview, Washington, D.C., April 20, 1967, by Ed Edwin, DDEL.
4. FRUS 1952-1954, II, 2: 1778; Bogart, *Premises for Propaganda,* 24.
5. FRUS 1955-1957, IX: 507; Bogart, *Premises for Propaganda,* 124.
6. FRUS 1955-1957, IX: 537; Oral History interview with Theodore Streibert.

7. FRUS 1952-54, II: 1189-99, 1170-77; Theodore Streibert, Oral History Interview, Columbia University, Dec. 10, 1970, by Don North, DDEL; "The Atoms for Peace Program," Quantico Report, November 1955, Box 73, Papers of C. D. Jackson, DDEL.

8. Robert A. Divine, *The Sputnik Challenge* (New York: Oxford University Press, 1993); Peter J. Roman, *Eisenhower and the Missile Gap* (Ithaca, N.Y.: Cornell University Press, 1995); John Newhouse, *War and Peace in the Nuclear Age* (New York: Vintage Press, 1990), 117-24; John Foster Dulles to Lyndon B. Johnson, Oct. 26, 1957, Box 15, John Foster Dulles Chronological Series, DDEL.

9. George V. Allen, "Books and the American Image," *Atlantic Monthly*, May 1961, 77-80; Bogart, *Premises for Propaganda*, 174-77.

10. FRUS 1952-1954, II, 2: 1778; Oral History Interview with George V. Allen No. 2, by Philip A. Crowl, April 7, 1966, Box 2, Allen-Angier Family Papers, Duke University Library Special Collections; Allen, "Books and the American Image," 77-80.

11. FRUS 1952-1954, II, 2: 1780; Allen, "Books and the American Image," 77-80.

12. "Motion Pictures in the Overseas Information Program," Box 15, Charles Hulten Papers, Harry S. Truman Library Institute (HSTL); OCB memorandum, White House Office, NSC Staff: Papers, 1948-1961, DDEL; Bogart, *Premises for Propaganda*, 116, 126; Memorandum for C. D. Jackson, Jan. 18, 1954, Box 99, White House Central Files, Confidential File, 1953-1961, Subject Series, DDEL; "USIA Film Program," Jan. 20, 1954, Box 99, White House Central Files, Confidential File, 1953-1961, Subject Series, DDEL.

13. *New York Times*, April 17, 1957; "Revised Rebuttal by [Leo] Crespi," undated, Box 2, Subject Files, 1953-1963; Sorenson, *The Word War*, 107; "The Cabinet, Record of Action," Jan. 22, 1957, Box 8, Cabinet Series, DDEL; Cabinet Minutes, Jan. 18, 1957, Box 8, Papers of Dwight D. Eisenhower (Ann Whitman File), Cabinet Series, DDEL.

14. *Department of State Bulletin*, Sept. 7, 1953, 321-22; FRUS 1955-1957, IX: 504; 521-22, 562.

15. Eugene W. Castle, *Billions, Blunders, and Baloney: The Fantastic Story of How the United States is Squandering Your Money Overseas* (New York: Devin-Adair Co., 1955); *Congressional Record* 101, 84th cong., 1st sess., A 1078-79, Part 4, 4607; FRUS 1955-1957, IX: 521-22, 565; Rep. John J. Rooney to Dwight D. Eisenhower, April 12, 1957, Box 910, Central File, 1955; United Press report, April 1, 1957, Box 15, Hulten Papers, HSTL.

16. Dwight D. Eisenhower, *Waging Peace, 1956-1961* (Garden City, N.Y.: Doubleday, 1963), 136-38; Sorenson, *The Word War*, 95-96; Phone Calls, May 18, 1956, Box 15, Dwight D. Eisenhower Diary Series, DDEL.

17. Allen interview; *U.S News and World Report,* Jan. 10, 1958, 22; *Newsweek,* Jan. 26, 1959; FRUS 1955-1957, IX, 614; "Legislative Leadership meeting," June 5, 1958, Box 3, Ann Whitman File, Log Series, DDEL; *New York Times,* Nov. 22, 1957.

18. On Soviet propaganda and cultural efforts in the developing world, see Frederick C. Barghoorn, *The Soviet Cultural Offensive: The Role of Cultural Diplomacy in Soviet Foreign Policy* (Princeton: Princeton University Press, 1960), 188-225.

19. William J. Lederer and Eugene Burdick, *The Ugly American* (New York: Norton, 1958).

20. Foreign Service dispatch from Havana by Francis Donahue, July 11, 1957, Box 1, Foreign Service Dispatches, Records of the United States Information Agency, RG 306; Thomas G. Paterson, *Contesting Castro: The United States and the Triumph of the Cuban Revolution* (New York: Oxford University Press, 1994), 47-48; NSC 5611, Part II, "Status of U.S. National Security Programs on June 30, 1956."

21. NSC 5611, Part II, "Status of U.S. National Security Programs on June 30, 1956"; Leon Hunsaker dispatch, July 7, 1956, Box 1, FSD.

22. NSC 5611, Part II, "Status of U.S. National Security Programs on June 30, 1956."

23. Richard Nixon, "Talk with Christian Herter," April 6, 1954, Box 3, White House Office, NSC Staff: Papers, 1948-1961, DDEL; Anspacher dispatch from Phnom Penh, May 24, 1957, Box 1, Foreign Service Dispatches, DDEL.

24. NSC 5611, Part II, "Status of U.S. National Security Programs on June 30, 1956."

25. Abbott Washburn to Dwight D. Eisenhower, Aug. 21, 1957, Box 99, DDE Papers, Subject Series, DDEL, FOIA request.

26. NSC 5611, Part II, "Status of U.S. National Security Programs on June 30, 1956."

27. FRUS 1955-1957, IX: 595-96.

28. George A. Mann, "Placement of Anti-Communist Material in Period of Shepilov Visit to Syria," July 17, 1956, Box 1, Foreign Service Dispatches, RG 306.

29. John D. Silvera, "Color—A Factor in U.S. Psychological Warfare," Psychological Warfare School, Fort Bragg, N.C., Box 673, White House Central Files, Official File, DDEL.

30. "Developments in U.S. Racial Relations with Some Implications for Psychological Strategy," June 27, 1952, Box 27; Silvera, "Color—A Factor in U.S. Psychological Warfare."

31. VOA Polish service broadcast, May 22, 1954, Box 73, VOA Records, RG 306.

32. Ibid.

33. C. D. Jackson to Abbott Washburn, Jan. 30, 1956, Box 90, Jackson Papers, DDEL.

34. Leo Crespi, International Research Institute Intelligence Summary [undated], Box 8, Intelligence Bulletins, Memorandums, and Summaries, 1954-1956, RG 306.

35. Stephen E. Ambrose, *Eisenhower: Soldier and President* (New York: Simon and Schuster, 1990), 444-48.

36. FRUS 1955-1957, IX: 613; "Summary of Discussion and Conclusions Reached at Regional PAO's Meeting," Box 1, Foreign Service Dispatches, RG 306.

37. "Opinions About East-West Affairs," Jan. 20, 1958, Box 3, World Project Files, 1953-1956, RG 306; Leo Crespi, IRI Intelligence Summary; "Post-Little Rock Opinion on the Treatment of Negroes in the U.S.," January 1958, Box 1, Program and Media Studies, 1956-1962, RG 306.

38. "Feature Packets," Box 3, RG 306.

39. "The Negro in America, 1961," Media Brief No. 13, Box 1, Program and Media Studies, 1956-1962, RG 306.

40. Report by Gilbert E. Bursley, USIS Leopoldville, May 4, 1956, Box 1, Foreign Service Dispatches, RG 306.

41. Ibid.

42. "Summary of Discussion and Conclusions Reached at Regional PAO's Meeting."

43. "Memorandum of Conversation Between the President and T. S. Repplier," Aug. 3, 1955, Box 99, White House Central Files, Confidential File 1953-1961, Subject Series, DDEL; Repplier memorandum [undated], Box 30, Ann Whitman File, DDEL.

44. "Memorandum of Conversation Between the President and T. S. Repplier," Aug. 3, 1955; Repplier memorandum [undated], Box 30, Ann Whitman File, DDEL; "'People's Capitalism': This *Is* America," *Collier's,* Jan. 6, 1956.

45. "This *Is* America," 34; "Excerpts from Sherman Adams speech over Mutual Broadcasting Network," Dec. 1, 1955, Box 90, C. D. Jackson Papers, DDEL; Laura Belmonte, "'Almost Everyone Is a Capitalist': The USIA Presents the American Economy, 1953-1959," paper delivered before Society for Historians of American Foreign Relations, June 23-25, 1994.

46. "Excerpts from Sherman Adams speech."

47. "The President's Reaction to the Repplier Proposal"; C. D. Jackson to Abbott Washburn, Jan. 30, 1956, Box 90, CDJ Papers, DDEL.

48. "America's New Economic Age," [1957], Box 4, Feature Packets, RG 306.

49. "History of U.S. Labor Day," Box 7, Feature Packets; see also Box 2, Feature Packets, both in RG 306.

50. Box 17, Feature Packets, RG 306; Belmonte, "'Almost Everyone Is a Capitalist.'"

51. Box 27, Feature Packets, RG 306.

52. Box 5, Feature Packets, RG 306.

53. "This *Is* America," 34; "Communist Propaganda in the Cold War," Streibert Report to President and Cabinet, July 1, 1955, Box 5, Ann Whitman File, DDEL; Barghoorn, *Soviet Cultural Offensive,* 60-98.

54. FRUS 1955-1957, IX: 505; FRUS 1952-1954, II, 2: 1773-74.

55. FRUS 1955-1957, IX: 508; FRUS 1952-1954, II, 2: 1775-77, 1791-92; USIS Conference, April 30, 1953, BCN 90, Papers of J. William Fulbright, University of Arkansas.

56. *New York Times,* Dec. 22, 1954; Report to President's Cabinet on President's Emergency Fund for Participation in International Affairs, undated [1954], Box 19, White House Office, Cabinet Secretariat: Records 1953-1960, DDEL.

57. FRUS 1955-1957, IX: 508; Walter B. Smith memorandum, Sept. 3, 1954, Box 12, White House Office, NSC Staff: Papers 1948-1961, DDEL; Eisenhower to Sinclair Weeks, undated draft [1954], Box 13, Ann Whitman File, Cabinet Series; Eisenhower memorandum, Aug. 10, 1954, Box 3, Ann Whitman File, Diary Series, DDEL.

58. Streibert and Weeks, "Agreed Policy Guidelines for International Trade Fair Program," April 14, 1955, Box 12, White House Office: NSC Staff: Paper, 1948-1961, DDEL.

59. Report to Cabinet on President's Emergency Fund for Participation in International Affairs; "Communist Propaganda in the Cold War," Streibert Report to Cabinet, July 1, 1955, Box 5, AWF; *Department of State Bulletin,* July 22, 1957, 150-51.

60. FRUS 1955-1957, IX: 600; "Memorandum of Conference with the President," Aug. 31, 1956, Box 17, DDE Diary Series.

61. Streibert to all PAO's, Jan. 10, 1956, Box 90, C. D. Jackson Papers, DDEL; "This *Is* America, 34.

62. Andrew Berding to Henry Loomis, "Pre-Test of People's Capitalism Exhibit," undated, Box 2, World Project Files, 1953-1963, RG 306.

63. Ibid.

64. "The People's Capitalism Exhibit," March 1956, Box 2, World Project Files, 1953-1963, RG 306.

65. Streibert to all PAO's, Jan. 10, 1956; "Study Design of Visitor Survey—U.S. Exhibits at Trade Fairs," July 5, 1956, Box 3, Subject Files 1953-1963, RG 306.

66. "Highlights of USIA Research on the Presidential Trade Fair Program," November 1958, Box 1, Special Reports 1955-1959, RG 306; "The Impact of the USIS Exhibit 'Youth USA' at the 1960 Berlin Industrial Fair," April 1961, Box 2, Program and Media Studies, 1956-1962, RG 306.

67. "Visitor Reaction to the U.S. Versus Major Competing Exhibits at the 1958 Zagreb Trade Fair," December 1958, Box 1, Program and Media Studies, 1956-1962, RG 306; "Highlights of USIA Research on the Presidential Trade Fair Program," November 1958, Box 1, Special Reports 1955-1959, RG 306.

68. *Christian Science Monitor*, Dec. 11, 1959; Katherine Howard, "The 'Fair' Way of Making Friends," Box 26, Katherine G. Howard Papers, 1917-1974, DDEL; Dennis Merrill, *Bread and the Ballot: The United States and India's Economic Development, 1947-1963* (Chapel Hill, N.C.: 1990), 150-52.

69. Howard Cullman, "The United States at the Brussels Universal and International Exhibition, 1958: A Report to the President of the United States," May 30, 1959, Box 721, Central File, Brussels, RG 306.

70. Ibid.; Robert W. Rydell, *World of Fairs: The Century of Progress Expositions* (Chicago: University of Chicago Press, 1993), 193-211.

71. Cullman, "The United States at the Brussels Universal and International Exhibition, 1958"; Rydell, *World of Fairs*, 193-211.

72. *Washington Post*, Jan. 26, 1958; Roderic O'Connor to Bryce Harlow, May 7, 1957, Box 70, Central Files, International Trade Fair, RG 306; May 22, 1957, telephone call with Lyndon B. Johnson, Box 10, Telephone Calls, Herter Papers, 1957-1961.

73. Cullman to Eisenhower, July 15, 1957, Box 720, Central Files, DDEL.

74. Cullman to Eisenhower, Nov. 10, 1957, Box 720, White House Central Files, Official File, DDEL; Barghoorn, *Soviet Cultural Offensive*, 89.

75. *New York Times*, Nov. 10, 1957; *Washington Post*, Jan. 26, 1958; Rydell, *World of Fairs*, 200.

76. Cullman, "The United States at the Brussels Universal and International Exhibition, 1958"; Rydell, *World of Fairs*, 202; *New York Times Magazine*, April 13, 1958; UPI Commentary by William Anderson, Box 721, White House Central File, Official File, Brussels, DDEL.

77. Cullman, "The United States at the Brussels Universal and International Exhibition, 1958."

78. George V. Allen report to Eisenhower, June 29, 1958, Box 721, Central File, Official File, Brussels, DDEL; UPI commentary by William Anderson.

79. Howard Cullman to Sherman Adams, May 21, 1958, Box 721, Central File, Official File, Brussels, DDEL.
80. *Cleveland Plain Dealer,* June 8, 1958; UPI commentary by William Anderson.
81. Rydell, *World of Fairs,* 208.
82. "Telephone Call from the President," April 7, 1958, Box 13, John Foster Dulles Telephone Calls Series, DDEL; Cullman to Adams, May 21, 1958.
83. Letter from Brussels to Eisenhower on "Unfinished Work" exhibit, Aug. 16, 1958, Box 721, Central File, Official File, Brussels, DDEL.
84. Ibid.
85. Rydell, *World of Fairs,* 209-10; "Memorandum of Conference with the President," June 25, 1958, Box 24, White House Office Staff Secretary Subject Series, Alphabet Subseries, DDEL.
86. Rydell, *World of Fairs,* 209-10.
87. Allen, "Memorandum of Conference with the President," June 25, 1958.
88. Ibid; Michael L. Krenn, "Unfinished Business: Segregation and U.S. Diplomacy at the 1938 World's Fair." I would like to thank Professor Krenn for providing me a copy of his essay.
89. Guides' letter to Eisenhower; UPI commentary by William Anderson.
90. Guides' letter to Eisenhower.
91. Ibid.
92. UPI summary by William Anderson; "Memorandum of Conference with the President," June 25, 1958; Allen report to Eisenhower, June 29, 1958.
93. State Department summary attached to Cullman to Adams, May 21, 1958; Allen, "Memorandum of Conference with the President," June 25, 1958.
94. Allen report to Eisenhower, June 29, 1958; Cullman, "The United States at the Brussels Universal and International Exhibition, 1958."

Chapter 6

1. *Department of State Bulletin,* July 15, 1957, 119; Yale Richmond, *U.S.-Soviet Cultural Exchanges, 1958-1986* (Boulder, Co.: Westview Press, 1987), xi, 4-6; Frederick C. Barghoorn, *The Soviet Cultural Offensive: The Role of Cultural Diplomacy in Soviet Foreign Policy* (Princeton: Princeton University Press, 1960), 22-23.
2. *Department of State Bulletin,* July 15, 1957, 119; J. D. Parks, *Culture, Conflict, and Coexistence: American-Soviet Cultural Relations, 1917-1958* (Jefferson, N.C.: McFarland, 1983), 166-67.
3. *Department of State Bulletin,* Oct. 21, 1957, 635; Parks, *Culture, Conflict, and Coexistence,* 168.
4. *Department of State Bulletin,* Nov. 18, 1957, 800-803; a Soviet university intellectual recalled that *Amerika* "was virtually unavailable at ordinary kiosks.

... Neither could one subscribe to it without [CP] authorization." Interview with Dr. Leonid Sidorov, Kazan State University (Russia), by the author, Akron, OH., May 14, 1994.

5. *Department of State Bulletin,* Nov. 18, 1957, 800-803.
6. *Department of State Bulletin,* Feb. 17, 1958, 243-47.
7. *Department of State Bulletin,* Feb. 17, 1958, 243-47.
8. *Department of State Bulletin,* March 10, 1958, 381-84.
9. FRUS 1958-1960, X, 2: 1-6.
10. *Time,* Feb. 10, 1958, 19-20.
11. For an overview of the cultural agreement, and its implementation in later years, see Richmond, *U.S.-Soviet Cultural Exchanges.*
12. Operations Coordinating Board (OCB) memorandum, Dec. 1, 1954, Box 20, White House Office, National Security Council Staff: Papers, 1948-61, Dwight D. Eisenhower Presidential Library (DDEL); Salisbury comments, plenary session, "Report on the National Conference on Exchange of Persons," Institute for International Education, New York, Feb. 25, 1955, BCN 57, 753, Fulbright Papers, University of Arkansas.
13. OCB memorandum, Dec. 1, 1954; General Records of the Department of State, RG 59, 961.50/7-1256.
14. Eric Johnston to George A. Morgan, Oct. 9, 1953, Box 20, White House Office, NSC Staff: Papers, 1948-61, DDEL; Elmer Staats to Eric Johnston, Aug. 19, 1954, Box 20, White House Office, NSC Staff: Papers, 1948-61, DDEL.
15. *Department of State Bulletin,* 1958, 248; Nov. 3, 1958, 696-98; George Allen, Memorandum of Conversation with the President, May 7, 1958, Box 24, White House Office Staff Secretary, Subject Series, Alphabet Subseries, DDEl; FRUS 1958-1960, X, 1: 184; *Newsweek,* Jan. 26, 1959, 100.
16. RG 59, 511.613/4-1658; *Time,* April 21 and 28, 1958; *The Reporter,* May 29, 1958; FRUS 1958-1960, X, 2: 10-13.
17. FRUS 1958-1960, X, 2: 67-70; Barghoorn, *Soviet Cultural Offensive,* 302.
18. RG 59, 511.613/5-958.
19. Martin Bauml Duberman, *Paul Robeson: A Biography* (New York: Ballantine Books, 1989). See pages 467-70 on Robeson's 1958 tour of the USSR.
20. Barghoorn, *Soviet Cultural Offensive,* 268-335; RG 59, 511.613/7-285; RG 59, 511.613/10-655; RG 59, 511.613/12-2755; RG 59, 511.613/3-2056; RG 59, 511.613/1-1058.
21. FRUS 1958-1960, X, 2: 1; Memorandum of Conversation, Jan. 27, 1958, Box 30, DDE diary series, DDEL; Telephone Calls, Feb. 25, 1958, Box 10, Papers of Christian Herter, 1957-61, DDEL; Memorandum of Conversation,

Jan. 17, 1959, Box 15, White House Office, Staff Secretary, International Trips and Meetings, DDEL.

22. Rhodri Jeffreys-Jones, *The CIA and American Democracy* (New Haven: Yale University Press, 1989), 133, 157-60.

23. Gordon Gray, "Memorandum of Meeting with the President," May 26, 1959, White House Office, Office of Special Assistant for National Security Affairs: Records, 1952-61, Box 4, Special Assistants Series, Presidential Subseries, DDEL; FRUS 1958-1960, X, 2: 1, 7-8; Telephone Call, Mar. 4, 1958, Box 30, Dwight D. Eisenhower Diary Series, DDEL; "Legislative Leadership meeting," June 5, 1958, Box 3, Papers of Dwight D. Eisenhower, Log Series, DDEL.

24. FRUS 1958-1960, X, 2: 25-36.

25. Parks, *Culture, Conflict, and Coexistence,* 17; FRUS, X, 2: 10-13; "Current Status of East-West Exchanges," Jan. 1, 1960, Box 12, U.S. Council on Foreign Economic Policy, Randall Series, Subject subseries, DDEL.

26. FRUS 1958-1960, X, 2: 9-16, 52-53.

27. *New York Times Magazine,* Aug. 11, 1957.

28. Richard Stites, *Russian Popular Culture: Entertainment and Society Since 1900* (Cambridge: Cambridge University Press, 1992), 132; Timothy W. Ryback, *Rock Around the Bloc: A History of Rock Music in Eastern Europe and the Soviet Union* (New York: Oxford University Press, 1990), 18; Sidorov interview.

29. *New York Times Magazine,* Aug. 11, 1957.

30. *The New Republic,* July 15, 1957, 12-15; *New York Times Magazine,* Aug. 31, 1958 and Aug. 11, 1957.

31. *New York Times,* July 27, 1959; Leo Crespi to Gordon Ewing, June 12, 1959; Ralph K. White to Gordon Ewing, June 12, 1959, both in Box 6, World Project Files, 1953-63, Records of the United States Information Agency, RG 306.

32. "Joint USIA-State Message," Sept. 17, 1959, Box 6; "Seventh World Festival of Youth and Students for Peace and Friendship, Vienna—1959," Research Notes, 1958-62 [undated], Box 2, both in World Project Files, 1953-63, RG 306.

33. Barghoorn, *Soviet Cultural Offensive,* 1-8.

34. FRUS 1958-1960, X, 2: 26.

35. "Memorandum of Agreement Between U.S.-USSR Representatives Pertinent to the Staging of a U.S. Exhibit in Moscow," Box 1, RG 306; *Department of State Bulletin,* Oct. 13, 1958, 577, and Nov. 3, 1958, 696.

36. L. A. Minnich, Cabinet Minutes, Jan. 23, 1959, Box 12, Cabinet Series, DDEL; Abbott Washburn, Oral History Interview, Washington, D.C, Jan. 5, 1968, by Ed Edwin, DDEL.

37. "Transcript of Tape Recording: White House Conference on Moscow Fair," January 1959, Box 7, RG 306.

38. Washburn interview; *Department of State Bulletin,* Nov. 3, 1958, 696; Neil J. Sullivan, *The Dodgers Move West* (New York: Oxford, 1987), 99-105.

39. Llewelyn Thompson to George Allen, Oct. 30, 1958, Box 13, White House Office, NSC Staff Papers, 1948-61, DDEL.

40. McClellan letter, undated, Box 2, RG 306.

41. "Transcript of Tape Recording: White House Conference on Moscow Fair," January 1959, Box 7, RG 306.

42. Ibid.

43. "McClellan Report on the American Exhibition," undated, Box 19, Sprague Committee Report, DDEL.

44. James G. Richter, *Khrushchev's Double Bind: International Pressures and Domestic Coalition Politics* (Baltimore: The Johns Hopkins University Press, 1994), 101-25; Raymond L. Garthoff, *Assessing the Adversary: Estimates by the Eisenhower Administration of Soviet Intentions and Capabilities* (Washington: The Brookings Institution, 1990-91), 31-52; William Burr, "Avoiding the Slippery Slope: The Eisenhower Administration and the Berlin Crisis, November 1958-January 1959," *Diplomatic History* 18 (Spring 1994): 177-205; William Burr, "New Sources on the Berlin Crisis, 1958-1962," *Cold War International History Project Bulletin* (Fall 1992), Woodrow Wilson International Center for Scholars, Washington, D.C.; John Newhouse, *War and Peace in the Nuclear Age* (New York: Vintage Books, 1990), 121-24; Peter J. Roman, *Eisenhower and the Missile Gap* (Ithaca, N.Y.: Cornell University Press, 1995).

45. "McClellan Report on the American Exhibition."

46. *Department of State Bulletin,* Jan. 26, 1959, 132-34.

47. "Transcript of Tape Recording: White House Conference on Moscow Fair."

48. Ibid.

49. "Policy Guidance for the U.S. Exhibit in Moscow in 1959" [Confidential], Box 7, RG 306, FOIA.

50. Ibid.

51. RG 59, 511.612/11-1758.

52. RG 59, 761.00/2-959.

53. Ibid.

54. "Transcript of Tape Recording: White House Conference on Moscow Fair"; Edwin P. Kretzmann to Christian A. Herter, May 21, 1959, Box 19, Cabinet Series, DDEL.

55. President's Special International Program, 7th Semi-Annual Report, July 1, 1959 to Dec. 31, 1959, Box 14, Sprague Committee Report, DDEL.

56. White House press release, May 21, 1959, Box 722, White House Central Files, Moscow Trade Fair, DDEL; "Transcript of Tape Recording: White House Conference on Moscow Fair"; "President's Special International Program, 7th Semi-Annual Report."

57. Robert Griffith, "Dwight D. Eisenhower and the Corporate Commonwealth," *American Historical Review* 87 (February 1982): 87-122.

58. "McClellan Report on the American Exhibition."

59. Memorandum by John S. Eisenhower, Feb. 3, 1959, Box 39, Papers of Dwight D. Eisenhower; Washburn, Memorandum for the President, Jan. 22, 1959, Box 721, Central File, Official File, Brussels, DDEL.

60. Eisenhower memorandum; Washburn interview; "Transcript of Tape Recording on Moscow Fair."

61. "McClellan Report on the American Exhibition"; Kretzmann to Herter, May 21, 1959.

62. "Proekt Postanovleniia Sekretariata TSK KPSS, 'O merakh v sviazi s predstoiashchim otkritiem sovetskoi vystavki v N'iu Iorke i amerikanskoi vystavki v Moskve'" ("Draft of the Decree of the CPSU Central Committee, 'On Measures to be Taken In View of the Forthcoming Opening of the Soviet exhibition in New York and American Exhibition in Moscow'"), May 23, 1959, Tsentr Khraneniia Sovremennoi Dokumentatsii, Moskva (Center for the Storage of Contemporary Documents, Moscow); *New York Times,* June 3, 1959.

63. "Soviet Counter Moves to American Exhibition in Moscow," June 15, 1959, Box 7, RG 306; RG 59, 861.191-MO/7-159; Barghoorn, *Soviet Cultural Offensive,* 92.

64. "McClellan Report on the American Exhibition."

65. Katherine G. Howard, "The 'Fair' Way of Making Friends," Box 26, Katherine G. Howard Papers, 1917-74, DDEL; Washburn interview.

66. Minutes of May 22, 1959, Cabinet meeting, Box 13, Cabinet Series, DDEL; Diary entry, June 15, 1959, Box 10, DDE Papers, DDEL; "The President's Extemporaneous Remarks to the Group Going As Guides to the Moscow Exhibit," June 15, 1959, Box 42, DDE Diary Series, DDEL. (I found no record of the guides' responses to Eisenhower's questions.)

67. RG 59, 861.191-MO/7-165; RG 59, 861.191-MO/7-255; RG 59, 861.191-MO/7-2559; "Airgrams and Cable" file, Box 1, Records Relating to the American National Exhibition, RG 306.

68. Memorandum, June 2, 1959, Box 722, Central Files, Moscow Trade Fair, DDEL.

69. Thurmond to Herter, July 16, 1959; George Allen to Francis E. Walter, Jan. 6, 1959, Box 722, Central Files, Moscow Trade Fair, DDEL.

70. Walter to Allen, June 25, 1959; Allen to Walter; Walter to Herter, July 1, 1959, all in Box 722, Central Files, Moscow Trade Fair, DDEL.

71. Telephone Calls, June 25, 1959, Box 12, Herter Papers, DDEL; RG 59, 861.191-MO/7-259.

72. FRUS 1958-1960, X, 1: 290; Dwight D. Eisenhower to Rep. Francis E. Walter, July 16, 1959, Box 722, Central Files, Moscow Trade Fair, DDEL; Minutes of May 22, 1959 Cabinet meeting, Box 13, Cabinet Series, DDEL.

73. RG 59, 861.191-MO/7-359; Phone Calls, July 2, 1959, Box 12, Herter Papers, DDEL.

74. Memoranda of conversation, July 27, 1959; July 11, 1959, both in Box 10, DDE Papers, DDEL.

75. RG 59, 861.191-MO/2-2559; Kretzmann to Herter, May 21, 1959; Minutes of May 22, 1959, Cabinet meeting; *America,* Sept. 5, 1959, 6-7.

76. *Time,* Aug. 3, 1959, 14.

77. "Transcript of Tape Recording of White House Conference on Moscow Fair."

78. Washburn interview; "McClellan report on U.S. exhibition in Moscow."

79. "Memorandum for the Record," April 4, 1959, Box 6, JFD Subject Series, DDEL; Richard M. Nixon, *Six Crises* (New York: Doubleday, 1962), 24; Llewelyn Thompson to Christian Herter, April 9, 1959, Box 11, DDE Papers, Dulles-Herter Series, FOIA; Herter, "Memorandum for the President," April 9, 1959, Box 11, DDE Papers, Dulles-Herter Series, DDEL; RG 59, 861.191-MO/4-2259; "Memorandum of Conversation with the Vice President," July 30, 1955, Box 6, John Foster Dulles Subject Series, DDEL.

80. Llewelyn Thompson to Christian Herter, May 14, 1959, Box 16, White House Office, Office of the Staff Secretary, Records, 1952-1961, DDEL, FOIA; Thompson to Herter, May 4, 1959, Box 7, White House Office, Office of the Staff Secretary, Records, 1952-1961, DDEL.

81. FRUS 1958-1960, X, 1: 332; Dwight D. Eisenhower, *Waging Peace, 1957-61* (Garden City, N.Y.: Doubleday, 1963), 408.

82. RG 59, 033.1100-NI/5-859.

83. Washburn interview; Nixon, *Six Crises,* 235-91.

84. *Time,* Aug. 3, 1959, 11-16; Nixon, *Six Crises,* 252.

85. Nixon, *Six Crises,* 252.

86. *Time,* Aug. 3, 1959, 11-16; *New York Times,* July 25, 1959.

87. *Time,* Aug. 3, 1959, 11-16; Nixon, *Six Crises,* 254-58.

88. "McClellan report on the American Exhibition."

89. "Message from the President to be Read by the Honorable Richard M. Nixon at the Opening of the American National Exhibition in Moscow," July 25, 1959, Box 722, Central Files, Moscow Trade Fair, DDEL; *Department of State Bulletin,* Aug. 17, 1959, 228-32.

90. *Time,* Aug. 3, 1959, 15.

91. Ibid.; Nixon to Eisenhower, July 26, 1959, Box 28, Administrative Series, DDE Papers, DDEL; FRUS 1958-1960, X, 1: 372-73.

92. FRUS 1958-1960, X, 1: 377-79; Nixon to Eisenhower, July 26, 1959; Nixon, *Six Crises,* 274-77.

93. *Department of State Bulletin,* Aug. 17, 1959, 232-36; Nixon, *Six Crises,* 278-81.

94. *Newsweek,* Aug. 10, 1959, 32.

95. FRUS 1958-1960 X, 2: 190-218; Nixon, *Six Crises,* 284-87; *Department of State Bulletin,* Aug. 24, 1959, 270-71.

96. FRUS 1958-1960, X, 2: 214, 221-23.

97. FRUS 1958-1960, X, 1: 382; FRUS 1958-1960, X, 2: 218-19; Nixon report, Minutes, Aug. 7, 1959, meeting, Box 14, Cabinet Series, DDEL.

Chapter 7

1. "Dokladnaia zapiska Orlova i Shokova o khode podgotovki k otkritiiu sovetskoi vystavki v N'iu Iorke i amerkanskoi vystavki v Moskve." ("On the Progress of Preparation for the Opening of the Soviet Exhibition in New York and of the American Exhibition in Moscow"), Report to the Central Committee of the CPSU, May 23, 1959, Tsentr Khraneniia Sovremennoi Dokumentatsii, Moskva (Center for the Storage of Contemporary Documents, Moscow, hereinafter TSKHSD).

2. Ibid.

3. Ibid.

4. Ibid.; "Postanovlenie TsK KPSS, 'O kontrmeropriatiiakh v sviazi s amerikanskoi vysavkoi v Moskve'" ("Decree of the CPSU, 'On Countermeasures in Connection with the Forthcoming United States National Exhibition in Moscow'"), Central Committee [undated], TSKHSD.

5. "O kontrmeropriatiiakh v sviazi s amerikanskoi vystavkoi v Moskve."

6. Ibid.

7. Ibid.; "Proekt postanovlenniia TsK KPSS 'O merakh v sviazi s predstoiashchim otkritiem sovetskoi vystavki v N'iu Iorke i amerikanskoi vystavki v Moskve,' podgotovlennyi G. Zhukovym i A. Orlovym." ("Draft of the decree of the CPSU Central Committee, 'On Measures to be Taken In View of the Forthcoming Opening of the Soviet Exhibition in New York and American Exhibition in Moscow,' prepared by G. Zhukov and A. Orlov"), May 23, 1959, TSKHSD.

8. "O kontrmeropriatiiakh v sviazi s amerikanskoi vystavkoi."

9. Ibid.

10. "Soviet Counter Moves to American Exhibition in Moscow," June 15, 1959, Box 7, RG 306.
11. RG 59, 861.191-MO/4-1359.
12. Ibid; General Records of the Department of State, RG 59, 761.00/2-959; Memorandum by John S. Eisenhower, Feb. 3, 1959, Box 39, Papers of Dwight D. Eisenhower (DDE Papers), DDEL.
13. RG 59, 861.191-MO/7-159; RG 59, 861.191-MO/6-1259; McClellan report on U.S. Exhibition in Moscow, Box 19, Sprague Committee report, DDEL.
14. RG 59, 861.191-MO/6-125; RG 59, 861.191-MO/4-1059.
15. RG 59, 861.191-MO/6-2959; Thompson to Secretary of State, July 8, 1959, Box 7, Records of the United States Information Agency, RG 306; RG 59, 861.191-MO/7-859.
16. "Proekt postanovleniia sekretariata TSK KPSS 'O merakh v sviazi s predstoiashchim otkritiem sovetskoi vystavki v N'iu Iorke i amerikanskoi vystavki v Moske'" ("Draft of the Decree of the CPSU Central Committee, 'On Measures to be Taken in View of the Forthcoming Opening of the Soviet Exhibition in New York and American Exhibition in Moscow'"), May 23, 1959, TSKHSD; Albert Harkness to Abbott Washburn, Aug. 4, 1959, Box 7, RG 306; Thompson to Secretary of State, July 16, 1959, Box 7, RG 306; *New York Times,* July 25, 1959.
17. *New York Times,* July 25, 1959; RG 59, 861.191 MO/7-2559.
18. Associated Press wire dispatch [undated]; Llewelyn Thompson to Secretary of State, Aug. 5, 1959, both in Box 7, RG 306.
19. RG 59, 861.191-Mo/8-359; McClellan to N.I. Muravjev, All Union Chamber of Commerce, July 30, 1959, Box 7, RG 306; undated AP dispatch, Box 7, RG 306.
20. Thompson to Secretary of State, Aug. 5, 1959, Box 7, RG 306; "McClellan Report on the American Exhibition," undated, Box 19, Sprague Committee Report, DDEL; Interview with Dr. Leonid Sidorov, Kazan State University (Russia) by the author, Akron, OH., May 14, 1994.
21. "McClellan Report on the American Exhibition."
22. Klosson, "Seven Days at Sokolniki"; President's Special International Program, 7th Semi-Annual Report, July 1, 1959 to Dec. 31, 1959, Box 14, Sprague Committee Report, DDEL.
23. Gustavus Tuckerman, "On the Lessons Taught by the Exchange of US-USSR National Exhibitions," Oct. 3, 1959; Llewelyn Thompson to Secretary, April 15, 1959, both in Box 7, RG 306; RG 59, 861.191-MO/8 359; President's Special International Program, 7th Semi-Annual Report, July 1, 1959 to Dec. 31, 1959, Box 14, Sprague Committee Report.

24. "Spravka otdela propagandy i agitatsii Moskovskogo gorodskogo komiteta KPSS ot 14 avgusta 1959 g., 'O vypolnenii meropriatii po agitatsionno-propagandistkoi rabote sredi naseleniia na period deistviia gosudarstvennoi vystavki SSHA v Moskve.'" ("A Note of the Department of Propaganda and Agitation of the Moscow Regional CPSU Committee, 'On the Completion of Measures on Agitation and Propaganda Work Among the Population for the Duration of the National United States exhibition in Moscow'"), August 14, 1959, Tsentral'nyi arkhiv obshchestvennykh dvizhenii (Central Archives of Public Movements, Moscow, hereinafter MGAOD).

25. Ibid.; RG 59, 861.191-MO/8 359.

26. Harrisburg (Pa.) Patriot News, Aug. 23, 1959, Box 7, RG 306.

27. "Dokladnaia zapiska o rabote kommunistov IKAN'A na amerikanskoi vystavke 19 avgusta 1959 g. brigadira gruppy IU. Levada v Proletarkskii RK KPSS" ("Memorandum on the Work of Communists in the Institute of Culture of the Academy of Sciences on the American Exhibition of August 19, 1959, IU. Levada"), undated, Op. 139, D. 13, MGAOD.

28. Ibid.; "Vpechatleniia ob amerikanskoi vystavke ot chlena KPSS Poliakova A.P." ("Impressions of CPSU Member A.P. Polyakaov from a Visit to the United States Exhibit") undated, Op. 139, D. 13, MGAOD.

29. Life, Sept. 21, 1959, 56-62; the classic work on poverty in the United States during this period is Michael Harrington, The Other America (New York: Macmillan, 1962).

30. "Dokladnaia zapiska . . . IU. Levada"; Katherine G. Howard, "The 'Fair' Way of Making Friends," Box 26, Katherine G. Howard Papers, 1917-74, DDEL.

31. "Dokladnaia zapiska . . . IU. Levada."

32. Life, Sept. 21, 1959, 56-62; USIA to State Department, Aug. 16, 1959, Box 7, RG 306.

33. Abbott Washburn, Oral History Interview, Washington, D.C., Jan. 5, 1968, by Ed Edwin, DDEL.

34. Life, Sept. 21, 1959, 56-62.

35. RG 59, 761.00/9-3059; RG 59, 861.191-MO/9-859.

36. "McClellan Report on the American Exhibition"; Washburn interview; Howard, "The 'Fair' Way of Making Friends."

37. "Informatsiia gruppy partiinogo aktiva Glavlita SSSR" ("Information of a Group of Party Activists of the Glavlit" [Office of Censorship]), Aug. 19, 1959, File D. 4; Op. 139; Ed., Khr. 13, MGAOD.

38. Ibid.; "Vpechatleniia . . . Poliakova."

39. Informatsiia gruppy partiinogo aktiva Glavlita SSSR.

40. "O poseshchenii kommunistami Ministerstva kul'tury RSFSR amerikanskoi vystatki v 'Sokol'nikakh'" ("On the Visit to the United States Exhibition in

Sokolniki by A Group of Communists of the RSFSR Ministry of Culture"), undated, File D. 4; Op. 139; Ed., Khr. 13, MGAOD.

41. "Dokladnaia zapiska . . . IU. Levada."

42. Ibid.

43. Howard, "'Fair' Way of Making Friends"; Harrisburg (Pa.) *Patriot News*, Aug. 23, 1959, Box 7, RG 306.

44. Ralph K. White, "USIA Report on the American Exhibition in Moscow: Visitors' Reactions to the American Exhibit in Moscow," Sept. 28, 1959, Box 14, Sprague Committee, DDEL.

45. O poseshchenii kommunnistami Ministerstva kul'tury.

46. "Dokladnaia zapiska . . . IU. Levada"; White, "USIA Report on the American Exhibition in Moscow."

47. "Dokladnaia zapiska . . . IU. Levada."

48. "Iz informatsii sotrudnikov MID v partkom" ("Information for the Party Committee of the Foreign Ministry"), undated, File D. 4; Op. 139; Ed., Khr. 13, MGAOD.

49. RG 59, 861.191-MO/7-2759; McClellan Report on the American Exhibition.

50. "McClellan Report on the American Exhibition"; White, "USIA Report on the American Exhibition in Moscow."

51. "McClellan Report on the American Exhibition"; RG 59, 761.00/2-959.

52. RG 59, 861.191-MO/8-2059; "McClellan Report on the American Exhibition."

53. White, "USIA Report on the American Exhibition in Moscow."

54. Ibid.; RG 59, 861.191-MO/8-159; RG 59, 861.191-MO/7-2759.

55. RG 59, 861.191-MO/8-159.

56. White, "USIA Report on the American Exhibition in Moscow."

57. RG 59, 861.191-MO/8 861.191-MO/7-2759.

58. Howard, "'Fair' Way of Making Friends."

59. Ibid.; RG 59, 861.191-MO/8-2059.

60. IBM Press Release, Aug. 11, 1959, Box 7, RG 306; Howard, "'Fair' Way of Making Friends."

61. "Fashion Industries Presentation of the American National Exhibition in Moscow," Prospectus, Box 2, RG 306; RG 59, 861.191-MO/7-2759.

62. Linda Salzman press release, Box 1, RG 306.

63. Ibid.

64. Ibid.

65. *Time*, Sept. 7, 1959, 54; "McClellan Report on the American Exhibition"; President's Special International Program, 7th Semi-Annual Report.

66. Ed Sullivan, "My Journey to Moscow," *Reader's Digest*, March 1960, 52-56; *McCall's*, November 1959, 52, 160; RG 59, 861.191-MO/6-1259; President's Special International Program."

67. RG 59, 861.191-MO/8-1059; White, "USIA Report on the American Exhibition in Moscow."

68. White, "USIA Report on the U.S. Exhibition in Moscow"; RG 59, 861.191-MO/8-2859.

69. Commerce Department release, Aug. 25, 1959, Box 64, Eisenhower Papers: Records, 1953-61, Subject Series: Russia, DDEL.

70. RG 59, 861.191-MO/9-459.

71. Ibid.

72. Ibid.; Report by Hans N. Tuch, embassy attaché, undated, Box 7, RG 306.

73. White, "USIA Report on the American Exhibition in Moscow."

74. Report by Hans N. Tuch.

75. "McClellan Report on the American Exhibition"; RG 59, 861.191-MO/9-1159.

76. White, "USIA Report on the American Exhibition in Moscow."

77. RG 59, 861.191-MO/10-654; 861.191-MO/7-2759l; Press release, Office of the American National Exhibition in Moscow, Sept. 3, 1959, Box 5, RG 306.

78. RG 59, 861.191-MO/8-2059; FRUS 1958-1960, X: 36-40; Howard, "'Fair' Way of Making Friends."

79. News clippings, Box 3, RG 306.

80. USIA Annual Report, Year Ending June 30, 1960, White House Office, Special Assistant for National Security Affairs, Box 9, Records: 1952-61, National Security Council Series, Status of Projects Subseries, DDEL; White, "USIA Report on the American exhibition in Moscow."

81. Ibid.

82. FRUS 1958-1960, X, I: 384; "McClellan Report on the American Exhibition."

83. RG 59, 861.191-MO/10-659.

84. "Some Developments Affecting the Soviet Consumer Since Summer 1959," USIA Office of Research and Analysis, Feb. 11, 1960, Box 2, Sprague Committee Report, DDEL.

85. Gustavus Tuckerman, "On the Lessons Taught by the Exchange of US-USSR National Exhibitions," Oct. 30, 1959, Box 7, RG 306; White, "USIA Report on the American Exhibition in Moscow."

86. Tuckerman, "On the Lessons Taught by the Exchange of US-USSR National Exhibitions"; Washburn interview; "McClellan Report on the American Exhibition."

87. Sprague Report, 1960, Box 14, DDEL.

Chapter 8

1. James G. Richter, *Khrushchev's Double Bind: International Pressures and Domestic Coalition Politics* (Baltimore: The Johns Hopkins University Press, 1994), 118-25.

2. FRUS 1958-1960, X, I: 204, 310, 324-25, 507; *Department of State Bulletin,* Feb. 1, 1960, 147.

3. FRUS 1958-1960, X, 1: 274-76; FRUS 1958-1960, IX: 162-65.

4. FRUS 1958-1960, X, 1: 393-95.

5. FRUS 1958-1960, X, 1: 45, 438-39, 485-92; "Summary of Planning for the Khrushchev Tour," Feb. 25, 1959, Box 8, White House Office, Office of the Staff Secretary, Records, 1952-61, FOIA; *Khrushchev in America* [text of Khrushchev's speeches during his U.S. tour] (New York: Crosscurrents Press, 1960).

6. FRUS 1958-1960, X, 1: 409-31; 438-39.

7. Stephen E. Ambrose, *Eisenhower: Soldier and President* (New York: Simon and Schuster, 1990), 492-94; FRUS 1958-1960, X, 1: 468-69.

8. John Newhouse, *War and Peace in the Nuclear Age* (New York: Vintage, 1990), 143.

9. See Khrushchev's revealing comments and his account of the Camp David exchange with Eisenhower in *Khrushchev Remembers* (Boston: Little, Brown and Co., 1970), 518-19.

10. FRUS 1958-1960, X, 2: 41-46; Report on Conversation, May 14, 1959, Box 16, White House Office, Office of the Staff Secretary, Records, 1952-1961, Dwight D. Eisenhower Presidential Library (DDEL), FOIA.

11. Herter-Allen phone call, Oct. 3, 1959, Box 12, Papers of Christian Herter, DDEL; Staff Notes No. 656, Oct. 17, 1959, Box 26, White House Office, Staff Research Group: Records, 1956-61, DDEL.

12. "Memorandum of Conversation," Sept. 26, 1959, Camp David, Box 9, White House Office, Staff Secretary, International Trips and Meetings, DDEL; FRUS 1958-1960, IX: 51; Ambrose, *Eisenhower,* 492-94.

13. *Department of State Bulletin,* Dec. 7, 1959, 848-49; Ibid., Dec. 28, 1959, 951-59; FRUS 1958-1960, X, 2: 59-62.

14. Abbott Washburn, Oral History Interview, Washington, D.C., Jan. 5, 1968, by Ed Edwin, DDEL.

15. FRUS 1958-1960, X, 1: 510-39; Stephen Ambrose with Richard H. Immerman, *Ike's Spies: Eisenhower and the Espionage Establishment* (New York: Doubleday and Co., 1981), 265-92; Michael R. Beschloss, *Mayday: The U2 Affair* (New York: Harper and Row, 1986); Robert S. Hopkins, III, "An Expanded Understanding of Eisenhower, American Policy, and Overflights,"

paper delivered before Society of Historians of American Foreign Relations, Annapolis, Md., June 1995 (forthcoming in *Intelligence and National Security*); *Department of State Bulletin,* July 28, 1958, 146-47.

16. FRUS 1958-1960, X, 1: 155, 170, 261-63.

17. *Department of State Bulletin,* April 17, 1959, 264-65; Ambrose, *Eisenhower,* 506.

18. Beschloss, *Mayday,* 327-54; Chester Pach, Jr., and Elmo Richardson, *The Presidency of Dwight D. Eisenhower* (Lawrence, Kan.: University Press of Kansas, rev. ed., 1991), 216-22. The Kremlin eventually traded Powers for a captured Soviet agent, but not until after the 1960 election. In his memoirs, Khrushchev claimed that by detaining Powers he had helped John F. Kennedy defeat "that son-of-a-bitch Richard Nixon." See *Khrushchev Remembers,* 458.

19. Richter, *Khrushchev's Double Bind,* 126-52.

20. Ibid.; *Life,* Dec. 18, 1970, 488.

21. FRUS 1958-1960, X, 1: 499-516, 555.

22. FRUS 1958-1960, IX: 439-52, 506; *Department of State Bulletin,* May 23, 1960, 816-17; Ibid., May 30, 1960, 852; Robert A. Divine, *Blowing on the Wind: The Nuclear Test-Ban Debate, 1954-1960* (New York: Oxford University Press, 1978), 314.

23. Ambrose, *Eisenhower,* 515; Richter, *Khrushchev's Double Bind,* 126-62.

24. FRUS 1958-1960, IX: 505; FRUS 1958-1960, X, 2: 67-70.

25. FRUS 1958-1960, IX, 508; USIA Newsletter, September 1961, Box 1, Monthly Employee Newsletters, RG 306; USIA Annual Report, Year Ending June 30, 1960, Box 9, White House Office, Special Assistant for National Security Staff: Records: 1952-61, NSC Series, Status of Projects Subseries, DDEL.

26. "Conclusions and Recommendations of the President's Committee on Information Activities Abroad," Box 14, Records of the President's Committee on Information Activities Abroad (Sprague Committee Report), DDEPL.

27. Among the best guides to a voluminous historiography are Stephen G. Rabe, "Eisenhower Revisionism: A Decade of Scholarship," *Diplomatic History* 17 (Winter 1993): 97-115; and John Robert Greene, "Eisenhower Revisionism, 1952-1992, A Reappraisal," in Shirley Anne Warshaw, ed., *Reexamining the Eisenhower Presidency* (Westport, Ct.: Greenwood Press, 1993).

28. Michael S. Sherry, *In the Shadow of War: The United States Since the 1930s* (New Haven and London: Yale University Press, 1995), 190-94.

29. Sherry, *In the Shadow of War,* 190-96; Ambrose, *Eisenhower,* 536-37.

30. FRUS 1958-1960, X, 2: 26; Box 5, Papers of Dwight D. Eisenhower, Cabinet Series, DDEL.

31. Robert T. Holt and Robert W. Van de Velde, *Strategic Psychological Operations and American Foreign Policy* (Chicago: University of Chicago Press, 1960), 45; December 23, 1960, Box 26, Sprague Committee Report.
32. Quoted in Katherine G. Howard, "The 'Fair' Way of Making Friends," Box 26, Katherine G. Howard Papers, DDEL.

Afterword

1. The best works on East-West cultural relations in the post-Eisenhower years are Yale Richmond, *U.S.-Soviet Cultural Exchanges, 1958-1986* (Boulder, Co.: Westview Press, 1987); Henry T. Bernstein, *And None Afraid: Soviet-Western Suspicion and Trusting from Red October to Glasnost Dialogue* (Oxford: Baardwell, 1991); David D. Newsom, ed., *Private Diplomacy with the Soviet Union* (Lanham, Md.: University Press of America, 1987).
2. The moral questions raised by the impact of U.S. culture abroad are quite important, but beyond the scope of this book. A good introduction to the issue is Tomlinson, *Cultural Imperialism;* see also Benjamin R. Barber, *Jihad vs. McWorld* (New York: Times Books, 1995), and the works cited in the Introduction, footnote 9.
3. Timothy W. Ryback, *Rock Around the Bloc: A History of Rock Music in Eastern Europe and the Soviet Union* (New York: Oxford University Press, 1990), 27; Svetlana Alliluyeva, *Twenty Letters to a Friend* (New York: Penguin Books, 1967), 23.
4. *Khrushchev Remembers: The Glasnost Tapes* (Boston: Little, Brown and Co., 1990), 137.

INDEX

Acheson, Dean, 15, 37, 46, 88, 190
Adams, Sherman, 134
Adenauer, Konrad, 73, 85-88, 93-97
Advertising Council, 60, 133, 139
African Americans, 115, 118, 125, 137, 171-72, 195-96
  American National Exhibition in Moscow and, 198-204
• USIA propaganda and, 129-32
  "Unfinished Work" display at Brussels exhibition, 145-50
Aksyonov, Vassily, 115-16
Albania, 41, 45-48, 60, 113, 160
Allen, George V., 11, 13, 36, 105, 124-26, 144, 147, 149, 158, 161-62, 165, 172-74, 178, 218-19
Altschul, Frank, 59-61
American National Exhibition (1959), xiv, xv, 162-213, 223, 227-31
American-Russian Institute, 6
American Society of Newspaper Editors, 14, 90
Amerika, xiv, 7, 32, 117-19, 152-53, 218-19, 222, 228-29
Armstrong, Louis, 144, 159, 204
"Atoms for Peace," 94-95, 140-44
Austria, xi, 18, 81
Austrian State Treaty, 91, 96-97

Barrett, Edward W, 13-15, 17, 20-21, 37, 40
Benton, William B, 5, 9, 11, 15, 20, 30-31, 35
Berlin Blockade and Airlift, 11, 32, 46, 60, 73
Berlin crisis (1958-61), 163-64, 181, 216, 218
Bohlen, Charles, 32, 54, 69, 91, 98, 107, 115, 154
Brezhnev, Leonid, 231
British Broadcasting Corporation, 22, 32, 35, 49-52, 55, 59, 82-83, 114-17
Brown v. Board of Education of Topeka, 130-31, 146

Brussels Universal and International Exhibition (1958), 141-50, 165, 167, 169, 172, 175, 195, 197
Bulganin, Nikolai, 97, 100
Bulgaria, xv, 10, 48, 60, 113, 231
Byrnes, James F, 30, 129

"Campaign of Truth," 14-17, 35-38, 125
Camp David summit (1959), 216-21, 226
Captive Nations Declaration, 177, 179, 181, 216
Carroll, Wallace, 18
Castle, Eugene, 125
Central Intelligence Agency, xv, 9-10, 12-23, 17-18, 23, 57-65, 69, 78, 84-85, 157, 177, 220
Chambers, Whittaker, 53
China, 11, 21-22, 38, 46, 65, 91, 127, 135, 160, 215, 221, 225
Churchill, Winston S, 91-93, 97
"Circarama", 138, 144, 175, 186, 188, 202, 204, 208
Cliburn, Van, 156
Cohn, Roy, 53-54
Cominform, 5, 96
Committee on International Information Activities (Jackson Committee), 24-27, 55, 63, 66-67, 125, 225
Committee on Public Information, 1
Communist Party of the Soviet Union (CPSU), 96, 156, 170, 185-87, 190, 192, 197-201, 204, 207, 227-28, 231
Compton, Wilson, 20-21, 54
Conant, James B., 72-73, 97
Congress for Cultural Freedom, 58, 82
Conover, Willis, 115-17
containment, xiv, 12, 21-22, 68, 95
  see also "dual containment"
Creel, George, 1
Crusade for Freedom, 59-60, 84
Cuba, 126, 222
Cullman, Howard, 141-50

cultural agreement (1958), xiv, 153-54, 157, 227, 229
cultural infiltration, ix-xvi, 38, 46, 52, 55, 102, 110-19, 137, 150, 154, 160, 165, 168-69, 182-83, 223-32
Czechoslovakia, 9-11, 32, 40-41, 44, 49, 51, 62, 65-67, 70-71, 80, 83, 86, 96, 112, 117, 187, 229

Darlan, Jean, 3, 30
Department of Defense, 17, 19, 109
Department of State, xiv, xv, 2, 6-8, 12, 16-17, 19, 23-27, 31-32, 36, 46, 50, 53, 66, 68, 75, 79, 92, 95, 102-6, 108-110, 114, 117, 123, 126, 138, 142-43, 145, 151-52, 154-60, 164-65, 168, 170, 172, 177, 210, 219, 222, 225
Disney, Walt, 138, 175, 188, 204
Donovan, William D., 3, 13
"dual containment," 92
Dulles, Allen, 22, 57, 78, 111
Dulles, John Foster, 15, 21-22, 53, 57, 62, 70, 123, 138, 152-53, 158-61, 166, 168, 170, 176, 178, 215, 225
    disinterest in overseas propaganda, 25-27
    East German uprising (1953) and, 71-81
    Eisenhower defers to, 26-27, 225
    fears Eisenhower compromise with Soviets, 98-99
    Geneva conferences (1955) and, 97-101, 104-8
    opposes negotiations with USSR, 89-111

East-West exchange, 101-19, 152, 157-60, 218, 222, 224, 227, 229-30
Egypt, 81
Ehrenburg, Ilia, 33, 102
Eisenhower, Dwight D., 3, 15, 20, 27, 37, 53-55, 57-58, 71, 81, 86, 98-99
    American National Exhibition and, 161-83
    "Atoms for Peace," 94-95
    Camp David summit with Khrushchev, 216-221, 226
    "Chance for Peace" address, 89-96, 225
    defers to Dulles, 26-27, 225

East German uprising (1953) and, 70-79
Farewell address, 226
Geneva Conference (1955) and, 97-101
militarization and, 225-27
psychological warfare and, 21-25, 68-101
rejects negotiations with USSR, 89-93
relations with C,D, Jackson, 22-23, 57-58
U-2 incident, 219-223, 226
USIA and, 25-27, 121-50
Eisenhower revisionism, xiii, 224-25
Emmanuel, King Victor III, 3, 30
Estonia, 42, 48
evolutionary approach, see cultural infiltration
Ewing, Gordon, 75-76

Feature Packets, 134-36
Federal Bureau of Investigation, 8, 43, 50
Federal Republic of Germany (West Germany), xi, 18, 46-47, 69, 72-77, 84, 87-95
films, U.S., xvi, 124, 127-28, 133, 154-55, 156, 223
Finland, 96
France, xi, 4, 11-13, 72, 81, 100, 106, 108, 131, 222
Franzusoff, Victor, 34, 36, 51
Free Europe Press, 65
Free Europe University, 66
Fulbright Act, 8-9, 11
Fulbright, Senator J, William, 8, 20

Georgia, Soviet republic of, 37, 48, 160
Geneva Conference (foreign ministers, 1955), 101, 104-08
Geneva Conference (heads of state, 1955), 97-101, 110, 123, 225
German Democratic Republic (East Germany), 18, 40, 86, 163, 224
    1953 uprising in, 70-79
    place in U,S, strategy, 88-95
Gomulka, Wyladislaw, 78-79, 109-11, 182, 224
Gorbachev, Mikhail, 230
Gray, Gordon, 17, 19, 24
Great Britain, 5, 11, 13, 72, 81, 91-92, 100, 106, 108, 155, 189, 222
Gromyko, Andrei, 152, 185
Guatemala, 57, 127

guides, American National Exhibition (1959), 171, 193-200, 212

Harvard College, 16, 36, 38-39, 157
Herrick, George, 35-36, 54
Herter, Christian, 147, 170, 172-73, 176, 222
Hitler, Adolf, 4, 41
Hoover, J. Edgar, 158
Howard, Katherine G., 197, 199, 210
Hughes, Emmett John, 90
Hungary, 10, 48-49, 51, 60, 63, 109-13, 117, 128, 136, 160, 224, 227
1956 rebellion in, 79-86

IBM RAMAC computer, 144, 169, 175, 180, 204
India, 15, 140-41
International Information Administration, 20-21, 25
International Telocommunications Union, 34
Iran, 57
Israel, 78, 81, 128
Italy, xi, 3, 12-13, 30

Jackson, C. D., 22-24, 54-55, 57, 60, 69-72, 75-76, 89, 92, 95, 97-98, 101-3, 109, 130, 134, 225
Jackson committee, *see* Committee on International Information Activities
Jackson, William, 24, 105
jamming, of radio signals, xii, 17, 33-37, 47-55, 62, 64, 76-77, 110, 114, 219, 222-23, 229
jazz, xiv, 50, 62, 115-19, 140, 159, 189, 204, 227-28
Johnson, Lyndon B., 125, 151, 154
Johnston, Eric, 155-56
Joint Chiefs of Staff, 17, 69, 220

Kadar, Janos, 80, 113
Komsomol (communist youth league), 116, 188, 193
Kennan, George F., xiv, 12, 32, 59, 70, 89, 93, 95
Kersten Amendment, 67-68
Khrushchev, Nikita S., xv, 77-85, 96-107, 116, 121, 151, 160-64, 194, 207-9, 226, 228, 231
final tour of American National Exhibition, 211-12

"kitchen debate" with Nixon, 175-82
U-2 incident, 219-222
U.S. tour and meetings with Eisenhower, 215-19
Killian, James, 16
"kitchen debate," xv, 176, 179-80
Korean War, xiii, 16, 19, 21-22, 37, 45-46, 87-88, 90-91, 225

Lachaise, sculpture, 205, 209
Lacy, William S. B., 152, 165, 168
Larson, Arthur, 125
Latin America, USIA activities in, 126-27
Lend-Lease, xi, 6
"liberation," xiv, 12-13, 21-22, 68-69, 95-98, 104, 107, 154, 223, 224
Lithuania, 41, 48, 200
Little Rock incident, 131-32, 146, 148
Lodge, Henry Cabot, 69, 216

MacArthur, Douglas, 4, 19
Malenkov, Georgi, 88-89, 96, 107
Marshall Plan, xi, 5, 14-15, 19, 33, 45, 212
Masaryk, Jan, 41
Massachusetts Institute of Technology, 16, 18, 23, 36, 53, 98, 141
May, Mark, 32-33
McCarran Acts (1952), 102-4, 109, 152
McCarthy, Joseph R. 52-55, 121-24
McClellan, Harold Chadwick, 162-80, 189-92, 197, 201, 206-12
Mikoyan, Anastas, 158, 176
militarization, xiii-xv, 89, 99, 224-27, 231-33
Mindszenty, Cardinal Joseph, 80, 84, 113
"missile gap," 164, 226
Molotov, Vyacheslav, 106-8, 164
Motion Picture Association of America, 155
Mundt, Rep. Karl, 10, 20
"Music USA," 115-19, 227

Nagy, Imre, 80-81
National Committee for a Free Europe, 59-67
National Security Act (1947), 12
National Security Council (NSC), 12, 17, 19, 25-26, 69-70, 101, 108, 113, 122, 126, 177, 223,
NSC 10/2, 13
NSC 66, 36
NSC 68, xiii, 14-18, 20, 24
NSC 114/2, 18

NSC 143/2, 69
NSC 160/1, 92
NSC 162/2, 93
NSC 174, 93-94, 101
NSC 5505/1, 101
NSC 5534/1, 98
NSC 5602/1, 101
NSC 5607, 109
NSC 5608/1, 101
NSC 5811/1, 110, 113
Nazi Germany, 2, 4, 33, 41
Nazi-Soviet Pact (Non-Aggression Pact), 6, 41
New Look, 95, 123
Nitze, Paul, 14
Nixon, Richard M., xv, 108, 124, 127, 151, 170-73, 209, 211
  "kitchen debate" and tour of USSR and Poland, 176-83
North Atlantic Treaty Organization, xiii, 33, 45, 67, 77, 79, 81, 88, 91, 93, 95, 98, 100, 128, 164
nuclear arms race, 94-100, 123, 216, 218, 226

Office of Strategic Services, 3, 59
Office of War Information, 2-6, 16, 26, 29-30
"Open Skies," 99-100, 123
Operations Coordinating Board, 25-26
overseas libraries, USIA, 123-24

"peaceful coexistence," 103, 121, 170, 215, 221-22, 226
"People's Capitalism," 133-41, 145
Pepsi Cola, 169, 175, 179, 186, 189, 193-94, 200, 228
Philippines, 4, 15, 127, 132
Plaut, James, 147, 149
Poland, xv, 39-41, 51, 60-62, 67, 78-79, 86, 96, 109-12, 130, 182-83, 187, 224
Powers, Gary, 220-21
Pravda, 43, 91, 103, 160, 188-89
Princeton Conference on Psychological Warfare (1952), 23, 89
Project TROY, 16-18, 36
propaganda, ix-x, xii-xiii, 1, 99-100, 159, 225-27, 229
  American National Exhibition, 166-80

Amerika magazine, xiv, 7, 32, 117-19, 152-53, 218-19, 222, 228-29
"Atoms for Peace," 94-95
"Campaign of Truth," 14-17
"Chance for Peace" address, 89-94
  impact of Cold War on, 5, 11-27
  in World War II, 2-4
  Radio Free Europe, 59-63, 66-67, 70, 78-79, 82-86, 111, 114-17, 229
  Radio in the American Sector (of Berlin), 63-67, 115-17, 229
  Radio Liberation, 59, 73-77, 229
  Soviet counterpropaganda at American National Exhibition, 185-213
  Voice of America, 29-55, 114-15, 218-19, 222, 227-29
  See also listings under psychological warfare and USIA
Psychological Strategy Board, 17-19, 23, 23
psychological warfare, 3, 4
  decline of, 87-120, 122-23, 137, 141, 154, 182, 223-25, 229
  and efforts to achieve "liberation," 57-86
  Eisenhower administration and, 21-27
  Truman administration and, 12-21
  See also propaganda
Psychological Warfare Division, 3-4, 22

Quantico Vulnerabilities Panel, 97-99, 104-5, 123

Radio Free Asia, 65, 182
Radio Free Europe, 59-63, 66-67, 70, 73, 78-79, 82-86, 111, 114-17, 182, 224, 229
Radio in the American Sector (of Berlin), 59, 73-77, 229
Radio Liberation, 63-67, 82, 115-17, 229
Rakosi, Matyas, 79-80, 84
Rapacki, Adam, 111-12
Rapacki Plan, 112
Robeson, Paul, 156-57
Rockefeller, Nelson, 22, 24-25, 97-100
rock 'n' roll, 159, 206, 228
Rooney, Rep. John J., 125, 142-43
Roosevelt, Franklin D., 2, 29
Rostow, Walt W., 89-90, 97-99, 141
Rumania, 10, 43, 48-49, 60, 80, 110-13, 136

Salisbury, Harrison, 103, 154
Sargeant, Howland, 52, 63-64
Schine, G. David, 53-54
Shub, Boris, 64
Smith-Mundt Act, 10-11, 13, 31-32
Smith, Senator H. Alexander, 10, 31
Smith, Walter Bedell, 15, 19, 22, 60, 69
Sokolniki Park, 163-65, 169-80, 185-92, 197, 201, 203, 206-19, 223, 228
Solzhenitsyn, Alexander, 64
Southeast Asia, USIA activities in, 127-28
South Korea, 15, 46, 127
Soviet National Exhibition (1959), 170-71, 180, 210
Soviet Society for Cultural Relations with Foreign Countries (VOKS), 6-7
Sputnik, 123, 126, 132, 142, 149, 152, 164, 170, 177, 226, 228
Stalin, Joseph, 6-7, 16, 60, 70, 78-79, 84, 87, 97, 102-3, 107, 121, 224, 228, 230-31
Stassen, Harold, 65, 81, 99
State Department, *see* Department of State
Stevenson, Adlai, 83, 190
Streibert, Theodore, 21, 104-7, 121, 125, 136-37, 140
Suez crises, 81, 126, 128, 132
Sullivan, Ed, 143, 206
Swiatlo, Joseph, 62

test ban treaty, 221-22, 226
Thayer, Charles W., 32, 54
Third World, 81, 124, 134, 216
Thompson, Llewelyn, 156, 162, 166-68, 173, 176-77, 181, 190, 192, 203, 210, 221-22
Thurmond, Strom, 172
Tito, Josip Broz, 61, 80, 94, 96, 101, 111
Truman, Harry S., xiii-xv, 20-21, 30, 46, 51-52, 63, 67-68, 87-88, 93, 129, 223, 225
"Campaign of Truth," 14-17

and postwar information program, 4-17

U-2 incident (1960), 219-23, 226
"Unfinished Work" exhibit (Brussels), 145-50, 172, 195
United Nations, 9, 39, 45-46, 63, 65, 68, 80, 82, 85-86, 91, 95, 152
United States Advisory Commission on Information Activities, 15, 32
United States Congress, xiv, 4, 10-11, 13-16, 19-20, 26, 30, 68, 121-25, 138, 142-43, 168, 227
United States Foreign Service, 2, 11, 89, 126
United States Information Agency, xv, 21, 26-27, 79, 82, 104-7, 117, 121-49, 160-62, 165, 168, 172-73, 199, 202, 208-12, 218-19, 223, 225, 227
United States Information Service, 2, 10-11

Voice of America, xiv, xvi, 2, 11, 13, 18-21, 26, 29-55, 59, 63, 78-79, 82-83, 86, 114-15, 122, 127, 130, 160, 218-19, 222, 227-29
Volunteer Freedom Corps, 68-70
Vishinsky, Andrei, 67-68

Walter, Rep. Francis E., 172-73
Warren, Earl, 130
Warsaw Pact, 77, 80-81, 96
Washburn, Abbott, 24, 65, 121-23, 161-62, 168-70, 173, 176, 189, 196-97, 209, 212
Weisner, Jerome, 53, 141
Wilson, Woodrow, 1
World War II, xi-xiii, 16, 29, 33, 69, 87, 95, 98, 154, 224-25, 228, 232

Yugoslavia, 15, 49, 61, 94, 96, 111, 231

Zarubin, Georgi, 152-53
Zhukov, Georgi A., 185, 218-19

Printed in the United States
1516400004B/55-108

9 780312 176808